P9-CCW-750

Praise for *Live from Baghdad*

"Entertaining . . . a candid memoir, hammered out in picaresque detail . . . manic, revealing."
—*The New York Times*

"*Live from Baghdad* made me feel like a leopard with no spots. Robert Wiener's heroic account of his days in Baghdad has provided me endless enjoyment. Wiener is a hero and a living monument to the balls and best instincts of our trade."
—Hunter S. Thompson

"*Live from Baghdad* grabs you with its hell-bent, rough-house, irreverent, and yet poignant account of that amazing experience"
—*Los Angeles Times*

"Television news at its core . . . exciting . . . immediate and emotional."
—*The Washington Post Book World*

"A candid, personal, and lively . . . behind-the-scenes look at the network's ground-breaking coverage."
—*San Francisco Chronicle*

"Wiener [is] about as macho as combat reporters come . . . but [his] machismo never comes off as sexist or unpleasantly egotistical, though, because it is so good-humored."
—*Los Angeles Times Book Review*

"By turns terrifying and hilarious."
—*Playboy*

"Thoroughly engrossing . . . a vivid chronicle of a great journalistic coup. With lots of raucous humor and a refreshing absence of modesty."
—*Publishers Weekly*

"Bytes and bombs, bureaucrats, and booze dominate Wiener's lively account of the months he spent in Baghdad . . . A refreshingly candid memoir told with pride but also an often disarming flippancy."
—*Kirkus Reviews*

"Using rapid-fire prose Wiener captivates readers with dramatic inside details of how CNN became the first ever news organization to offer live, moment-by-moment coverage of a war behind enemy lines."
—*Booklist*

"If Damon Runyon had lived today, he might have been Robert Wiener. . . . Wiener is generous in his praise to his colleagues and to himself. He should be."
—*The Houston Chronicle*

"A breathless, as-it-happened account of CNN's news operation in Baghdad before and during the Gulf War."
—*The Christian Science Monitor*

"Wiener perfectly captures the tension and insanity of being at the center of an impending firestorm . . . few readers will question the enormous courage and dedication of the news people who risked their lives to report the war from behind enemy lines. Even fewer readers will be able to put down this ballsy, funny, and exhilarating account of the frenetic days and nights spent in the bull's eye of America's war effort."

—*The Flint Journal* (Michigan)

"One of the best books to come out of the Persian Gulf war . . . a detailed Stolichnaya and Gauloises augmented chronicle of how television news gets to the box in your home." —*The Tampa Tribune*

"A lively, fast-paced reconstruction of events . . . an often brash, sometimes poignant glimpse into the fiercely competitive battle to broadcast news from behind enemy lines." —*Macleans News Magazine*

"Fast-paced, irreverent, and sometimes hilarious."

—*The Veteran Journal*

"A Tomahawk missile of a memoir . . . conveys immediacy with a wallop." —*The Atlanta-Journal Constitution*

"A tale of vice, victories, and vanities . . . [Wiener] provides a fascinating wealth [of information] about the day-to-day frustrations building a high-tech operation in a Third World hotel suite."

—*The Montreal Gazette*

"Robert Wiener is the producer-genius who persuaded a reluctant Saddam Hussein to let CNN cover the Baghdad bombing live—allowing the world to watch the war in 'real time' from the comfort of their living rooms. Wiener's razzle-dazzle account accurately captures the hysterical mood of the Iraqi capital as the countdown to war ended in a blast of bombs. If you want to know how CNN pulled it off, read *Live from Baghdad*."

—Peter Arnett

LIVE

FROM

BAGHDAD

Making Journalism History Behind the Lines

ROBERT WIENER

St. Martin's Griffin New York

For information, address St. Martin's Press, 175 Fifth Avenue, New York, N.Y. 10010.

www.stmartins.com

Library of Congress Cataloging-in Publication Data

Wiener, Robert.
Live from Baghdad: gathering news at ground zero / Robert Wiener.
p. cm.
ISBN 0-312-31465-5
1. Wiener, Robert. 2. Cable News Network. 3. Persian Gulf War, 1991—Personal narratives, American. 4. Television producers and directors—United States—Biography. I. Title.
PN4888.T4W548 1992
070.4'499567043—dc20 91-27310
CIP

First published in the United States by Doubleday, a division of Bantam Doubleday Dell Publishing Group, Inc.

First St. Martin's Griffin Edition: December 2002

10 9 8 7 6 5 4 3 2 1

This book is dedicated with love to
Elaine,
Jesse, Jake,
and
my parents

And
to the memory of Ed Turner
and John Holliman

ACKNOWLEDGMENTS

Television news is by nature a group venture. You can have the best reporter/writer in the world, but if the pictures aren't there, the story is diminished. The pictures may be the best, but if the sound isn't crisp, the story also suffers. The words, pictures, and sound may be fine, but the edit can make or break it. Everything can hum, but if the producer isn't sharp, the story may never make air.

In Baghdad, I was blessed with the opportunity to work with some of the best producers, correspondents, photographers, sound technicians, videotape editors, and the most courageous field engineer in the business. I hope this book does justice to their professionalism and commitment; and in particular, the seven CNN staffers—Ingrid Formanek, John Holliman, Peter Arnett, Mark Biello, Kris Krizmanich, Nic Robertson, and Bernard Shaw—who were there beside me to share a dream.

I owe a great deal to CNN president Tom Johnson, who went above and beyond the call of duty when he flew to Florida and helped save my father's life; to Ed Turner, my friend and colleague, who has saved my professional skin more times than I'd like to admit; and to Eason Jordon, my immediate boss, who is as crazy about this business as I am. I would also like to thank CNN vice chairman Burt Reinhardt for his support over the years. My thanks also go to all the men and women at my favorite network who worked around the clock to support those of us behind the lines.

Writing, by nature, is a solitary enterprise. But I was fortunate to have the love and support of friends and family. Primarily, my partner, Elaine Butler McCarthy, the best news spouse in the business and the best editor I ever had; and my sons, Jesse and Jake, who helped count pages and offered to provide drawings to accompany my text. I hope this book helps them understand and one day forgive me for the missed birthdays, school assemblies, and good-night kisses because Daddy had to get on an airplane . . . again. I also got fine advice, support, and encouragement from my best friend and fellow desperado, Thomas D. "Uncle Jesse" Herman, with whom I look forward to landing again on Omaha Beach on June 6, 1994 (which we did); Norman Brokaw, who was among the first to believe that a person on the other side of the camera had a compelling tale to tell;

and of course the team at Doubleday: David Gernert, Joel E. Fishman, and Estelle Laurence.

It's been a long haul from hardcover to paperback, and for their efforts I thank Mel Berger and Gary Stuart at William Morris, and Marc Resnick at St. Martin's Press.

Had Home Box Office not turned *Live from Baghdad* into celluloid, it's a safe bet that this updated edition would never have been published, so thanks to Jeff Bewkes, Colin Callender, Jonathan Krauss, Richard Pepler, Nancy Lesser, Quentin Schaffer, and the film's director, Mick Jackson. Special thanks are also offered to Carmi Zlotnik and Liz Crawford, with whom I first discussed the film during a memorable trip to Normandy with the survivors of Easy Company.

For their unyielding support I also salute my fellow screenwriter and co-producer Richard Chapman and his wife, Nancy, of the great state of West Virginia.

And final thanks to Nicolas George, former managing editor of ABC Radio News, who taught me a most valuable lesson when I first started out in this business, a lesson that I've tried to pass on to others. "All stories are essentially the same," Nick said. "Only the people are different. If you concentrate on the people, the story will tell itself."

CONTENTS

AUTHOR'S NOTE

This book is based on notes and diaries I kept while on assignment in Baghdad. I also referred to "The Gulf Crisis Memopack" compiled and produced by Chris Drake and his staff in Cyprus, as well as to *The Baghdad Observer*. *Live from Baghdad* is a personal memoir. It is not meant to be a comprehensive history of events leading up to the war, but rather a look behind the scenes from one journalist's point of view. I have tried to faithfully reconstruct all dialogue as it happened; any errors herein are my own.

THE IRAQIS

SADDAM HUSSEIN
President, Republic of Iraq

TARIQ AZIZ
Foreign Minister

NIZAR HAMDOON
Deputy Foreign Minister

LATIF NASIF JASSIM
Minister of Culture and Information

NAJI AL-HADITHI
Director General, Ministry of Culture and Information

SADOUN AL-JENABI
Press Liaison, Ministry of Culture and Information

DR. SA'DOUN ZOUBAYDI
Translator to Saddam Hussein

MRS. AWATTIF SAMIR
Director, International Exchange Dept., Iraqi TV

MINDERS

Mr. Alla
Mr. Faiz
Mr. Mazin
Mr. Nasir
Mr. Thamir

DRIVERS

Abu Ali
Halaf
Jasim
Kareem

PART ONE

January 16, 1991

INTRODUCTION

It was the most agonizing decision I would ever have to make.

On January 16, 1991, at 11:05 A.M. Eastern Standard time, presidential spokesman Marlin Fitzwater strode into the White House briefing room and, for the second time in seven days, urged reporters to leave Baghdad immediately. His first warning had come before the United Nations deadline and was largely ignored. But this time, the news froze journalists at the Al-Rasheed Hotel like jackrabbits caught in the glare of oncoming headlights. Stunned and panicked, they ran down the corridors of the hotel, many deciding then and there to "pull the plug." Within hours most of the major news organizations would decide to leave the Iraqi capital, in some cases ordered out by their headquarters.

"This is it . . . we're outta here," veteran CBS producer Larry Doyle barked as he bounded into our office. "The New York desk just got the call from Washington . . . so did ABC. It was a special code: *Everyone's fine at home except the kids have the sniffles*. That means it's coming down tonight. We're packing up. Did your guys get it in Atlanta?"

No one at the CNN home office had ever mentioned a code to me. *The kids have the sniffles?* Sniffles? There's a candy-ass code if I ever heard one. Who the hell comes up with these things? In Vietnam the signal to pull was "White Christmas" piped over Armed Forces Radio. If you hear that, we were told at the time, head for the U.S. Embassy; the final evacuation is on.

Throughout the crisis, CNN had gone out of its way to keep us up to date on anything that might affect our safety. But the code was a new wrinkle. Jeez, could Atlanta have fucked up?

"Nah, I don't know anything about it," I told Doyle. "So you and ABC are history. What about NBC, or the Brits?"

"They haven't decided yet. But we're trying to round up cars and leave tonight . . . by caravan to Amman."

"They're going nuts in the lobby," CNN cameraman Mark Biello reported, marching into our workspace. "Everyone wants to know if CNN is going to stay."

Who's everyone? I wondered. There weren't that many of us left. Most of the print media, or "scribblers," as we called them, had left by the fifteenth. *The New York Times, The Washington Post, The Wall Street Journal, The Los Angeles Times*—all had gone. Only *USA Today* had a representative in Baghdad, which says a lot about the state of American journalism these days. The small gaggle of European media meisters were long gone too, having left with the Japanese by the time the UN deadline expired.

"Mark, I don't know yet. We plan to stay, but let's take it one step at a time. Peter and I have been through this before. Just because everyone else is bouncing off the walls doesn't mean we have to get swept up in it. We don't have to make a decision immediately."

"Listen, guys," Peter Arnett interrupted, "absolutely nothing's changed between yesterday and today except for Fitzwater's announcement. It's obvious the White House doesn't want us here. They don't want any reporters here, but that doesn't mean we should panic. I say we stay and that's that!"

I marveled at Peter's self-confidence, but he and I had different responsibilities. "Hang on one second, Peter. There are eight of us here and the decision to stay or go is an individual one. There are several factors to consider, not the least of which is whether we have the means to commit journalism. There's no point being here unless we can do our jobs. I think we can, but I need to get it nailed down as much as possible."

"Yes, you're perfectly right, Robert. All I'm saying is that I've seen this panic before and it's easy to get caught up in it."

By now, all eight of us were in Room 906 of our workspace, one of five rooms comprising the CNN office suite. I looked around the room trying to read the faces of my colleagues. Only Peter's was devoid of any hint of doubt. But why not? At fifty-six Arnett was the ultimate war correspondent, a bare bones, meat-and-potatoes former wire service reporter whom CNN had hired in its early days, hoping his reputation and his Pulitzer prize would add prestige to an operation most in the industry had scorned as a nonstarter. I had known Peter in Vietnam and had worked with him at CNN in 1985 when I produced our coverage of the Mexico City earthquake. Brash, brilliant, and absolutely fearless, Peter was once described by Morley Safer as "probably the toughest, fairest, most consistent of all the hundreds of reporters who covered the [Vietnam] War. He is a feisty but modest man," Safer wrote, "with the face of a boxer who'd taken as much as he'd given."

"What does he mean, 'with the face of a boxer'?" Peter howled when I once read him that quote. " 'The face of a boxer'?" Arnett had developed an ego.

In addition to Peter, CNN had two other correspondents on the ground.

Bernard Shaw, our principal Washington anchor, did not come to Baghdad to cover a war. He arrived on January 11 specifically to interview President Saddam Hussein. But Bernie was still a reporter at heart. His heroes were Walter Cronkite and Edward R. Murrow. Bernie had displayed extraordinary courage by coming to Baghdad and staying as long as he did. He could have left by the UN deadline, but he held tight on the promise that he would be given an interview with Saddam on the sixteenth or seventeenth. This prompted a great deal of gnashing of teeth on the home front, where his family was, quite literally, terrified. A true gentleman, Bernie was always concerned about the welfare of the CNN troops, inquiring if so-and-so had gotten enough sleep, or eaten properly, or if the desk was keeping in touch with our families. Bernie was at the peak of his profession. Thoughtful, deliberate, penetrating, unflappable, he was solid as a rock . . . the perfect anchor.

John Holliman rounded out the troika. This was his second tour in Baghdad and he wanted the story so badly he could taste it. But he was also venturing into uncharted waters.

Holliman had the least experience working overseas but perhaps the best attitude. "Just tell me what to do and I'll do it, Robert," he said to me many times. "This is all new to me, so I'm counting on you to point me in the right direction." John was always pushing to go the extra mile, to file one more report, to do one last live shot. His unflagging work when all the hostages had been released the month before had impressed us all. He was also the consummate radio pro . . . a real motor mouth.

"Remember, the first rule of television is to keep Holliman's face off television," he would joke when it came time to edit. "If you have the pictures, just cover me."

John occasionally liked to play the fool, yet he was anything but. He had a gee-whiz quality about him that was open and sincere. In short, John was our "Everyman."

The technical crew consisted of cameraman Mark Biello, videotape editor Kris Krizmanich, and engineer Dominic (Nic) Robertson. Mark was based in Germany and had distinguished himself on countless occasions during the revolutions in Eastern Europe. Whether he was working as a shooter, editor, tape librarian, feed coordinator, or wearing the many other hats he donned as events warranted, you could count on Mark to be all over a story like a puppy with a new toy. He had eagerly volunteered to come to Baghdad with me on the first wave in August. "First to go! Last to know!" he joked back then. "We're the fuckin' pathfinders . . . yeah!" His latest battle cry was "Geee Haad!" More than a few folks thought Mark was unhinged.

Kris Krizmanich, who lived in Atlanta, had also been around the block. She had worked in Afghanistan and the Soviet Union and had come to Iraq early in the crisis. As videotape editor, Kris was not only responsible for editing our reports but also for taking them to Iraqi TV each night to feed via satellite.

Kris was not scheduled to be in Baghdad as the January 15 deadline passed, but volunteered to replace a colleague who felt it was prudent to depart. "I'll commit for a week past the deadline," she said. "After that, I'll play it one day at a time."

Nic Robertson was our field engineer, or, as John Holliman called him, our "satellite maven." He was extraordinary in many respects. Most guys in Nic's position are in hog heaven if you tell them there's plenty of AC and catering is on the way. Not Nic. Not only was he a technical wizard and the only staff engineer who would *accept* a Baghdad assignment, he was also a born-again journalist. "What piece are we doing tomorrow?" Nic would ask. "Has Bernie decided on his questions for Saddam? What's his first one going to be? Do you think they'll take us to Kuwait?" Nic had done yeoman duty in Romania, the Soviet Union, and points East. His contract said he was there to provide the technology to get the story out, but, like all good journalists, Nic was really there to witness history first hand.

Then there was my comrade-in-arms, Ingrid Formanek, a producer in our Rome bureau. Ingrid and I had traipsed around the world pushing it to the edge more times than I'd care to remember, but I wouldn't trade a second of it. Anyone who has ever known Ingrid—and once you have met her you will not soon forget her—has another "Ingrid story" . . . like the time she rousted the Polish ambassador out of bed to secure a few bottles of Wyborowa from his embassy's larder for a New Year's Eve party. A brilliant field producer and accomplished linguist, Ingrid is one of those romantic figures a novelist would be hard-pressed to invent. Always dressed in black, with silver bracelets up her arms, the Damsel, as some of us call her, has the spirit of a wild mustang and the soul of a wide-eyed child. Always efforting one more shot, one more soundbite, changing one last edit, Ingrid strives for perfection. And sometimes—especially when she works with the poet laureate of CNN, correspondent Richard Blystone—lo and behold, she finds it. Whatever CNN had accomplished in Baghdad thus far was due in large part to the drive, tenacity, and sensitivity of this incredible woman.

"WELL, MR. ROBERT," Bernie asked dryly, "what is the plan?"

"A few of us are going over to the ministry soon. Apparently, they're also concerned by the number of people taking flight."

"Well, my brother, keep me posted. I presume you'll ask about the interview. If it's not tomorrow, I want that charter here at first light."

"I plan to bring it in anyway, Bernie. It will have the flyaway on it, at the very least."

The flyaway was CNN's portable television earth station. It would allow us to broadcast live from Baghdad as we did from so many places around the globe. For months we had been negotiating with the Iraqis to bring it in, but permission was always denied due to "security concerns." Just two days earlier, the authorities had relented and told us to prepare it for shipment. The problem was, after the Iraqis had said "no" so many times, the flyaway originally destined for Baghdad had been sent elsewhere and CNN now found itself in the unenviable position of having received permission to independently transmit live pictures from Baghdad—a television first—without having the equipment readily available to do so.

"Is this for sure?" Eason Jordan, vice president, international news gathering, had asked me. "'Cause I gotta tell you, we don't have a flyaway anywhere we can spare. I've got pool commitments in Saudi and I can't break down Amman. I mean, are these guys really serious?"

"What can I tell ya? They say to prepare it for shipment. Listen, surely there must be one somewhere we can buy."

"Good grief," Eason had countered. "That's about four hundred thousand dollars, not to mention the cost of getting it to Amman, then on to you."

"Well, I guess we'll have to bite the bullet."

"Understood. Okay, I'll get back to you."

Less than an hour later, Eason had told me CNN was indeed buying a flyaway and we could expect it within seventy-two hours. When I'd told Ingrid, she'd rolled her eyes.

A moment after my conversation with Bernie, Tom Johnson, CNN's president, came over our open line and asked me to call him from a room where we could speak privately. "What is your assessment, Robert?" he asked, his voice strong but strained.

"I can only repeat, Tom, what I've told you before. The Iraqis want us to stay, and they say they'll do their best to protect us. We have a good professional relationship with these folks. I can't give you any guarantees but I can't believe, having been here for so many months, they will treat us as anything but journalists. I can't see them holding us as hostages, or, worse, POW's. As I say, no guarantees, Tom, but that's what my gut tells me."

"Robert . . . again I want to emphasize, anyone who wants to leave is free to leave."

"Understood."

There was silence on Tom's end of the line. I knew he was under tremendous pressure. Only later would I learn how much . . . that the President of the United States had personally called Johnson, imploring him to shut down CNN's Baghdad operation.

"Robert . . . tell me again: which news organizations are there and which are leaving?"

I ran down the laundry list.

"Tom," I asked, "are you going to order us out?" As I spoke those words, I secretly hoped Johnson would. It would take an enormous weight off my shoulders. For an instant, I thought, journalism be damned. I want to see Elaine and the boys. But Johnson was still undecided.

"Can you call me back after your meeting at the Information Ministry?" he asked.

As I drove to the ministry, my head felt like it was in a vise. The panic at the hotel, the Saddam interview, the flyaway, the possibility of Bernie getting stuck in this shit for months. . . . Jesus, I could see the headline already: CNN ANCHOR TRAPPED INCOMMUNICADO IN HOTEL BASEMENT WHILE WAR SURGES IN PERSIAN GULF. We'd look like idiots. TV critic Tom Shales would be in seventh heaven. The roller coaster was nearing the top of the first loop and the ride down was going to make the Giant Cyclone looked like a cakewalk. And this ride didn't come equipped with a safety belt.

"So . . . are you all going to bow to your government's wishes and leave?" Naji al-Hadithi asked dryly, "or are you going to stay and report the story fairly?"

Hadithi was the Director General of the Ministry of Culture and Information, the number-two man. A former diplomat who had been posted in London, Naji spoke impeccable English and had a dry sense of humor. He was also editor of *The Baghdad Observer*, Iraq's only English-language newspaper, and had more than a passing knowledge of how the Western press operated and the pressures of the deadline demon. He posed this question to the four of us seated in front of him: two reporters from the British networks, an NBC News producer, and myself.

"Obviously we wish to stay, Naji, but our offices must have the assurance, the guarantee, that we may continue to perform our jobs." John Simpson of the BBC was on a roll. "I think I speak for all of my colleagues here when I say that we're committed to the story, but we must have your cooperation. I mean, will you be able to provide telephone and satellite transmission service?"

"I have told you before that we will provide telephones both at the Al-Rasheed and here at the ministry," Naji answered. "We will also hold daily briefings at the ministry. We will do everything we can. This is a commitment on our side. In addition, I am trying to arrange cars to Amman each day to deliver videotape. But if that's not satisfactory and you feel that you want to leave, or must obey your government, then of course you are free to leave. We won't put anyone's name on a blacklist," he added, smiling. "And what are CNN's plans, Robert?"

"In principle, we're here to stay, Naji," I said. "Obviously we have certain concerns, but I prefer to discuss those with you privately, if you don't mind."

"I think this meeting concerns all of us," Simpson interrupted. "Obviously, we're all in the same boat."

"Look, John, let's be realistic," I said. "First of all, there is no way anyone can 'guarantee' anything, especially if there's war. I believe Naji when he says he'll do his best to provide telephone service, but we all know the phone system is going to be one of the first things to go once the bombing starts. That's why you and I have INMARSATs [a suitcase-sized satellite phone]. Secondly, I think running cars to Amman is a fine idea—I hope it works—but no one knows for sure what the actual situation will be like: if the highways will be bombed, if there will be chaos on the roads. I don't have to tell you, John, that the situation's going to be fluid."

"Why don't we all go and see the minister," Naji interjected.

As we walked to the elevator, I waylaid Naji a moment. "What about the interview with the President?" I asked. "And I'll need assistance and an escort to bring in our television station. The plane is coming in tomorrow morning."

"Mention these things to the minister," Naji whispered.

Latif Nasif Jassim, Minister of Culture and Information and childhood friend of Saddam Hussein, was wearing a heavy green army overcoat over his Revolutionary Command Council military uniform. "Welcome, welcome," he said to us as our group entered the room. "I want you all to know that you are welcome here. You may work in Baghdad and we shall help you." He spoke for a moment in Arabic with Naji, then abruptly began again in English. "Good night," he said, and shook hands all around.

As the other journalists filed out, Jassim grabbed my arm. "Robert, you are going to stay, yes?" he asked plaintively.

"Yes, we plan to, Mr. Minister," I replied, "but there are certain matters I must discuss with you. As you know, we have our television station coming in tomorrow morning on a chartered airplane. I'm going to need a truck and an escort to provide the clearance at customs. I want to avoid spending hours at the airport."

"Yes, we shall see," Jassim answered. "We are working on all the permissions and in a few days everything will be ready."

His answer struck me as if a cattle prod had been put to my gonads. "A few days?" I asked incredulously. "With all due respect, sir, I was told we already had permission. That's why my network went out and spent more than four hundred thousand dollars to buy the equipment. The flyaway is being loaded onto the plane as we speak. Furthermore, sir, much can happen within a few days."

"In principle, you have the permission," Jassim said. "We must simply . . . ah, make certain all is in order."

"Is there any way you can work on that tonight? Time is vital."

"Yes, yes. Naji will help you."

"Sir," I continued, "another matter. Have you heard from the President's office concerning the interview with Mr. Shaw? Tomorrow is the seventeenth, as you know."

"Yes, the interview will take place at the end of the month or the first week in February. The President is very busy these days."

That's it, I thought. That's it. It's war! All the speculation about Saddam doing an about-face within forty-eight hours of the deadline is bullshit. For weeks, the Iraqis had been saying that January 15, the UN deadline, was just another date on the calendar and there was a feeling among reporters and diplomats, both in Baghdad and elsewhere, that Saddam would at first thumb his nose at the deadline, but then make a dramatic concession within two days. I had secretly hoped this was the blockbuster Saddam would deliver during his interview with Bernie. Now it was up in smoke.

"That's very disappointing news, Mr. Minister. I'm afraid Mr. Shaw will not be able to remain in Baghdad."

"Someone else may do the interview," Jassim answered. "You have other reporters here, and, of course, you're here, Robert."

Yes, I'm here all right, I thought. God help me!

I bade farewell to the minister, and Naji accompanied me down the corridor.

"I gotta tell ya, Naji, this is not good news. It's worse than that. I can't believe your President's actually going to war. It's crazy! It's insane! It's 'no win'!"

Naji just shrugged his shoulders.

"Listen," I said, "one last thing. I must have your word I may obtain exit visas for my people *at any time* should they wish to leave. Agreed?"

"Of course. Good night, Robert." He shook my hand. "*Inshaallah*, we shall both survive."

I felt nauseous as I returned to the hotel. Numb, frightened, and heartsick. In the lobby, newsmen were lined up at the cashier's desk to settle their accounts. Porters were struggling with equipment and anvil cases. The Ministry of Information desk by the entrance was manned as usual, but the "minders" weren't smiling or joking among themselves. I said my ritual hellos and shook hands as I passed by, and took the elevator up to the ninth floor.

Everyone was in the workspace, with Bernie huddled in front of the "four-wire," our open telephone hookup.

"Bernie's gonna do an interview with Cronkite in a few minutes," Ingrid said. "What'd Naji say?"

"Well, it's not good news," I answered. "First, no interview. Maybe the end of the month or the beginning of February . . ."

"Oh, Jesus!" Ingrid exclaimed.

"And as for the flyaway, they're still working on permission. It'll happen, but God knows when."

"Well," Bernie interrupted, lighting a cigarette, "I'm leaving tomorrow. What time is the plane coming in?"

"I'll make the arrangements and let you know. I first need to call Atlanta and speak to Tom. Look, there is some good news. Naji is trying to provide a shuttle service to Amman to ferry out tapes and he's given me his word that exit visas will be granted immediately—at any time—for anyone who wants to leave."

"That's perfect," Peter said. "That's very good news, Robert. Look, guys, the interview is a disappointment but we can still do our jobs. Bernie, you came here for a specific purpose and we salute you, but I think you're right to leave. You should leave. As for the rest of us, we can continue doing what we've been doing, right, guys?"

"I don't know," Kris said softly. "I mean, if they're going to shuttle tapes to Amman, they'll be edited in Amman. What am I going to do here? We won't be feeding from Iraqi TV."

"Hold on one second," I interrupted. "We'll all talk about this in a few minutes. I want to emphasize that anyone who wants to leave with Bernie in the morning should do so. I don't want anyone to feel under any pressure whatsoever. I want you all to search your souls and use your heads and your hearts to make a decision. Now, I'm going in the other room to place a call to Atlanta. Do we have a hard start for the Cronkite interview?"

"They're trying to set it up now," Bernie said.

As I walked next door to place the call, Mark collared me. "You know Fabrice is leaving." Fabrice Moussus was a legendary ABC News cameraman who, among other things, had shot the riveting footage of Anwar Sadat's assassination. Fabrice was a friend of Mark's and one of the reasons Mark was still in Baghdad. Having Fabrice nearby was a comfort. "I don't know, Robert," he continued. "I don't think I feel good about this. You understand, don't you?"

"Of course I do. I have a lot of misgivings too, but let's talk about it later, okay?"

"Do you think Arnett's crazy?"

"Nah," I laughed. "If Peter were crazy I wouldn't have asked him to come here in the first place. He's just . . . um, enthusiastic. Listen, I need to make this call, but we'll thrash this out later."

"All right. In the meantime, I'm going to set up some cameras by the windows. I'm putting them on both sides of the hotel, and I'll stick the handycams in the edit bay and crew room so we're covered from all angles."

While I waited for the hotel operator to get Atlanta on the line, I tried to come to grips with my own emotions. I had been in Baghdad since August and knew the beat inside-out. Throughout the crisis, there was never any doubt in my mind that this was the place to be. Covering a war from behind the lines would be a journalistic first. And for a while, thanks to our "four-wire" open line to the States, we'd be able to voice it live—at least until the communications tower was destroyed. People had told me I was nuts, that I was suffering delusions if I thought the Iraqis would actually permit coverage. Even some colleagues at CNN thought I had crossed into the Twilight Zone. But my network had backed me and seven people were risking their lives, due, in some measure, to the commitment I had made to the story. Now it looked like most, if not all, of the press was leaving and we'd be alone. Alone. Sitting on Ground Zero in what would surely be the biggest shit storm in the history of aerial bombardment. I was fairly certain the bombers wouldn't go for the Al-Rasheed. A hotel housing civilians couldn't be a target. It made no sense. But pilots on one of the U.S. aircraft carriers did a double take when a colleague told them that's where we were staying.

"Are you serious?" one had asked. "We're using that hotel as a landmark when we go for the bridges. We're gonna come right over it."

Somehow, until Fitzwater's announcement it had seemed almost like a game, a good sparring match. But the news from Minister Jassim meant Saddam wasn't throwing in the towel. Fuck, I thought. I don't want to be here. It was the same feeling I had along Highway 13 in Vietnam when Dave Kennerly, Art Higbee, and I were trapped in a shell hole under North Vietnamese fire so close and intense you could almost hear the enemy loading their mortars. It was the same feeling I had in Romania when, during the revolution, we were yanked out of our car more than thirty-two times while partisans cocked a gun to my head as they checked our papers. The same feeling I had running down nine flights of stairs at the Sheraton Hotel in Mexico City while the earthquake split the hotel in two and blew out the windows.

But somehow this was worse. As frightening as Vietnam was at times, the press still had a support system. As perilous and uncertain as Romania could be, the partisans welcomed us. An earthquake is terrifying, but it begins and it ends. A minute of hell, and it's over.

This was different. I wasn't afraid of the Iraqis. I was afraid of the American bombs. And what if Saddam hit Tel Aviv with chemicals? Would I sit in the Al-Rasheed under a mushroom cloud dropped by the Israelis?

My legs felt numb. At the same time, I knew that CNN had to stay in Baghdad. We couldn't abandon the story, especially if NBC or even the Brits decided to stay. I could imagine the full-page ads in *The New York Times*, with the peacock in full feather. NBC NEWS: THE ONLY U.S. NETWORK REPORTING LIVE FROM THE IRAQI CAPITAL. Jesus, what a nightmare! Everything CNN had tried to achieve for ten years was riding on this. Unless, of course, we were ordered out. Now, there would be a way to save face, I thought. "Yeah . . . well, we were prepared to stay," I could hear myself explaining to friends, "but we were ordered out." A great dinner in Amman with our colleagues, a "job well done" from the network brass, and welcome home! It all seemed so easy.

Yet another network had ordered me out of Saigon in 1975 and I had always regretted it. Peter and I had talked about that a few days earlier.

"You know, Robert, I'm here because of you and I'm here to stay," he said. "I just hope they don't order us out. I hope they'll have enough sense to leave the decision to us on the ground. What do you think?"

"I think they'll leave the decision to us, Peter. We've invested a lot of time here, and I think Tom and Ed will go with our recommendations."

"Well, if they order us out, I'm not going to leave. What do you think will happen if you and I 'miss' the plane?"

"I don't think we're going to get fired if we keep reporting from Baghdad," I laughed, "if that's what you mean. Look, we'll deal with that later."

Later, of course, was *now*!

"United States on the line," the hotel operator chirped. Tom Johnson, Ed Turner, CNN's executive vice president, and Eason Jordan, my immediate boss, were gathered around a speaker phone in Atlanta.

"Robert," Tom said, his voice almost cracking, "I am not, repeat not, going to order you out. Anyone who wants to leave is free to leave, but I am not going to order you out. Do you understand?"

"Yes sir. Have you gotten any indication of what NBC or the Brits will be doing?"

"Robert, this is Eason. NBC is leaving the decision up to its guys in Baghdad, but ITN [London's Independent Television News] . . . and now it looks like the BBC as well, are pulling their people. After the Cronkite interview, ITN would like to use our four-wire so they can communicate with London about arrangements. I've told them it's okay as soon as it's convenient. It will not be used for news, just for talking with their desk."

"Understood."

"Robert, this is Ed. What did they say at the ministry about the interview with Bernie?"

"It's not going to happen. Maybe at the end of the month or in February, for Chrissake. I also had some bad news on the flyaway. They're still working on permission, so I suggest you hold it in Amman for the time being. I don't want to waste time at the airport getting into a flap with customs while I make sure that Bernie and whoever else wants to leave gets on the plane."

"Fine, we're not bringing the flyaway in," Eason interrupted.

"Who is leaving with Bernie?" Ed asked.

"I don't know yet. We're going to have a meeting shortly and decide. My feeling is that some of our folks want to leave."

"What are *you* going to do?" he asked.

"I haven't made up my mind yet. Obviously, it's a tough decision. I'm still trying to work it out."

"Robert, this is Tom. Who did you see at the ministry? Naji al-Hadithi or the minister?"

"Both of them, Tom, and it's obvious they want us to stay. They're even talking about laying on cars to ferry tape to Jordan."

"Tell me again about the hotel," he implored.

"Well, as I've said, the Al-Rasheed's got an excellent bomb shelter and the hotel itself is built like a fortress. . . ."

"Let me interrupt you, Robert. I assume this call is monitored, so I'm going to be as circumspect as I can. You know there are a lot of . . . um, inviting . . . well, there are areas all around the hotel that the coalition is very interested in. Is there any possibility of moving to another location?"

"I've already discussed it with the authorities and we're free to move, but in my view it's impractical for two reasons. The first is that our four-wire is here, and I don't think these folks will have time to install it elsewhere. Secondly, I've checked out the Sheraton, and, while we've considered taking a room there as an alternative camera position, the shelter isn't as strong as the Rasheed's. We'd also be cut off on the other side of the city if the bridges are taken out. I know what you're driving at, Tom, but it's simply not a viable option."

"I understand. Is there anything we can do for you?"

"Well, I'd certainly call Linda and let her know Bernie's coming out tomorrow. I know she'll be terribly relieved."

"We've been in touch with all your families," Tom said. "And we'll be staying in touch."

"Okay, guys," I said, "I'll speak to you again after our meeting. . . ."

"Robert," Ed interrupted, "I'm going to transfer this call into my office. Do you have a second?"

While I waited for the connection, I thought it must be as tough on them as it was on us. They were privy to intelligence and briefings that I knew they would share with us if they could, but they could tell us only so much. All of our calls were monitored. Some of us thought even the cars were bugged. I had never met Tom Johnson face to face. He had joined CNN shortly before I left for the Middle East but Ed and Eason were old and loyal friends. Both had gone to bat for me more than once, and Ed in particular had even put his job on the line when I'd gone too far out on a limb that easily could have been sawed off from under me. I could ask for no wiser colleague or better friend when the chips were down than Ed Turner. And as scared as I was, I felt now was the time to repay him.

"Hi, Robert," Ed said, as he picked up the line. "How ya doing, my friend?"

"Can we go home now?" I joked, soliciting from Ed the expected gale of laughter. "I tell ya, seriously, I feel like my fuckin' brains are gonna burst out of my skull. We've been through some tough ones together, Ed, but this one's a bitch. My only consolation is knowing that if I buy the ranch, it's gonna drive the accounting department crazy for years."

"They have enough problems with your expense accounts in English. We could submit them in Arabic," he laughed. "So," Ed asked, turning serious, "what's going on?"

"Well, Peter's here to stay but I don't know about the others. This Fitzwater thing's got a lot of folks spooked. There's panic in the air, Ed. It's not pleasant."

"What have you decided?"

"I haven't made a firm decision. My inclination is to stay but I need to speak with Elaine."

"You understand," he said, speaking slowly and deliberately, "everyone there knows you are CNN Baghdad. If you leave, the place will collapse like a house of cards."

"I know that, Ed. I still need to speak with Elaine but I can give you this assurance: I guarantee that I'll keep CNN competitive on this story. I don't know how many of us might be here, but as long as it's possible, we'll have a presence. Peter and I were talking about it the other day. It would be disgraceful if we abandoned the story to the competition."

"It would be," Ed agreed.

Just then John Holliman came bounding into the room. "Bernie's going to do Cronkite. Hey, who are you on with?"

"It's E.T.," I told him.

"Tell Ed I've made my decision. If Robert stays, I stay. If Robert goes, I go. Come listen to Cronkite."

I passed on Holliman's remarks. "Like you said, Ed," I added, "it's a house of cards."

I placed a call to Elaine, then stepped next door to listen to the interview. Bernie and Walter talked for a while about the Fitzwater warning, the role of the press, and the government. And then Cronkite made it personal.

"The decision to stay in a place that is clearly a major danger zone," he said, "where one's mortality has to be considered on the line, is probably the toughest decision that any newspaperman or reporter ever had to make."

I looked at my colleagues gathered around the four-wire. The impact of Walter's words hit everyone hard. That's exactly what we're doing, I thought, coming to grips with our mortality. Walter spoke of the press being the front line of the people's right to know, no matter what the dangers, then added this caveat.

"I suppose," he continued, "there comes a point where it becomes foolhardy to risk one's life to do that job if it's almost certainly fatal at the end. But I can't make that judgment for anybody today."

Did Cronkite think we were going to die? Was he trying to send us a message? I didn't think so, but there were some in the room who were clearly unsettled by what they had heard.

"Don't grandstand this one," he admonished Peter. "Save your skin."

When the interview concluded, I spoke to Elaine. She had been watching CNN and was obviously frazzled. It didn't help matters any that a former colleague of mine had called her in tears, pleading that CNN should order us out.

"Well, babe, I can't stay on long. We're about to have a meeting. As of now, Bernie's leaving but I don't know who else."

"What are *you* going to do?" she asked.

"I don't know. I don't know. My gut is telling me to get out but I feel I should stay. Everyone's looking to me and the pressure is incredible. But I haven't made a final decision. I just wanted to hear your voice. How are the boys?"

"They're fine, they're such great kids," she said. "Listen, don't worry about us. We'll be okay, and whichever way you decide is really okay with me. But please try to give yourself a quiet moment before you go into that meeting. Babe," she added gently, "I know you'll make the right decision."

Elaine never ceased to amaze me. I knew I was putting her through hell but she was a brick. God knows, being married to me was no picnic. How in hell did she put up with it? I marveled. We said our good-byes.

The crew from ITN came into the workspace to use the four-wire to speak to their office. "So, what is CNN going to do?" Brent Sadler asked.

"We haven't decided yet," I told him. "We're about to have a meeting."

"They've ordered us out," Brent said. "We're going to see about at least keeping a Jordanian cameraman here."

I turned over the four-wire and closed the door after me as I stepped into Room 904, our edit suite. All of the staff had assembled there.

"Can I just say something?" said Peter, addressing the group. "If you go to Amman, in a few days you're going to want to come back. Trust me. I've seen this before, in Vietnam, this panic. Now Robert has set up a great operation. Everything is in place. This is a fantastic opportunity—"

"Peter," I interrupted. "This is not the way I want this meeting to go. Everyone has his or her concerns and all those concerns are legitimate in my view. It is not for me or anyone else to question them. We're all here in Baghdad by choice and we're open and honest with one another and feel good about each other. Since August, that has been the basis for working here. I want to hear from everyone, and no one should feel pressured one way or the other. Whatever decisions are made, you should be proud. You've done yourself and journalism a great service."

"Well, I've made my decision," Peter said as he stood up. "I'm staying." And with that, he left the room.

I took a deep breath. "Okay. Let me tell you where I stand." I paused for a moment. That's not fair, I thought. "Let me back up. First I want to hear from all of you." I looked around the room and caught Biello's eye. "Mark?"

"The thing is, I really don't know what we'll be able to do . . . just how much, if anything, they'll allow us to shoot. You know Fabrice is leaving and all of the other Western cameramen too. I spoke to Allison and she's really freaked. I mean, I'll come back but as of now I don't feel too good about this place."

"That's understandable, Mark. So you'll leave tomorrow with Bernie?"

He nodded.

"Kris," I asked, "how are you feeling?"

"I'm here as an editor," she said, "and by the looks of things there's not going to be much to edit, much less feed. You said the flyaway's not coming, and we all know the TV station is going to be bombed, so what's for me to do? Any tape is going to be shipped to Amman, right?"

"I don't know for sure, but that's not the issue."

"Well, I came here to do a job and I don't think I'll be able to do it. There seems to be no point for me to be here. I'd like to leave."

"That's no problem, Krissie. I can't thank you enough for having come when you did and helping us out. This network owes you a lot. Ingrid, you're looking so unhappy."

"Well, Wienerish, you know I was prepared to stay and you know I love working with you, but I also have to tell you that Blystone's leaving changed a lot for me."

Richard Blystone was a correspondent in our London bureau who had come to Baghdad as part of the "final rotation." Because of a family crisis, he could not run the risk of getting stuck in Iraq indefinitely. Arnett had come in to replace him.

"I know how you feel about Bly, darling," I said. "We all love him."

"Look," Ingrid said, "I'll come back. I just think it's better to sit in Amman a few days. Furthermore, Wienerish," she laughed, "I like shitholes, not death traps!"

Nic Robertson had been listening closely to all of this, and I really didn't know which way he would go. "Nic," I said, "your thoughts?"

"Well, I came here because of the flyaway, and who knows? We may still get the flyaway in soon. It would be a pity to have it here and not be able to use it. I also think I can help out a lot on the INMARSAT and the other gear, especially now that Mark is leaving. I feel comfortable with Peter and anyone else who decides to stay. So . . . I'm prepared to stay and play it day by day."

"That's terrific news, Nic. I thank you." I turned my attention to John, who was standing by the window. "Mr. Holliman, I presume your decision remains the same?"

"Absolutely . . . if Robert stays, I stay. If Robert goes, I go. As you say, you've got great instincts and I've got no instincts, so I'll just follow you."

All eyes were now focused on me. "Well, this has been as difficult for me as it has been for all of you. I gotta tell ya that I've got a lot of misgivings about this, not the least of which is my concern for my family.

You know Elaine's a trooper, but God forbid anything should happen to me . . . I can't imagine depriving Jesse and Jake of a daddy." I tried to check my emotions but the strain was overpowering. I took a deep breath and hoped the thumping in my chest would go away.

"But I'm also aware of the fact many of you are here because I asked you and that especially goes for Peter and Nic, who came in at the last minute. I'll be honest with you. I don't particularly want to be here right now but it would be unconscionable for me to bring people to Baghdad and then abandon them. So I too will remain. I thank you all very much and I love you all very much."

That was that. I walked across the hall to find Peter.

"Peter," I said, "John, Nic, and myself are staying here with you. The others will leave in the morning with Bernie."

"That's fantastic, Robert! I knew you'd stay. You couldn't live with yourself otherwise. It's perfect . . . and we even have Nic for the equipment. It's just perfect," he said vigorously, shaking my hand. "You'll never regret it."

"Yeah, my friend, I know. It's gonna be fabulous," I laughed.

I walked into Room 906 and sat down at the four-wire. "Baghdad to Atlanta . . . Baghdad to Amman," I called.

"Atlanta here. Go ahead, Robert, it's Eason."

"Amman here."

Very slowly, at dictation speed, I ticked off the roll call I knew they were waiting for. "The following people will be leaving Baghdad tomorrow: Bernard Shaw, Mark Biello, Kris Krizmanich, and Ingrid Formanek. The following will remain in Baghdad: Peter Arnett, John Holliman, Nic Robertson, and Robert Wiener."

There was silence at the other end of the line. "Atlanta . . . Amman, do you copy?"

"Atlanta copies."

"Amman copies."

"Peter," I said to our senior producer Peter Humi in Amman, "I'll get back to you shortly to talk about arrangements for the charter, but plan to have it on the ground at first light."

"Very well, Robert. I'll be here," he replied.

So the die is cast, I thought. And the network is covered. I lit a cigarette and looked at Bernie. "It's been a hell of a night," I said, calling room service to order some ice.

"That and more," Bernie agreed, "that and more."

"Well, I think we'll be all right," I ventured. "Just cross your fingers that the airport stays open another few hours."

Less than ninety minutes later, Baghdad came under attack.

PART TWO

August–September 1990

1

If we could somehow pull it off, I mused at the time, it would be the journalistic equivalent of walking on the moon . . . to cover a war "live" . . . in real time, from behind the lines . . . from the enemy's capital! Not even Murrow had done that, but I could easily imagine ole Edward R. lickin' his lips at the prospect. In December 1989 CNN had covered the bloody Romanian revolution live, transfixing viewers as the people of Bucharest rose up and toppled the dictator Nicolae Ceauşescu. We were set up on the terrace of the Intercontinental Hotel in the center of the capital, beaming pictures via satellite of tank columns rolling down snow-covered Nicolae Balcescu Boulevard.

Those were heady days for all of us there, but covering a full-scale war was something else. How on earth would we even get permission? And if we did, who the hell would actually do it?

The announcement from the cockpit snapped me out of my reverie. "Ladies and gentlemen, fasten your seat belts, please. We're about to land at Saddam International Airport in Baghdad." It was about 2 P.M., August 23.

It had taken herculean efforts to get as far as we had. Eight days earlier I had flown to Amman by private charter from Cairo, and had spent every waking moment since then camped out at the Iraqi Embassy in the Jordanian capital. Hundreds of journalists were trying to get visas for

Baghdad, but the Iraqis wouldn't budge. Ted Koppel and Dan Rather had been allowed in briefly to interview Foreign Minister Tariq Aziz, but that was it. Obtaining a visa to Iraq was next to impossible during the best of times, but since the invasion of Kuwait, Baghdad had slammed the door and bolted it. We tried everything. Executives in Atlanta pursued all of their contacts. Even Jordan's King Hussein, a friend of Ted Turner, interceded on our behalf. Nothing seemed to work. My editor was going ballistic. "We've just got to get in there," Eason Jordan howled over the phone one particularly frustrating afternoon. "This is bullshit! ABC and CBS are kicking our butts on this one. How is it possible they got in and we can't?"

"Aziz invited them, Eason. It's that simple. Don't *we* have anyone who knows Aziz?"

"I'm told Rowland Evans does. We're going to pitch him."

Rollie Evans, syndicated columnist and the liberal conscience of CNN's "Evans and Novak," had just returned to Washington, D.C., after conducting exclusive interviews for the network with King Hussein and Egyptian President Hosni Mubarak. As we would learn later, Tariq Aziz had *wanted* to talk with Evans even before doing Koppel, but Rollie, darting around the Middle East, was hard to pin down. "I'll call you back after we speak with him," Eason said.

Eventually Evans became our ticket to Baghdad, though it would still take a couple of days to work out the bureaucratic snafus. He was due to join us in Amman on August 24, but, sensing that other news organizations were also on the verge of obtaining visas, we decided to fly out as soon as possible. A few hours before our departure, I stopped by the CBS suite in the Intercontinental Hotel to get a fill from Tom Bettag. Bettag was then the executive producer of the "CBS Evening News with Dan Rather." He'd returned from Baghdad a few days earlier and we had often helped each other out on the road.

"Get in touch with Joe Wilson at the U.S. Embassy," Tom said. "Good man. Very helpful. They have phones that you can use to dial the States direct. Forget about calling from your hotel. Steve Thibault is the press attaché. Nice guy. Colonel Jim Ritchie is the military attaché, but you'll probably be dealing with Wilson and Thibault. Here are some telephone numbers."

While I jotted them down, I asked Tom if the embassy folks had any special needs. "Wilson likes cigars," he said, "Ritchie too. You can get some good Havanas at the airport duty-free. Oh, here's a name you'll need, Mrs. Awattif Samir; she runs the show at Iraqi Television."

"What's the feed situation like there?" I asked.

"A mess. It's a frustrating ordeal."

God save me from Third World feedpoints, I thought. Every producer in this business has at least one classic "horror story" about a feedpoint someplace. The chaos that ensues when the members of the free press descend en masse on some hapless, ill-equipped television station and go berserk deciding who feeds what, to where, on what format and when, is not a sight for the faint-of-heart. In Prague, for example, it had caused a senior official of Czech TV to beg me for sedatives.

"So, how long do you plan to stay?" Tom asked.

"The visa's good for thirty days."

"I'd get in and out quickly. It looks like war could be pretty close."

As I was leaving CBS I ran into John Reid, a producer with their special events unit. John is among the best in the business, a pro at putting together remotes, be it a presidential trip or a major breaking story. "Hey, Robert, what's going on?" he asked.

"Heading for Baghdad," I replied.

Reid did a double take. His expression showed genuine concern. "Robert, don't go in, please don't," he beseeched. "It's not a good idea, not now. Really. Don't do this."

"We'll be okay. Look, you guys had your shot. I've got to get CNN on the boards." But if John felt this strongly, I thought, it was not a good omen.

I was thinking about this and more as the Iraqi Airways 747 taxied to the jetway. There were four of us from CNN on the flight, including correspondent Jim Clancy, Mark Biello, and Trey Haney, an editor/sound tech. We had all worked together in various shitholes before, but this was going to be a new experience—in fact it eventually became known as "the Iraqi Mind Fuck." It had started even before we embarked in Amman. As we handed over our first-class boarding cards, an Iraqi airline official summarily informed us we would be "downgraded" to economy. "An official delegation will be on board. They must have first-class seats," he said.

"I beg your pardon," I replied, "but we have confirmed first-class tickets."

"No, you go economy," he insisted.

"I'm very sorry," I replied, "but we are confirmed in first class. As you can plainly see, we have first-class boarding cards . . . so with all due respect, first class is how we shall fly."

"No, you go economy," he said again.

"Look, are you going to reimburse us for the difference in fare?"

"You just go economy," he repeated.

By now our little duet had caused a major bottleneck, and I sensed the crowd around us beginning to get ugly. The situation called for quick action.

"This man," I pointed to Jim Clancy and shouted, "*this man has a heart condition*! If you possess a shred of human decency, you'll permit him, and his assistants, to travel first class!"

The official surveyed Jim, who, at over two hundred pounds, carries a sizable girth. He was sweating like a pig, weighed down by his carry-on luggage, personal computer, and bags from the duty-free shop.

"Okay . . . I find other seats for delegation," he said. "You go first class." I humbly accepted my colleagues' congratulations as we took our seats on the upper deck, where I noticed we were not the only journalists who had managed to obtain visas. John Simpson of the BBC was on board along with Mohammed Amin, a cameraman for VISNEWS (a television news agency that supplies video to clients worldwide). I didn't know if John or Mo also had heart conditions, but they too had avoided flying steerage.

SADDAM INTERNATIONAL AIRPORT was a pleasant surprise. Modern, almost futuristic for a Third World country, the terminal was immaculate and gleaming. As we rushed to the immigration line marked "Foreigners," a man approached us.

"Excuse, please," he asked. "Journalists?"

"Yes, hello," I answered. "We're with CNN." I made the introductions.

He looked again at the paper he was clutching.

"CNN? No BBC?"

"The BBC is here too. They're coming off the plane."

"You wait here, please," he said, and disappeared to make a phone call.

"What'd I tell ya?" Clancy sighed. "It's starting. We'll be here for hours." Jim had worked in Baghdad before. The experience, he told us, was not amusing. "The last time I was here we spent eight fuckin' hours at the airport. You see, they didn't expect us today. We were supposed to come in with Evans." He reached for a Gauloises Blonde. "You got a light?"

By now the BBC had joined us. "The minder has gone to call the ministry," Clancy told Simpson. "Be prepared for a long wait." Simpson took it in stride and began jotting in his notebook.

"You've been here before, haven't you, John?" I asked.

"Oh yes," he replied. "About six months ago, we came to shoot a documentary. When we left they confiscated all our tapes at the airport."

"*All* of them?"

"I'm afraid so. Forty of them, actually."

"Jesus!"

Just then, Thamir, the man from the ministry, reappeared and ushered us to baggage claim. Hundreds of passengers surrounded the rotating belt and were piling their possessions onto oversized but rickety self-service carts. We were carrying about thirty cases of heavy equipment, not to mention personal effects, and could have used some help. "Are there any porters available?" I asked Thamir. "We have an enormous amount of gear."

"No porter. You use cart." He pointed to the end of the terminal, where the cart supply was quickly disappearing.

"We're gonna need about a dozen," I said to Mark as we ran down the hall.

It took more than an hour to collect our things. "All right, let's head for customs," I said.

"No, no," interrupted Thamir. "Other passengers go first. You wait."

Trey looked uncomfortable. "Well, there's nothing we can do but wait," I said. "Are you okay?" I asked him.

"That guy gives me the creeps," Trey whispered.

I noticed a bank of telephones and went off to call the U.S. Embassy. The one phone that worked didn't require a coin. A nice touch, I thought. Joe Wilson came on the line promptly. ". . . So, if you don't mind, I'd like to come over tonight," I said.

"We'll be here," Joe replied, "but I warn you, we're very busy."

"I've got a box of Havana cigars with your name on it," I told him.

"You've said the magic word," he laughed. "Come by anytime."

Another two hours passed before the men of the Republic of Iraq Customs Service finished checking the remaining passengers. By then Thamir had returned our passports to us, each bearing an entry stamp. Satisfied that not a soul beside ourselves was still in the terminal, he informed us we could now proceed. This is going to be a nightmare, I thought.

The Iraqis wanted to look at *everything*. They began with the equipment. In the television game there's no such thing as traveling "light." The bare minimum means a camera, a sound deck, a tripod, a light kit, and a case or two of tapes. If you're going to edit in the field, you need an edit bay, comprised of two machines. If you're going to stay put and use a feedpoint for a week or two, it helps to have another machine there too. Then there are the assorted cases of extra cables, batteries, bulbs, spare parts, and tools. If you're going to set up a temporary office, it helps to have stationery supplies and even clocks, not to mention shipping bags and tee shirts or hats that you give to local hires. If the driver for another network is wearing a cap with the network's logo and your driver doesn't have one, you're going to hear about it fast.

All this we had, and more. Because the Evans interview with Aziz would be a two-camera shoot, we had two of everything, plus a vast amount of tape, a handycam, and a nifty little machine from Sony called a still store, which in the event of war would allow us to transmit video pictures one frame at a time over a simple telephone line. Not for the first time though, and despite my repeated requests, the home office forgot to include the instruction manual for this twenty-thousand-dollar marvel of technology. But it kept Iraqi customs busy for hours and eventually made a great magazine stand, so all was not lost. (When I began writing this book, one of my colleagues asked if I would mention him by name. All I'll say is, please don't forget the manual again.)

"Modem? Modem?" For some reason, the Iraqis were paranoid about modems. They looked for modems everywhere. Not only in Clancy's computer but even in shortwave radios and tape recorders. Eventually, as scores of reporters filtered into Baghdad, the customs inspectors became more sophisticated and harder to fool. They also got a kick out of Trey's "Third World kit," a huge orange anvil case stocked with tuna, raisins, nuts, cheese, chocolates, and bottled water. "Look at this," one inspector laughed, examining the mineral water. As if in the cradle of civilization, on the banks of the Tigris, you couldn't find a glass of water! Finally, satisfied that Mark Biello's underwear wasn't a threat to national security, we were allowed to pass.

"We must hurry," Thamir informed us. "You have appointment with Minister of Information."

"Whoa," I said. "Jim and the others can see the minister, but I've got to get the equipment to the hotel. Where are the taxis, Mr. Thamir?"

"No taxis. You no have car?"

"No, can I rent one?" I asked innocently. "Or better yet, a van?"

"No, you take taxi."

This was getting us nowhere fast and the prospects were not promising. We were the last ones out of the airport and, with no other flights due that day, there wasn't a soul in sight. The only taxi we were likely to get was some fool who would wait for a plane that wasn't coming. Suddenly, I spotted a small bus disgorging what appeared to be the airport's cleaning staff. "I've got an idea, Mr. Thamir," I suggested. "I'd like to rent that bus."

"No, bus not for you. You take taxi. I go telephone for one."

"We're gonna need seven of 'em," I yelled as he vanished into the terminal.

Five minutes later Thamir returned with a satisfied grin. "Taxis coming soon," he said. While we waited I tried to make small talk. "So, do the people here expect war?" I ventured.

"Everything possible," he replied.

"And what do you think?"

He shrugged his shoulders.

One by one, three orange and white Hondas drove up to the curb. "Taxi? Taxi?" the drivers shouted. "We're gonna need more than three," I told Thamir.

"Others come," he said. "You put in luggage quickly. We must not be late for minister."

We grappled with the loading process for nearly forty minutes. It took six cabs to hold all the gear. Clancy, Thamir, and the crew hopped in the seventh and headed for the ministry. "I'll set things up at the Sheraton," I shouted. "Meet me as soon as you can."

I took my seat in the lead car of the convoy as we drove into town. Even with the windows rolled down there was no relief from the scorching heat. It felt like a blast furnace. Huge billboards of hand-painted portraits of President Saddam Hussein dotted the modern expressway. We seemed to be the only cars on the road. Then a sign: "WELCOME TO BAGHDAD, Capital of Arab Saddam." I looked over my shoulder, relieved the other cabs were on our tail. As we approached the city, the traffic became heavier, and the driving more reckless. Instead of using turn signals, I observed, the Baghdadis honked their horns. My driver shook his head when I asked if he spoke English.

"Sheraton?" was all he could muster.

I expected to see soldiers everywhere but there were only a few scattered here and there. On the other hand, Saddam Hussein was everywhere. On what seemed to be each corner, along every street and boulevard, in front of all government buildings, near every major intersection, portraits of Iraq's Maximum Leader looked down upon the populace. Saddam in a business suit, in the uniform of a field marshal, on his knees in prayer, on horseback, in an overcoat, and even in a sharkskin suit, Saddam's countenance was omnipresent. From some rooftops he pointed, from others he waved. From still others, he beckoned and he blessed. The portraits were a powerful and palpable force.

"His Excellency President Saddam Hussein doesn't ask for the paintings," one of our minders told me early on. "He is a simple man but the people love him so that they rush to put them up." A few months later, during the course of a story, we were told that Saddam personally approved much of the artwork. I have never seen a cult of personality so assiduously refined.

The Ishtar-Sheraton off Abu Nawas Street was a modern sixteen-story affair, across the road from the Palestine Meridian. Both hotels were home to hundreds of foreign hostages held in Baghdad since August 9. The Iraqis maintained that these people were simply "guests." "Hostages do not stay at hotels, drink beer, and enjoy themselves," Tariq Aziz said during a stop in Cairo. In fact, for nearly eleven days, even President George Bush declined to refer to the detainees as "hostages," saying he did not want to inflame the situation. Finally, on August 20, Bush used the "H" word for the first time. "Whatever these innocent people are called, they are, in fact, hostages," said the President.

I told the cab drivers to unload the equipment and motioned that only after it was in the hotel would they all get paid. The Sheraton's lobby was dominated by a large formal photograph of you-know-who.

"Good afternoon," I said to the reception clerk. "The name is Robert Wiener from CNN, American television. I have a reservation, five rooms and a suite, preferably overlooking the mosque." The clerk thumbed through his card file.

"I'm sorry, sir," he said, looking up. "You say you have a reservation?"

"Yes," I lied. "If you can't find it under Wiener, check under CNN. This happens all the time. I'm also going to need several porters," I added, as he stared at the gear that was coming in.

"I'm sorry, sir. I still can't find your reservation."

"Please check once more," I said, sliding a twenty-dollar bill across the counter.

"Very well, sir. I believe I can accommodate you," he replied, handing me a registration form. "How will you be paying, cash or charge?" Over his shoulder was the familiar blue and white welcome from American Express.

"Charge," I said, offering my card. He stared at me a second, then as if he'd forgotten something, abruptly turned around and snapped his fingers. In an instant, an assistant removed the American Express sign.

"We no longer accept credit cards," he said. "I hope you understand, it has become difficult for us to receive the payments. Cash would be acceptable?"

"Cash it will be, my friend."

By now the equipment was in the lobby and the drivers were clamoring to be paid. I enlisted the clerk's help as a translator. "They say twenty-five dinars each taxi is what your guide at the airport promised them."

"Fine, what's that in dollars?" I asked.

"One Iraqi dinar equals three U.S. dollars," he replied.

"Jeez! Seventy-five dollars for a twenty-minute ride from the airport sounds a bit steep, my friend. I occasionally get screwed on the road but not necessarily in a hotel lobby," I laughed.

"Well, that's the official rate," he said. "The Bank Rashid is around the corner down the hall."

I helped separate the gear from the crew's personal luggage and had the porters deliver it to our individual rooms. "The fifth sleeping room is for Mr. Evans," I said. "He'll be arriving tomorrow." I then paid the drivers the tidy equivalent of four hundred and fifty dollars, which would no doubt once again cause the interoffice mail to flow from the accounting department.

"This is Mr. Wiener in Suite 501," I said calling housekeeping. "Could you please send someone up as soon as possible. I'd like the bed removed and some additional chairs, tables, and lights brought in. Could you also inform room service that I need a large bucket of ice, six Pepsis, and a chicken sandwich? I'd be most grateful if you'd take care of this immediately. Thanks very much." I then dialed the operator. "I'd like to place a call to the United States, please."

"No lines to U.S.A.," she replied. Well, Bettag was right, I remembered. So much for that.

By now the porters had delivered the gear. They struggled with the heavy cases and I tipped them well. On the road, a good tip can go a long way. Tens of dollars can often save you thousands, especially if you need a long distance call, porter, or taxi to get to a feedpoint or airport *now*. I walked out to the balcony and opened the louvered doors. As requested, the suite overlooked a beautiful mosque, which dominated a roundabout, complete with the prerequisite billboard of Iraq's President. Perfect for a "stand-up" I thought. A great "live shot" position.

I fumbled with the television set a minute. As the picture came into focus, I couldn't believe my eyes!

There was Saddam Hussein speaking to a group of what appeared to be British hostages: men, women, and children. Through an interpreter Saddam told them their presence in Iraq was to "prevent the scourge of war . . . Your presence is not a source of pleasure for us," the President added. "What would make us happy is to see you back in your country or on the streets of Baghdad during normal times."

Several of the hostages looked uncomfortable, nervous. One said he was appreciative that Saddam had come in person to speak with them. Another asked about the children who had school in the fall. "We'll make efforts to ensure the children are not deprived of their education if they are still here at the beginning of the school term," said Saddam. He said he would try to treat the hostages the same way Iraqis are treated.

The President insisted that Iraq's invasion had not taken anything away from the United States or Britain. "The Arab nation is one nation. British colonization has tried to divide the Arab nation . . . Kuwait has come back to her motherland . . . We don't want war, although we know we can smash the aggressor.

"Regrettably," Saddam said, "no one has conducted any dialogue with us." He called dialogue based on the precondition Iraq must withdraw from Kuwait "blackmail."

The hostages were being held at an undisclosed location. They were dressed casually, some in shorts; in fact one man was even bare-chested. During the "conversation" a few children continued playing with games. It was riveting television and I took notes furiously.

"Bush and the others will learn a great deal from Iraq on the humanitarian level," Saddam told the group, "and the Arabs and Iraqis will teach them how to be closer to God."

Saddam shook hands with several of the hostages and promised to allow videotape and radio messages to be sent to their families. He posed for a group photo and then, in a moment that would eventually be frozen on the covers and front pages of magazines and newspapers worldwide, put his arm around the shoulder of a trembling five-year-old named Stuart Lockwood. "Stuart will, I'm sure, be happy to have as a part of his . . . personal history that he played a role in maintaining peace," the President said, smiling.

Holy shit! I thought. This is amazing stuff. I wondered for a moment if we had it in Atlanta and concluded that we probably did. From the beginning of the crisis CNN had closely monitored whatever was available from Iraqi television.

Around me, the staff from housekeeping was transforming our suite into a workspace. I still hadn't heard from Clancy. Just then the telephone rang.

"Robert Wiener?" the caller asked. "My name is Faiz from the Foreign Ministry. I am in the lobby and would like to speak with you." I invited him up to our "office." Less than five minutes later a short, haggard-looking guy who appeared to be in his forties knocked at the door. He had an odd growth on his balding head, like a knitted piece of excess skin. He shook hands matter-of-factly but declined my offer of coffee.

"You are here to interview Foreign Minister Tariq Aziz," he said, "but you weren't expected until tomorrow. Where is Mr. Evans?" I explained Rollie would arrive the following day or perhaps the day after, depending on connections.

"While you are here you may not take pictures outside without someone with you. That is a rule," he said. "I hope you understand. Also, no pictures from the hotel of the river or the buildings near it." I asked if we could do a stand-up with the mosque in the background. He said that wouldn't be a problem.

"All right, you stay in the hotel tonight and I will contact you in the morning," he added.

"I'm going to need to go to the television station, Mr. Faiz. Our correspondent is conducting an interview with the Minister of Information and we'll obviously satellite it to CNN."

"I will telephone the TV," he said, walking over to the phone. "They expect you between eleven and eleven-thirty tonight," he explained after a brief conversation. "They say there is telex from CNN."

"Do we have a firm date and time for our interview with Mr. Aziz?" I asked. "It would be helpful if I could let CNN know."

"We will talk tomorrow when I contact you," he replied. "But remember, no pictures outside."

"Agreed," I told him and we said good-bye.

By now it was close to nine, about two hours before the "bird" was booked. Where the fuck was Clancy? I took a bite of the chicken sandwich. It was dry and unappetizing. I walked out to the balcony. Even at night Baghdad was oppressively hot. Traffic circled the roundabout, the street noise punctuated by the staccato honking of automobile horns. As I smoked a cigarette, I heard the crew coming down the hall.

"Great interview with the minister," Clancy shouted.

"Fuck the minister!" I shouted back. "You're not gonna believe what was on TV. It's dynamite! And I've got great notes."

"Do we have a bird?"

"Yes, and not much time." Clancy and I hammered out a script while the crew set up for his stand-up. "We've got to assume Atlanta's got the pictures," I said. "We'll give 'em the ins-and-outs of the soundbites."

"Jassim said they're not pulling out of Kuwait," Jim said.

"So, what else is new?"

"It'd be great to interview some of the hostages," Clancy ventured. "The hotel is full of them."

"We don't have time tonight," I said. "We'll pencil it in for tomorrow."

While Clancy clicked away at his computer, I checked my watch. It was going to be tight but you could always count on Clancy. He was one of our front-line correspondents and the network's fireman. He had been with CNN since its salad days, posted in various domestic and foreign bureaus, including a stint in Beirut. He loved CNN but constantly bemoaned the fact he wasn't paid as well as some of his colleagues. When the day was done and the feed long over and Jim had a few under his belt, you could make bet he'd eventually get around to the saga of the drunken Eskimos.

"A drunken Eskimo could do what those guys do in Washington," he would bellow. "All that money for standing in front of the White House or State Department. It's bullshit! A drunken Eskimo could read those releases. I'd like to see one of those guys dropped into Bulgaria in the middle of the night, without a producer, and told to have a report ready in forty minutes. Hah! They're nothing but a bunch of drunken Eskimos!"

We went over the script, laid down his track, and recorded a stand-up close on the balcony. I told Jim to head for the U.S. Embassy and call Atlanta.

"We'll lay down whatever we can here," I said, "but you'll need to pass on some edit instructions. I don't know how the phones are at Iraqi TV. I imagine you'll be at the embassy awhile. I'm sure Atlanta's hungry for beepers [live phone reports]. Oh, one other thing. Take the cigars!" Jim hurried out the door while Trey and I did a "rough cut" of his package, and Mark organized the feed gear. Then the three of us also headed into the night.

2

It was only a ten-minute cab ride to Iraqi Television, but it took another twenty minutes to get through the door. Security conducted a thorough search of our gear. It was about twelve minutes before the start of the scheduled transmission and I was getting frantic. For me, it was always a matter of pride, not to mention good economic sense, to be ready to feed "at the top" of a bird whenever possible. When ordering a satellite, there's usually a set fee for the first ten minutes and an additional charge for every minute used after that. After almost ten years with CNN I was well schooled in the company's Waste Not/Want Not mentality; well . . . at least, Waste Not. It always amazed me how other networks would often nonchalantly "sit" on a bird, unconcerned that literally thousands of dollars were being spent needlessly.

This was on my mind as we lugged the gear from one building to the next and up two flights to Master Control. As Mark and Trey put together the feedpack, I ran down the hall to find the person in charge. A slight, bespectacled middle-aged woman, who, I thought, was unusually well dressed for a feed coordinator, beckoned me into her office.

"Hello, I'm Robert Wiener with CNN," I said, extending my hand.

"Welcome Mr. Robert. I am Mrs. Awattif."

Mrs. Awattif Samir, I would soon learn, was more than a feed coordinator. She ran the International Department of Iraqi TV and ran it with an iron fist. During those early days she was also the official censor. As the crisis dragged on and the pressure upon everyone, including Mrs. Awattif, became more intense, others sometimes referred to her as the Dragon Lady, or worse. CNN, too, was subject to censorship, occasionally for pictures that confound me to this day, but from that very first meeting Mrs. Awattif treated us with respect and courtesy, and we in turn tried to do the same.

"The telex from Eason Jordan says you will feed on INTELSAT," Mrs. Awattif informed me.

"That's fine. Is there a phone in the feedroom I could use to call London?"

"No, I will call London from here," she offered. "What is the number?"

While Awattif placed the call, I ran down the corridor to check on Mark. He and Trey were patching cables. "We'll be ready in about two minutes,"

Trey said. Mrs. Awattif joined us to screen the tape and found nothing offensive.

"I'll have to coordinate from down the hall," I told them. "We're going INTELSAT to London. Put a countdown in the gate as soon as you're set." I double-timed it back to the office just as the phone began to ring.

"Hi, it's Robert in Baghdad. Who's handling the feed?" A moment later I was on with Rod Huntress, who told me he was seeing "hash." We should be ready in a minute," I told him. "Let me know when you see a 10 in the gate. By the way, did Clancy get through to Atlanta?"

"Yeah, they've got all the instructions," Rod said. "This bird's patched straight through to them. So, what's Baghdad like?"

"I'll let you know after the feed. Still nothing?"

"Nothing. Oh yeah, now I see your countdown but there's still a lot of hash. It looks like it's on your end."

"Jesus! Hold a sec . . ." I ran down the hall again.

"London's seeing the ten count but it's covered by hash," I told the guys. "Are you sure we're patched out correctly?"

Trey rechecked his cables. "Should be," he said. I tried to sprint back to the office, acutely aware that as a three-pack-a-day man my sprinting career had long since ended. I told Mrs. Awattif what the problem was and she picked up a second phone.

"Rod, we're double-checking but I'm told we're fine on this end."

"Well, I still see hash but let's roll for levels. Maybe it'll clear up."

Fuck! I thought, and began another lap. "Roll, roll," I yelled as I approached Master Control, then turned around to continue the relay. "Hold it," I said. "This is not gonna work. Mark, you do the feed. Trey, you come with me and wait halfway down the hall. Otherwise I'm gonna have a heart attack."

"There's a problem with INTELSAT," Mrs. Awattif said as I entered the office. "Because of the United Nations embargo, they don't confirm our order. Why not feed ARABSAT to Jordan?" she asked. I thought for a second, then picked up the line to London.

"Listen, Rod, it ain't gonna work with INTELSAT. I'll spare ya the details. Get Atlanta on the line and have them contact CNN Amman. Amman should call Jordan TV and have them patch through to our flyaway at the Intercontinental. We're gonna feed ARABSAT. That's the only way this is gonna work." I put down the phone a second and went to the door. "Trey," I yelled. "Tell Mark to stop feeding and take it back to a ten. We're going on another bird."

It took a few minutes before all was ready. "They're seeing you in Amman," Rod said. "They have speed. Roll!"

"Roll! Trey, roll," I yelled. "How are the levels, Rod?"

"Amman says everything's looking good. Keep rolling. By the way, do you have a running time?"

"Hang on. Keep rolling, Trey," I yelled. "Everything's fine. Rod, the package runs two and change. I don't have an exact time."

"Okay. They're going to pass on a nat-sound refeed [without the reporter's narration]," Rod said.

"Fine, have Amman check tape and give me a 'buy.' "

"That's a buy and good night at thirty-three," he said a minute later.

"Okay, thanks very much. We'll speak to you later. Good night."

"Did everything go all right?" Mrs. Awattif inquired.

"Thank you, just fine," I replied. "What we call 'a piece of cake.' " I used her phone to place a last call to Atlanta.

"Hey, nice job," said Eason. "We're gonna book ARABSAT for the next week, between 10:45 and 11:15 P.M. local. We're also hearing Iraqi tanks are going to surround Western embassies in Kuwait tomorrow. Frankly, we're worried this could be the spark that ignites it."

"That was one of the most fucked-up feeds I've ever gone through," I said to Mark as we headed back to the hotel. "I asked Mrs. Awattif if a phone could be installed in the feedroom. She's gonna see what she can do. I tell ya, at my age there's no way I can go through that every night."

Even though it was after midnight the lobby looked like Grand Central Station. Dozens of hostages lounged on couches, while dozens more drained large bottles of local Iraqi beer in the downstairs bar. A physician from Switzerland approached me and introduced himself. "You're a journalist, aren't you? I worked with a relief group in Kurdistan. I heard the Swiss are permitted to leave but our ambassador is not even in Baghdad. Do you know if it's true?"

"I'm afraid I don't," I told him, "but give me your room number and I'll get in touch if I hear anything." Along with the Europeans, the hotel was also home to a number of Third Worlders, refugees from India, Pakistan, Bangladesh, and the Philippines. Large families occupied a single room while their children ran amok in the hallways.

Jim was still at the embassy and the crew was starving. "Let's hang on the feedbag, boys," I said, calling room service. "Forget about the prices. There's no way we can afford to eat on our per diems. Atlanta will have to pick up the tab. I'll clear it with 'em in the morning." While we waited for sandwiches to arrive I cracked open a bottle of Stoli. "This is going to be another hardship post," I joked. "The hotel is already out of tonic."

Clancy breezed in about half-past two, exhausted but clearly exhilarated. "They loved the package," he exclaimed. "Couldn't believe we turned it around so fast. They had me doing phoners at the top of each hour. Oh, Wilson says thanks for the cigars. I said you'd see him tomorrow. Are we out of ice?" We continued the ritual for another hour, then decided to get some sleep.

"I feel good about this one, Robert," Jim said as I walked him to his room. "I'd like to see those guys in Washington do what we did today. Hah! They're nothing but a bunch of drunken Eskimos."

"The eggs look nervous and the hotel's out of juice," I said. "May I offer you a cup of coffee?" As promised, Faiz appeared at our workspace, and he had brought a friend.

"This is Mr. Mazin," he explained, introducing us. "Both Mr. Mazin and I will be your guides. If I can't be here, Mazin will."

"That's what I call fabulous service! Do you also work for the Foreign Ministry?"

"I work at the protocol office," Mazin said, eyeing me suspiciously. "I think you have not been to Baghdad before?" he asked.

"You're absolutely right. This is my first visit. How long have you been in Iraq?" I asked.

"I live here!" Mazin exclaimed. "Do you not know I am an Iraqi?"

"I thought you might be," I laughed, "but as a newsman I need to confirm these things." There was something about Mr. Mazin that intrigued me. I couldn't quite put my finger on it, but my gut told me he had a sense of humor. Either that or I'd found the perfect straight man.

"What is your program for today?" Faiz interrupted.

"Well, as you know we spoke with the Information Ministry yesterday. Today I think we'd like to drive around the city, take some pictures, and interview some average Baghdadis. We'd also like to interview some of the hos . . . er, guests here at the hotel. Would that be feasible?" Both Faiz and Mazin nodded their agreement.

"Where exactly do you want to go in Baghdad?" Mazin inquired.

"This is Friday," I said. "Perhaps we could stop by one of the larger mosques and shoot the noon prayers. Is there someplace else special where people usually go today?"

"The pet market is every Friday. It is very old and very famous."

Pet market! I could hear Elaine screaming in my head, pet market! In the middle of a damn crisis you went to a pet market?

"Perfect," I said. "When shall we leave?"

"Mr. Mazin will meet you here at eleven-thirty," Faiz said. "This afternoon I hope to know about the interview with His Excellency Mr. Tariq Aziz."

I telephoned Clancy and gave him a fill. "I'm heading over to the embassy," I told him. "In the meantime you can knock off some hostages here at the hotel." I gave him the room number of the doctor from Switzerland. "I'll meet up with you later."

"Taxi! Mister, Taxi! Where you want to go?"

"The U.S. Embassy please," I said to the fat man. "So, I see you speak English. What is your name, my friend?"

"I Jasim. I make you good price." As we headed to the embassy, Jasim gave me his spiel. "I can take you anywhere. In Baghdad, to Jordan border, to border with Iran. I very good driver. You can to telephone me at home." He offered his card. "I have other car, not taxi car. Good car, air-condition car. If you want, I get."

"Let me think about it," I said. "How much would you charge?"

"You pay dollar, yes? One hundred fifty dollar. I drive all day, all night. When you want me, I here. I stay by hotel. Is good price." I offered him a hundred dollars a day, the usual rate for the road.

"Hundred dollar too little. Only thirty-five dinar. You take hotel car, you pay maybe twenty dinar every time. For little trip even. You pay to me one hundred and fifty dollar I take you anywhere. I here all time, day and night. We at embassy in five minutes. I very good driver. You see."

"All right, Mr. Jasim, you've got yourself a deal. Wait for me in front of the embassy. I won't be long."

The embassy compound housed two main buildings, the chancery and the United States Information Service, or USIS. A private driveway separated the two. Only a handful of American diplomats was still in Baghdad. Even the U.S. Marine security detachment had left. A few Iraqi guards were in front of the compound but the door to the chancery was open and unmanned. I made my way through the ground floor past large plastic sacks of shredded documents. The embassy was apparently already in a "read and burn" mode. I walked upstairs, introduced myself to the ambassador's secretary, and asked for the chargé d'affaires.

Joseph Charles Wilson IV was the Deputy Chief of Mission and ranking U.S. diplomat in Baghdad following the departure of Ambassador April Glaspie, who was ordered home for consultations on July 30. Prior to his tour in Iraq, Wilson had been posted in Brazzaville, Burundi, and South Africa, where he worked mainly as an administrative officer. Now the forty-two-year-old career diplomat faced a daunting challenge. Wilson was America's point man to negotiate the freedom of hundreds, if not thousands, of American citizens trapped in Iraq and Kuwait. He had gone without sleep for the past thirty hours and looked exhausted.

"Hi, Joe Wilson," he said, extending his hand as he ushered me into the ambassador's private office. "I'm sorry but I can't spare much time this morning. We're bringing up a number of our staff and dependents from the embassy in Kuwait."

"How many?" I asked.

"A little over a hundred. We're trying to work that out."

"Will they be allowed to leave Baghdad?"

"Yes. At least that's what I've been told by the Foreign Ministry, but you can't count on anything around here until it actually happens."

"What's the latest you've heard about the situation in Kuwait itself?"

"Well, as you probably know, Iraq has ordered all embassies to cease operations by midnight tonight. They say they're going to cut off their electricity and water. We also have indications that diplomats remaining in Kuwait will lose their immunity as of the deadline."

"But we're still going to keep our embassy open, right?"

"Absolutely. Ambassador Howell will remain with a small staff."

"I understand that tanks may be surrounding some embassies there. If Iraq forcibly entered our embassy, what then?"

"Well, that's up to the President," Joe said, "but if you ask me, I think it's war! Look, you can use what I've told you but please attribute it to 'Western sources.' I don't want to go on the record at this stage."

"How about 'Western diplomats'?" I asked. "It puts more meat on the bones."

"Okay, if you have to," he said.

Wilson was preoccupied and I felt it was best to wrap things up. "So, I gather we can use the phones here?" I asked.

"Yes. I told Jim Clancy yesterday, we'll make the same accommodations for CNN as we did for ABC and CBS. I work across the hall, so you can use the phone in this office. We also have some phones at USIS. Please log your calls and we'll bill you later, Also, there's no filming permitted on the embassy's grounds, and that means here as well as the ambassador's residence. I'll give you my home number but please don't call unless it's urgent. I've been putting in twenty-hour days and my time at home is precious."

"Got it. Enjoy the cigars, by the way?"

Wilson laughed. "Yeah, thanks. I smoked one last night over a cold Heineken."

Joe went back to work and I checked in with Atlanta. It seemed surreal sitting with my feet propped up on the ambassador's mahogany desk with both the U.S. and State Department flags behind me. I made a mental note to take a picture one day.

I then strolled over to USIS to meet Steve Thibault. Steve bore the title of assistant press attaché, but, with no press to speak of requiring care and feeding, he spent most of his time providing consular services to American citizens, including the hostages. Before entering the foreign service he had worked at the Boston Public Library; fluent in Arabic, he had been eager for an assignment in the Middle East. Steve was affable and helpful but, as I immediately discovered, the art of diplomacy was not his forte.

"This government is fucked!" he replied when I asked for a briefing, "and if it comes down to it, we're gonna kick their goddamn ass. They think it's one big game but we're not playing around here."

"What can you tell me about the situation on the ground?" I asked. "Are the economic sanctions biting?"

"Yeah, they're starting to hurt," he said. "Prices have doubled in many shops. Chicken and rice are way up. There's only a two-month supply of canned goods available. Some of the hotels have run out of soft drinks. I hear even mineral water is getting scarce. They just don't understand," he said, "and it's going to get worse. And every day these pathetic demonstrations in front of the embassy. I mean, it's a joke. Last week they sent the so-called poets and writers. Yesterday there were about a hundred kids, like five and six years old. What the hell do they understand? You know, they stand out there chanting 'Down Down Bosh! Down Down Bosh!' as if it's going to make us change our mind. I mean, we're dead serious about this. They've got to get out of Kuwait. They've got to release the hostages."

"How many Americans are we talking about?"

"We estimate about six hundred in Iraq and about twenty-five hundred U.S. citizens in Kuwait."

"And how many Americans are being held at strategic sites?"

"We think around forty-one. Most of them were brought up from Kuwait the first week in August and taken to the Mansour Melia Hotel here. They've since disappeared."

"Steve, I understand you've got some Americans who've taken refuge in diplomatic quarters. If possible, we'd like to do some interviews."

"Well, that's up to them," he said. "They had a bad experience with CBS and it's soured them. But let me check. Why don't you call me this afternoon."

"What happened with CBS?"

"When Rather was here, his crew said they would take some video of the guys just to give to their families, and they agreed. But then the pictures turned up on the evening news. They're really bent out of shape about it. They feel they were used."

"Shit. Were you there at the time? Did that really happen?"

"Oh yeah, I was there. I think that was the understanding, but I don't know for certain. But it sure left a bad taste in everyone's mouth."

"Well, see what you can do," I said. "We obviously need to talk to these folks. We'll even come without a camera, and just play it by ear. Okay?"

Thibault agreed and I thanked him for his time. "By the way," he said, "I'm sure Joe told you the phones are always available. The door here at USIS is usually locked. Just punch in the code one-three-five and turn the handle."

The drive back to the Sheraton took us through the Inacarata district. The small grocery stores, many of them managed by Indian nationals, looked well stocked; their window displays were a showcase for imported liquor and beer, artfully arranged in pyramids. Every few blocks you'd see a small breadline, but the people who waited appeared patient and orderly. There was no discernible sense of panic. In Ali Baba Square, we passed the magnificent fountain by Mohammad Ghani, his tribute to tales from the *Arabian Nights*.

Jim and the crew had interviewed some British hostages but it hadn't been easy. Many were afraid of retribution, and their remarks were tempered. I pulled soundbites with Mark while Clancy returned to the embassy to do an early beeper.

Around noon both Faiz and Mazin reappeared at our workspace. Faiz seemed concerned that we weren't ready to roll, and that Jim had gone to the embassy again.

"Why do you go all the time to the American embassy?" he asked with more than a trace of menace. "Do you work together there?" I concluded his remark was a calculated one, if not a veiled threat. After all, Iraq had already hanged one British journalist it accused of being a spy. But I decided not to let him get under my skin. We're in the truth business, I thought. The best policy is to play it straight.

"As you probably know," I said, "there are phones at the embassy we can use to call the States. We also get briefed by officials there. This crisis, I'm sure you'll agree, is a two-way street. We need to hear from our own government, as well as yours."

"This crisis will show your government is not as powerful as it thinks," Faiz said sternly. "Why do you support the corrupt sheiks? They do nothing for their people. I think you're only after the oil."

"With all due respect, I'm not here to debate foreign policy," I said. "But I must tell you, if your tanks attack the U.S. Embassy in Kuwait, the crisis could seriously escalate, and that would bode ill for all of us. But in the meantime, I see Mr. Jim has returned, so why don't we hit the streets."

Jasim rounded up a second taxi and we drove to Sa'adoun Street, one of Baghdad's main thoroughfares. It was clogged with shoppers and browsers, including some soldiers. "No pictures of soldiers," Faiz admonished. While Mark rolled tape outside a music store, some good natural sound that might open the report, I looked for people to interview, preferably in English. In the shops and restaurants, the replies were identical. "We don't want war," people told Clancy, "but if there is war, we are prepared for it." There was no sense of gloating, no sense of posturing. "We endured eight years of war with Iran, a terrible war in which missiles landed here in Baghdad," said one man. "We will do it again if we have to." All professed loyalty and admiration for Saddam Hussein. He was their champion, a man who would stand up for Arab rights. Faiz and Mazin were present for each of the interviews but spent most of their time handling crowd control. Wherever we walked, we were mobbed.

From Sa'adoun Street we drove to the Al-Imman Al-Adham Mosque to catch the end of Friday prayers. In the small square adjacent to the mosque we interviewed a fruit vendor. Whether from fear, or ignorance, he looked to Faiz before answering every question. Though he too expressed devotion to Saddam, his replies would be left on the cutting room floor.

It was murderously hot as we sped to the pet market. Jasim kept a cooler in the trunk filled with mineral water and soft drinks, but with the temperature well over a hundred degrees, I constantly felt dehydrated. A few weeks later, during another visit to the market, one of our minders would purchase two parakeets and leave them in the car for fifteen minutes while the crew wrapped up shooting. When he returned, the birds were sleepin' with the fishes.

The pet market was nothing exotic: birds, fish, rabbits, chicks, roosters, and a couple of mangy dogs. The best it had to offer were cages handcrafted in wood, tin, or bamboo. The market was a natural magnet for children, as was our camera. Mark looked like the Pied Piper as they whooped and hollered in front of his lens. It was impossible to get a clean shot. Faiz and Mazin again played traffic cops, but they were swimming against the tide. No sooner did they fend off one group of adolescent rubberneckers than another bunch would take up the ballyhoo. But the market made interesting "B roll," good pictures and sound that would add to the texture of Clancy's report.

"ROLLIE SHOULD BE THERE TONIGHT," Eason said later when I called from the embassy. "Do we have a time yet for Aziz?"

"No, not yet. What's the latest on your end?" I asked.

"It's still a standoff at the embassies in Kuwait, and it looks like the Security Council is going to pass a resolution authorizing the use of force to interdict Iraqi shipping."

"Jesus! Is there still the feeling war may be imminent?"

"I'm afraid so," Eason said. "Oh, one other thing. We're hearing Kurt Waldheim is due in Baghdad and will meet with Saddam. It looks like he's trying to take out a group of Austrian hostages. See what you can do about getting a camera in. Maybe we can throw a few questions at Saddam."

I ran down the elements for Clancy's package and what I had learned from my earlier briefings. The desk sometimes slipped when it came to passing on information from one shift to the next, and I wanted Eason firmly in the loop.

"What about the American hostages?" he pressed. "We really need to hear from them."

"With luck, you'll see them tomorrow," I said. "I assume you'll want Clancy for beepers tonight, as often as possible . . . same drill as yesterday."

"Affirmative! Good luck."

"That was a hell of a flight," Rollie laughed as he began to unpack. "For some reason I didn't expect the plane to be crowded, but it was filled to capacity. So, kiddo," he asked, "what's going on?" Evans was not long on small talk and I was in no mood for it anyway. The Aziz interview, Clancy's package, tonight's feed, nailing down U.S. hostages, the Waldheim visit . . . the network monkey was on my back again.

"I want to do Aziz and get out," Evans said. "I can't afford to be away from Washington too long. My partner and I have a column to write, and there's no percentage getting stuck in here, not for me right now." I brought Rollie up to date on the day's developments.

"Well," he said thoughtfully, "Bush's presidency could well die in the sands of Saudi Arabia. It's a bold but very dangerous game. What do you think, kiddo?"

"To be honest with ya, Rollie, after a couple of years in Vietnam, I don't have much confidence in the U.S. Army. Look at Panama, for Chrissake! Almost half the casualties were the result of our troops shooting each other. The Air Force might be somewhat better, but I'm not overly optimistic. If there's war, I think we could get our asses kicked."

"You know, Vietnam is a paradise compared to Saudi Arabia," he said. "It's the most godforsaken place you've ever seen. The duty has got to be hell. There's nothing for those GI's to do. You can't get a drink. You can't get laid. There are no women, no nightclubs. And even if we win," he added, "what then? Is Bush going to permanently station forty thousand American troops in Iraq? I'm not sure he's thought that far ahead."

"I tell ya, Rollie, you certainly hear a lot over here about a double standard with regard to Israel. And the fact is, the Arabs have often gotten the short end of the stick. One word that kept popping up on the streets today was 'dignity.' It's clear many people believe Saddam can bring them that."

"Of course there's been a double standard," Rollie agreed, "but this is not about dignity, human rights, or international law. If Cameroon invaded Gabon, do you think we'd send hundreds of thousands of troops to defend territorial integrity? This is about oil and our strategic interests."

Rollie needed to nap before checking in with Nizar Hamdoon, the Deputy Foreign Minister. Hamdoon had been Iraq's ambassador to Washington, D.C., and the two were old friends. I walked down the hall to touch base with Clancy and review parts of his script. With Mazin there to translate, we then watched the local news. It began, as I would learn it always did, with the nightly homage to the man at the top: a smiling Saddam receiving the enthusiastic accolades of the multitudes. Astride a white stallion, the President, in the full regalia of a field marshal, led an impressive display of military hardware, including tanks and ballistic missiles, down Baghdad's official parade route. A few moments later, the martial music switched to a more festive tune and Saddam was shown, now attired in a natty white linen suit, clapping in time to the music as hundreds of schoolchildren sang and pranced around him.

"His Excellency President Saddam Hussein's birthday," Mazin intoned reverently. The third act consisted of "Saddam Does Mecca," a zany toga party in which the Prez and his inner circle, clad in what looked like bedsheets, did the two-step around the holy *Kaaba* during the annual haj. That's the last he'll see of Saudi Arabia for quite a while, I thought. Then it was on to the news.

Several countries, including Jordan, Switzerland, and the Philippines, were reported to have closed their embassies in Kuwait. The Iraqi News Agency said diplomats' families at embassies remaining open there would be allowed to leave, but male employees would be prevented from doing so until their governments officially closed the mission. The broadcast ended with a replay of Saddam and the British hostages from the previous night.

"I'll need some 'file' from Kuwait," Jim said. "Do you know what they have?"

"The U.S. Embassy for sure," I said. "We can throw up a graphic for the others." While Jim continued writing, I ordered room service and asked Mazin to join me. He declined.

"Why you not eat downstairs at the buffet, Mr. Robert?" he asked. "There is better selection in restaurant. It is not good you eat sandwiches all the time." I explained that I had calls to make and schedules to plan. I told him about the Waldheim visit and asked if we could cover the meeting.

"This is not up to me," he replied. "It is up to the President."

"Well, how do I contact the President's office?" I asked.

"You cannot contact the President," he laughed. "Who you think you are? Mr. Evans is already here to see His Excellency Tariq Aziz. Now you want to see His Excellency President Saddam Hussein. What, you think CNN can see whole government? The government is very busy, you know."

"Look, Mr. Mazin," I said. "I don't think it's an unreasonable request. I'm sure if you popped up in Washington, President Bush and his Cabinet would rearrange their entire schedule."

"I think . . . I think you are a crazy man," Mazin laughed. "You think Bosh wants to see Mazin?"

"You know, the name is Bush, not Bosh," I said.

"I know what his name is, but Bosh is, what you call, a joke. The word *bosh* in Arabic means 'nothing.' " Mazin laughed uproariously. "He is President Nothing!"

"Well, I'm gonna be Producer Nothing unless I can get into the Waldheim meeting. Are you sure there's nothing you can do?"

"Very well," he said, getting up to leave. "I will telephone and do my best."

It was already becoming routine: Jim tracked his piece and took a cab to the embassy; I stayed to help edit and feed the package. The heat had taken a toll on everyone, especially the crew who lugged the gear. Mark and Trey were troopers, yet I sensed Trey was still uneasy.

"What's up?" I asked.

"There's something about this place," he said softly. "I just don't like it. Those goons in the lobby give me the creeps. How long do you think we'll be here?"

"Gee, I have no idea. I'd say for a while but we can discuss it. We've got the Aziz interview, and then we'll play it by ear."

"Shit," he muttered.

The routine at the television station didn't change either. Again, we were given the once-over by security before hauling the feedpack to the second floor. Mrs. Awattif was in Master Control and, best of all, she was on a telephone. Thank God for small favors, I thought.

"Welcome, Mr. Robert," she said, shaking hands. "As you can see, everything is confirmed for your transmission." While the crew hooked up the equipment, Awattif screened Clancy's report.

"This . . . no," she said, after viewing a man eating a sandwich. "This picture cannot be transmitted." I was dumfounded. It was an innocuous shot Mark had taken at the pet market, of a food vendor and his customer.

"What is the problem?" I asked. Awattif simply waved her hands. "No . . . not this," she said. I again asked for an explanation but she offered none.

"You may use this to call Amman," she said, offering me the telephone. As Jim's package rolled into space, Awattif positioned herself by the video patch. As the offending shot appeared, she abruptly pulled the plug, turning the picture to "hash." A second later, she inserted the plug reestablishing the video. We fed the complete story twice, with a third feed for natural sound, as Awattif dutifully censored the man with a sandwich each time. Amman finally gave a "buy and good night." I'm sure they were as perplexed as we were. We decided to leave the feedpack at the television station. It would save time at security and save me, I thought, from an eventual hernia.

Rollie returned to the hotel about the same time we did. He had dined with Hamdoon and wanted to speak privately.

"From what I gather," he said, "there seems to be a conflict of sorts between the various ministries. The Foreign Ministry has one approach, more conciliatory, I think, while the Information Ministry takes a harder line. You know, Nizar and I go back a ways. He gave me his word of honor that if war breaks out, he'll try to protect us. But I don't know how good those guarantees will be, kiddo."

"What'd he say about Aziz?"

"Nizar said to call him tomorrow afternoon, but he doubts it will take place before Sunday, if then. Tell me," he asked, "do we have someone who can accompany me around the city in the morning? I want to walk the streets, get the scent of things, if you know what I mean." I liked Rollie immensely. He wasn't necessarily the toughest of interviewers but unlike some others who had achieved his prominence, he knew that to feel a story, you had to pound the pavement. I told him I'd make Mazin available after breakfast.

The phone was ringing as I walked into 501. It was Sue Tinson, a producer for ITN. London's Independent Television News and CNN have what's called a reciprocal agreement. We often share each other's material, including airing correspondents' reports. Sue had arrived that afternoon and spent what was left of her day with the British ambassador. We compared notes with my U.S. brief.

"Our embassy says its first priority is getting the hostages out," she said. "Apparently the Iraqis have indicated that Bush and Thatcher should make a conciliatory gesture like permitting food and medicine. In return for that, there might be some movement."

"Did you interview any British hostages?" I asked.

"We're going to do some tomorrow. A number are camped out on the embassy grounds. What about you?"

"We're working on it, but I've been up to my ass in alligators since we arrived."

"Yes, I saw your hostage report yesterday using the Iraqi TV material. Grand stuff," she said. "Let's do keep in touch."

I called for ice while we waited for Clancy. It had been another long day, albeit a satisfying one. I was pleased with Jim's report, both the content and the writing. I chuckled when I thought about Faiz's earlier comments, as Mark had begun shooting billboards of Saddam. "Why newspeople so interested in posters of the President?" he'd asked. "Is this so unusual?" Tonight our viewers would be the judge of that. If Baghdad wasn't unusual, I thought, what was? I'd been censored before, but never because of a sandwich.

"This is very bad, very bad," Faiz exclaimed, jabbing his finger in my face. "This United Nations resolution . . . very bad. If you attack, we will send tens of thousands of you home in coffins!"

"Hey, give me a break," I joked. "I haven't even had my coffee yet!" But Faiz was fuming and in no mood for humor.

"You will see," he shouted. "You cannot push us to our knees anymore."

"*Please!*" I interrupted. "I didn't pass the goddamn resolution. There's no point hollering at me, my friend. Take it up with the Security Council."

I was still trying to get my head to work, and Faiz's little sideshow wasn't helping any. I had ordered juice, then remembered the hotel was out of it. It was only seven-thirty and Jim and the crew were still asleep.

"When is Mr. Mazin coming?" I asked, to change the subject. "I'd like him to escort Mr. Evans around Baghdad."

"He will be here soon," he said. "What is your program for today?" I told Faiz we wanted to shoot in the souk but kept our plans for the American hostages to myself. I had a feeling it would be like rubbing salt in the wound. We agreed to link up in a couple of hours. Jesus, I thought. First tanks surround the embassies in Kuwait and now this UN resolution authorizing naval force. It didn't feel good. I placed wake-up calls to the crew and left for the embassy.

At the compound, things were hopping. The convoy carrying American diplomats and their dependents from Kuwait had arrived in the early hours and was parked bumper-to-bumper from one end of the private driveway to the other; an assortment of Chevy station wagons, Jeep Cherokees, and sedans filled with suitcases, cartons, coolers, duffel bags, animal cages, and even stuffed animals. People were scurrying between the chancery and USIS; among them, Steve Thibault. "This is a bad time right now," he told me. "We're trying to get these people out of town."

"How many came up?" I asked.

"About one hundred and eight."

"And they'll drive to Amman?"

"More likely to the Turkish border."

"Look, I know you're up to here with it, but what about the guys at the ambassador's residence?" I asked. "I'm being squeezed by the home office."

"We'll try to go over this afternoon," Thibault said, "but, like I said, it's up to them whether they want to be interviewed."

ATLANTA READ THE WIRES on the morning call. Security Council Resolution 665, which authorized the coalition to intercept and inspect all shipping bound for Iraq and Kuwait, had passed by a vote of 13–0. Cuba and Yemen abstained. Kurt Waldheim was now en route to Baghdad, and Iraq again stated that diplomats still in Kuwait had lost their immunity.

"So, how's it going?" Eason asked as he picked up the line. I told him the Faiz coffin story and laughed like a hyena. I'm sure if I were on his end, I'd find it problematic, but retelling the episode had me in stitches.

"You know, Eason, this may be premature, but we ought to think about getting a second correspondent here. Between the beepers and feeds, there's more than enough for two."

"Yeah, we've thought about that. The problem is, there's not a single correspondent who's willing to go."

"No one in Amman will volunteer?" I asked incredulously.

"Negative!"

"Jesus! Murrow must be rolling over in his grave."

"Tell me about it! You know," he continued, "you wouldn't believe the atmosphere over here. Everyone's beating the war drums. I've never seen anything like it." That's fabulous, I thought. Just what I needed to hear.

I rousted the crew and had them head for the embassy. At the very least, we would need shots of the American convoy for our evening wrap. Thibault had said no interviews, so Mark simply set up as near as we were permitted to the driveway and rolled. Jim knocked off a few beepers for the early shows before we all left for the souk, first stopping by the hotel to pick up Faiz.

A few hours later, after depositing our trusty guide, we returned to the U.S. mission. "Okay," Thibault said, "here's the deal. We'll drive over to the ambassador's residence and if someone wants to be interviewed, we'll do it at my apartment. I'll personally take them over in my car, which has diplomatic plates, so they'll be in no danger. But remember, no filming at the residence."

Ambassador April Glaspie's annual salary of $83,600 is a matter of public record, and her villa, in one of Baghdad's poshest neighborhoods, was testament to the fact that public service has its perks. Set beyond a high wall, the compound, with its manicured lawns and verdant foliage, was magnificent. The main house was classic, with its huge foyer dominated by a grand staircase. To the left of the entrance was an immense and lavishly furnished living room; to the right, an intimate den. The dining room and rear patio were the perfect size for wining and dining, and the large modern kitchen contained every convenience. Upstairs there were several bedrooms and baths, the ambassador's tiled in robin's egg blue. The swimming pool and tennis court were discreetly tucked away behind the garden. Since the hostages had taken up residence, however, the ambassador's house looked more like Animal House. Most of the furniture was pushed to the side and replaced by mattresses. There were six of them in the living room alone. Others were stacked up along the hallway while the bedrooms, including Ms. Glaspie's, were redecorated for the occasion in what can only be described as flophouse contemporary. The place looked like the aftermath of a chaotic pajama party.

Many of the hostages were on the rear patio, some playing cards, a couple playing Ping-Pong, others sipping beer. Most were in the oil or construction business and, along with their blue jeans and baseball caps, several sported the inevitable gold chain and Rolex. Just a bunch of good ole boys stuck in Bag Dad, Eye Rack. Thibault made the introductions and emphasized that no one was under any obligation to do an interview. "It's really up to you guys," he reminded them.

"What do we gain by doing an interview, Robert?" one of them asked as Steve walked away. "I mean, there's no sense calling attention to ourselves, is there?" It was a legitimate question and the guy had a point. Here they were, trapped, not knowing if there would be war or peace, not knowing if Saddam would pluck them from their diplomatic haven and handcuff them to a wall in a poison gas factory, and they were being asked to go on television and say what? What could they say? That they were desperate to go home, that Saddam was fucked, that we should bomb the shit out of Baghdad? Whatever they said would be seen by the Iraqi authorities, and they feared the possible repercussions. "I don't think there's one goddamn thing we can say that's gonna help us any," another said. I could see convincing them was going to be a tall order.

"Look, guys, I'll be honest with ya," I told them. "I agree there's probably nothing any of you can say that will help your particular situation. I mean, even if you made a personal appeal to the Iraqi government during an interview with CNN, I doubt it's going to change a thing. And I also understand your anxiety about saying anything negative that might affect your safety here or your colleagues' safety. I'm not here to put words in your mouths," I emphasized. "But I believe there is a benefit to doing an interview and this is it. Right now you guys are only statistics. You're only a group of Americans "taking refuge in diplomatic quarters." You're an abstract. I don't relate well to abstracts and I don't believe many people do. You've got to put a face on these things. There's a person behind every number. You're not just hostages, you're human beings. And the people at home need to be reminded of this. To do that, they need to see you and hear from you. Even if it's nothing more than just hearing who you are and that you're doing your best to cope. Furthermore, I don't see how that, in any way, could have a negative effect so far as the Iraqi government is concerned."

They listened sympathetically, and as I searched their eyes I sensed a chink in the armor. "You mean, we would only say who we are and that we missed our families. That's it, right?" one asked me.

"If that's all you're prepared to say, fine. I think we could talk in very general terms about what brought you to Iraq and what you've been doing here and so on. Look, I guarantee that I'm not gonna put you on television and throw you a curveball. I'm not gonna put you in front of the camera and then ask if you think Saddam Hussein should have his dick chopped off. I give you my word."

"Well, okay," one laughed. "I wouldn't have a problem . . ."

"Excuse me, may I speak with you a moment?" We were suddenly interrupted by a man I had never seen before. He motioned me to follow him inside the house.

"Uh-oh," one of the hostages chuckled. "The boss man."

"We will not be doing any interviews," he told me. "I'd appreciate your not bothering my men."

"I wasn't aware I was bothering anyone," I said, introducing myself. "And what is your name, sir?"

"I'd rather not say," he replied. "For security reasons."

"Security reasons?" I asked, astonished. "At least tell me your first name. That won't violate security, will it?"

"Uh . . . Stu," he said, tentatively.

"Well, Stu," I pressed, "with all due respect, it's my understanding that anyone who agrees to be interviewed has the right to do so. That's basically freedom of speech." By now, Thibault had joined us and laid out the ground rules for Stu.

"We'll see about that," Stu huffed, and trotted back to the patio.

"Who is that schmuck?" I asked Steve.

Thibault rolled his eyes. "I was afraid of that," he said. "Stu was the head honcho at Bechtel and most of the guys outside worked under him. He's a real piece of work. He's got them all convinced if they open their mouths, something awful is gonna happen. I mean, the guy is totally paranoid and he's doing his best to make them paranoid too."

"Jesus, the situation is tense enough without some martinet making it worse," I said. "The U.S. Embassy is providing security for these folks, no? Who the fuck gave Stu the authority to make the rules?"

"He's got no authority," Thibault said. "What he's got are a bunch of guys afraid of going over their boss's head." By the time Thibault and I returned to the group, it was evident ole Stu had put the whammy on things, and even Clancy's formidable powers of persuasion failed to budge the captives.

"I'm sorry," one hostage told us. "I just can't buck him. It really is a crazy situation," he said, pointing to a guy hanging shirts on a nearby clothes line. "We got a hundred-and-fifty-thousand-dollar-a-year laundry-man over there," he laughed. "And there's a hundred-thousand-dollar-a-year cook in the kitchen. It's not every day you go for a swim where the lifeguard makes over a hundred grand. Again, I'm sorry, guys," he said. "I hope you understand."

"Well, don't let Stu get you down," I said. "Keep the faith. We're going to be around for a while and can stop by another day. Perhaps one of you will have a change of heart."

Clancy and I poked around the house looking for others to interview. Thibault had said not everyone at the residence worked for Bechtel, but, to a man, each of the Americans declined to go on camera. I was getting desperate. "Jesus, we're gonna look like idiots if we can't come up with some hostages," I said. "Eason and Ed will skin me alive." Jim made one final sweep of the grounds but again came up empty-handed. We were on the verge of leaving when I decided to take one last look in the living room. Two men I hadn't seen earlier were talking quietly.

"Excuse me," I said. "I'm with CNN. . . ."

"Sure, I'd be happy to do an interview," one of them told me. "I don't work for Stu and, furthermore, I think his attitude is inappropriate."

Fifty-eight-year-old Bob Vinton from Sante Fe, New Mexico, was a news producer's dream. Bright, articulate, and forthright, Vinton had moved to Baghdad from Saudi Arabia several months earlier. He worked in the petrochemical industry, had spent many years in the Middle East, and was conversant with the people and the problems of the region. When Iraq announced it would not permit foreigners to leave the country, Vinton sought shelter at the ambassador's residence, but lately he'd been returning to sleep at his own apartment nearby. He was fed up with Stu and his petty politics, and said he had nothing to fear from the Iraqi people. He suggested we shoot the interview at his place, where his fridge was stocked with a case of cold Heinekens.

Vinton was as well spoken on camera as he was when we first met, and the interview was a keeper. "Sure, I'm concerned," he said, "but in this situation you've got to take it one day at a time. I'm trying to lead a normal life as much as possible. I go to my office every day. I do my marketing. I have Iraqi friends and I try to see them."

Clancy asked Bob if he feared being taken to a strategic site and held as a so-called human shield. "I suppose the possibility exists," he said. "That's why I initially went to the residence, but I can't spend my days just cowering. I'm a man. I think if it happened, though, I would have the stamina and courage to see it through."

This guy would make a fabulous reporter, I thought, as I listened to the interview. Vinton had an eye for detail and a feel for nuance. He was familiar with the beat and could express himself clearly. "How about doing some live telephone interviews with CNN from the phones at the U.S. Embassy?" I asked him. "You could be CNN's eyes and ears on the hostage front, if you get my drift. I need to run it by Atlanta, but we could set up some specific times for you to call in and just basically shoot the shit. You know, tell our viewers how you spent the day, how food prices have changed in the market, how your colleagues are holding up."

Vinton thought it a fine idea, and we agreed to meet at the embassy later. "I can even drive you guys around town if you like and show you the sights. I've noticed some small but perceptible changes on the street." As the crew was packing up, two of Bob's friends came to the house. Mike Nickman and Gus Cero had been at the residence earlier and were curious about the interview. "You should talk to these guys," Vinton insisted. "You know CNN. They're straight shooters. People are interested in what we have to say." Because of Vinton, both Mike and Gus also agreed to go on the record, although Gus preferred to be shot in silhouette, and we happily agreed.

"This stuff is fanfuckingtastic!" I said to Jim as we returned to the Sheraton. "I can't believe it. What a godsend!"

"Yeah, it's terrific," Clancy agreed. "We really lucked out."

"Well, you know what they say, ole buddy, the harder you work, the luckier you get."

WE WEREN'T SO LUCKY with former Nazi Storm Trooper, and now Austria's President, Kurt Waldheim. His meeting with Saddam Hussein to seek the release of some ninety Austrians being held in Baghdad was closed to the press—the local foreign press, that is. A sizable contingent of reporters and television crews traveling with Waldheim got a shot at a joint news conference with the two leaders, which, of course, was also carried on Iraqi TV. Both Waldheim and Saddam said they hoped for a diplomatic way out of the crisis, and then Iraq's Revolutionary Command Council advanced diplomacy to a new plateau by announcing that anyone who sheltered foreigners held in Iraq or Kuwait would be hanged. Saddam got the headlines, Waldheim got his hostages, and I got another knot in my stomach.

But there was some good news on another front. "It looks like Aziz is on for tomorrow," I told Eason later in the day. "I'll bring up the Saddam interview and the possibility of going live when I meet with Hamdoon at the Foreign Ministry. We have a fabulous live shot location at the Sheraton. It's a terrific backdrop. You've got the mosque, the Saddam billboard, the traffic circle . . . the works. It'd be dynamite."

"Great! How's tonight's piece shaping up?" he asked.

"It's got it all. You'll have to insert file from Kuwait and Iraqi TV, but the interviews with Vinton and the others are excellent. Jim and the crew are doing a helluva job. Listen, I gotta tell ya, though," I said, trying to speak in measured tones, "there are moments when it doesn't feel too good. It has nothing to do with our rooms being bugged, or the phones being bugged, or even working with these minders. What's really frightening is the possibility of getting stuck in here if war breaks out. You wouldn't go to the U.S. Embassy, that's for sure. Even Thibault said the last place he'd want to be is in the ambassador's office, watching five thousand Iraqis charge the embassy to tear him limb from limb."

"I hear you," Eason said.

"It's just incredible tension," I said. "Maybe it has something to do with being the only Americans in Baghdad right now. I bet the other nets were slitting their wrists over Clancy's report with the hostage video."

"You wouldn't believe the fallout over our airing that stuff," Eason said. "There's been all kinds of criticism . . . that we're being used by Saddam, that we're running his propaganda . . ."

"That's bullshit! Our viewers are intelligent enough to judge that hostage video in the proper context."

"Of course it's bullshit!"

"So who's doing the criticizing?"

"The other nets, for one. Steve Friedman of NBC gave a long interview in which he said it was irresponsible for us to air the stuff live and said that was the common judgment of most news executives."

"Fuck Steve Friedman!" I laughed. "Where the hell is NBC on this story anyway? That news organization has a major problem, and the problem is it's dying."

"Well, Friedman is saying NBC can't get into Iraq because it did a major investigative piece a while ago and ruffled a lot of feathers in Baghdad. He says the Iraqis know they can't use NBC."

"Piss on Friedman! Look, Brian Ross and his producer . . . what's his name, Ira Silverman, often do a terrific job, but who the fuck is Steve Friedman to talk about journalistic integrity or investigative reporting? What the hell did he investigate when he ran the 'Today' show? Hemorrhoid medications? Listen," I said, getting back on track, "about this tension thing. I have a feeling that Trey would like to get out of here as soon as possible."

"We just got here!" Eason exclaimed. "We don't want to leave!"

"We're not going to leave," I said. "We're here to do a job and we'll do it, and that goes for Trey too. He's a trooper. All I'm saying is, after the Aziz interview we ought to think about getting a replacement for him. He's got a new baby, you know, and his wife is alone in Paris. The guy has a lot on his mind, and possibly getting stuck in Baghdad is a burden he and his family can do without."

"Okay, I hear ya," Eason said. "Let me work on it."

AS EXPECTED, Vinton aced the live phoner. The questions often bordered on the bizarre, shaped, no doubt, by the anchor's erroneous impression that all of the hostages were in a state of siege, stockpiling food and water, as they waited for Armageddon. But Vinton set him straight, offering an accurate and reasoned description of what he was personally experiencing. When the interview concluded, Atlanta gave the nod and Bob Vinton became a fixture on CNN—until a few days later, when he was picked up at home by security police and taken to a strategic site. I telephoned his wife, Sue, racked by guilt that my asking him to become so visible contributed to his abduction. I expected Sue Vinton to be furious with me when I related the news, but on the contrary she said she lived with her television glued to CNN and was really pleased with the coverage we provided. "I'm sure Bob will be all right," she assured me. "He is very strong and courageous." Sue Vinton would be proved right.

The evening transmission, our third now from Baghdad, worked like a charm, but censorship was becoming more rigid. "He is diplomat," said Mrs. Awattif after screening in advance the silhouetted image of Gus Cero. "No interviews with diplomats permitted. Where did you take these pictures, at the American embassy?"

"The interview was done at a private home," I explained, "and the gentleman is not a diplomat."

"Out . . . out!" Awattif insisted, pulling the plug. Luckily, she was a second too late and one frame of Gus's video went over the satellite. Atlanta was able to "freeze" it, and since the audio wasn't cut, the report was complete. Our colleagues at ITN were not as fortunate. Their report included a long interview with the British ambassador, which, of course, got the ax. When the correspondent complained bitterly, his stand-up close was also chopped.

"What did I say?" he implored Awattif. "You can't do that."

"Out . . . finish," was all she would reply.

You've got to know when to hold 'em, and know when to fold 'em, I thought, as I watched this display. When you worked in Baghdad, you operated under certain constraints. None of us in the press liked those constraints, but it was quickly apparent that browbeating Mrs. Awattif would get you nowhere fast. The Iraqis would accept a protest if it were lodged in a professional and reasoned manner. That doesn't always work if you're on deadline, but it pays off in the long run. Awattif Samir, after all, was not a person to be trifled with. She didn't make it up the ladder at Iraqi TV by being a pushover.

ROLLIE HAD SPENT a fruitful day walking in Baghdad. "He's an unusual character, that Mr. Mazin of yours. Did he tell you that during the Iran-Iraq war, he machine-gunned dozens of Iranian kids who were sent to the front?"

"Well, Rollie, you know what they say about the Middle East: the longer you're here, the less you understand." I told Evans about Vinton, the other hostages, and the chilling announcement by the Revolutionary Command Council.

"I might use some of that in my column," he ventured.

"So what do you think?" I asked. "Are the battle lines drawn?"

"I'm afraid they might be, kiddo. Let's see what Mr. Aziz has to say about it tomorrow."

"It's unbelievable," Thibault fumed. "These goddamn people just changed the rules on us. Either that or the Foreign Ministry can't make its decisions stick." For the "dips" at the U.S. Embassy it had been another long night. The convoy from Kuwait had been turned around at the Turkish border. The Iraqis allowed only fifty-five of the one hundred and eight people to leave the country. "They said only dependents and minors could go," Steve explained. "There were three kids, aged eighteen to twenty-one, who were forced to return to Baghdad. They all got back around two-twenty this morning."

"I don't know what more I can add," Joe Wilson said glumly. "Tariq Aziz had given his word these people could leave. It's an interesting situation when a promise from a Foreign Minister of a country to the ranking U.S. diplomat is meaningless."

"So where do you go from here?" I asked.

"Back to the Foreign Ministry," Joe said. "As you know, Robert, our highest priority is the evacuation of all U.S. citizens. I've been meeting with the Iraqis at least once a day, sometimes three times a day."

"As far as I'm concerned," Steve exclaimed, "this government can kiss my ass!" He smooched his palm and slapped his rear. Wilson and I were struck speechless by his exaggerated pantomime.

"Joe, I don't suppose you'll be taking Steve along to supervise these delicate diplomatic negotiations?"

"I don't think so," he laughed. "We're going to let him handle the people out there," Wilson said, gesturing out the window at the Iraqi demonstrators gathered below. We were sitting in the ambassador's office as the chants of "Down Down Bosh" grew louder and louder. "Who is it today?" he asked Steve.

Thibault peered out the window. "School kids and their teachers," he said.

"You know, Robert," Joe said, turning serious, "this is a proud, well-educated, and cultured society. And when all of this is said and done, we're going to have to reestablish some kind of relationship with them. Brainwashing five-, six-, and seven-year-old kids is not a positive thing."

The crew shot the demo while Clancy phoned in another beeper. Because the Aziz interview could come at any time, we restricted our movements to the embassy and the Sheraton. Iraq seemed to be easing its grip on the foreign embassies in Kuwait. Several tanks had pulled back and electricity was restored. The wires were reporting that Yasir Arafat had come to Baghdad to meet with Saddam and discuss the hostages. Did all this add up to a reason for hope? Rollie hunkered down at the hotel, working on his questions for Aziz.

"I'm not going to be confrontational," he told me as we finally left for the Foreign Ministry. "You never get anything by being confrontational." I had seen Rollie in action only once before when I produced his interview with then Israeli Defense Minister Yitzhak Rabin. It was during the height of the Palestinian uprising and, as we drove from Jerusalem to the studio in Tel Aviv, we discussed the military situation on the ground and the controversial "beating policy" instituted by Rabin.

"He's taken a lot of heat on that one," Evans told me. "I expect to press him on it." But when Rollie brought up the question of Palestinian human rights, Rabin handily flyswatted the query and that was that. I was hoping Evans wouldn't let Aziz off the hook so easily.

From the elegant and hushed suite of chambers occupied by Tariq Aziz on the fifth floor of the Foreign Ministry, the crisis in the Gulf seemed as remote as Mars. We set up our cameras in a small study adjoining his office. The room, to this day, I remember as the most quiet place I have ever been. For the first time since I arrived in Baghdad, I couldn't hear a sound outside. There were absolutely no distractions. What a superb milieu for conversation, I thought. Rollie introduced me to Nizar Hamdoon, who watched intently as we rearranged the furniture and checked the lighting and camera angles. For some reason, Hamdoon objected to Iraq's flag being in the background, and an aide dutifully removed it. It was curious. Did Hamdoon think the flag projected a militaristic edge he wanted to avoid? "It isn't necessary for this interview," was all he would say when I asked.

Minister Aziz stepped out of his office and Nizar made the introductions. While the crew continued setting up, Aziz, Hamdoon, Rollie, and myself retired to the conference room next door. Coffee was served as Aziz lit a Davidoff cigar.

"I want some news today, Mr. Minister," Rollie admonished him. "Are you going to make news today, sir?"

"There is nothing new," Aziz chuckled as he puffed on his stogie.

I liked Aziz instantly. I'd been told he was tough, shrewd, and articulate—a master diplomat and negotiator, whose name translates to "Glorious Past." In fact, as the crisis unfolded, I privately referred to Aziz as Mister Past, since the future looked like it was going down the crapper. Aziz had worked first as a journalist, then as party propagandist for Saddam Hussein during the underground war against the Hashemite monarchy. After the Ba'ath seized power in 1968, Aziz eventually became Iraq's Minister of Information. He was the only Christian among Saddam's inner circle, although I once refrained from asking him if releasing the hostages wouldn't be the Christian thing to do. Aziz had a dry sense of humor and a twinkle in his eye.

"I think I have seen you before," Aziz said, looking at me while Rollie explained my position in Baghdad. Indeed he had. Several days earlier in Amman, Aziz had announced that a surprise news conference would take place within the hour. Naturally, CNN wanted to cover it live. We broke all records getting to the Plaza Hotel, but unfortunately, a vital piece of gear needed for the transmission was broken. Will King, our senior international editor on the desk in Atlanta, saved the day: couldn't we just take the audio live? he asked. Atlanta would throw up a slide of Aziz to cover the picture. This would be heresy at another network, of course, but Will was right on the money. Aziz was liable to say something important, something that could either defuse or escalate the crisis. The news was potentially more important than the picture, and at CNN the news was what mattered. We had managed to get two telephones into the ballroom, and it was a simple matter of channeling the Aziz audio through one of them. I had used the second phone to coordinate coverage with Atlanta. The news conference was jammed to the rafters as the world anticipated a possible breakthrough. Aziz coolly surveyed the gathering and then did a double take as he gazed upon a bald, middle-aged man three feet in front of him sporting sunglasses and a Hawaiian shirt and holding two phones to his ears.

"Yes, we carried your news conference live, sir," I now recalled to the minister.

Unfortunately, neither that news conference nor the interview with Evans provided any breakthroughs. Aziz again insisted the United States must withdraw from Saudi Arabia before negotiations over Kuwait could begin. He criticized Washington and the UN for not enforcing resolutions that applied to Israel and the occupied lands. And he forcefully maintained that Iraq would never succumb to threats or pressure. The only spark during the thirty-minute exchange came when Rollie asked about the hostages.

"We call them guests," Aziz interrupted him.

"We, sir, call them hostages," Evans countered.

It wasn't exactly one of journalism's shining moments, but CNN finally had Iraq's Foreign Minister one on one, on the record. I made my pitch to Aziz and Hamdoon about an interview with Saddam and the possibility of bringing in a flyaway for live coverage. They reacted positively to both requests.

"I will be seeing the President in a day or two. Will you still be in Baghdad?" Aziz asked Rollie. Evans said he was leaving for Jordan but could return on a moment's notice. I told the minister I planned to remain as long as possible.

"Be my guest!" Aziz exclaimed. And we all had a laugh over that one. I made an appointment to get together with Nizar, who also urged me to see one Naji al-Hadithi, at the Ministry of Information. "I'll telephone Naji myself," he volunteered. "He can help with your request to do live programs."

Back at the Sheraton, I suggested that Evans might want to hang around a day or two on the chance Saddam agreed to an interview. "Aziz seemed rather receptive to the idea," I said.

"I don't know, kiddo. If we get the interview I'll come back, but I want to get the hell out of Baghdad." My gut told me I should urge Rollie to stay, and we should mount a full court press. It was one of the rare times I didn't follow my instincts and it caused a colossal fuck-up. A couple of days later, Dan Rather flew into town and CBS became the first network to interview Iraq's President.

"See if you can get Arafat," Eason urged when I next checked in. "Let me give you some numbers." He reeled off seven of them, including one at a "safe house" Arafat reportedly used when he came to Baghdad. On top of his other responsibilities, Eason was also CNN's resident expert on the Palestine Liberation Organization. He talked regularly with PLO spokesman Bassam Abu Sharif and, although the relationship was sometimes a stormy one, Eason's contacts were invaluable. When he worked the phones trying to track down the elusive chairman, as I heard him do a few months later, it was like listening to a virtuoso performance. Crisp, businesslike, and insistent, Eason almost always got his man. Some folks in the field who didn't know him well found his phone manner a bit chilly, but one of the things I liked most about Eason was that he didn't pull his punches. He had enormous responsibilities for a person who was only thirty. He had taken control of CNN's international coverage during a particularly difficult period for the company, and never looked back. He was a consummate newsman and a fierce competitor. Eason couldn't stomach coming in second. Like me, he would agonize if we dropped the ball and become elated when we scored a touchdown. Maybe he didn't always appreciate the hardships of life in the field, but his judgment was always sound and if you needed the support, you could count on Eason to provide it.

I left messages with the PLO, but getting an actual commitment from Arafat was like trying to nail down the wind. At the U.S. Embassy, things were stalled on the hostage front too. Wilson had gotten nowhere during his meeting at the Foreign Ministry. Having received the interview with Tariq Aziz, the network's demand for phoners from Clancy even abated. For a change, all of us were back in the workspace by midnight. We'd been going at full throttle almost round the clock from the moment we arrived in Iraq, and could finally have an early night. So naturally, Clancy and I hit the juice until four in the morning.

"Please call me back in ten minutes," I begged the hotel operator who telephoned with my wake-up call. I was amazed I could muster even that much. My head was throbbing, my muscles were sore, and my eyes hurt. In fact, my left eye was sealed shut, caked in a layer of pus from a viscous sty that had troubled me for weeks. King Hussein's personal physician had offered to lance it back in Amman, but eye surgery in the Middle East isn't included on my list of Top Ten pleasures I'm inclined to pursue after hours. The bugger had gotten worse since our arrival in Baghdad, festering into a hard red lump the size of a grapefruit. Fortified by the massive doses of potato juice I'd consumed with Jim the night before, I'd decided to practice a little medicine on my own: a safety pin from the hotel's sewing kit had seemed like the perfect tool. Now, I was in the grip of a hellish hangover, made even worse by the loss of half my vision. It took every ounce of strength I had to crawl to the shower.

"Oh . . . why did we do that?" Clancy groaned over coffee. He seemed in even worse shape than I did. "I think you better do something about your eye. It looks really fucked up. Maybe Mazin can get you some antiseptic."

"Yeah, I'll check with him later. Let's discuss what we'll do today." Jim thought another report on the hostages would be in order and I agreed. Television news has only two things going for it that beat the written press. It's the best medium in the world for capturing emotion, and it's immediate. The hostage story was emotional headline material and at CNN, if you've got a headline story, you'd better know how to milk it. It might be tough coming up with more Americans, but it was worth a shot. And then, there were always the Europeans. I also wanted to get some fresh shots of breadlines. That and the market might cover a possible graph on the sanctions. Arafat was still a possibility, of course, and we'd see if Wilson had any news that might affect our plans. On a breaking story, nothing is locked in stone, and we had the whole day in front of us.

"What time is Mazin coming by?" Jim asked.

"As soon as he gets back from the airport," I said. "He took Rollie out there at six this morning." Evans was concerned about the flight. He thought something might go wrong at the last minute, and he wanted Mazin with him just in case. "I even gave Rollie a thousand bucks in the event of an emergency."

It was still too early to telephone Hamdoon or al-Hadithi, but the PLO, as the saying goes, never sleeps. When I called to ask about the chairman, however, I was simply told, "He not here."

Clancy and the crew left for the embassy, and what was becoming the habitual anti-American demonstration out front. I gobbled more aspirin as I deciphered *The Baghdad Observer*.

"OOOOOOH!" MR. MAZIN EXCLAIMED, "I think something very wrong with your eye. I think you must go to hospital." I politely assured Mazin that that was out of the question, but I would welcome some medication.

"Of course, you must to go soon to hospital anyway," he tittered, "for your AIDS test!" I recalled the sign at the reception desk: MANDATORY AIDS TEST REQUIRED FOR VISITORS STAYING IN IRAQ MORE THAN FIVE DAYS. Spare me, I thought. Throughout my career I have seen people mutilated, executed, and even decapitated. I have seen 'em sliced, diced, and later on ice. But a blood test makes me go weak in the knees.

"Give me a break," I laughed. "I'm not gonna take an AIDS test. Surely that doesn't apply to professional journalists of my standing."

"Don't worry," he assured me. "When we go to hospital they only give you appointment for AIDS test . . . maybe in two or three months. You not take test now." He laughed.

"Not now . . . not ever," I told him, and then explained what we'd want to shoot on the streets.

"Tell me other stories you want to do while you in Baghdad," Mazin said. "It will be easier for you, easier for me, if I know in advance." I thought for a moment as I sipped my coffee.

"Well, in addition to interviewing your President and visiting Kuwait, we'd like to talk with some of the 'guests' being held at strategic sites. If that presents a security problem we wouldn't have to divulge the location, but would simply interview the people."

"I think you already interview several guests here in Baghdad. Now you want to interview 'special guests'?" He laughed.

"Of course we do, Mr. Mazin, because they're special!"

"I don't think that's possible," he said, "but I ask."

"How about a story on the Army and military preparedness? There'd be enormous interest in that," I ventured.

"I think we take you soon to see Popular Army. In one or two days, maybe."

"You know," I said, turning serious, "what about a story on the Jewish community of Baghdad? Do they attend religious services on Friday night or Saturday?"

"Who?"

"The Jews."

"Oh, the Jewish! Yes. They have . . . what you call, synagogue, where they pray. I think they pray on Saturday," he said.

"Yeah, Saturday's the day, all right."

"Yes, this is good story. Is possible, I think."

"Well, terrific! That should give you some stuff to work on. We wouldn't want you wasting the government's money just idly lounging around the hotel drinking Turkish coffee, would we?" I joked.

"Oh, Mr. Robert," he laughed. "When I first meet you, I think you crazy man . . . and you want to drive me crazy too! But now I like you."

"I assure you the feeling is mutual, my friend."

"It looks like the State Department is going to expel several Iraqi diplomats and issue travel restrictions for those remaining," Clancy said. "Wilson expects Baghdad will reply in kind. He's already been told our 'dips' can't travel more than twenty-five miles outside Baghdad's city limits, and permission to go further will require seven days' advance notice."

"What else did you learn?" I asked.

"Let's see," he said, checking his notes. "There are nine Americans accredited to the U.S. Embassy here. Oh, they think there are about two hundred people of all nationalities now being held at strategic sites. Of those, they estimate forty-one are Americans."

"Nothing new on the folks from Kuwait?"

"No, although there are still about a hundred people of various nationalities taking refuge on the grounds of our embassy there."

"Did Atlanta have anything for us?"

"Not really. They've been playing the shit out of the Aziz interview."

I placed a call to Nizar Hamdoon and was put on hold—where I was treated to the tune of "Home on the Range." The Iraqi Mind Fuck strikes again! Nizar begged off lunch or dinner, saying he was much too busy, but suggested I drop by his office to chat a few minutes. Only later would I learn why they were working overtime at the Foreign Ministry. In less than twenty-four hours Iraq would declare Kuwait its Nineteenth Province, officially annexing the tiny state. Iraqi cartographers were already putting the finishing touches on the country's new maps.

"How are you, Bob?" Nizar asked as I was ushered into his anteroom. Now there are only two groups of people on Planet Earth who call me "Bob": military and law enforcement officials, or those who don't know me well. Dealing with the former, I begrudgingly accept the misnomer; the latter I quickly correct. I decided to let Iraq's Deputy Foreign Minister call me whatever he liked. I thanked Hamdoon again for his assistance arranging the Aziz interview.

"What did you think of the interview?" he wanted to know.

"What did *you* think of it?"

"It was . . . all right," he said glumly. My curiosity was piqued.

"Did you expect the minister to say something he didn't?" I inquired. Hamdoon took a puff on his Marlboro, but didn't answer the question.

"So, Bob," he asked, changing the subject, "how long will you stay in Baghdad?" I told him CNN was in for the duration and felt an interview with President Saddam Hussein was of paramount importance. I also explained the need for us to go live and the advantages such coverage would provide. "It would be an excellent opportunity for your President, ministers, and other officials to be interviewed and explain Iraq's views to the world."

"I agree," Hamdoon said. "Tell this to Naji when you meet with him later." I could tell Nizar's mind was elsewhere and it was time to wrap things up.

"I hope I may call upon you from time to time and solicit your views, on or off the record."

"I don't do television interviews," he smiled, "but feel free to call me if I can be of any assistance."

WHEN I WAS SHOWN into Naji al-Hadithi's office he was not alone. John Simpson and Mohammed Amin were already sitting there. Shit, I thought. I didn't want a public forum when I discussed our coverage plans. From the expressions on their faces, it was obvious that the BBC and VISNEWS felt likewise, but we were in the same boat.

"So," Naji asked, "I suppose CNN would also like to visit Kuwait?"

"Absolutely. Is that in the cards?"

"We shall see," Naji said coyly, fingering a strand of turquoise worry beads. "What can I do for you, Robert?"

I decided not to mention the interview with Saddam, figuring Aziz and Hamdoon were already in the loop, but I needed to get cracking on the flyaway. It galled me this wasn't a private meeting, but I pressed on.

"Sir, as I'm sure you know, CNN has requested permission to bring in its portable television station. I've been told you can assist me in this matter," I added, trying to be as discreet as possible. If looks could kill, Simpson and Amin would have made me a dead man.

"Yes, of course, but we have not received a formal written request," he said.

I figured I'd already gone this far, so what the hell? "If there's a telephone with an international line I might use, I could have that request telexed within the hour."

"Please," Naji offered, "you may telephone from my secretary's office." As I copied down his telex number, I felt as if I'd scored a major coup. This is gonna happen, I thought, and what's more, the guy's even letting me use his own phone to do it!

"Eason," I said, trying to contain myself. "You'll never guess where I'm calling you from." He was as excited as I was when I related the news.

"Who are we going to get to run the flyaway?" he asked. "Aside from

Nic Robertson, there's no one else who will come!" It usually takes two engineers to set up and man the uplink, and we'd had unhappy experiences with several of these guys when it came to working in danger zones. During the Romanian revolution, for example, we couldn't find a single flyaway engineer who would travel to Bucharest. Ultimately, Charlie Hoff, who runs Newsbeam, CNN's affiliate service, and Tim Wilson, our chief satellite engineer—both executives, really—were the only two with the balls to do the job. (Nic was employed by NBC at the time.) In fact, in Cairo, where I produced our live coverage of the emergency Arab summit on August 10, one of the engineers said he would "officially oppose" any move to transport the flyaway to Iraq.

"Why on earth would you do that?" I'd asked.

"The flyaway is my responsibility," he huffed. "What if the Iraqis confiscate it? It's my ass on the line."

"Give me a break," I laughed. "Do you think the company would make you pay for the thing out of your own pocket?" The truth was, he was simply scared stiff.

"Let's worry about the staffing later," I told Eason. "We need to get the telexes out ASAP." We consulted a few minutes about the points we needed to stress, and Eason took care of the rest. In no time, our request was on the desks of Iraqi TV and the Ministry of Information.

The telex concluded by respectfully asking for immediate approval so we could ship in the uplink that very day. In retrospect, how naive I was to assume doing business in Baghdad could move that quickly. Before we were through, more than one hundred telexes would cross the desks of assorted ministries.

"Jesus! Look at this," I shouted at Clancy. "Saddam's on TV again and he's got more hostages with him." The setting was decidedly different from the first get-together, when the President visited his captives at a strategic location. This time, some hostages had been brought to him and were seated along both sides of what looked like a palatial ballroom, as Saddam held court.

"We are open-minded," he tried to assure them. "We have not closed the doors to any ideas but [everything] is complicated by the American presence [in Saudi Arabia]. We are not newcomers to the region," he insisted. "We know the world needs crude oil, but at a reasonable price." Saddam's translator was the same bespectacled gentleman with an English accent who'd caught out attention on the first "hostage show."

"The issue of Kuwait is an Arab issue," he admonished. "The United Nations is a pawn of the United States and now we are under threat. You," he said, gesturing around the room, "are serving a noble cause!"

"At least, why can't the children leave," one woman asked tentatively, "to return home and continue their education?" Saddam seemed to ponder the question, but his response was vague. He simply stated that he was "deeply affected" by their ordeal. Once again, he posed with the group for a *photo de famille* and then the television screen was filled by a slide showing a bouquet of flowers.

Clancy began revamping his script while the crew set up for a stand-up close on the balcony. "I'm going to check in with Atlanta," I told them. "I'll be back within forty minutes." As I rushed through the lobby, I noted with chagrin that a horde of journalists was checking in. Our "exclusive" was over.

"Ingrid and Peter Humi will be there in a day or two," Eason said, "but I can't find any correspondents. Blystone's still on vacation and the guys in Amman say no. C.D. is en route to Amman from Miami. We're not even gonna ask, just tell him to head for Baghdad once he arrives."

"What about a replacement for Trey?"

"See what you can work out with C.D.'s crew, or maybe Nic can help. We're also trying to get Krizmanich in there to edit."

It had been exhilarating having the story virtually to ourselves for the past five days, but I welcomed the help. The competition, I knew, was going to get fierce. Ingrid would be a godsend, but it was pure bad luck having Richard Blystone out-of-pocket. He, Clancy, and Peter Arnett were the network's old war horses, but Arnett was locked into Jerusalem. "There's no way we can spare him," Eason said.

AT THE FEEDPOINT, the atmosphere had changed appreciably. The main entrance to the TV station was grid-locked by Japanese journalists, all shrieking in fractured English to make themselves understood by the Iraqi guards, who wouldn't have understood a word of it even if Alistair Cooke were speaking. "I go Tokyo! I go Tokyo!" they wailed, dispensing a flurry of business cards to the stone-faced soldiers. "Pleeease, I must go Tokyo!" Well, I thought. It was fun while it lasted. I gingerly made my way around the Land of the Rising Sun and bolted for Master Control, waved on by one Iraqi guard who instantly recognized me.

Upstairs, a producer from ABC looked like he was going to burst into tears. "It's all right, Terry. It's all right," Mrs. Awattif said, trying to comfort him. "We'll try again later."

"You don't understand," he pleaded, trying to compose himself. "Later is too late." He buried his head in his hands.

"Problems with the feed?" I asked Awattif following the customary niceties.

"Please," Terry Wrong interrupted. "I know the bird is yours in less than a minute, but I've got to get these anchor links for Forrest [Sawyer] down. If I don't, the show is completely fucked. Can you give me a break?"

"They're seeing you in Amman," a technician suddenly shouted. Terry looked up at me, his eyes wide as saucers.

"Go ahead," I said, checking my watch. "But one pass only, my friend. One pass only." While Sawyer droned on, Awattif screened Jim's report.

"Tomorrow we may have important announcement," she whispered. "You can telephone me in afternoon."

"Thanks a lot," Terry said, sounding like he'd been reborn. "I owe you one."

"Duly noted," I replied, taking over the phone line to Amman. "Roll for levels, Mark. . . ."

On my way out I ran into Fabrizio del Noche, a senior television correspondent for Italy's RAI. Fabrizio had spent a lot of time in Israel covering the Intifada and we'd become good friends. Since then, we'd run into each other along the line, in places like Bucharest or Jo'burg. He was a stylish writer, as well as a stylish dresser, and had excellent contacts to boot. A true bon vivant, you could always count on Fabrizio to be of good cheer, even in the most dire of places, but he seemed uncharacteristically low-spirited. He gestured me away, to where we would not be overheard.

"I heard from a very reliable source, it looks like war very soon," he said gravely.

"Can you tell me more?"

"The source works where we first met, and he's not an Arab."

"Foreign Ministry?" I whispered.

He nodded, yes.

"Many thanks. I'll be in touch."

I dropped off Mark at the Sheraton and continued to the embassy. Israeli intelligence was not something to be dismissed out of hand. Their track record was a given. I called Eason immediately, keeping in mind the embassy phone was undoubtedly tapped.

"Better have Register check it out," I said. Larry Register, our Jerusalem bureau chief, was very tight with Israel's Deputy Foreign Minister. In fact, as the crisis continued Bibi Netanyahu appeared on CNN so often, he often seemed like a paid consultant.

"Okay, I'll pass it on," Eason told me. "We'll talk in the morning."

"CBS is here," Trey said as I entered our office. "Rather and some guys were looking for you. They're in 1408." I poured myself a drink and took the elevator upstairs. Dan and crew were huddled around a dining table, polishing off fare from room service that I didn't even know was on the menu.

"Hey, pull up a chair," Dan said. "May we fix you something, Robert?" I begged off, toasting their arrival instead. Traveling with Dan were Tom Bettag, John Reid, and Dave Caravello, a producer from their Washington bureau. "So what's going on?" John asked.

For the past several months, CNN and CBS had been conducting an experiment of sorts. Because of the mounting costs of covering major news events, we'd often "pooled" our resources. CBS used our flyaway during the Romanian revolution. We fed off theirs during Nelson Mandela's release. They served us during the East German elections. We serviced them again in Bucharest when Romanians went to the polls. And so it went, back and forth, from hostage arrivals in Wiesbaden, Germany, to the emergency Arab summit in Cairo. Purists at both networks decried the relationship, but I wasn't particularly concerned about it. Having been present at all of the aforementioned events, I thought it was still possible to help each other out (especially when we each had one crew) while keeping a competitive edge. I brought them up to date on the most recent events.

"I hope we can be of some help to you too," Dan said graciously as I bid them good night.

"We've been informed that an American hostage has died," Steve Thibault said. "The Iraqis say it was a heart attack." Until today, this would have have been privileged information, but I was now joined in the ambassador's office by producers from CBS, ABC, and even NBC, where these days, as the saying goes, "If it's news, it's news to NBC News." We pressed for more information.

"Look, all we know," Thibault explained patiently, "is that we hope to have the body by the end of the day, but at this point it does appear to be a heart attack. We're treating this as a normal consular matter pertaining to the death of a U.S. citizen abroad. Obviously, we're not going to release a name until the family has been notified." A minute later, Joe Wilson entered the room.

"Good morning," he said, introducing himself. "As Steve probably told you, a U.S. citizen has died. Now I've got several things I need to take care of. If you'd like, I'll brief you this evening over at USIS . . . informally, over some beer. Will you stock the fridge?" he asked Thibault. Wilson answered some general questions about the status of "dips" at the embassy and matters relating to hostages, and said good-bye. "I promise you," he told the group, "we'll talk later."

Thibault went over the ground rules again—everything attributed to Western sources or diplomats—and explained the procedure for using the telephones, then the meeting broke up. All of us eagerly marched to USIS to inform our headquarters.

BY THE TIME WE RECONVENED later that night, the death of an American was no longer the headline. Possibly moved by the personal appeal of the woman hostage the day before, Saddam Hussein declared all foreign women and children would be free to leave Iraq and Kuwait. That was the carrot. The stick came in two parts: Iraq officially declared Kuwait its Nineteenth Province and announced that it would expel a number of U.S. diplomats in a tit-for-tat reaction to Washington's decision to declare some Iraqi "dips" persona non grata. Suffice to say, bedlam had prevailed at the feedpoint. "You see, Mr. Robert," Awattif had reminded me, "I told you today would be important."

"So," JOE WILSON SAID as he popped the top off a Heineken, "you could characterize my talks with the government as frank, assertive, aggressive, and direct." He took a long slow pull on his cigar. "This government is traditionally paranoid. There's virtually no contact with the presidency. I can't tell you why Saddam made the decision [to release women and children], but we're seeking to clarify the offer.

"As far as the death of the U.S. citizen is concerned," Wilson went on, "we still don't have positive identification. We hope to have it tomorrow. Naturally, I have officially protested the death to the Foreign Ministry."

"Joe, this guy died of a heart attack, right?" I asked.

"That's our understanding."

"Was there any indication the heart attack may have occurred because he was denied certain medication during his captivity?"

"No, that doesn't seem to be the case. . . ."

"And you're treating the death as a normal consular matter . . . a U.S. citizen has unfortunately died while abroad, correct?"

"Yes. . . ."

"So, with all due respect, why are you lodging an official protest?" I asked.

"Because we still don't have all the facts, Robert," he said testily. "And these days, there's no such thing as normal behavior. We have twenty people in Iraq and Kuwait with serious medical problems. We've brought up their cases with the Ministry of Health. The government of Iraq has given us no satisfaction that it will change its policy with regard to these cases. That's why a protest over this death may be helpful. It just may prevent others," he snapped.

Wilson was in no mood to be put on the defensive, especially in front of media heavies like Rather and Forrest Sawyer, who were listening intently to our little exchange. But I wasn't looking for a confrontation. Was an official protest really called for, or was the chargé doing a bit of posturing? Since my arrival I had never seen Joe take the tone he just had.

"Joe got sucked up in this media thing," Thibault had told me a few days earlier. "He was in heaven when Rather and Koppel were first here. I think that's why he even allowed CBS to shoot on the grounds of the ambassador's residence. He knew it was off limits, but he did it anyway. And Washington came down on him for it."

It was easy to sympathize. The media needed Joe, and courted him. The embassy was, after all, our "lifeline," our communications link to the outside world. We needed Joe's input, his insights, his overview. It was only natural that he felt flattered. Being on a first-name basis with network anchors can be heady stuff for civilians. Hell, it could even be heady for some journalists. The press is traditionally at odds with the government, but in Baghdad we were throwing in our lot with Uncle Sam. Were we sometimes getting too close? I wondered, as the crisis unfolded.

Rather diplomatically changed the subject and asked about the embassy expulsions.

"Interestingly enough," Joe said, "they've ordered our commercial attaché out, even though he's already left. Not that there's that much trade between Iraq and the U.S. going on these days," he laughed. And we all laughed with him.

"I've got at least four people plus equipment coming in later," I told Mazin. "We'll have to arrange for pick up."

"No problem," he said. "We now have three cars. You become big boss in Baghdad," he laughed.

"I think the guy whose picture's in the lobby is the real big boss, but I appreciate the compliment."

Now that the other networks were firmly entrenched, our workload would increase significantly. In addition to the constant phoners and the nightly package, CNN would want a morning spot to remain competitive. The pictures might be thin, but they weren't a problem. By mid-morning, every cameraman was lined up at the U.S. Embassy to shoot the "spontaneous" demonstration. Some shots of the embassy itself, its walls topped with concertina wire, and Old Glory flapping in the wind would "cover" what came out of the morning briefing. If needed, we'd throw in a little Iraqi TV from the night before. Mix with some fresh street scenes of people buying food. Sprinkle a hostage soundbite or two. Add a stand-up. And presto, we had a package! As Linda Ellerbee says, "It ain't brain surgery."

According to Wilson, there were some two hundred and fifty women and children in Iraq who were eligible to depart. Baghdad Radio announced the government was in the process of bringing many of them to the capital from military and industrial sites, but several of the women vowed to remain with their husbands. The embassy was told to prepare lists of those people who wished to go. Many were calling the U.S. mission for clarification. The vast majority of Americans, including a significant number of women and children, were still hiding in Kuwait, or in custody there. The American "dips" in Baghdad were working with their European allies to arrange for the evacuation of everyone eligible.

"So, you think Iraq is serious about this?" I asked Joe.

"We'll see," he replied cautiously. "It wouldn't be the first time they changed the rules on us."

The announcement by Saddam was like a shot in the arm for Clancy. It got his adrenalin pumping again. He skillfully weaved together his morning spot, and we fed it to Atlanta. I touched base with both Nizar and Naji, but they had no new information about either the flyaway or the interview with Saddam. I'd already booked rooms for our incoming troops but decided belatedly we'd need additional workspace. Within a few days, CNN would have two correspondents, two crews, two producers, and a videotape editor in Baghdad. A portrait of Andrew Jackson helped secure an adjoining suite from the man at Reception. With more journalists arriving each day, the Ministry of Information set up a desk in the Sheraton's lobby. "Sign up here for a visit to the Popular Army!"

"Are you ready for this one?" Eason asked. "Jesse Jackson should be there tonight or tomorrow, and it looks like he's gonna meet with Saddam. He's also trying to take some hostages out with him. The crazy thing is, Jackson's traveling as a journalist, if you can believe it. He's doing this for his new TV show."

"Give me a break," I laughed.

"No, I'm serious. He's got three cameras with him to document the entire trip."

"Jesus!"

"Anyway," Eason said, "see if you can get together with him. We're not necessarily interested in Jesse, but maybe we can use him to get to Saddam. I gotta tell ya, there might be a slight problem, though. Apparently Jackson's folks contacted CNN and asked us to help underwrite his trip. Obviously we said no, so I don't think we're among his favorite people right now."

"Great. So what are ya tellin' me? My assignment's Mission Impossible?"

"Well," he laughed, "if anyone can pull it off, you can, my man. Good luck—"

"Wait . . . wait," I interrupted him. "I need to speak to E.T. Can you transfer me up there?" I lit another cigarette while I waited for the connection.

"Hiya, Robert. How are you holding up? Still fried?"

"Yeah, Ed," I laughed. "What about you?"

"We're all fried here," he chuckled. The man has a memory like an elephant, I thought. During the course of a conversation several days earlier, I'd mentioned to Ed that Clancy and I were exhausted. "Fried" was the operative word. It was amazing that Ed Turner was as good-natured as he was. As executive vice president in charge of all news-gathering operations for the network, Ed's job made what the Flying Wallendas did seem like the Amateur Hour. His was an even more delicate balancing act, shaping CNN's editorial direction and honing its coverage. He always had a million things on his plate, from hiring correspondents to creating new bureaus, or simply providing a supportive shoulder for a colleague going through a divorce. Just like CNN, Ed's job never ceased. On top of that, Ed had to deal with the press. It was disconcerting enough that he had to begin most interviews by explaining that he was no relation to CNN founder Ted Turner (a fact that invariably turned up in parentheses), but since the network had aired the video of Saddam and the hostages on August 23, Ed had spent a good deal of time defending the decision. That the decision was the correct one he had no doubt, but I could tell the pounding we'd taken in some quarters rankled him. During the latest edition of Meet the Guest, Saddam had said he was prepared to debate George Bush, a suggestion the State Department later termed "sick."

"I was holding my breath his next two words weren't going to be 'on CNN,' " Ed told me. "We've got to be careful about not becoming a participant in this story."

"I know what you're driving at," I said, "but we are participants, whether we like it or not. We're using them, they're using us; it's the same damn thing in Saudi or Washington, isn't it?"

"I'm just cautioning you of the need to be aware of our particular responsibility," he said flatly.

"So Eason tells me you wouldn't underwrite Jesse's travel expenses," I quipped. "Why not? Did I blow the budget with my last charter?"

"Yes, I've been meaning to discuss that with you," he laughed. I briefed Ed on what I foresaw in the days ahead, and asked if he had any suggestions.

"Is there something in Western logic that prevents us from being able to understand what the Arabs are saying between the lines?" he asked. "Surely the Arabists at the State Department must have great input?" It would not be the last time Ed would pose this question. "No, you guys are doing just fine," he said a moment later. "Give my best to everyone, and keep up the good work."

"I don't understand why they won't at least allow food and medicine in," said a British hostage sitting in the Sheraton's lobby. "Releasing the women and children was a show of good faith. We ought to respond in kind. Maybe then he'd let us all out of here." Saddam's announcement, as welcome as it was, would play havoc with many emotions. For husbands whose families were with them in Iraq, there was enormous relief knowing their loved ones would soon be out of harm's way. But for wives and children who would leave husbands and fathers behind, there was only anguish. The hostages, more than anyone else, were caught in the middle.

Why not permit shipments of food and medicine? I myself wondered. Would that truly weaken the embargo and hence the coalition's resolve? Or would a humanitarian gesture prompt from Saddam a reciprocal kindness? The United Nations Security Council, led by the United States, was taking a hard line. Then again, the members of the Security Council had never heard of American hostage Gus Cero, the man we'd interviewed a few days earlier. They would never learn, as he did during his daily telephone call home, that his father had died. Nor that Gus, still a captive, would not attend the funeral.

"Hey, we might have a problem," Mark said as he entered the office. "The cameraman from VISNEWS was turned back at the airport when he tried to leave."

"Mohammed Amin?" I asked. "The guy who was on our flight coming in?"

"Yeah. I don't know all the details, but he's down at the Ministry of Information desk right now. If they're gonna keep journalists here, we're all in deep shit."

It has to be a bureaucratic snafu, I thought as I headed downstairs. The alternative would be too grotesque. More than once, we'd discussed the possibility of our being detained as "guests," but I'd always dismissed it out of hand.

"Can you imagine," I'd joked to Dave Caravello, "Dan held hostage with a gun to his head, pleading with George Bush to just do something?" But Caravello was not amused, and from the look on his face, neither was Mohammed Amin, who at that moment was venting his frustration at three moon-faced officials seated behind the desk. "This is very improper," he chastised them. "Very improper, and quite wrong!"

"So, exactly what happened?" I asked.

"At the airport, they took me into a room where they held me for hours," he explained, clearly exasperated. "They wouldn't tell me why. It was very disturbing. Finally they said I didn't possess a proper exit visa."

"Didn't your minder get you one?"

"He said that he had. Oh . . . they say it'll be sorted out by morning and I can leave on tomorrow's flight," he said wearily. "This place is unbelievable!" I made a mental note to double check with Mazin. Trey would be leaving the next day and I wanted to be certain he'd encounter no problems. His nerves were already frayed. I went back upstairs to check with Clancy, who would also be leaving in the next day or so. His wife was expecting a baby, and his assignment in Baghdad had opened a floodgate of emotion. But Clancy, always the trooper, had put his commitment to the story first.

"He say it now Province Nineteen," Mazin explained as he translated a long dissertation outlining what the Iraqi TV announcer said was Baghdad's historical claim to Kuwait. "Oh... Mr. Jesse Jackson will be here soon. Perhaps he meet with His Excellency President Saddam Hussein," he cooed. The evening news seemed to feature more martial music than I'd heard before, over an endless procession of tanks and Scuds. Even the people's militia got into the act. "Five million people have been given guns," Mazin said proudly.

"I seem to detect a perceptible change in attitude."

"No... no," he disagreed. "Is quite normal." Clancy put the finishing touches on his script and gave it to Kris Krizmanich, who'd arrived earlier with Nic from Amman to edit. She, Mark, and Nic then left for the feedpoint.

"I'll catch up with you at the embassy later," I told Clancy. "I want to link up with Humi, C.D., and the crew."

"SO I FIGURED, what the hell?" C.D. bellowed. "I think it's gonna be at least another two weeks before these fuckin' rag heads get the shit bombed out of 'em. It's a crap shoot, but I say better to be here now than get stuck in here later. I mean, these people have got their heads so far up their ass. Clearly, Saddam Hussein has got to be insane. You whacky Iraqi, you smoke cracky?" he laughed. I couldn't believe what I was hearing. I had never met C.D. before, though I'd heard he had a reputation as a "cowboy." But this little outburst was beyond the pale. Even the normally unflappable Peter Humi looked nonplussed.

"Listen," I said as calmly as possible, "I think you should bear in mind that everything said in this room is being listened to. All our phone conversations are monitored as well. There's even a feeling that the cars are bugged. I think perhaps our interests would be better served if you expressed yourself a bit more... er, diplomatically." C.D.'s eyes darted around the room, as if looking for hidden microphones.

"I'm sorry," C.D. replied. "I understand. It's just that this fuckin' place ... I mean, can you believe all the portraits of Hussein in the streets? Jesus H. Christ!" I introduced myself to the crew, Stuart Clark and Rod Nino, both based in Atlanta.

"He's been like that since we got on the plane," Rod said to me privately. "Sometimes he's just out of control." That's fabulous, I thought. CBS has Rather. ABC has Sawyer. And I've got the journalistic equivalent of General Curtis LeMay.

"SO WHERE'D YOU GET THIS GUY?" I asked of both Ed and Eason, who were conferenced on the line.

"Just let me know," Ed said angrily, "and I'll pull him out of there. . . . That behavior is inexcusable. It's bullshit, and I won't have it!"

"Well, I've spoken to him. Let's just hope he got the message."

"He had better," he replied, hanging up.

"Hey, I've got some good news," Eason volunteered. "Doug James should be in there soon. He telephoned me, all pissed off, saying it was a misunderstanding in Amman that he didn't want to come. Ingrid will be with him, along with a crew."

"Great. We'll be in good shape."

"I'll say. You'll have Ingrid and Peter, two correspondents, two crews, plus Nic and Kris. That's a bigger bureau than you had in Jerusalem."

"Hey, I'm not bucking for Baghdad bureau chief."

"Whaddya mean?" he laughed. "You've already been nominated."

The impending evacuation of women and children continued to dominate the morning briefings. "We've been telling most people to go to the residence office to obtain their exit visas," Thibault said. "They should stay in touch with us and we'll advise when we know more. We still have no specific information to release about the evacuation from Kuwait. We're trying to contact the people there via the VOA and other newscasts. And we're looking into charter flights to Basra or Baghdad." Attendance at the briefings was growing each day. The evenings when Wilson would brief us over a few cold brewskies would soon be a memory, although he always tried to make himself available whenever we called. The Marines who'd arrived in the diplomatic convoy from Kuwait had taken over security, instructing the locally hired embassy staff to inspect all bags for cameras and tape recorders. At USIS, a man I had never seen before was compiling a list of spare automobile parts from the embassy's warehouse. Even in the midst of chaos, bureaucracy reigned supreme.

The demonstrations in front of the embassy were growing larger too, though the themes remained the same. "Down Down Bosh!" "Yes Yes Saddam!" "We Need Medicine!" "We Need Baby Milk!" Occasionally, Thibault would descend from his perch and engage the demonstrators in lively debate. As for Wilson, he continued to knock heads with Iraqi officials, a frustrating and demoralizing experience at best.

"So you're seeing Naji al-Hadithi, huh," Joe said after I'd expressed the opinion that Iraq seemed to be showing some flexibility on the hostage issue. "Why don't you ask him the following questions: Why had most of the women been told nothing about their departure? Even the Iraqis admit some children are suffering from dysentery. Why not permit a separate plane to evacuate them immediately? Yeah, go ahead," he added testily. "Ask him if Iraq will allow charters to fly here without preconditions." The day before, Iraq intimated it might grant landing rights to foreign charters, if the planes carried food and medicine to Baghdad.

"All I'm saying, Joe, is that perhaps Saddam's announcement should be seen as a positive step."

"What's positive about it? These people shouldn't have been taken in the first place." Wilson was right, of course, but I thought he was missing the point. In the Middle East, as in Asia, "saving face" is visceral. Perhaps "we" could afford to be more gracious. But Washington had taken a hard line and Joe wasn't going to buck it.

There were a myriad of details to be worked out. For instance, did the Americans in Kuwait need Iraqi exit visas to transit through Baghdad? After all, when they'd entered Kuwait earlier, it was still a sovereign state. Was it necessary that every female U.S. passport holder go individually to the residence office? The French and West German embassies were permitted to collect their nationals' exit visa forms en masse. "Negotiating with the Iraqis is like a boxing match," Joe would say more than once. "Nothing really gets settled until the final round." And so, he came out for the bell, sometimes three times a day, often tipping us in advance, so the networks could dutifully record his departure. His white Chevy sedan would be positioned in front of the chancery, and woe betide the chauffeur who forgot to unfurl the miniature Stars and Stripes on the car's tiny flagstaff.

By now, things were hopping at the Ministry of Information as well. Upon arrival in Baghdad, virtually every reporter or crew was summoned to meet Latif Nasif Jassim, as he dispensed, over and over again, the strict party line. "Kuwait is part of Iraq," he would lecture. "We shall never surrender. Kuwait has rejoined her motherland." At least half a dozen journalists were waiting to receive this "bulletin" as I arrived for my appointment with Naji. As usual, I perused the latest Iraqi "position papers," which were translated into English, French, German, and Spanish, until I was shown into al-Hadithi's office.

"Hello, Robert," Naji said, getting up from his desk to greet me. "Still surviving?"

"Yes," I laughed. "Still surviving." Naji deferred all details about the mechanics of the hostage release to the Ministry for Foreign Affairs. He would say only that all of the women and children detained at their "special locations" would probably be in Baghdad within twenty-four hours.

"What can you tell me about Jesse Jackson?" I asked. "Why is your President going to meet with him?"

"Jackson is the leader of the Democratic party, is he not? He has great influence on President Bush." I thought for a moment he was pulling my leg, but Naji was dead serious.

"C'mon, Jesse Jackson is not the leader of the Democratic party. He is an important politician . . . some might say, even a great man, but I assure you he has no influence whatsoever on George Bush. Furthermore, he's not even traveling in his capacity as a politician, but as a so-called journalist . . . a talk-show host for his new television program, for Godsakes!"

"Are you sure?" Naji asked, with a look of astonishment.

"Absolutely. You know, with all due respect to Mr. Jackson, if President Saddam Hussein wants George Bush and the rest of the world to hear his views, then CNN is the better forum. You know, Naji, without sounding presumptuous, I think it is terribly important that your President goes 'on the record.' If war erupts, it will be catastrophic." Naji mulled it over while he sipped his tea.

"How long would the interview last?" he asked.

"An hour, at least."

"Would it be edited?"

"Certainly not if we carried it live. But I assure you, even if it were taped, we will run the President's remarks in their entirety."

"Very well," Naji said. "Have your office send me a formal request." I noted that Eason already had, the day he telexed our request for the flyaway.

"I have not seen it," he said, shuffling through the sea of paperwork that covered his desk. "Please, Robert. Have them send it again. I will see what I can do." As Naji walked me to the door, I asked again about the flyaway.

"Have patience," he smiled. "Do not worry. *Mah-a-salame.*"

"You're gonna have to send another telex," I told Eason, as I spelled out the terms. "Mr. Mazin came up with a name at the ministry's telex room. In the future, we'll be able to verify if the damn thing is actually delivered to Naji's desk."

As I walked through the lobby, CBS was shoving a shitload of gear into the elevator—enough, it seemed, for a studio shoot. It was not a good sign, I thought, but decided not to ask. If Rather were going to interview Saddam, I'd know shortly. Sure enough, at the embassy several hours later, Caravello gave me the bad news. Rather had nailed Saddam.

"I'D BE INTERESTED to know what prompted you to give CBS the interview first?" I asked Naji the following day. "Was it just because Rather was here?"

"That was part of it. But truthfully, Robert, CBS offered better terms."

"How could they possibly have offered better terms than what we proposed?" I asked incredulously.

"They offered an hour of air time."

"We offered an hour too."

"No, your telex said a half-hour."

"I DON'T BELIEVE IT," I exploded at Eason. "What happened to the hour?"

"Well, the feeling here was that we'd commit to a half-hour and go longer if it was warranted."

"Give me a break," I sighed. "We give a half-hour to Mike the Mechanic."

"Well, don't let it get you down," Eason consoled me. "Just keep on pushing."

"How are you, Wienerish?" Ingrid whooped as she bolted into the workspace. "The airport was a madhouse . . . the same squirrely-looking guys at customs from the first time I was here a year ago with Clancy. I think one of them remembered me. Jesus tits!" she hollered. "*Provisions!*" She pulled two cartons of Gauloises out of her duffel, along with the mandatory order of potato sap. "I've got some magazines and newspapers here somewhere," she exclaimed, searching her bag. "What the fuck? I'll find them later. So whaddya think of Baghdad? It's a shithole, but it's a groovy shithole, huh? Goddammit, Wienerish, I can't believe they wouldn't call me in from my vacation to get here earlier. I spent the whole time in New York going to the dentist or reading the wires. Nice work in Cairo, by the way. So, what's going on?"

"Well, women and children have been told they can leave, but the logistics are still being worked out. The first couple of days here were really tense, but it's eased somewhat. There are phones we can use at the embassy. The chargé is Wilson. Thibault handles the press. They're both upstanding. The feedpoint's a mess. You can take over that responsibility. You like rat-fucks if I remember, right?"

"And gang-bangs," she laughed.

"Well, you'll be in hog heaven. You can even have both at the same time! Hey, seriously, I should take you over to the embassy to meet Wilson."

The four-car motorcade pulled into the private driveway and stopped at the door of the U.S. Embassy. As his personal camera crews immortalized the scene, Jesse Jackson emerged from a silver Mercedes and strode purposefully into the building for a private briefing with Joe Wilson. I watched the proceedings from a window on the second floor of USIS, along with Steve Thibault and a couple of hacks. "He asked for the meeting and Joe was happy to oblige," Steve explained. "But we've told Jesse, if he wants to use the phones, he has to come up here to the press room like the rest of you guys. There will be no special privileges."

"You don't expect us to believe that?" I laughed. "I don't recall our cars ever being allowed onto the embassy's grounds."

"Okay . . . so we've allowed him a small privilege," Thibault replied good-naturedly. Jackson had met earlier with Nizar Hamdoon and told reporters he had come to Baghdad to "listen and learn." Now he would hear Wilson's take on the story. I sought out Jackson's producer to get the poop on the meeting with Saddam.

"I wouldn't hold out much hope for your getting into that one," he said. "But give me your number and maybe we'll have something for you later on." Jackson's crews, meanwhile, were frantically taking pictures of the daily demonstration while bona fide news crews, in turn, videotaped the Jackson people.

"What a trip!" a Jackson cameraman told me when I asked how things were going. "We have no idea what the schedule is. Jesse just says, 'Let's go!' and we go. It's really wild."

Yeah, it's really wild, I thought. Eason says, get Arafat . . . no Arafat! Eason wants Saddam . . . Rather gets Saddam! Now Eason wants us to use Jackson to get to Saddam, and that ain't gonna happen either! "I can't put your problems on the air," a former boss once reprimanded me. It hardly mattered that my current superiors were far more supportive, I felt as bad now as I had back then.

"Oh my God, I can't believe it," Ingrid shrieked, covering the telephone mouthpiece. "It's Jackson's people. They want to know if we're interested in doing an interview."

"Now?" I asked in amazement. "It's after one-thirty in the morning."

"Yeah. They say to come right over."

"Okay, let's do it!

"What the fuck is this all about?" I asked no one in particular as we gathered the gear. In less than ten minutes, we were out the door and heading across town. Jackson was staying at the Al-Rasheed, a government-owned hotel usually reserved for dignitaries and official delegations. Even in darkness, the building looked impressive. Definitely a notch or two above the Sheraton. The lobby was practically deserted except for a man I instantly recognized as the President's translator. A small octagonal gold pin engraved with a likeness of Saddam adorned his left lapel. He was hunched over a counter, checking off names on a list. While Ingrid and the others headed for the reception desk to locate Jackson, I introduced myself.

"Hello," he said graciously in a clipped English accent. "I am Dr. Sa'doun Zoubaydi."

"It's a pleasure to meet you. I've seen you on television quite a bit these past days. Are you here with the President?" I asked hopefully.

"No, not at all," he smiled. "I've been assisting Mr. Jesse Jackson."

"Are those the names of the . . . er . . . guests Mr. Jackson will be taking with him?"

"We shall see. That's what I'm working on."

"Well, we have an appointment with Mr. Jackson right now, but would it be possible for us to get together in a day or so? Perhaps we could do a story about you."

"About me?" he asked with astonishment.

"Absolutely," I said, remembering a feature I'd once seen that profiled Gorbachev's translator. "You're close to the President. You're familiar with his thinking. You're now very well known. I think there'd be enormous interest."

"Very well, Mr. Robert," he agreed, jotting down his telephone number at the Ministry for Foreign Affairs. "You may call upon me."

I hurried to catch up with Ingrid and the others as they took the elevator up to Jackson's suite. "Great news," I told them. "This guy, Zoubaydi, is key. It'll pay off down the line. Whatever J.J. might say, meeting Zoubaydi is worth the price of admission." Jackson was closeted with his staff and wouldn't be available for several more minutes. An aide asked us to return downstairs and set up off the lobby. While the crew, Cynde Strand and Dave Heaberlin, rearranged the furniture, correspondent Doug James jotted down some notes. Then we waited some more.

Even at two-fifteen in the morning, after what had surely been a grueling day, Jesse Jackson was impressive. He'd spent some three hours with Saddam Hussein, and had come away convinced that unless diplomacy was pursued aggressively, war was inevitable.

"Our disregard for a comprehensive Middle East policy is about to catch up with us," he told Doug. It was unnecessary for Bush to resort to name-calling and rhetoric, he asserted. "Here is a man who is really at center stage . . . He has the power to spare the world a war," he said.

Jackson said he was traveling to Kuwait in the morning and he'd submitted a list of Americans in ill health there whom he wanted to take home. Not surprisingly, he spoke of the need for "one world . . . a quilt of many colors" and other familiar themes anyone who's ever covered Jesse Jackson can probably recite by rote.

"Most of us know nothing of the long-standing border dispute between Iraq and Kuwait . . . there's a whole history of that dating back to when Britain carved up the territory," he added. "While Kuwait can't retroactively lose its nation status, there's a history of anguish there, and there are some tensions that should have been negotiated more fully between the two countries. I think Kuwait underestimated Iraq's fury, and I think Iraq underestimated America's ability to mobilize the world against annexation. And now," he emphasized, "I think we may be underestimating the price we may pay fighting a war in that sand." The rhetoric, he stressed again, was clouding the issues. "I want to believe a tree by the fruit it bears, not by the bark it wears," he insisted.

It was really a stellar performance, I thought. Perhaps that was what troubled me. It seemed too much of a performance. As Doug completed the interview, I decided to ask one final question.

"Sir, you've been around the world and around the block. You've met with world leaders as well as the average man. You can look people in the eyes and get a good sense of them. Now, Reverend Jackson, you've just met with Saddam Hussein. Do you trust the man?" Jackson had literally been beaming as I began the windup, but the pitch caught him off guard.

"Well . . . I am in no position, I . . . I . . . I . . . can you cut this a moment?" he asked. I had never seen Jackson react this way. It was as if all the self-assurance on display for the past thirty minutes had suddenly evaporated. But this, after all, was a spontaneous interview. I'd be damned if I'd turn off the camera.

"I'd like to stay rolling if you don't mind, sir."

"I wish you wouldn't," Jackson said. " 'Cause . . . I, I just lost my thought. I don't want to make this a big confrontation. I'll answer the question. . . ."

"We'll certainly be glad to fix anything we need to in the edit . . . but it's a simple question, sir, with all due respect. Do you trust Saddam Hussein?" Jackson was furious, but with the camera still rolling there was nothing much he could do about it. His aide, Kenneth Walker, attempted to intercede.

"Look, Jesse's very tired," he interrupted. "I think that's it for tonight."

"C'mon," I said, "you called us! It's a simple question. Do you trust Saddam Hussein?" Jackson reflected another moment before finally answering.

"I trust him," he said, speaking very deliberately, "to operate within his own interests, but any relationship between nations must be mutually verifiable, and that becomes the protection in such an arrangement." He concluded by saying he hoped American officials "with portfolios" would spend as much time as he had with Iraqi, Kuwaiti, and Saudi officials. And with that, he disconnected his microphone and said good night.

"How about letting us on the plane to Kuwait?" Ingrid asked Walker.

"We'll see in the morning," he said, and left to join Jesse.

"Can you believe it?" Cynde laughed. "I'm glad you didn't let him off the hook, Robert. Way to go."

"Well, however he answered he was getting into deep water, but hell, it was a legitimate question. The man just spent three fuckin' hours with Saddam Hussein. Surely he has a feel for the guy. And that business about stopping the camera is absolute bullshit. We're not making a movie here!"

"I THINK WE BOTH DESERVE A NIGHTCAP," I said to Ingrid when we got back to the Sheraton. "That whole episode was so goddamned bizarre."

"Just more of the mind fuck, Wienerish," she laughed.

"I thought that was limited to one side only."

"Nah, it infects everything it touches."

"IT'S INGRID FOR YOU," Humi said, handing me the phone. "She's at the airport."

"They're gonna let Morton Dean [of ABC News] on the plane as a pool reporter. Should I see if I can hop on board?" she asked.

"Are they letting a crew on with Morton?"

"No, no crew. Jackson's folks are going to shoot it for everyone."

"In that case, stay where you are, sweetheart. Dean's a capable guy and he's filing for all of us. I have a feeling it's gonna be a madhouse at the terminal when the hostages arrive. We'll be better off if you stay there."

It was already shaping up to be a hectic day. Jackson would be leaving at eleven for his flight to Kuwait, where, according to embassy officials, he hoped to evacuate several ill Americans and return to Baghdad. There he would be joined by more than fifty U.S. hostages for the trip back to the United States. Wilson and other diplomats had been working around the clock to sort out the paperwork in conjunction with the Ministry for Foreign Affairs and other allied embassies. It was hoped a large number of U.K. passport holders would be on the flight as well.

Many of the passengers had assembled at a downtown hotel, where the Iraqis permitted the press to interview them. What ensued was a journalistic free-for-all, a chaotic gang-bang in which hostages were trampled, feelings were bruised, and officials from the Ministry of Information finally learned, up close and personal, the meaning of the term "rat-fuck," an expression Mr. Mazin had never heard before. Even hard-nosed reporters admitted it was not their finest moment.

"But why they act that way?" Mazin asked plaintively.

"Beats me," I replied. "I think it's in the genes."

In Kuwait, Jesse Jackson prayed with Ambassador Nathaniel Howell as the two clutched hands through the compound's locked gate. Naturally, with everyone on deadline, the operation ran hours behind schedule. By the time all of the evacuees finally gathered at the airport, it was almost time to feed. But Ingrid, true to form, managed to make the bird. The footage of Jackson in Kuwait City would be distributed by ABC during a stopover in London.

At the U.S. Embassy, Marcia Kunstel of Cox Newspapers and Joe Treaster of *The New York Times*, both of whom had accompanied Jackson, were writing their stories. I asked Marcia if she'd do a live phone interview with CNN.

"Gee, I don't know," she said. "I'm coming up on deadline and what's more, my mother will have a fit if she hears I'm in Baghdad."

"What are you talking about? She's going to read your dateline tomorrow morning when she picks up her newspaper."

"No, my mother never reads our papers," she laughed. "Why don't you ask Treaster." Joe was about to file his story, but said he'd help us later, in a pinch. In the meantime, Eason had a great concern.

"ABC is telling us the pictures from Kuwait are theirs exclusively," he screamed. "Are you sure they're pool?"

"Hey, Morton!" I shouted at Dean, who was sitting a few feet away from me. "Can you please ring your people in London and tell 'em the facts of life?"

"Call 'em back in ten minutes," I told Eason. "Morton's taking care of it." Jesus Christ, I thought. Maybe it *is* in the genes.

7

"This scum-bag Nazi-like regime is courting vaporization!" Steve Thibault ranted as we waited for Wilson. "Can you imagine the gall of these people? They told the women their husbands needed to be with them when they went to the residence office, and then they abducted the men right in front of them!"

The New York Times had already reported the incident, but I had sought out Wilson to get independent confirmation. There was nothing more frustrating for CNN than having to quote another news organization when it had its own people on the ground, but events were unfolding so quickly it was impossible to nail down everything. It often amazed me that some other TV outfits sometimes ignored news altogether if they didn't have a lock on the story themselves. But, while CNN had no problem attributing the report, you could bet the show producers in Atlanta were hammering the desk demanding to know why *we* didn't have it first.

While I was at the embassy, the crews worked on a story about food rationing, which had begun on September 2. The government had already distributed ration coupons, but inexplicably denied us permission to photograph them. At considerable risk, Mr. Kareem, one of our drivers, allowed us to shoot his personal ration card, though it was by no means certain the shot would get past the censors. (It eventually did.)

"Unlike you in the West," Naji had lectured me earlier, "we don't need hamburgers to survive. After all, this is the fertile crescent," he laughed. "We can eat dates if we have to. The sanctions are blackmail. We will never succumb to them."

"Yes, they can probably hold out in terms of food," Wilson agreed. "But the sanctions will hit them hard in the area of spare parts, lubricants . . . that sort of thing. I mean, I'd advise you to think carefully if you're going to be shuttling in and out on Iraqi Airways," he laughed. "Those planes aren't in the greatest shape to begin with."

"Tonight we go to the synagogue," Mazin said, out of the blue. "You remember? You asked to do story on the Jewish. Everything is arranged. We must leave in one hour."

"Tonight!" I exclaimed. "This is Monday!"

"Yes, yes. I know today Monday."

"Well, Jews don't usually worship on Monday nights—"

"Yes, they will be at synagogue," he interrupted me. I had a sinking feeling, but I had to ask.

"Mr. Mazin, you didn't round up these people and force them to go to the synagogue, did you?"

"Yes, yes. You wanted to do story. . . ."

"Jesus Christ! *Ingrid,*" I screamed. "We have a *major problem!*" I gave her the details.

"Oh, Jesus," she wailed. "What are we going to do?"

"Well, it's pretty clear what we're not going to do. But you'll have to go over there . . . without a camera. Apologize for the inconvenience and misunderstanding. See if you can line up a family we can visit at home on Friday night, and shoot at the synagogue Saturday morning." As calmly as possible, I then defined journalistic heresy to Mazin and explained that even in Baghdad, we would never, ever stage a news event.

"So, how'd it go?" I asked Ingrid when she returned a few hours later.

"They were all there, all right," she laughed, "dressed up in their Saturday best. I don't think they quite understood what they were supposed to be doing, but I've taken care of everything. It's all set for Friday."

"I owe you one," I said, lifting my glass, "*L'chaim.*"

WITH HUMI AND INGRID now firmly in place, I could spend more of my time lobbying for the Saddam interview, as well as for the flyaway. I spoke with Naji or Nizar almost daily, while Eason continued to pepper the authorities with the appropriate telexes. By now, NBC was also on the case, in the form of Gordon Manning, an exec from New York. Manning, whose long career at CBS had taken a nosedive after the Sally Quinn/ "Morning News" fiasco, was renowned at NBC for having delivered Mikhail Gorbachev to Tom Brokaw after months of persistent lobbying. In the industry, his telexes were known as "manninggrams." Gordon was accompanied by a Palestinian translator from Amman who seemed to be on a first-name basis with everyone. This, coupled with Manning's deep reservoir of experience, didn't help me sleep any better. Getting beaten by Rather was bad enough, but to play second to NBC News was unthinkable. At times, I found myself trying to read, upside down, the pile of Gordon's correspondence scattered across Naji's desk, hoping to learn something. But from what I gathered, his requests were pretty straightforward. In the months that followed, all of the networks would try to impress the Iraqi government by presenting ratings and opinion polls that heralded each network's achievements. It was part of the game called "groveling for interviews." CNN was not immune, though I found it distasteful the one and only time I got into the swim. At the behest of Atlanta, I explained to Naji that 76 percent of Americans were getting their news primarily from television and that 30 percent of those viewers were tuned to CNN. According to the folks at Gallup, ABC News, with 18 percent of the audience, was a distant second.

"This is all very interesting," Naji laughed, waving a typewritten sheet of paper. "This morning ABC News showed me the same poll, but the figures were quite the opposite."

It was about 7 P.M. when Naji summoned me to his office.

"So where is Rowland Evans right now?" he wanted to know. From the tone of his voice, I could tell it was more than a casual query.

"Does this mean what I think it does?" I asked anxiously.

"I think it would be best if he came to Baghdad now. If you wish, he may bring his colleague, Mr. Novak, with him."

"That's fabulous news. I take it the interview with the President has been confirmed. Will it be live?" I asked.

"No. Our technicians from Iraqi TV will shoot it for you. You may then send it on the satellite just like Dan Rather." I thanked Naji profusely and sped to the embassy to inform Atlanta.

"It's a 'go' with Evans and Novak," I shouted to Eason. "Naji said they should catch the first plane."

"How's the feed gonna work?" he asked. "Since they'll shoot it on SECAM [a television standard that differs from NTSC, the U.S. norm], where do we convert—in Baghdad or Amman?" I suggested he conference us with John Reid at CBS Amman. John had fed Dan's interview from Iraqi TV.

"Those motherfuckin' cocksuckers," Reid exploded. "Those goddamned sons-of-bitches. Fuck those assholes! I'll never forgive them for what they did to Dan." As John told it, Dan had, in fact, been put through the wringer. Informed twice that the Saddam interview was on, then off again, he'd then been summoned to the Foreign Ministry late at night for what he was told was a routine briefing. The Iraqis would send a car, and Dan was to come alone. His producer, Tom Bettag, should wait at the Sheraton for news of the interview. But Rather never made it to the Foreign Ministry. In fact, as the car drove past the building, no one would tell him where he was being taken. For a moment, the thought occurred to him that he might have been kidnapped.

"The next thing you know," Reid said, "they brought him into a room and the cameras were rolling. Those motherfuckers did everything they could to put Dan off balance." I recalled that Rather had seemed uncomfortable when the interview began. (It was broadcast on Iraqi TV the following day.)

"Well, all things considered," I commiserated, "I think the interview was fine."

"Well, fuck them and their motherfucking goddamn country!" Reid bellowed.

"What about the feed?" I asked.

"Nothing to it. Just convert in Amman."

"Whew!" Eason laughed when he caught his breath. "And I thought *you* had a foul mouth."

"Anyway, you track down Evans and I'll call you back in a few minutes. I'm gonna check with Hamdoon about picking up the visas." I listened to "Home on the Range" for more than five minutes before Nizar finally came on the line. He sounded quite agitated.

"As far as I know, there is no interview right now," he informed me. "Naji was mistaken. I just got off the phone with him."

"Is it a matter of days?" I asked. "What about Evans and Novak?"

"I think it is better they remain in Washington. They will only be wasting their time if they come to Baghdad."

"ANYWAY, IT'S PROBABLY FOR THE BEST," Eason said when I called back. "The feeling here is that we ought to wait until after the Bush-Gorbachev summit, so Saddam will have something to react to. I'm sorry if I forgot to mention it."

While I pondered the grotesque possibility of being put in the position of having to tell Saddam Hussein to go take a flying fuck, I overheard Forrest Sawyer on the telephone across the room. "You don't understand," he said plaintively. "No, you don't understand. [Pause] You can get killed here! [Pause] You can die here! [Pause] I appreciate that. [Pause] Tell Roone, I really appreciate that . . . but no. It's final. I'm leaving tomorrow.

"They just don't get it," Forrest said to me, shaking his head as he walked out. Sawyer wasn't the only correspondent with a bad case of nerves. NBC's Keith Miller, his producer, and crew also decided to pull the plug, leaving his network (except for Gordon Manning, who departed soon after) naked as a jaybird.

"What the hell am I supposed to do?" asked David Page, an NBC producer who arrived in Baghdad a day later. "I've got no correspondent, no crew, and no editor. Ain't it great?" Page was one of NBC's finest producers, and a wonderful guy to boot.

"Well, you could either slit your wrists, or join us for cocktails."

"I'll be there in an hour," he laughed.

BAGHDAD WAS AN EMOTIONAL ROLLER COASTER. It was hard to get a fix on it. Some days, it seemed as if there would surely be a negotiated way out of the crisis. There just had to be. Other days, it felt as if war was imminent. The atmosphere was spooky. One afternoon, a team from ITN was caught taking pictures without their minder. They were driven far out of the city and interrogated for almost three hours before being released. During an interview with the Minister of Culture and Information, Joe Treaster was told by Latif Jassim that Iraq knew the *Times* man also worked for the FBI. Treaster flew out of Baghdad two days later.

"I don't know what his motives were," Joe told me later in Amman. "But I wasn't going to stick around to find out. He's the same guy who went after Bazoft." Farzad Bazoft was the Iranian-born British-based journalist who'd been tried for espionage and hanged by the Iraqis in March.

But aside from Faiz's outrageous threat that first week to send tens of thousands of us home in coffins, I never felt menaced by Iraqi officials. I suppose the closest I came was during a conversation with Naji in late November. As I was leaving his office, he asked about the origins of my last name. "It means 'from Vienna,' " I told him matter-of-factly.

"Is that where your parents are from?" he wanted to know.

"No, they were born in the U.S.A."

"And your grandparents?"

"They came from Eastern Europe," I said, and changed the subject. I always assumed Naji knew I was Jewish, though on my visa application form I'd left the "Religion" question blank and Anglicized my grandfather's name, Jacob, to Jack. But, although I didn't flaunt it, I made no secret of my background.

"When I first laid eyes on you, with your Hawaiian shirt and two pairs of sunglasses," Joe Wilson once reminisced, "I said to myself, 'There's a New York Jew.' " In fact, there were several Jewish journalists who eventually came to Baghdad, including Carl Bernstein and CNN's Richard Roth. Roth was on a trip to Basra when, after finishing lunch, he asked for a receipt.

"Aha! You're Jewish!" his minder confronted him. Richard was taken aback a moment before the man added, "But you're one of the good Jews."

Since our arrival in Baghdad, the Ishtar-Sheraton had served us well. It was a short drive from the U.S. Embassy and only minutes away from the feedpoint. By night, Abu Nawas Street was illuminated by thousands of small white bulbs strung like Christmas lights, as Baghdadis feasted on grilled *masgouf* at the score of restaurants that lined the banks of the Tigris. Driving past, it was easy to imagine life in better times, and it made me nostalgic for those languid evenings in Vietnam when I would stroll down Nguyen Hue to the Saigon River, tantalized by the scents of Southeast Asia and joyous in the knowledge and romance of being young and free, and

Vietnam 1970. UPI's Art Higbee and the author take cover in a shellhole along Highway 13.
David Hume Kennerly

The Romanian Revolution. The author in Palace Square, Bucharest, December 1989. *Ingrid Formanek*

First to Go . . . Last to Know! Correspondent Jim Clancy, the author, and Mark Biello depart for Baghdad on August 23, 1990. *Trey Haney*

Checking in. The author calling CNN Atlanta from the desk of U.S. Ambassador April Glaspie, August 1990. *Author's collection*

The author with his favorite portrait of Saddam Hussein, at the Ministry of Information. *Ingrid Formanek*

Producer Elisa Gambino, CBS soundman Juan Caldera, and Cynde Strand in Baghdad. After the war erupted, Caldera was captured on the Saudi-Kuwait border along with correspondent Bob Simon and held prisoner by the Iraqis for forty days. *Author's collection*

Party Hearty. The author surrounded by colleagues in September 1990 at Baghdad's Ishtar-Sheraton Hotel: David Heaberlin, Stuart Clark, Doug James, Cynde Strand, Rod Nino, and Miss Ingrid. *Author's collection*

Hello Atlanta! Jim Clancy, Ingrid Formanek, and the author call in from the workspace at the Al-Rasheed. Before the four-wire was installed, telephoning the United States was one of the most frustrating parts of the job. *Author's collection*

"Cybil's" Birthday. Videotape editor Tracy Flemming is overwhelmed at a surprise birthday party. It wasn't her birthday, but the affair served to lift "Cybil's" spirits. *Author's collection*

Mr. Kareem. Our faithful driver, flanked by Tracy and Ingrid. Kareem worked for CNN from August 1990 through the end of the war and became a dear friend to us all. *Author's collection*

Naji al-Hadithi, Director General, Ministry of Culture and Information. Naji was subsequently appointed as Iraqi's foreign minister. *Republic of Iraq*

"Dream-O-Vision: TV at Ground Zero." The collage that kept on growing. *Author's collection*

"Minder" Mazin. With the author in early September. *Author's collection*

U.S. charge d'affaires Joe Wilson outside the U.S. Embassy with the videotape of President George Bush's address to the Iraqi people, September 15, 1990. *Klaus Raisinger Reuter/Bettmann*

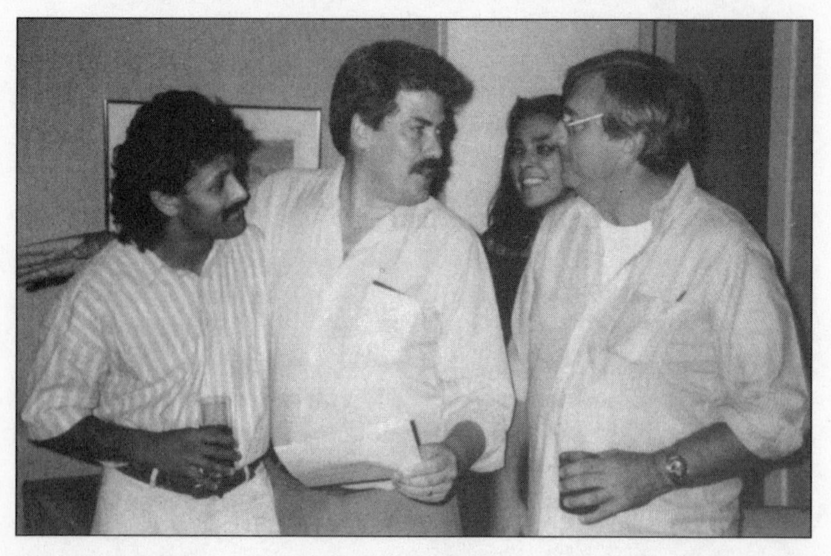

The DSB Quartet. Cameraman Tyrone Edwards, Jim Clancy, Ingrid Formanek and Richard Blystone in harmony, October 1990. Tyrone was later captured and held by the Iraqis along with some forty other journalists traveling from Kuwait to Basra at the end of the war. *Author's collection*

precisely where I wanted to be. I'd like to come back to Baghdad, I thought, when there's not a crisis, when I'm not on deadline. Maybe even bring Elaine and the boys. No doubt about it, Baghdad could be captivating.

But by the time I returned to the hotel, where the room service menu had become more than a little stale and the ice machine was perpetually empty, those thoughts had evaporated. It was time for a change, I reckoned. For one thing, the lighting was driving us all loco. All the fixtures were fluorescent, bathing everything and everyone in an unforgiving stark blue-white glare. For another, the only amenity left in my room was an "automatic" TV, which mysteriously turned itself on and off at odd moments.

So I was easily swayed when a certain Mrs. Nihad recited the charms of the Al-Rasheed while she plied Doug James and myself with a chilled bottle of French Chablis. I'd gotten a taste of the hotel when we'd interviewed Jesse Jackson and I'd liked what I'd seen. Now, surveying the menu, which included everything from smoked salmon to grilled *entrecôte béarnaise,* I liked it even more. What sold me, however, was the promise that as guests at this government-owned hotel, we'd be given the highest priority when telephoning the United States. What's more, the rates were competitive with the Sheraton. Doug and I declined Nihad's offer of lunch on the house to tour the ninth floor, three-room suite that eventually became our permanent office. It offered a commanding view of the swimming pool and gardens, a modern revolving restaurant nearby that we affectionately dubbed "the Giant Mushroom," and a small airport used by various dignitaries as well as members of the Revolutionary Command Council. The hotel was a stone's throw from the presidential palace, the Ministry of Culture and Information, and the television station. Immediately next door was the Ministry for Foreign Affairs. Located behind a high wall, the Al-Rasheed didn't offer the greatest of live shots, but what the hell? A palm tree could say Baghdad.

The hotel was built for the 1982 nonaligned summit, and it seemed as if as much money had been spent on security as on furnishings. The door to each room was at least six inches thick, and every floor boasted an individual security desk just off the elevators, complete with its own "Assault Alarm" button. Naturally, there was a private heliport and control tower. Only after we moved in did we discover that guests could be locked *into* their rooms as well. And no one could explain a series of miniature red and green lights imbedded in the ceiling of every bathroom.

After the bowling alley, tennis courts, discotheque, hairdresser, photo stand, airline office, bank, craft store, boutique, and jewelry store, not to mention the Scheherezade Bar and two restaurants, the series of bomb shelters were a major selling point, all equipped with wall-to-wall carpeting, toilets, and individual generators. Frankly, I would have been sold solely on the basis of the bath soaps, but I figured it would soon be a buyers' market. Nihad agreed to supply free coffee and, even better, she'd accept American Express. If you were going to go down in flames, I figured, why not have a mink-lined coffin?

"Hey, listen to this," I laughed, reading aloud from *The Baghdad Observer*. " 'A Spanish-born Peruvian businessman claims to have set the world's record for joke telling for the second year in a row following a nonstop hundred-hour joke-telling marathon. During his hundred-hour session at a hotel in Lima, Peru, Felipe Carbonell said he told eight thousand jokes in Spanish, English, French, Italian, and Portuguese. Carbonell, who broke his earlier record for cracking jokes for seventy-two hours, said, 'Laughter in a crisis-ridden country such as Peru is an elixir to help us bear the burden.' Peru is plagued by guerrilla violence and its economy is in shambles."

"Why you read that to me?" Mazin chirped.

"Maybe you should invite this guy to Baghdad. He sounds like a great morale booster."

"What's going on?" Ingrid asked, entering the room.

"I was just telling Mr. Mazin here about this fabulous comedian in Peru. . . ."

"Does Mr. Mazin know your Ceauşescu joke?" she interrupted.

"I don't think so, but here goes. . . . What do you get when you cross a penis and a potato? Give up? A dictator!" I howled.

"A dic, what?" Mazin puzzled.

"Oh, never mind. It's only funny in Romania."

IF THE TRUTH BE TOLD, flying Felipe Carbonell to Iraq wouldn't have been such a bad idea, after all. We could all have used a little comic relief. We'd been putting in long days at the airport, recording gut-wrenching scenes of emotional farewells as the exodus of women and children continued. One morning before heading to Saddam International, we'd assembled at the embassy as about forty U.S. citizens, either married to Iraqis or of Iraqi descent, loaded their baggage onto a chartered bus for the first leg of their long journey home. Most of them had flown to Baghdad earlier that summer to visit loved ones. It was a poignant moment as relatives clutched children and infants, fearful they would never see them again. One woman had to be pried apart from her naturalized American daughter, only to reach out to her again, for a last hug and embrace. On the sidewalk near the rear of the bus, a grandmother, clad in an *abaya*, was on the verge of collapse. Finally, after almost an hour, the passengers took their seats on the bus and waved good-bye. But their families would not disperse. They lingered in front of the embassy, talking among themselves, commiserating about the tragedy that had befallen all of them.

"Leaving your children is like leaving part of your life," one man told me. "But I'll see them again one day. *Insha'allah.*"

MY VISA TO IRAQ was valid for thirty days, but after two weeks Mazin informed me it was time to leave. It didn't seem to matter that the Foreign Minister himself had assured me I could remain as long as I liked.

"The Information Ministry says journalists can stay ten days only," he said. "You can come back, Mr. Robert. It will be good for you to return home for a while." I didn't protest. I was anxious to see my family.

On August 8, my wife and two children and I had moved into our new apartment in Berlin, where CNN had established a bureau to cover the developing story in Eastern Europe. One hundred forty-three boxes, plus furniture, had finally made it from Jerusalem, where I had been bureau chief for two and a half years. That night, after Elaine and I got the boys to bed, we sat on top of the cartons, exhausted. We'd begin unpacking in the morning. But at 7 A.M. it wasn't Jesse or Jake who woke us as usual, but Paul Dieterich, our Berlin sound tech, who buzzed the front door. Unable to reach me on the mobile phone, the desk had told Paul to get to our flat and instruct me to leave for Cairo immediately. CNN wanted live coverage of the emergency Arab summit, scheduled to begin the following day. I'd been gone ever since.

With Ingrid also planning to depart to attend a friend's wedding in Greece, CNN dispatched producer Alec Miran to work with Peter Humi. Alec was permanently assigned to our Special Events Unit, but preferred the rough-and-tumble of breaking news to the stage-managed world of presidential travels and U.S.-Soviet summits. A gifted and inveterate workaholic, Alec had produced CNN's award-winning live coverage of events in Tiananmen Square. We had worked together on several occasions since, and I considered him a good friend.

With Alec in tow, I bid farewell to Wilson and Thibault, Naji and Nizar, and the staff at Iraqi TV. "May you have a safe journey, Mr. Robert," Mrs. Awattif said to me, "and come back to us soon." Mazin insisted on accompanying me to the airport, and saw to it that I was whisked through the departure formalities with a minimum of fuss. What he was unable to do, however, was convince Iraq Airways that under IATA regulations, possessing a first-class ticket means the airline does have a certain obligation to seat you in first class. Well, I mused, if they possessed a shred of human decency. . . .

PART THREE

September–October 1990

8

By the time I returned to Baghdad about two weeks later, it was clear that, if anything, the crisis was escalating. In a joint communiqué following their summit in Helsinki, Presidents Bush and Gorbachev agreed Iraq's invasion of Kuwait would not be tolerated and said the United Nations might have to take further action if the economic sanctions failed to budge Baghdad. On September 9, Iraq and Iran reestablished diplomatic relations, and three days later an Iranian leader, Ayatollah Ali Khomenei, called for a "holy war" against the United States. On September 14, Iraqi troops burst into the home of the French ambassador to Kuwait and kidnapped three French citizens. President Mitterrand angrily called the raid "an act of aggression." France immediately expelled almost thirty Iraqi diplomats and announced it was deploying troops and warplanes to Saudi Arabia. On September 16, during a videotaped message played on Iraqi TV, President Bush told Iraqis that although there could still be a peaceful end to the crisis, they now stood "on the brink of war." The Iraqi News Agency denounced Bush as a "liar." The same day, Margaret Thatcher called Saddam Hussein a "ruthless, barbaric dictator."

The UN Security Council, meanwhile, adopted four new resolutions: it approved sending food and medicine to Iraq and Kuwait as a humanitarian gesture; condemned Iraq's raids on embassy compounds in Kuwait (Iraq officially apologized to France on September 24); offered assistance to countries suffering economic hardship due to the embargo of Iraq; and on September 25, imposed an air embargo against Baghdad. Iraq decried the air embargo, Resolution 670, as "an act of war."

On the hostage front, the State Department said about nineteen hundred Americans had been evaucated but some nine hundred remained in Iraq and Kuwait. According to the U.S. Embassy in Baghdad, at least one hundred and one Americans were now being detained at strategic installations.

During a series of visits, Yasir Arafat, King Hussein, former Algerian president Ahmed Ben Bella, and various delegations, including Japanese and British politicians, all flew to Iraq to meet with Saddam Hussein. Ultimately, his response remained unchanged: Kuwait is part of Iraq.

My return flight to Baghdad left Amman four hours late. By the time I'd cleared customs and Mr. Jasim had deposited me at the Al-Rasheed, it was almost 11 P.M. But in spite of the delays, the long lines and hassles at customs, I was genuinely glad to be back. By now, Baghdad was familiar territory. In fact, I considered it my "beat." And that in itself would ultimately give CNN a significant advantage over many of our competitors. Throughout the crisis, a number of reporters traveled to Iraq with the hope of safely completing their ten-day stints, then getting out of town. We, on the other hand, had made a genuine commitment to the story. From the day we'd arrived, through the end of the war, CNN maintained a continuous presence in Baghdad. What's more, many of the same people came back again and again. I am convinced this made a difference to the Iraqi authorities. After all, if war broke out, we'd be laying it on the line alongside them. In fairness, however, there were indeed compelling reasons for not wanting to be there. The dangers notwithstanding, several reporters called Baghdad "the ugly dateline." The censorship, the restrictions, the constant surveillance, the feeling of often being manipulated . . . all contributed to many journalists' distaste for the place, and their desire to blow Dodge as soon as possible. On the other hand, there was censorship in Saudi, censorship in Israel, and restrictions and constraints all over the map. Baghdad wasn't always ideal, but you could still do your job. What really tightened the sphincters was more basic: Baghdad was Ground Zero.

And so said Air Force Chief of Staff General Michael Dugan during an interview with *The Washington Post* in mid-September. In the event of war, not only would American bombers unleash what he called massive raids against the Iraqi capital, the United States would also target Saddam Hussein himself. For speaking out of school, the general was sent to the showers, but the import of his words was heard loud and clear on the banks of the Tigris. The Iraqis at that point may not have believed him, but the guardians of the Fourth Estate sure as hell did.

"WELCOME, MR. ROBERT. WELCOME!" driver Kareem greeted me as I stepped into the hotel's lobby. He was standing by the Ministry of Information desk, which was manned by several familiar faces from the Sheraton.

"So, you guys are all here too," I said, shaking hands with everyone.

"After CNN move, all journalists come to the Al-Rasheed," one official told me.

"That's fabulous. So, how are your families? How's everyone holding up?"

"Everything good. *Hamdelaylah*. What they say in United States? Will there be war?"

"I don't know, but that seems to be the direction. Unless you guys have had second thoughts about the Nineteenth Province."

"You know, Mr. Robert, we don't want war. All Iraqis want peace."

"Yeah," I agreed. "Everybody wants peace. But peace on whose terms?" I excused myself and checked in at Reception.

"Good to see you again," Mrs. Nihad said. "We have nice room for you, next to your office."

"So I see business has picked up since we last met."

"Yes, it's very good," she beamed. "But even better if we have peace."

"Hey," Ingrid shouted as she ran through the lobby. "We're on our way to see Nizar. We'll be back soon." She was accompanied by Richard Blystone, a reporter from our London bureau. It was good to see him finally on the case. A veteran foreign correspondent who'd joined CNN after a successful career at the Associated Press, Bly was far and away the network's most talented writer. Covering anything from the fortieth anniversary of D-Day to a natural disaster in the Third World, Blystone's scripts were always a cut above the rest. During his first few years at the network he'd been unfairly pegged as a feature writer, but his riveting work during the CNN Farewell to Communism World Tour '89 had dispelled any doubt about his ability to cover breaking news. Bly was the only correspondent who could go head-to-head against a master wordsmith, like Bob Simon of CBS, say, and often come out on top. The two of them, in fact, went back together many years. But if Simon looked like the quintessential successful television correspondent—urbane, handsome, and sartorially turned out—Blystone was quite the opposite. On the road especially, he was usually grossly overweight, invariably disheveled, and attired in whatever garb his bloodshot eyes happened to focus on when he awoke in the morning. To put it simply, Richard was a diamond in the rough, and all of us who worked with him not only grew professionally, but felt proud to call him friend.

I THREW MY BAGS INTO ROOM 923 and walked down the hall to our office. The three-room suite was divided into an assignment desk/editorial area

(906), an edit suite (904), and an equipment room (902), which also doubled as a crew lounge. "This isn't bad," I said to Clancy, "but we're gonna need more space. Is there anyone we know living next door?"

"A couple of minders are sleeping in 908," Jim said, "but they'd probably be willing to move. They've already complained about the noise."

"Well, it's only gonna get worse," I laughed, fixing myself a drink. "I'll make the arrangements in the morning." A moment later, we were joined by Tyrone Edwards and Phil Turner, two of the network's ace shooters.

"So how's it going, guys?" I asked.

"It's an interesting place, all right," Tyrone said with a grin. "So you really like working here, huh?"

"Well, it does have its benefits," I said, calling room service to order a *chateaubriand*. I hadn't eaten in over twelve hours.

"I take it you skipped the meal on the plane coming in," Phil chuckled.

"Yeah, you know me, Floyd. I'm a finicky eater. Who was it who dubbed those little Iraq Airways sausages 'hostage fingers'? It's certainly apropos."

"Hey, Weenie!" cried Tracy Flemming as she gave me a hug. "Welcome back. Uh-oh, I see you never got that sty taken care of. I guess we'll have to call you 'Stymie' from now on," she giggled.

"Go ahead. It's a great road-name."

On the road, we called each other a variety of monickers. During the revolutions in Eastern Europe, Blystone had christened me "Captain Wacky" as I shepherded our little band from one hot spot to the next. Ingrid was baptized "the Damsel," as in "Dark Damsel of Danger," for her proclivity for dressing in black, as well as for her romantic persona. Later, during "An Iron-Curtain Odyssey," a series of special reports she produced for Blystone, she was also dubbed "Dingir," an anagram for her first name. Phil Turner was known alternately as "Floyd" or "Kakanada Slim," after his birthplace in India. Tracy Flemming became "Cybil Simpson." Cynde Strand was her best friend, "Pearl Plum." Doug James was intrepid reporter "Willard 'Three Scoops' McHenry." Mark Biello was knighted "Axel Bigrod." Our Paris cameraman, André Brauns, answered only to "Action." Tim Wilson, a good ole Southern boy, and Charlie Hoff, who sported a leather jacket and fedora, were called respectively, "Homer" and "Indiana." Correspondent Christiane Amanpour was known as "Kissy," the name her father called her as a baby. Richard Roth was "the Dick of Death," as opposed to "Red Dick," an alias for Blystone when the two worked a story together. Blystone also answered to "Bly," "Bubba," "Buck," "Lance," "Arthur," "Raoul," "Roy," and sometimes "Grandpa-pa." In some cases, the sobriquets were less than flattering. One reporter, diminutive in stature and always clad in a trenchcoat, was immediately dubbed "Stumpy McGruff" after the crime-fighting dog, while a certain bureau chief, known for his fondness for gossip and more apt to wring his own hands than anyone's neck, was called "the Old Woman of Europe." Clancy, for some reason, was always just Clancy.

"HAMDOON SAYS IT'S TOTAL BULLSHIT!" Ingrid screeched as she returned with Blystone. "Jesus, this place is surreal. This morning Wilson turned up at the briefing wearing a noose around his neck. I told him he was the best-dressed man in Baghdad." What prompted Joe to go off the deep end was a note delivered to Western embassies by the Iraqi government reminding diplomats that anyone sheltering foreigners was subject to hanging. Baghdad had also asked for the names of nondiplomats who had sought refuge in the residence. "Nizar said it was a misunderstanding," she said. "They're not going to start hanging diplomats."

"Well, you can't win 'em all," I laughed. "What else did Hamdoon have to say?"

"They're apparently encouraged by Mitterrand's speech before the General Assembly," Bly said. The French President had told the UN an Iraqi withdrawal from Kuwait could lead to a comprehensive settlement in the Middle East, including a resolution to the Palestinian problem and Israel's right to peace and security. "Nizar said it reflects several elements of Saddam's August 12 initiative." (Saddam had said he was ready to resolve the crisis in the Gulf if Israel withdrew from the occupied lands and Syria pulled out of Lebanon.)

"Well, that's never gonna happen," I said. "Israel's not going to fold its tent just like that, nor should it. Did Hamdoon say anything about establishing diplomatic relations with Jerusalem?"

"No, we never got that far."

"Any other headlines . . . ?"

"There's still nothing on the Saddam interview," Ingrid interrupted. "I told Nizar you just got in and would call him tomorrow. By the way, Bubba and I are leaving in the morning for Basra."

"That's a good hit. How'd ya arrange that?"

"Everybody's going," Blystone groaned. "Another dog and pony show."

By the time I got to the morning briefing, Wilson and Thibault were playing to standing room only. "They're still bringing people up from Kuwait on a regular basis," Steve said. "They're taken to the Mansour Melia Hotel, where we can sometimes visit them, but where they go from there, who knows?' Thibault was asked what advice, if any, he had for these "special guests."

"Well, we usually tell them they're going to face spartan conditions and they should be prepared to share warm clothes. And we advise them to hide whatever dollars they can. Sometimes, they can establish a relationship with their guards and the money can help. We also tell them they may be asked to make some sort of statement."

"Many foreigners in Iraq suffered from a form of Stockholm Syndrome even before this crisis started," Joe interjected. "To begin with, every foreigner here must have an Iraqi sponsor, and, as an employee, you're subject to the whims of that sponsor. A lot of these guys are past retirement age in the States. They feel they got a good deal by working here in the first place. They're already tied in emotionally."

"It's really a mind-fuck," Thibault added.

"Speaking of mind-fucks," I asked, "how's Stu holding up?"

"You mean, in the Bechtel Bunker? I'm afraid there's no change there," he laughed.

"Joe, what's your take on the Mitterrand proposal?"

"That's not a question for me. It's best directed at Washington."

"Well, apparently the Foreign Ministry feels it could form a basis for an end to this thing."

"I can't comment," Joe said. "What I can say is that I'm not aware of any movement to find a solution. . . . The situation is still fraught with danger."

"Okay," I said to Clancy. "The women and children have been evacuated. Thibault says those who wanted to get out have gotten out. The sanctions are only biting in terms of spare parts. Baghdad thinks the Mitterrand proposal is worth looking into, but Wilson says there's zip on the diplomatic front. Abul Abbas is threatening terrorist retaliations if Iraqi airplanes are attacked. We're all over the goddamn map here. So what's the focus of our piece tonight?"

"I think you've just answered your own question, Robert," Clancy said wearily. "The focus of our piece tonight is whatever Mr. Blystone brings back from Basra. As for me, I'm heading down to the souk. I'll check in later."

WHILE WE WAITED for Bly and Ingrid to return from Basra, Clancy cobbled together a script. "It ain't gonna be pretty," he said, "but it has all the elements." Iraqi TV reported the government had reversed an earlier decision to prohibit foreigners from purchasing rationed food. "Food will be provided equally for all," the announcer said, "including diplomatic missions, foreigners . . . and all those who arrived as guests of Iraq."

"That's at least the third time they've backed down after taking the hard line," I said to Clancy. "First, the hostages, then that bullshit about possibly hanging 'dips,' and now this ration business. I find it interesting, no?"

"Well, they still haven't backed down on Kuwait," he said.

"I don't know. I've got a feeling we should be doing more on this Mitterrand thing. Hamdoon's been tied up all day and I really wanted to discuss it with him." The more I thought about it, the more sense the French proposal seemed to make. Of course, it didn't stand a snowball's chance in hell of succeeding. The United States rejected any linkage between Iraq's withdrawal from Kuwait and other regional issues, and Israel was no more willing to accept an international conference under UN auspices than it was willing to unilaterally give up the West Bank or Gaza Strip. Furthermore, there was absolutely nothing to indicate any Arab country was even willing to sit down, let alone make peace with the Jewish state. For a moment, I whimsically imagined all parties suddenly seeing the logic of what Mitterrand proposed, and avoiding war. But if my years in the Middle East had taught me anything, it was that logic takes a back seat to emotion, and the region was an emotional quagmire of passionate points of view with little tolerance for any opposition. Oh yeah, they all wanted peace: the Arabs, the Israelis, the Palestinians . . . but on their own terms. In my darkest moments I thought a war wouldn't be so bad after all. Let 'er rip, clear the decks, and start anew. What was the old joke about Northern Ireland? Take everybody in favor of peace and put them on ships in the North Atlantic. Next, allow everybody left to kill one another. Then . . . sink the ships.

"Excuse me, does anyone here know anything about computer printers?" Carl Bernstein asked as he entered our office. I had never met Bernstein before, the man who, along with partner Bob Woodward, had blown the roof off Watergate. Here was a journalistic legend, a Pulitzer prize-winning role model for countless up-and-coming newspeople, including myself, who devoured *All the President's Men* when it first appeared in print and took a vicarious thrill in the reporters' exploits when their story was immortalized on the big screen. Since Watergate, Carl had had his ups and downs, including an ill-fated move to ABC News as its Washington bureau chief, and a messy and highly publicized divorce from writer Nora Ephron, whose novel *Heartburn* (which was also made into a movie) chronicled his alleged philandering and deceit. Bernstein was in Baghdad on assignment for *Time*, where he was currently employed as a correspondent in its New York bureau. Coincidentally, I had just finished reading *Loyalties*, his latest book.

"Howdy. Robert Wiener," I said, introducing myself. "No, I know absolutely nothing about computers or printers, but Jim Clancy over there in the next room is probably the most knowledgeable guy in Baghdad when it comes to that stuff. Hell, he even travels with a mainframe."

"Is that so?" Bernstein laughed.

"Yeah. Hey, Jim," I shouted. "Willya help out Mr. Bernstein?"

"I take it you're the head of this operation?" Carl asked.

"We all sort of work together. It's a socialist kind of thing."

Within a moment Clancy appeared, and, after listening to Bernstein's problem, quickly offered five possible explanations why his printer wasn't working properly. "I'm sure I can fix it," he said. And with that, he and Carl left for Bernstein's room.

"What's so funny?" I asked Tracy, who'd been watching the exchange.

"I can't explain it," she laughed. "It's just that the guy always seems to be needing help for something. For the past couple of days, even before you got back, he's been popping around asking for this or that."

"And we should help him, sweetheart. The problem is you've got no respect for your fuckin' journalistic elders!"

"Give me a break, Weenie."

"No, I'm serious. I think you're in need of some discipline."

"Please, Weenie! Don't start that again," she laughed. "I've got a tape to log."

"So what's the story with Mr. Mazin?" I asked Ingrid later that night after she'd returned from Basra. "What exactly happened?"

"To the rodent?" she laughed. "Well, apparently Mazin was ripping off the drivers, at least Kareem and what's-his-name, the other guy who quit after you left. He was pocketing about fifty bucks a day from each of them."

"And Jasim?"

"No," she said, "we've always paid Jasim directly. Mazin was in charge of the other two."

"Well, where is Mazin now?"

"He's working inside the Ministry of Information. We don't have an assigned minder anymore. You sort of pick one up from the minder's pool at the desk in the lobby."

"So, who have we been working with?"

"For the most part, a guy named Nasir. Clancy says he's okay, but I think he's a bullshit artist."

"Well, say what you will about Mazin, he got the job done, story-wise. By the way, how'd the piece on the Iraqi Jews turn out?"

"Oh, great, Wienerish. You should take a look at it. Doug wrote a beautiful script. I'm told Israel TV even ran the piece several times."

"That's fabulous. Well, I'd like to meet this Mr. Nasir."

"You will," she said, ordering more ice. "He's gonna stop by to discuss our 'program' with you."

A SHORT TIME LATER, a squat, fat-jowled, curly-haired, mustachioed little man sporting a heavy five-o'clock shadow appeared in our office and, within two minutes of introducing himself, asked for a shot of vodka. This was not a good sign, I thought, a definite breach of protocol, but what the hell? By now, we all had a few under our belts, and the atmosphere was, well, convivial.

"*Mi casa es su casa*," I said to Nasir as I poured him a drink. "So, tomorrow we'd very much like to visit a farm for a story on increased production in view of the economic sanctions. Would that be possible?"

"Yes, that is no problem," Nasir said. "I know big farm about one hour from Baghdad."

"What do they grow there?"

"Everything," he said. "Is good farm. ITN did story there last week. Please," he said, gesturing to the Stoli, "another drink?"

"Help yourself." Nasir scooped up a handful of ice and drained what was left in the bottle.

"So, how long have you been a devout Muslim?" I inquired.

"What? You no have more vodka?" Nasir replied.

"For you? Absolutely." I cracked open another bottle and served him a stiff double. "You're sure you'll be okay in the morning?" I asked. "We'll have to leave very early."

"We go at maybe eleven," he slurred. "Is time enough."

"That's very late. In most of the world, farmers begin at dawn."

"No, you see. We go at eleven. Everything will be good."

"Well, I can see you've had a long day," I said as I escorted him toward the door. "We'll meet you in the lobby at eleven, sharp. I'm counting on you."

"See what I mean?" Ingrid laughed.

"Yeah, you're right, but let's give the guy the benefit of the doubt. How long's he been into the sauce?"

"Don't know, but ITN must have corrupted him." The Brits drank like there was no tomorrow.

The alarm jarred me awake at 6 A.M., but despite the excesses of the previous night I was anxious to get moving. The sun was already up and a warm breeze blew through the open window as I made for the shower. Fifteen minutes later I walked down the hall to the office, which, as usual at that hour, looked like a disaster area. Trays of half-eaten food, empty bottles, melted ice, overflowing ashtrays, discarded magazines and papers were strewn all over the place and the air was rancid with the stale smell of smoke, sweat, and suds. I threw open the windows, put on a pot of coffee, called housekeeping, and ordered breakfast. I then stepped into the bathroom of Room 902, our in-house infirmary, and gobbled my daily dose of vitamins, aspirin, and antidiarrhea medicine. By the time the Sudanese waiter arrived carrying an enormous tray filled with rolls, toast, hard-boiled eggs, ersatz orange drink, and tea, we were ready for business. Bly was usually right on his heels, his years in the Navy having instilled in him the dubious virtue of being up-and-at-'em at first light. His morning staple: peanut butter and Nutella chocolate spread on toast. As the day progressed and his appetite increased, the Nutella was discarded in favor of canned anchovies, a lethal combination that made us all nauseous. Like an old married couple, we spoke little as we each digested *The Baghdad Observer*.

"Good morning," said Carl Bernstein. "Any chance of a cup of coffee? I can't drink that stuff they bring you with room service."

"No problem. Be my guest."

"So what are you up to today?" he wanted to know.

"Nothing special. We're gonna file our Basra piece and we're working on an agricultural story. What about you?"

"I've got a couple of meetings with diplomats. I need to tie up some loose ends. By the way, how are you fixed for cash? Perhaps I could cash a check?"

"A personal check?" I laughed. "Gee, I don't know, Carl . . . unless Woodward's gonna co-sign."

"I've got traveler's checks," he smiled.

"Well, in that case, I think we can accommodate you. How much do you need?"

"Five thousand," he said, "or at least thirty-five hundred, if you can spare it. I've got a lot of expenses before I get back to New York, and I want to stop off in Cairo. What do you know about buying rugs there? Is that the place?"

"Well, Cairo's inexpensive but I've never bought rugs there. You should check with Mario downstairs at CBS. He's the rug maven in these parts." As Carl and I transacted business, Tracy sauntered into the office and poured herself a cup of tea.

"Thanks a lot," Bernstein said. "I'll see you later. Oh, and thank Jim again for the help with the printer."

"So what was it this time, Weenie?" Tracy asked. "A social call?"

"Not quite. He needed to cash a check."

"See, what'd I tell ya!" she laughed.

WHILE TRACY LOGGED THE TAPES from Basra and Bly returned to his room to write, I poured myself another cup of coffee and gazed out the window. Several hostages were already sunning themselves at the pool below while others splashed playfully in the water. A moment later, a trio of nurses from the Irish Hospital displayed their bikini-clad charms as they prepositioned their chaise lounges to take optimum advantage of the sun. One in particular, who we came to know later as Nurse Natalie, seemed to take forever as she meticulously lathered her already bronzed body with Bain de Soleil. Alongside the swimming pool, the two tennis courts were already occupied by players dressed in regulation whites, while other "guests" strolled in the gardens nearby. For an instant, it was easy to forget we were in the eye of the hurricane. I placed a wake-up call to Ingrid, who was to accompany Clancy, Nasir, and the crew out to the farm, and left for the embassy.

In the lobby downstairs, two European television crews were recording interviews with Yusaf Islam—who once answered to the name Cat Stevens. The Cat-Man had hopped on the Peace Train and was now in Baghdad as a self-proclaimed emissary of entente cordiale, happy to throw his two cents' worth into the pot, and eager to explain why to anyone willing to listen. Within days we too would air a soundbite from Señor Cat, ostensibly drawn from the Koran and God knows what else. When not meeting with Iraqi officials or dispensing interviews, Stevens could usually be found taking the air in the hotel's gardens, clad in a white galabaya and matching skullcap.

Abu Ali caught my eye and I signaled him to bring the car around. Abu Ali was our third driver, but unlike Jasim or Kareem, he spoke no English. Nevertheless, he was conscientious and hardworking . . . a good-natured fellow, eager to please. He was also terrified of the minders. It took several weeks to convince him it was not necessary to report to the Ministry of Information desk before every trip to let officials know precisely where he was taking us. Our conversations were limited to "Hello," "How are you?" "I am fine, *hamdelaylah*." My numerous attempts to advance beyond that were greeted only by a smile or nod, or, at the very best, sign language that indicated he realized the car's air conditioning should be turned up. He also understood "U.S. Embassy," "Ministry of Information," "TV," "Ministry for Foreign Affairs," "Airport," and "Hotel." Not for nothing was he paid a hundred and fifty dollars a day.

As usual, he declined my offer of a Gauloises as we drove to the embassy, opting instead for the locally manufactured ersatz version of Marlboros. As we passed the presidential palace, I noticed a huge crane hoisting a second anti-aircraft battery onto the arch over the main entrance . . . another great picture we would never be permitted to shoot. Understandably, the Iraqis were sensitive as hell about security. So sensitive, in fact, that the first time I drove past the compound and remarked to Mazin, "So that's the presidential palace, huh?" he replied, "Maybe." On another occasion, when Ingrid made a similar observation, another minder told her, "If you like me, don't ask me."

"The U.S. State Department is warning Americans there's mounting evidence that Iraqi-sponsored terrorism may begin shortly," the Atlanta editor on overnights told me when I called in from the embassy. "There's also speculation Saddam is trying to circumvent the embargo by importing goods through Jordan. Is there anything we can do on that?" Due to the nature of the story and the obvious problems with censorship on our end, I suggested the bureau in Amman should follow through on the report. But at the very least, we would try to feed pictures of whatever Jordanian imports might be available.

"Of course they're breaking the embargo," an Australian diplomat told me a few hours later, "and we're not talking about food or medicine. Just take a look at the main road from Amman. It's always jammed with lorries. Hell, the Foreign Ministry just got a new fleet of Oldsmobiles. Where do you think they came from? Now that would be a good story for you," he added. "Find out who has the franchise to import and sell General Motors cars in Jordan and you've got your sanction buster!"

In early November, on my way back to Berlin for a few days of R&R, I spoke to a Lufthansa representative at Amman's Queen Alia International Airport who was equally candid. "I see it every day. Iraqi Airways flies here with just enough fuel to make the trip, but when the plane returns to Baghdad it carries a full tank. Everyone knows they siphon off the remaining jet fuel in Iraq and use it for other flights, including those to Kuwait."

NOTHING NEWSWORTHY came out of the morning briefing; in fact most of the time was spent going over old information for several reporters who had just arrived. I walked back to USIS and tried to firm up appointments with Naji and Nizar.

As we returned to the Al-Rasheed, I asked Abu Ali to pull over in front of a small grocery. The shop was loaded to the gills with large cans of Florida orange juice, Scottish smoked salmon, jars of mayonnaise, beárnaise sauce, and other condiments, tins of tuna, Ritz crackers, Mars bars, Cheddar cheese, Greek kalamata olives, canned oysters, corned beef, not to mention several cases of Coca-Cola and Fanta. I picked up a can of Coke and turned it upside-down. The bottling date 02-08-90 was stamped in blue; the day Iraq invaded Kuwait. "Is everything here from Kuwait?" I asked the proprietor. He picked up his newspaper and continued reading.

The supervisor on duty at the minders desk leapt to his feet as I entered the lobby, wringing his hands. "Please, Mr. Robert, you must speak to

Miss Ingrid. She must not yell like she does. Is not right. Not here in hotel."

"What seems to be the problem?"

"I don't understand," he said. "Nasir say he take her to farm like you want, but she very angry. Please, you must talk with her." I took the elevator up to 906. Muzak was playing the theme from *Exodus*.

"*This is fucked!*" Ingrid howled. "The guy is absolute bullshit! First, he arrives ten minutes late for the shoot; then, by the time we get to the farm, there's no one there. They're having lunch or something."

"Were they going back to work after lunch?"

"Of course not. It's over a hundred degrees out there. They're farmers, Wienerish, not idiots!"

"Where is Nasir right now?"

"Who knows?"

"Okay. I'll speak with him later. In the meantime, the farm ain't gonna go away. You work with Bly on Basra. I'm going to have a bite, then meet with Naji. Hungry?"

"Who's ordering lunch?" Bly yelled from across the hall. Bubba's room was directly opposite the workspace and his door was invariably open. A moment later he padded in.

"Onion soup and ice cream? Or are you going to be adventurous and try something new?"

"No, that sounds fine," Bly said.

"Ingrid?"

"Cucumbers with cream, and a platter of melon and dates. Oh, and a Turkish coffee."

"What about Clancy and the crew?"

"They're downstairs at the buffet." I called room service and placed the order, including a cheese omelette for myself.

"You should speak to Naji about getting another minder," Ingrid lectured me.

"I'll take that up with Sadoun. With Naji, I've got other priorities."

While we waited for lunch, Blystone read us what he'd written about Basra, or, as he'd put it, "the legendary port of Sinbad the Sailor." The Iraqis had taken the press to Basra to witness the arrival of an Indian freighter carrying food and medicine. As usual, the trip had been tightly controlled, but Ingrid and Bly had managed to sneak an interview with an Indian Red Cross official who was less than flattering in his description of the "cooperation" he'd received from Iraqi authorities. After several procedural problems, the ship had eventually been off-loaded, part of its cargo destined for the needy in Kuwait City. But Baghdad had failed to provide trucks, drivers, in fact, any transportation, so the shipment was left piled up at the dock. "We need to check again with the Red Cross," Bly said, "and see if it has finally been moved."

As if it were preordained, Nasir and the food arrived at precisely the same moment. "How you call that?" he asked, pointing to the ice cream. "Is very good, no?"

"Listen," I said, trying to be diplomatic, "I must tell you I'm extremely displeased with how things were handled this morning. As I told you last night, farmers begin their day early in the morning. Last night you told me otherwise and I believed you. You've caused me to lose face in front of my co-workers."

"But . . ."

"Let me finish, please. I have no problem with your coming to our office, drinking our liquor, and socializing for that matter. But with all due respect, we're here to work, and if work means getting up at dawn, so be it!" Nasir stared at his feet. For an instant I felt sorry for the little bugger.

"I don't think it is right that Ingrid yell at me. . . ."

"Miss Ingrid happens to be CNN's farm specialist! It's only natural that she was perturbed about not being able to provide our global network with the coverage she'd promised. You told me you once worked for *The Baghdad Observer,* right? Surely, as a professional journalist you can empathize with her frustration."

"But . . ."

"Please, Mr. Nasir, let's not dwell on it. As a gentleman, I'll simply accept your word this will never, ever happen again. Agreed?"

"You want to go to farm tomorrow?" he asked contritely.

"I don't know yet. But I think you'd be well advised to get in touch with the people there and find out exactly what time they begin work, precisely what they are harvesting, and some other basic facts. Let's do journalism for Chrissake, okay?"

"Okay. I come to see you later."

On the way to Naji's office, I stopped off to see Sadoun al-Jenabi, whose bureau was on the same floor. Sadoun was in charge of day-to-day operations for the foreign press: issuing visas, assigning minders, organizing trips, and hustling newly arrived reporters into Minister Jasim's office for the traditional "meet and greet." He had recently been promoted to this new assignment and threw himself into it with unabashed zeal. His first order of business was redecorating his predecessor's drab digs. He threw down a couple of oriental rugs, and added half a dozen Naugahyde armchairs and a bookcase containing copies of Saddam's latest pronouncements and position papers on Kuwait translated into English, French, German, and Spanish. The two telephones on his desk rang constantly as he juggled appointments and set up interviews. Occasionally, when the pressure became too intense, he would simply lift the receiver off the hook a second, then hang up. He seemed to derive a certain satisfaction from this maneuver, although it only caused the caller to think he'd misdialed and immediately telephone again. Sadoun was a big, burly guy who spoke excellent English. Like Naji, he had a dry sense of humor, but you'd have to get him at a quiet moment to see it. Most of the time, he was being harassed by the guardians of the free press, who bombarded him with one request after another, from the trivial to the obscure. His standard reply to these queries was "Call me back after six-thirty."

"The office looks great," I said, extending my hand.

"Welcome back, Robert," he said, brushing aside my arm to give me a bear hug instead. "How was your journey? Uh-oh, you never took care of your eye!"

"Yeah, I know. It's okay. So tell me, how are you?"

"As you can see, it's business as usual." There were about five newsmen camped out in his office. "They're all waiting to see Mr. al-Hadithi," he whispered. "And all of these," he said, pointing to a pile of correspondence on his desk, "want to come to Baghdad."

"I need to see Naji too."

"Yes, yes. This is not a problem. You will go first. Come, sit down a moment. I want to ask you something." Sadoun leaned forward and lowered his voice. "What was the problem with Nasir and Ingrid? I'm told there was a big fight."

"Nasir didn't do his job properly. He jerked us around on a shoot and now we don't have a story."

"This is very bad," Sadoun said. "I will speak to him."

"Well, I've already spoken to him. But frankly, why can't we work with Mr. Mazin?"

"You know, we don't like to have you work with the same guide all the time. It creates . . . um . . . problems."

"What sort of problems?"

"It's not good if you become too friendly with a guide."

"Why not? You think Mazin's gonna divulge state secrets?"

"It's not that," he laughed. "Please, I will speak to Nasir. We want CNN to be able to do its work professionally. And now I will call Mr. al-Hadithi for you." He picked up his internal line.

"Please," he waved his hand toward Naji's office, "he is waiting."

"IT'S GOOD TO SEE YOU AGAIN, ROBERT," Naji said. "How is your family?"

"Just fine, thanks. How are you?"

"Still surviving," he smiled. Naji sat down behind his desk and called for tea. "So, what do they say in America? Will there be war?"

"Difficult to say. You know, I've been in Berlin, not the U.S."

"Yes, yes. But you are in touch with America," he insisted.

"I honestly don't know, Naji. Apparently, the Emir painted a very bleak picture of human rights abuses when he met with President Bush a few days ago."

"And people believe the Emir?" he asked incredulously. "Let's be serious, Robert. Even Bush must realize the al-Sabah family rules by corruption."

"Corrupt or not, the United Nations recognizes Kuwait as a sovereign state."

"The United States has bought the United Nations. Washington threatened and blackmailed countries to support its position."

"Are you saying Iraq wouldn't have gotten a fair shake if it had tried to resolve the Kuwait question through the UN?"

"Please, Robert. We are not stupid people."

"Listen, Naji, I'll be honest with you. I don't know enough about Iraq's so-called historical claim to Kuwait; maybe there is a legitimate case, who knows, but I gotta tell ya—and I'm speaking personally here, not as a representative of CNN—I happen to be a pacifist. I believe in dialogue. I believe in sitting down around a table and discussing grievances. I don't believe our world is best served by one country imposing itself militarily upon another. I didn't believe it when the United States was in Vietnam, and I think it was ill-advised for Iraq to take over Kuwait as it did. Sue me, I'm an idealist."

"My dear Robert, it was in the interest of the United States to support the al-Sabah family no matter how corrupt it was. It goes beyond what we are discussing now. Do you think it is right that a handful of sheiks control everything, that they spend their time in casinos around the world while most of the Arab world lives in poverty? Is that justice?"

I took a breath and wondered if we should continue in this vein. Well, why not, I thought, if something's worth doing, it's worth overdoing. "And do you think it was just for Iraq to threaten to destroy half of Israel?"

"It is Israel that threatens to destroy us," he countered.

"You don't seriously believe that?"

"Of course. They have already attacked us. They would like nothing better than to destroy what we have built." I felt we were getting into deep water, which would serve no one's interest, especially mine, and abruptly changed the subject.

"So, on another matter; how does it look for our interview with the President?" Naji reflected a moment as he fondled his worry beads.

"What did you think of Mitterrand's proposal?" he asked.

"It made sense to me, but I think he'll have a hard time selling it to Washington or Jerusalem."

"So that means the United Nations?" he laughed.

"Seriously, Naji, what about the interview . . . and our flyaway?"

"You must be patient, my friend."

"I get paid a lot of money to be impatient."

"We shall be in touch," Naji said, signaling me that our time was up. "Call me in a few days."

"So what'd Naji say?" Eason asked.

"Be patient."

"Good grief!"

"Listen, my gut tells me we're gonna get this thing sooner or later. We'll keep pushing, but obviously it's up to them."

"I hear ya. What about a trip to Kuwait?"

"Frankly, I didn't even bring it up. I sensed it wasn't the moment. I was also supposed to meet with Hamdoon, but he's postponed the meeting for a day or two. Has Rollie Evans heard anything from him?"

"Negative. By the way, we just got a telex from Iraqi TV. They're going to broadcast a major address by Saddam. It looks like his response to the Bush speech to the Iraqi people."

"Are we going to carry it live?"

"No. We're gonna take it in and see how long it runs. We'll turn it around later."

"Gee, I would have thought a long, rambling discourse by the President of Iraq broadcast live around the world would do wonders for the ratings. If nothing else, it'd be a hit with our critics."

"Yeah, right," he laughed. "When you get back here we're gonna let you answer all the mail personally."

"Well, shit, I'll check with Mrs. Awattif and see if I can get some more information. So, how's everyone holding up on your end?"

"We're all exhausted. No one's had a day off. Nothing worse than what you guys have been going through."

"And Susan and the baby?"

"They're fine, but I hardly see them. I really feel terrible about it, but I just can't seem to get away from this place."

"Yeah," I laughed. "I know the feeling."

President Saddam Hussein's "Message of Peace to the People of the United States of America" ran one hour and sixteen minutes. In addition to airing excerpts on most of its newscasts, CNN broadcast the speech in its entirety, though not during prime time in the United States. The address was vintage Saddam. He chastised President Bush for plotting against Iraq during his alleged role in the Iran-Contra affair. He rejected what he called "the Zionist encroachment upon the land of Palestine." He decried the hypocrisy of imposing sanctions against Iraq when no similar blockade had been imposed on either Israel or Syria, which continued to occupy Lebanon in spite of Security Council resolutions to the contrary. He blasted the West for trying to impose its will on the Arab Nation. He reasserted Iraq's historical claim to Kuwait and accused that country's sheiks of conspiring "to debilitate Iraq economically and politically." He explained that keeping foreigners, including U.S. citizens, against their will as "guests" in Iraq was intended to give the U.S. administration "a better chance for thinking," in order to prevent the outbreak of a devastating war. And he warned that if war erupted, it would be bloody and long.

The crisis, Saddam said, was a question of politics and not of principles, "contrary to what Bush has tried to tell us." With that in mind, Saddam said, "Let us then resort to dialogue, rather than to arms, as the road to common understanding and to acceptable solutions." He stressed that if the international community wanted to participate in resolving the crisis and the problems of the region as a whole, then all issues, "in Palestine, Lebanon, and the Gulf should be discussed together and on the same level in the Security Council with a view to arriving at the same principles and criteria to be applied to all issues, while taking into consideration the special nature and background of each one of them."

But Saddam did not repeat what he and his ministers had always said before; he did not say Iraq would never withdraw from Kuwait. If there were a moment in which the balance could have been tipped in favor of peace, this, I thought, was it. But once again, the West couldn't see the forest for the trees.

"It's bullshit. There's nothing new. It's what we've heard before," Joe Wilson said when I asked for his reaction. "That's my personal opinion, of course. Any official comments must come from Washington." But Joe might as well have been speaking for the U.S. State Department.

POUNDING, RAUCOUS, EAR-SPLITTING ROCK 'N' ROLL filled the fourteenth-floor hallway of the Al-Rasheed. As you approached the suite, the music, blasting from a pair of Fostex speakers cranked to the max, was almost deafening. The congenial hosts had provided well: large bottles of scotch, vodka, gin, cognac, Chianti, and the occasional liqueur were laid on the table; bottles of beer and mixers filled the bathtub. As usual, about two dozen guests were in attendance, though their numbers would swell and ebb throughout the evening. To the uninitiated, it might seem odd that almost all the guests were male, odder still that some were attired in women's clothing as they gyrated to the rhythm. But there was nothing strange about it, really. The Brits were just throwing another party.

In all my years on the road I have never seen anyone party harder than Jeremy Thompson and his crew from ITN. And it's a testament to his physical stamina, if not his outlook on life in general, that Jeremy was always up and about early the next morning, when lesser mortals, including myself, felt like Big Ben was ringing between their ears. At 3 A.M. the ITN office made Animal House look like a tea party. A few hours later, the place could have passed a Marine inspection.

"The lads and I washed up about four," Jeremy explained one morning over coffee. "We find it's best to do it immediately," he added laconically. "It's terribly demoralizing to awaken to such a mess."

After several tours in Baghdad, Thompson and his gang had merrymaking down to a science. They would first hold a party to celebrate their safe arrival. Naturally, the night before their departure called for a giant blowout too. Having filed a particularly rewarding story was an obvious cause for celebration—as was filing absolutely nothing on a slow day. Any birthday, any holiday, any national day . . . of any country . . . was reason enough to get ripped to the tits.

The festivities usually began around midnight when everyone was back from the feedpoint. There was no such thing as easing into it slowly. You didn't score points for nursing a drink. The objective was simple: get in, get drunk, get down. On at least one occasion, getting down literally meant jumping out. Only the cameraman from Britain's TV-AM can explain why he was sporting an underwater mask and snorkle as he propelled himself out the window fourteen stories above the ground. One moment he was there; one heart-stopping second later he was gone, only to magically reemerge after having grabbed hold of a ledge.

The parties provided a welcome release from the tension, of course. Until the end of November, when the Security Council passed Resolution 678 authorizing military action against Iraq only after January 15, we didn't know from one day to the next if war was imminent. That certainly contributed to the madness—but the fact was that most of the press corps were prime candidates for the Betty Ford Center anyway.

If the truth be told, one of the reasons some of us were in Baghdad and not in Saudi Arabia was the Potato Juice Factor. Vodka was a major concern. The CNN Farewell to Communism World Tour '89 was fueled by huge quantities of the clear liquid as we rolled our merry way through Hungary, Germany, Czechoslovakia, and Romania. In some places it was cheaper than potable water, and naturally better for the system.

"Your bar bills on the charter out of Romania almost bankrupted the network," Eason scolded me at the time.

"Jeez! That must have been a mistake," I said. "Catering was included, or should have been for a sixty-four-thousand-dollar airplane ride."

In Baghdad, a bottle of Stolichnaya cost about ninety dollars, and when we were going strong our little group was good for about four bottles a night. In Saudi Arabia, you might have to pass a fitness test to get into the combat pool, but there was no such requirement to join the cocktail pool in the Iraqi capital.

"The days of the potbellied, chain-smoking, booze-guzzling journalist are a thing of the past," reported one Associated Press writer in Dhahran, but Blystone and I were living proof the great tradition was not about to wither in Baghdad.

"Holy shit! Look at this," I yelled as the pictures rolled on the 8 P.M. Iraqi TV evening newscast. "It's Saddam in Kuwait. That's the first time we've seen him there! Thomas! Where the hell is Thomas?"

Thomas Dreger was a young German in his early twenties whom we employed to translate the news. Fluent in Arabic, he'd come to Baghdad to continue his studies, only to get caught in the crisis and become a hostage. Ingrid had discovered him during one of her jaunts around the capital and offered him the job. It was a fabulous opportunity for the kid; a hundred bucks a night, a hot meal, and a front-row seat at a major news story of historic proportions. I often kidded him that he was nuts to constantly petition Bonn to seek his release. Anyone with the slightest inkling for journalism would kill for this assignment. In fact, after his eventual repatriation to the fatherland, compliments of Willy Brandt, Thomas actually telephoned us in Baghdad asking to return. Unfortunately, Naji thought the idea of CNN applying for a reentry visa on behalf of a former hostage was "ill-advised."

Thomas usually monitored the news on the television set in 902, away from the constant din that pervaded our main editorial space two doors away. I would watch the news in 906, of course, close to the telephones and the "converter," which decoded Iraq's television signal and converted it to the compatible American standard. By hooking up a Sony BVU 35 to the converter, we were able to record Iraqi TV and edit the pictures directly into our evening package.

"Yes, yes, it's Kuwait," Thomas exclaimed, running into the room. "The announcer says he made the trip today." After touring the city by motorcade, Saddam alighted onto the beach, where he looked through a gunsite while inspecting his troops. One soldier reached out to kiss his hand.

"What's he saying now?" I asked Thomas excitedly.

"He's telling them Kuwait is part of Iraq and will always remain so."

"Are they the Republican Guards?" From the disheveled looks of the soldiers, I doubted they could even pass basic training.

"They don't say," Thomas said as he furiously took notes.

"This is great stuff," Ingrid whooped.

"It's fabulous!" I agreed. The picture abruptly cut to the inside of what looked like a conference room. Saddam was seated at the head of the table receiving a military briefing.

"His commanders," Thomas explained. "They say they are ready."

The pictures of Saddam Hussein in Kuwait were chilling. They sent a powerful message not only to the people of Iraq, but also around the globe. Was it simply a propaganda ploy, or was the man the West like to call "the Butcher of Baghdad" actually digging in his heels for a fight to the finish on the sands of his "Nineteenth Province?" Whatever message Saddam wanted to convey, it was gripping television.

Blystone quickly crafted a new lead to his story, which Tracy edited at breakneck speed. Then she and Ingrid rushed off to the feedpoint. The News-God had smiled upon us once again. It was a happy little group that gathered afterward in our office to toast to his good health.

"I suppose you led with the Kuwait stuff," Bernstein asked rhetorically, paying us another visit.

"What else?" I shrugged, pouring myself a shot. "Those were great pictures."

"The feedpoint was a zoo," Tracy repeated for the umpteenth time. "Everyone was trying to get that stuff on the bird."

"You got any more of that Toblerone chocolate left?" Carl asked. "Mind if I take one last piece?"

"Help yourself," I told him. "So, when are you shoving off?"

"Probably tomorrow, or the day after at the latest."

"Well, before you go, I wanted to ask you something."

"Anything. Shoot."

"You'd agree we've been pretty hospitable?" I asked dryly.

"Absolutely," Carl nodded.

"In the morning you stop by for coffee and we always have a fresh pot."

"Yeah."

"And we've always been generous sharing our contacts and observations, right?"

"All the time!"

"When you needed money, we were right there with thirty-five hundred big ones."

"You guys have been just great, Robert."

"Late at night, like now for instance, when you crave some chocolate, our larder is here for the pickin's."

"Yeah, as I said, you've been terrific."

"So, Carl, one simple question: *who the fuck was Deep Throat?*" Bernstein turned beet-red as the room exploded with laughter. For a moment, he was literally speechless. I could tell he was actually more than a mite uncomfortable as he tried to formulate a diplomatic response.

"That's okay, Carl," I reassured him. "It was just a thought."

"Appreciate it," he chuckled as he bid good night and turned to leave the room.

"Oh, Weenie, I can't believe you asked him that!" Tracy howled.

"Asking isn't the problem," I laughed. "I can't believe I let him off the hook. I'm getting too fuckin' soft for this business."

Sandwiched between demonstrations by the Popular Army and visits to farms, hospitals, and schools, the story seemed to shift to the diplomatic front as officials from France, Britain, and Japan crisscrossed the Middle East. Mostly, they reaffirmed their already stated positions; while Iraq's Deputy Prime Minister, Taha Yasin Ramadan, during talks with Jordan's King Hussein and Japanese Prime Minister Toshiki Kaifu, reaffirmed that Iraq was ready to fight rather than surrender.

Then, on October 6, after completing talks with Saddam Hussein, Soviet envoy Yevgeni Primakov said he was optimistic about a peaceful way out of the crisis. His visit to Baghdad, coming as it did on the heels of Yasir Arafat's most recent trip, fueled speculation that a breakthrough might be in the works. But the next day, Iraq again demanded that all foreign diplomatic missions in Kuwait cease operations. Publicly, at least, Baghdad was holding the hard line.

At various times, I'd tried to contact Sa'doun Zoubaydi, the President's translator. I'd left several messages before he eventually returned my call. He sounded unusually cheerful.

"How are you, Mr. Robert?"

"Just fine," I told him. "I was hoping we could get together."

"I am very busy these days," he insisted, "but perhaps in the next week or so." I asked if he'd heard any news about our request to interview Saddam.

"Frankly, I think you will have good news soon, but you must be patient."

"It sounds like you've wiretapped Naji's office," I laughed. "Those were his words exactly."

"It is good to have a consensus among government officials, is it not?" he quipped.

"That depends upon the subject of the consensus."

"Yes, yes, I quite agree," he tittered. "Mr. Robert," he added, turning serious, "I think you should contact Mr. Nizar Hamdoon. He has some news for you." We exchanged pleasantries for a few more minutes and promised to keep in touch.

"I PRESUME YOU'RE STILL INTERESTED in an interview with Foreign Minister Aziz," Nizar said, lighting another Marlboro.

"Absolutely. And we'd love to do it live, from Atlanta."

"Who would conduct the interview?" he asked. "We would prefer Bernie Shaw."

"I don't know Bernie's schedule but I'll pass that on to Atlanta."

"Tomorrow afternoon, then," Nizar said. "At three o'clock."

"We'd prefer to do it at five. That's our 'World Day' broadcast, which is carried on the international feed. It's a much better venue." Nizar got up from the couch, walked to his desk, and made a brief telephone call.

"Five o'clock is confirmed," he said matter-of-factly.

"We'll need the minister in the studio fifteen minutes beforehand. I'll need to check his microphone, etc."

"No problem, Bob."

"Will you be there too?"

"I don't think so. I'll be here," he smiled, gesturing to his television set, which was tuned to CNN, "watching."

"You know, you look tired, Nizar."

"These are long days," he sighed. "Very long days. I often sleep here at the office."

"So, what's your feeling? Will there be war?"

He puffed on his cigarette and shrugged. "That is up to Mr. Bush."

"Primakov sounded optimistic," I ventured.

"Well, there is much that remains to be settled," he replied flatly.

I DROVE STRAIGHT TO THE EMBASSY to telephone Atlanta. Ordinarily, getting through to the States from the Al-Rasheed wasn't a problem. But after ten minutes the line would be abruptly cut. "Your ten minutes finished," the operators would merrily chirp. Eason was ecstatic when I gave him the news. "That's terrific!" he exclaimed. "Good work." I confessed we'd basically been handed the interview on a silver platter, but he was jazzed nonetheless.

"So Bernie will do the interview?" I asked. He put me on hold while he checked with Ed Turner.

"Begleiter's anchoring 'World Day' tomorrow. Ed says Ralph will do it."

"But . . ."

"Ed doesn't want Hamdoon dictating who our anchors will be. Hey!" he exclaimed. "I just got a telex from Iraqi TV confirming the interview."

"Jesus, that was fast. I hope things go as smoothly tomorrow."

"I hear ya. Good luck!"

It doesn't take a genius to produce a live television interview. Once the satellite is booked, you basically need two telephones: one for IFB, the second for coordination. IFB stands for Interrupted Feed Back. It's that little gizmo the guest puts in his ear that allows him to hear the other end of the line—what's on the air and the person asking the questions. If it's working properly, that's all the guest hears. If it's not, the guest also hears himself, a second or so after he actually speaks . . . which is distracting and confusing at the same time. Even that, of course, is preferable to hearing absolutely nothing at all.

The second telephone is used to coordinate the live shot. That simply means the on-site producer, in Baghdad, for example, talks to the producer in Atlanta to make sure he's satisfied with the picture, the microphone level, and anything else that affects the quality of the shot. If a correspondent is doing a live shot and his IFB goes down (it sometimes happens), the producer on the "co-ord line" can either cue the correspondent or signal him to "keep talking," "stretch," or "wrap it up." This presupposes, of course, there's no Q&A with Atlanta, because the correspondent can't respond to questions he cannot hear. (Well, actually he can, through meticulous preplanning and an elaborate series of gestures and hand signals, but it's best avoided; it's the equivalent of crossing the Grand Canyon on a tightrope while blindfolded, during a hurricane . . . without a net.) The bottom line is, a reporter can sometimes do a live shot without an IFB, but if it goes down during an interview with a guest, you're fucked!

With that in mind, I wanted to make absolutely certain Tariq Aziz would be hearing Ralph Begleiter at five o'clock and not Robert Wiener going berserk as I pulled out what was left of my hair. I double-timed it over to Iraqi TV.

"Welcome, Mr. Robert," Mrs. Awattif beamed. "Yes, I know you have interview with His Excellency Foreign Minister Tariq Aziz," she exclaimed before I could even open my mouth. I accompanied her to the studio where the interview would be conducted. It was a cavernous room on the ground floor, about half the size of a football field. "This is our biggest studio," she explained proudly.

"We're going to need to construct a set that's a bit more intimate," I informed her gently. "I'll want to use 'chroma-key,' you know, a picture that's projected behind the minister."

"Yes, yes, you will have it," she assured me. "We will take care of everything, the camera, lights, everything. Do not worry."

"That's wonderful," I said. "Now, if we could talk about communications for a moment. . . . I'll need four telephones, direct-dial international lines with extra-long cords, right here in the studio. I presume the phone company, the PTT, won't have a problem accommodating that request for an interview with His Excellency, the Foreign Minister."

"Four telephones?" she asked, a bit bewildered.

"That's right, four of them. I'll need backups. You'll have to trust me on this."

"You shall have four telephones," she declared.

"That's great. Now, one final request. I'd like the phones and the crew here at 11 A.M."

"But the interview isn't until five o'clock."

"I realize that. But I want to be certain everything is perfect for Mr. Aziz."

"The technicians will be here at eleven," she promised. "My assistant, Achlam, will be here too, and I will come at three-thirty. Do not worry, Mr. Robert. Everything will be taken care of." If I had a dollar for every time I've been told that during my twenty-one years as a newsman, I could retire in baronial splendor on the Côte d'Azur. That the live shot would happen, I had no doubt. It always did. It was simply a matter of how much blood would be on the floor by the time the clock struck five.

I COULDN'T BELIEVE MY EYES. In fact, I was dumbstruck. At eleven on the button, right there in the studio on top of a small black table, were four cream-colored telephones. This is fabulous, I thought. They actually did it!

"You see," Achlam gestured with pride. "Mrs. Awattif promise you everything will be ready."

"That she did," I replied as I happily witnessed a team of Iraqi stagehands preparing the studio.

"This for 'chroma-key,' " she said, pointing to a large green backdrop being positioned behind a chair. "We have different pictures of Baghdad. You may choose what you like."

"That's great," I replied as we strolled over to the set. It was a simple affair, just what we needed: an oriental rug, a chair for the minister, and the "chroma-key" backdrop. We'd have plenty of time to play with the lighting and camera angles. Tyrone and Phil would be coming over within the hour to supervise the technical stuff. After that, they'd record the interview on videotape even though Iraqi TV was shooting it live. This was going to be a piece of cake, I thought.

I picked up a telephone, and waited for a dial tone. Nothing. Not a good sign. I checked the second phone. It was also dead. So were the third and the fourth. Suddenly, looking down, I understood why. As promised, four telephones had indeed been provided, but something was missing. *They were not connected to anything!*

I knew it. I knew it, I said to myself. I knew it was too good to be true! "There seems to be a small problem," I explained to Achlam as calmly as possible. "The telephones aren't connected."

"Yes, yes, I know," she replied. "The man from PTT will come later to make telephones work."

"What time is later?" I asked, trying to maintain an even keel.

"He come by four-thirty."

"*Four-thirty!*" I exploded. "The interview is set for five. I need those phones now."

"Please, Mr. Robert, do not be angry," she implored. "I will go to telephone PTT. You wait, please." Jesus fuckin' Christ, I thought. Give me a goddamn break. The minutes seemed to drag on forever while I waited for Achlam to return. I lit a Gauloise and tried to think of a contingency plan. If necessary, perhaps we could move the interview to another location. I remembered there were two phones in Mrs. Awattif's office upstairs. No, that wouldn't work. It'd be a technical nightmare for the cameraman, not to mention a security concern at that time of the day. Aziz's bodyguard would never go for it. Furthermore, we'd look ridiculous. I could see myself welcoming the Foreign Minister to the television studio, only to inform him we'd be conducting the interview in a cubicle on the second floor. It was out of the question. It began to dawn on me why no one had ever gone live from Baghdad before. I popped another Gauloise into my cigarette holder, but found it was awkward to smoke and hyperventilate at the same time.

"PTT say it send someone soon," Achlam insisted as she returned. "Everything will be fine. Do not worry. Oh," she suddenly remembered, "your CNN people are in front. Perhaps you should go to them."

"I've got a sinking feeling about the phones," I cautioned Tyrone and Phil, as I pantomimed slitting my wrists. "Other than that, everything seems to be okay."

"This isn't bad," Tyrone agreed, inspecting the set.

"We should readjust that little jobbie over there," Phil explained, peering up at one of the spotlights. "That's going to burn him out if it's set like that." For the next hour or so, the three of us fine-tuned the lighting and aligned the cameras. There was still no sign of anyone from the PTT.

"Come, Mr. Robert," Achlam beckoned me, "choose pictures for the background."

"What about the PTT?" I asked, glancing at my watch.

"Soon, soon he come."

"What time . . ."

"Please, Mr. Robert, he must to come . . . after he eat lunch."

"After lunch?" I asked, as the muscles in my stomach tightened. "What time will he finish lunch?"

"After two o'clock," she said softly.

"*After two!* You said the PTT told you he was coming right over!"

"Please, not be angry. Everything will be fine. Do not worry." I gazed at Tyrone, who sat shaking his head.

"I'm not angry," I tried to assure her. "But with all due respect, unless we have telephones, and by that I mean telephones on which you can actually talk to people, we can't do the interview with Mr. Aziz. It's really that simple."

"You will have telephones," she insisted again. "Do not worry. Please, come choose pictures."

It wasn't a difficult choice. There were only four slides. The first was a picture of a heavily congested highway underpass. Interesting, I thought, but not quite what I had in mind; I dismissed it out of hand. The second was an elaborate fountain, shooting geyserlike bursts of water high in the air. "Which fountain is that?" I asked Achlam.

"Is here in Baghdad," she said, after puzzling a moment. "I do not remember the name."

"Let's project it and see how it looks." As Phil sat in what would be Aziz's chair, the fountain electronically appeared behind him. In fact, it did even more than that. It seemed to grow directly out of his head, while water appeared to spout from both of his ears. "Oh, no," Achlam laughed. "It looks so funny!" I told her if she thought it looked funny behind Phil, imagine the hilarity it'd provoke behind Iraq's Foreign Minister. We quickly moved on to slide number three. "Baghdad at night," she said sweetly, as we surveyed a downtown roundabout bathed in the headlights of oncoming traffic.

"We're gonna have to stick to a day shot," I told her. "It's daytime here and it will be morning in the U.S. when we do the interview."

"Yes, yes," she admitted. "I think this picture is what you want." The last slide, it was true, was taken in daylight. It was a drab shot of a three-story nondescript building. "What building is that?" I asked. "It's not the Foreign Ministry."

"Pictures of ministries not allowed," she explained. "This, any building."

"I'm afraid 'any building' is not going to do, because if we project it behind Mr. Aziz, viewers will think it's the Foreign Ministry, and we know it's not the Foreign Ministry. We'd be misleading our viewers, you see." I decided to shitcan the slide and go with a plain blue background. Achlam happily agreed.

"This is just great," I said aloud as the clock in the studio read two-fifteen. The telephones were still unconnected, of course, and Achlam had mysteriously disappeared. "I've got to track down Mrs. Awattif," I told the guys with more than a trace of frustration. On the way to her office, I ran into Achlam.

"He come, yes?" she asked.

"No," I told her, trying to contain myself. "No one has come yet."

"Uh-oh," she said, sounding alarmed. "This no good."

"That's what I've been saying since eleven o'clock. I need to call Mrs. Awattif."

"I will telephone her to come to studio now," she said.

"Would you please? And try the PTT again." When will it end? I wondered. When will it ever fuckin' end?

LIKE MOST OF MY GENERATION, I dabbled with drugs in my youth. Now, of course, as a responsible journalist, my only vice was alcohol. But as I waited in that studio, as the clock struck three, if someone had magically appeared carrying a baggie full of Valium, I would have gladly gobbled them all—without water. Suddenly, a little man appeared lugging a spool of telephone wire. Quickly and professionally he connected all of the phones, leaving, as I'd requested, extra-long cords. I watched him methodically check each instrument, speaking quick-paced Arabic presumably to a supervisor at the PTT. He then carefully labeled each telephone with the appropriate number.

"You see, Mr. Robert," Achlam gently admonished me, as if speaking to a child, "no reason to be angry. I tell you, 'Don't worry.' "

"Well, I get paid a lot of money to worry," I joked, "but I sincerely thank you for your help." Tyrone pulled out his IFB kit and began attaching it to one of the phones while I picked up a second line to call Atlanta. A strange humming noise came over the line as soon as I dialed the international code. I hung up and tried again. That's odd, I thought. Then I noticed Tyrone was having the same problem. "Is there a special number I need to call the United States?" I asked Achlam, who by now was standing by my side. Her face seemed contorted in a curious expression.

"You, you cannot telephone United States," she stammered. "These telephones good only for Baghdad."

"*What?*" I howled. "I don't need to call Baghdad. CNN is in the United States." I could feel the veins in my temples swell as my chest started to thump. This is the last fuckin' straw, I thought. Whatever my company was paying me, it wasn't nearly enough.

"I go find Mrs. Awattif," Achlam cried as she sped for the door. A few minutes later Ingrid, Bly, and Clancy arrived.

"Not bad," Bly smiled as he approved of the setup. He and Jim hoped to chat with Aziz after the Begleiter interview.

"It's a nightmare," I told them. "*An absolute nightmare!*"

"Oh, Jesus," Ingrid exclaimed after hearing the tale. "What are we gonna do?"

"First of all, head for the embassy and try to commandeer both of the phones at USIS. Call Atlanta on one of them, and call me here on the other. At least we'll have some communication. Where we go from there, I don't know, but it's a start."

"Right," she exclaimed, quickly copying down the phone numbers before she ran to the car.

"I don't suppose there's any way to patch IFB from this phone to Ingrid, then on to Atlanta?" I asked Tyrone, knowing it was impossible before I'd even finished the question. "There's no way she could hold the earpiece of one phone to the mouthpiece of the other, and Aziz could hear Begliter?" Tyrone shook his head, but I could tell he was trying to think of something.

"Well, if we don't have IFB, you guys will do the interview," I said to Bly and Clancy. "I'll coordinate with Atlanta through the Damsel, and cue you by hand. It's bad luck for Ralph, but what can I tell ya?" Just then I spotted Mrs. Awattif.

"Hello, Mr. Robert, I hear you have problems."

"It's been a trying afternoon," I confessed. "I hope you can help us."

"Give me your number in United States," she said, picking up one of the phones. I quickly ripped a page from my notebook and jotted it down. Awattif dictated it to someone on the other end of the line, then put down the receiver. "They will call us back," she informed me. While we waited for the connection, Awattif inspected the studio. "You don't want a 'chroma-key' picture behind His Excellency Mr. Tariq Aziz?" she asked.

"Thank you, no. We've decided to use a simple blue background."

"Did Achlam show you the slides?"

"Yes, of course, but we've decided to go with this." Just then, the telephone rang. Awattif answered it.

"United States on the line," she said, handing me the receiver. Amazing, I thought. So you could make international calls; you just had to go through the operator. I asked the desk to transfer the call to a line dedicated solely to IFB and Tyrone connected the earpiece. A moment later he gave me a "thumbs up."

"Everything good now?" Awattif inquired. I nodded my head gratefully, and asked her to place another call on the second phone. Five minutes later, we had the connection.

"I WANT TO KEEP THIS LINE OPEN," I informed Will King on the International Desk in Atlanta.

"Is it necessary?" he asked. "We still have forty minutes before the bird goes up and I've got Ingrid on the other line."

"Yeah, it is," I told him curtly. Suddenly, the third phone began to ring. "Hold on a second," I barked.

"Hi, it's Ingrid," she shouted. "I've got Will on the other line."

"I know, I know. Hang on a sec. Hello, Will. Will?" I blurted into phone number two.

"I'm . . . I'm here," he said. "I still have Ingrid—"

"I just lost IFB," Tyrone interrupted. "The line disconnected."

"Oh, shit!" I cried.

"What!" Will exclaimed.

"No, not you," I shouted. "Will, could you transfer this call to IFB? I'll call you back on another line."

"Don't you already have IFB?"

"We just lost it."

"What?" Ingrid squealed. "You lost Will? I'm still on with him. Do you want to relay a message?"

"Ingrid, hold on," I howled. "Will, just transfer the call to IFB. The other phone went dead."

"Are we going to be okay for the live shot?" he asked.

"I don't know. That's what I'm trying to arrange. Please transfer the call."

"Ingrid, stand by," I insisted.

"I've got IFB now," Tyrone called out.

"Great!"

"What's going on?" Ingrid wailed.

"Hang on!" I asked Mrs. Awattif to call Atlanta again on phone number one. "We lost IFB on the first line," I told Ingrid. "You just stay on with Will."

"He put me on hold. He said he's busy."

"That's great," I moaned. "Well, keep the line open anyway."

"You sound like you're having a great time," Ingrid smirked.

"Yeah, it's a barrel of laughs."

"United States for you," Mrs. Awattif piped up.

"Hi, Will! I'm back," I informed him.

"Hey," he said. "You're okay with IFB?"

"Yeah, we're fine for the moment. Let's just keep this line open."

"You know, I'm still on with Ingrid."

"I understand. I'm just concerned about losing a line. I want to have backups."

"That's okay," Will said, "but I'm really busy right now. I'm going to have to put the phone down for a few minutes."

"Hello, Ingrid," I called. "You're still on hold?"

"Yeah. He picked me up a second, then put me down."

"Okay," I told her, finally catching my breath. "Let's just wait for Aziz."

AT FOUR FORTY-FIVE, Iraq's Foreign Minister, accompanied by his personal bodyguard and the Director General of Iraqi Television, entered the studio. He shook hands first with Bly and Clancy, noting that he'd been watching their reports. As usual, Aziz was immaculately groomed, and sported a beautifully tailored dark silk suit. I escorted him to his seat as he checked the time and lit a cigar. As I clipped on his microphone, I noticed his tie was from Christian Dior.

"Sir, we still have a few minutes before the interview," I said. "Our World Affairs correspondent, Ralph Begleiter, will be the anchor in Atlanta." Aziz continued to puff away while Tyrone fitted him with an earpiece for IFB.

"You should be hearing CNN programming," Ty explained. "How's the level?" Aziz indicated everything was fine as I picked up the phone again and spoke to Will.

"He's miked and in the chair," I said.

"You'll be up on the bird in another thirty seconds or so."

"Ingrid, you're still there, sweetheart?" I asked, grabbing the other line.

"I'm here."

"We see you now," Will informed me.

"Great, let's go into 'A Control' and do a mike check." Will conferenced the call with Simon Vicary, the executive producer of "World Day." Originally from England, Simon began his career as an intern I'd hired when I was bureau chief in Los Angeles.

"How are you, luv?" Simon asked in a mock cockney accent.

"Fine, thanks. What do you think of the shot?"

"Could be a bit tighter," he said. I relayed the instructions to the camerman through Mrs. Awattif.

"That's much better. Stop right there," Simon shouted. I gave Awattif a "thumbs up."

"Speak to him in his IFB, Simon."

"Mr. Aziz, this is Atlanta. Do you hear me?" I heard him say.

"Yes, I hear you," Aziz replied. "I hear . . . no . . . now I hear nothing." The Foreign Minister fiddled with his volume control.

"Are we in a break?" I asked Will. During commercials, the IFB was silent.

"No. We're still in program."

"Shit!" I muttered. "We lost IFB again. Ingrid!" I hissed into the other phone. "We just lost IFB. Stay on the line with me. Will," I said into his connection, "let's transfer this line to IFB." While Tyrone adjusted the

IFB kit from one phone to the other, I asked Mrs. Awattif to telephone Atlanta one more time.

"I can hear fine now," Aziz perked up.

"Ingrid, tell Will we've reestablished IFB." I overheard her pass on the information.

"Yes, yes, I can hear you, Atlanta," Aziz said into space. "One, two, three, four . . ."

"Everything's fine in Atlanta," Ingrid said.

"Thank Christ! How far away are we?"

"Hang on," she said. "About two minutes."

"United States for you," Mrs. Awattif said, handing me the other phone. For a split second there was a weird clicking noise on the line. I thought I heard it on Ingrid's phone too. That's funny, I thought.

"It's Robert for Will," I barked into the phone.

"Oh, hi, Robert. I think Will's busy doing a live shot," came the response from Atlanta.

"Yeah, I know. *My* live shot . . . he should be on with *me*!"

"Oh, okay. Hold on a second."

"You're about a minute away from the opening," Will said finally.

"Are we straight at the top?"

"About a minute in," Simon shouted.

"We're about two minutes away, sir," I said to Aziz, who acknowledged me with a nod.

"Now I can't hear anything," he said suddenly.

"Welcome to our viewers in the United States and around the world," I heard Ralph Begleiter begin.

"Fuck!" I swore. "Will . . . Simon, we've lost IFB again. Quick, transfer this line. Ingrid," I shouted, "we'll coordinate through you. We've lost it again."

"Jesus tits," she shrieked. Once more, Tyrone worked a miracle and set the world's record for making the patch.

"I can hear now," Aziz said calmly.

"Thirty seconds," Ingrid bellowed.

"What a fuckin' nightmare," I whispered to her.

"You're telling me!" she exclaimed.

"I can hear you in here too," Aziz said, turning to me as he pointed to his earpiece. "You're talking with someone." Oh, shit, I thought. That weird click. Somehow the lines got crossed.

"Fifteen seconds," Ingrid said. "Simon wants to know if you can tighten the shot."

"No," I growled. "The minister can also hear us on this line."

"Quiet!" I barked at Ingrid and everyone in the studio. "Let's make television!" A moment later, I heard Tariq Aziz say, "Good afternoon, Ralph."

UNFORTUNATELY, AFTER ALL THAT, the interview provided little news. Begleiter asked all the usual questions about withdrawing from Kuwait, releasing the hostages, and the chances for war. As usual, Aziz replied by giving the world an Iraqi history lesson, explaining the "guests" were serving a useful purpose, and maintaining that the eventuality of war was up to President Bush. Ralph was obviously trying to get in as many questions as possible during the limited time, and kept interrupting Aziz when the minister droned on. Ralph was right to try to keep the interview moving along, but the overall effect seemed contentious. At times it was more like a debate than a dialogue. When it ended and Aziz had removed his earpiece, Ingrid gave me her assessment. "Bullshit!" she snapped.

"You see, Mr. Robert," Achlam good-naturedly prodded me, "no reason to be angry. I told you, 'Don't worry.' "

"What can I tell you?" I smiled. "When you're right, you're right."

Much to my delight, Aziz gladly agreed to a second interview with Bly and Clancy. "It's easier for me," he said, "when I can look people in the eye." He lit up another cigar as Tyrone and Phil moved the cameras. I opened a fresh pack of Gauloises, offering one to Aziz's bodyguard. But he, along with Saddam's look-alike TV announcer, who had joined us in the studio, was a died-in-the-wool Marlboro man.

The second interview with the Foreign Minister didn't provide any banner headlines either, but the give-and-take, especially between Aziz and Bly, was stimulating. Aziz was relaxed, and perhaps feeling comfortable with his interlocutors, sallied forth into waters I'd never seen him navigate before. The three of them discussed not only the facts on the ground, but the deeper issues that set them in motion. Aziz was philosophical.

"You've got to understand," he said, "that pride, in this part of the world, is an important factor. It's in some cases the decisive factor. In this particular historical event, pride and historical rights are the main issues. They are more important to the Iraqi individual than having a nice meal. They are more important than having a vacation, more important than having a nice suit, or a nice apartment. I tell you, this is how we feel."

What Aziz said struck me as very important. If they want peace, Bush and the UN are going about this the wrong way, I thought. Poking a finger in Saddam's face and chastising him like an errant schoolboy was not going to get them anywhere. On the contrary, if anything, Saddam would only become more entrenched. For Iraq's President there was more at stake than Kuwait. It was a matter of pride. In the West, the concept of "saving face" is often dismissed as a simple Arab cultural stereotype, but in the Arab world a man is measured by the respect he commands. Saddam Hussein could not allow himself to be dictated to by the West. It would be unthinkable for him to "surrender," lock, stock, and barrel, to President Bush. By the same token, if Bush backed down he'd be seen as appeasing the man he'd denounced as the next Hitler. And George Herbert Walker

Bush had had quite enough, thank you, of the "wimp factor." So, in the interest of saving face, both men were on a collision course. Bush and the Security Council may have been reluctant when they said they were ready to use force to get Saddam out of Kuwait, but ole Tariq Aziz knew what the West couldn't fathom: Saddam would risk losing everything as a matter of pride.

"So what do you make of this?" asked Jeremy Thompson. "It's going to change the complexion of the whole story, wouldn't you agree?" We were gathered in front of the television screen watching pictures of what the world press immediately dubbed a "massacre." In the worst single episode of violence in Arab East Jerusalem since the Six Day War, Israeli security forces had killed 21 Palestinian protestors at the Al-Aqsa Mosque. Iraqi TV was broadcasting footage of the bloodletting, over and over again, and would continue to do so for weeks. "This will give Saddam a huge propaganda victory," Jeremy said.

"I suppose in the short term, but in the long run it ain't gonna change a thing," I said. "Trust me. There'll be some demonstrations. Israel will deplore the loss of life and conduct an investigation. They'll say it shouldn't have happened . . . if it did happen, there was a reason it happened . . . if it didn't happen now, it might have happened later . . . and they're sorry it happened at all. They'll conclude their policemen were provoked, but admit some may have been, perhaps, overzealous. Some poor *shmegegge* might even lose his job. Meanwhile, Washington will be embarrassed. The Security Council will condemn Israel. As usual, the Israelis will feel the whole world's against them. And a couple of months from now, it will all be forgotten. Both sides will just go back to hating each other."

"You're one cynical bastard," Thompson laughed.

"True, but I'm also a realist. Don't forget, I've lived there."

"I'm not so sure about this one," he said. "It could have serious repercussions for the Arab members of the coalition."

"Well, you can't be sure about anything, but I'm quite sure I need a drink." I picked up the telephone and requested a bucket of ice.

"Okay, I've ordered the cake," Ingrid whispered. "I'm taking Driver Kareem for an hour to pick up provisions." The occasion was Blystone's birthday, his fifty-fourth. Bly hadn't mentioned it to anyone, but Parisa Khosravi on the Atlanta desk had reminded me. "You should throw him a party," she suggested. And so we did, gathering in the workspace around eleven to surprise him with an enthusiastic, albeit off-key, rendition of "Happy Birthday." Bly was delighted. Tracy anointed him "King of

Sheeba" as she bestowed upon him a black and white checkered *kaffiyeh*, and Kris Krizmanich, on behalf of JTFC (Just The Fuckin' Crew), offered up a strand of edible worry beads she'd fashioned from bubble gum.

"This is just smashing," Bly laughed. The chocolate cake, prepared by the pastry chefs of the Al-Rasheed, contained enough sugar to keep a playground full of six-year-olds strung out for months, but the icing, which read "Happy Birthday Baghdad Bubba," was delicious. Tyrone dutifully captured the celebration on videotape.

"What about the groupies?" Bly joked. "Where are the groupies? I was promised a forty-five-year-old groupie with big knockers."

"Uh-oh," warned Ingrid, "another case of DSB."

DSB was a hideous and demoralizing ailment that afflicted most of the male journalists in Baghdad. The initials stood for Deadly Sperm Backup. True, you could cure it by hand, but it was considered preferable to seek a more traditional and communal form of relief. Even so, within days, sometimes even within hours, the symptoms would reappear. It was virtually impossible to suffer from acute DSB in Eastern Europe, where certified "healers" were available in every bar, but it was epidemic in Iraq. Female companionship was in short supply. Ingrid fended off would-be suitors with her standard reply: "It ain't war yet!" she'd bark at anyone who suggested joining her for more than a drink. (Once the war started, she changed this retort to a simple "Not now, I'm busy!") But DSB was on everyone's mind. One evening, Bly, Clancy, and I even composed a ditty about the malady sung to the tune of "There Is Nothin' Like a Dame."

We got sunlight on the sand
We got moonlight on the sea
We got hostages and vodka
and the dreaded DSB
We got Tracy, Kris, and Ingrid
Who are bold and unafraid
What can't we get?
We can't get laid

We got demonstrators plenty
We got minders, we got gin
We got lots of time to think about
the ways we'd like to sin
We got hard-boiled eggs and coffee
Mujaheddin *on parade*
What can't we get?
We can't get laid

We got good old Captain Wacky

With his pockets full of tricks
We got Roth and we got Blystone
We are up to here with dicks
We got Clancy and Toshiba
Performing Perverse Acts
What can't we get?
I suppose a blow job would be out of the question

"You guys!" Parisa jeered when we sang it to her over the telephone. "That's awful. I suppose that was your idea, huh, Robert?"

"Look, sweetheart, part of my job is being the morale officer around here. I'm just trying to keep spirits high."

The birthday party was going full blast when the telephone rang. I could barely make out what the caller was saying. "Quiet! Shush! Quiet!" I beseeched my co-workers.

"CNN, yes?" a thickly accented Arab voice asked.

"Yes, this is CNN," I replied. "Who is calling, please?"

"You requested an interview with President Arafat? The President will be in the lobby of the Al-Rasheed Hotel in ten minutes." (The PLO always referred to Arafat as the President of Palestine.)

"Who is . . ."

"In ten minutes," the caller said again, then hung up.

"Oh, Christ. It looks like we've got Arafat. Downstairs." No one was in the best of shape to conduct an illuminating interview.

"I'm fine," Clancy insisted, heading for his room. "I'll just throw some water on my face and put on a tie."

"Well, congratulations, Ingrid," I said. She had been trying for days to line up an interview.

"Captain Fatty's coming here?" Bly asked. Bly always called Arafat "Captain Fatty."

"That's what the man said."

"Who was it?" Ingrid interrupted. "I bet it was, what's his name, ah, Samir . . ." Just then, the telephone rang.

"CNN," I answered.

"Robert, it's Larry [Doyle of CBS]. I just wanted to make sure you got a call from the PLO. They phoned here by mistake looking for CNN. I gave them your number."

"Yeah, thanks very much," I told him.

"What's up?"

"Ah, nothing special," I said. The last thing I wanted was a goddamn press conference.

"Feel like a drink?"

"Maybe a little later. I've got some shit to take care of. Are you guys gonna be up for a while?"

"We'll be here," he said. "C'mon by."

IT WAS ALMOST ONE-THIRTY IN THE MORNING. "This is so fuckin' typical," Ingrid said as we waited downstairs. "Arafat never sleeps," she laughed. Thirty minutes later, we were still waiting.

"Maybe you should call the PLO," I suggested as we continued our vigil seated behind the Ministry of Information desk, which by now was deserted. Another fifteen minutes passed before Clancy authoritatively pronounced, "This is bullshit!" and informed us he'd be reachable in his room, if necessary. Somewhere around two-thirty, it began to dawn on us that we'd been had, but if not by the PLO, then by whom?

"Fuck!" exclaimed Ingrid. "It was Doyle."

"Goddamn it, you're right!" I wailed. We headed back to our office, where I called CBS. "Hi, Larry. . . ."

"It wasn't me," he protested immediately. "I swear."

"Yeah, who was it then?" I laughed.

"I don't know who it was, but it wasn't me."

"Right. Well, touché," I congratulated him. "I owe ya one."

The daily briefings at the embassy continued to revolve around hostages and sanctions.

"So," Joe Wilson explained, "to the best of our knowledge these are the numbers: ninety-three Americans, two hundred Japanese, seventy-seven Germans, sixty French, and three hundred-plus Brits. They're still being held at strategic sites. In addition, there are about twenty Americans in "safe haven" [the ambassador's residence], three hundred U.S. passport holders, mainly spouses of Iraqis who chose not to leave, between six and seven hundred Americans in Kuwait, and between eight and ten American diplomats in Kuwait. Of course, the embassy there is still without electricity and water.

"We've heard that," he noted in response to a question about whether Iraq had requested Western companies to provide lists of employees over the age of fifty-five, "but we don't know exactly what that means. We certainly haven't been told they're going to be released."

"Do you see any evidence Iraq may be softening its position?" a newly arrived reporter asked him.

"Softening? I just gave you a list of innocent people this government is holding against their will," Joe said curtly. "And may I remind you, Iraq continues to occupy Kuwait. No, I don't think that constitutes a softening of position. Okay, gentlemen," he said, getting up, "if you'll excuse me."

"You seem a bit ragged around the edges this morning," I told him after the others had left. "Are you okay?"

"I'm fine, Robert. It's just that sometimes these questions . . ."

"Yeah, I know what ya mean. Well, relax. Remember what Hemingway said: 'Grace under pressure.' "

"I'll remember," he laughed. "By the way, I heard about your Aziz interview, but I haven't gotten a transcript from Washington yet. Do you mind if I stop by the hotel one of these days to see it?"

"Not at all. Any time."

"How'd it go?" he asked.

"My personal opinion? Frankly, I thought the live interview with Begleiter was contentious and didn't advance a thing. Nizar even telephoned me afterward to say he thought it was, quote, 'rude and rough.' "

"Really?"

"But I think you'll find the interview with Bly and Clancy interesting. Yeah, do come by. I'll stock our fridge with some cold ones."

"So," I asked Joe, handing him another beer, "what did you think?" He took a long puff on his cigar.

"Nothing different from what they've been saying all along," he concluded.

"Perhaps, but what about that matter of pride?" I pressed.

"Yes," he said thoughtfully. "I agree Saddam has his pride, but he's also a megalomaniac. And I think he may be reaching the messianic stage."

It was early evening and I was finally seated in Naji's office in the Ministry of Information, after spending nearly an hour cooling my heels in the waiting room. "I am sorry for the delay, Robert," he said, sweeping his hand over the huge pile of paperwork stacked on his desk. "Please excuse me." As usual, I had come to press for the Saddam interview, the flyaway, and a trip to Kuwait. God knows how many meetings we'd already had to discuss these issues. "You know," Naji said coyly, "we found some interesting documents at the Foreign Ministry in Kuwait. They prove the corruption of the Sheik and his princes." Here it comes, I thought: John Simpson of the BBC had mentioned that Naji had tried to interest him in lurid tales of the al-Sabah family's sexual peccadilloes.

"What did you discover?" I asked innocently. He chuckled slyly as he leafed through some papers.

"We came across a letter from the Bulgarian ambassador to an official at the Foreign Ministry," he said, continuing to sort through the correspondence. "Apparently, one of the princes had engaged the services of a, er, a prostitute, a Bulgarian woman. The letter said the woman felt five thousand dollars was not sufficient," Naji smiled. "Not sufficient compensation for the loss of her, er, left nipple."

"Jesus!"

"Oh yes," he smiled. "It was either cut . . . or bitten off."

Spare me, I thought. I don't want to hear this.

"There's even more," he smirked.

"I'll pass," I said. "We're a family network."

"I understand," he laughed. "Most Western correspondents are not interested in such things."

"You should try selling it to the British tabloids," I joked.

"I know," he chuckled. "Unfortunately, those newspapers don't have correspondents in Baghdad. So, Robert, what can I do for you?"

"Just making the usual rounds, Naji. Take a guess." He reached for his worry beads and gazed out the window. For almost a minute, neither of us said a word. Finally, Naji turned and looked directly at me.

"Would it be Mr. Bernard Shaw doing the interview with President Saddam Hussein?" he asked.

"Is that a question or a request?"

"It is merely a question."

"I think it would be excellent if Bernie did the interview. Of course, I'll have to check with Atlanta, but I'm sure they'll agree. Furthermore, I'd suggest that Richard Blystone, one of our correspondents here in Baghdad, join Bernie in this venture."

"This is a good idea," he agreed.

"So, I take it we finally have our interview?"

"Yes, yes, dear Robert," he said, raising his voice. "Your interview has been approved."

Hallelujah, I nearly shouted.

"And Nizar Hamdoon concurs?" I asked, remembering the previous miscommunication between the two of them.

"I spoke to him two hours ago. He knows everything."

We spent the next several minutes working out the details. The interview would take place between October 20 and 27. It would be taped, not live, and Iraqi technicians would man the cameras. I had a problem with that, but decided this was not the time to raise the issue. The interview would run for at least an hour unedited, and be satellited as soon as possible. Naji would extend my visa so I could remain in Baghdad to oversee the project.

"It's been a long haul," I said. "I can't thank you enough."

"Not at all. You have been patient."

"Now, about the flyaway . . . ?" I half-joked.

"Not now," he laughed. "I think you have received enough good news for one day."

"Not really," I smiled. "On this story, there's never enough good news."

EASON SAID HE'D SET THE WHEELS in motion by sending telexes to Naji, Nizar, and Mrs. Awattif confirming the interview, and then brought up the subject of Bernie Shaw. "First we'll have to ask him if he even wants to do it," he said. "Ya know, sometimes he doesn't travel that well, and he'd be out of pocket for several days."

"Believe me," I said. "He'll want to do it. The combination of Bernie and Bly will be terrific."

"I hear ya," he said. "We'll be in touch."

"THE WHOLE PROCESS WAS EXCRUCIATING," I said to Ingrid later as we shared a nightcap. "First I had to sit through that goddamn nipple story, then, well you know Naji, the staring out the window routine, and finally . . . finally, he lays it out there. So, how'd the feed go?"

"The usual zoo, but nothing was censored tonight."

"Good. Did anyone have anything we didn't?" I asked.

"No. In fact, NBC and CBS didn't even file. ABC did another, 'Are the sanctions working?' story. By the way," she said, "I want to buy some little perfumes to give to Mrs. Awattif, Achlam, and the others. It's a nice gesture."

"Fine. The next person in from Amman can pick them up at duty-free."

"Got ya. Hey, Wienerish!" she scolded me as I replenished my drink, "aren't you forgetting something?" She held up her empty glass.

"I'm sorry," I said, reaching for the Stoli. "Terminal bad manners."

"Well, get it in gear."

"I'd like to get a lot in gear," I joked mischievously.

"Uh-oh! DSB alert! Forget it, Wienerish," she roared. "It ain't war yet!"

I was on the phone with Earl Casey in Atlanta discussing upcoming stories. Earl had recently joined the International Desk after having been away from the network for many months. Originally CNN's managing editor in charge of the National Assignment Desk, which he manned for years from dawn till dusk, Earl had finally experienced terminal burn-out. Among other things, he was writing a book about country and western singer Jerry Jeff Walker. A superb newsman, Earl had curiosity, intelligence, insight, and drive. On top of that, he was swell to work for. Even during a crisis, Earl always maintained an even keel, asked pertinent questions, and offered valuable advice. His latest assignment, reporting to Eason Jordan, who had once worked for him, surprised some of us, but everyone was delighted Earl was back at CNN. (In fact, after only a few months on the job, Earl was plucked off the International Desk, promoted to vice president, and appointed head of the National Assignment Desk once again.)

"I don't suppose," he said, "they'd allow us to put a camera on Aziz for a day or so, and just follow him around. I was thinking when I watched Blystone and Clancy's interview, he's a hell of an interesting guy. He goes back a long way with Saddam, doesn't he? It's got to be worth a profile." I agreed, and was telling Earl that I'd discuss it with Hamdoon when Tracy interrupted us.

"Sadoun's on the other phone. He says it's important." I told Earl I'd call him back, and picked up the second line.

"You must come quickly, Robert," Sadoun panted. "Mr. Naji wants to see you in his office. Now." I told him I'd be right over and rushed out the door. "Quickly, quickly," he greeted me at the ministry. "Mr. Naji is waiting for you."

"What's this all about?" I asked as he accompanied me down the corridor.

"Mr. Naji will explain," he said, ushering me into the office. Naji stood up from behind his desk and walked across the room to greet me.

"Thank you for coming, Robert," he said politely. "So," he asked as we took our seats, "how are things progressing with Mr. Shaw?" I'd already let him know Bernie was a "go" and didn't understand why he was asking me again.

"Bernie's all set. He'll be here by the nineteenth," I reminded him.

"Very good," he said flatly, and began the staring-out-the-window routine. This time he kept it down to about twenty seconds.

"Tell me, Robert, do you and a CNN crew still want to visit Kuwait?" he asked conspiratorially.

"Kuwait?" I repeated. "Of course, we'd love to go to Kuwait."

"You must understand, if you go, it is only to visit hospitals, to see conditions there and nothing else." So that was it. The Iraqis were reacting to several published reports that said babies in Kuwait City had been taken from their incubators and allowed to die, while the incubators were transported to Baghdad. "Those reports are pure fabrication," Naji insisted. "Nothing but lies. You may see for yourself."

"We'd have to visit several hospitals and be allowed to speak with many people to attempt to gauge the truth," I said.

"This will be permitted. You may go everywhere. But, Robert," he said sternly, "you must give me your word you are only going to do a story about hospitals. You may not talk about the military situation or take any other pictures. That's the only reason the Security Services have agreed to my request to let your team go." I quickly thought it over. On the one hand, I was under no illusions—we were being offered another dog and pony show. Nevertheless, if we visited many hospitals and did several interviews, we just might be able to glean the truth. On the other hand, what people really wanted to know was what was going on in Kuwait City, news about Iraqi troops, Kuwaiti citizens, and foreign hostages. And this, if we agreed to Naji's condition, we couldn't report. Still, since Jesse Jackson's brief visit there, no journalist had been to Kuwait to cover any story. CNN would be the first network to file from the occupied country. On balance, I thought, it was no contest. We'd do the hospital story, and who knows, maybe we'd get something more. I thanked Naji for his offer and agreed to the ground rules.

AS USUAL, the scheduled departure time bore no relation to reality. At the last moment, Sadoun, who was joining us on the trip, had inexplicably changed the program. Instead of taking off at seven in the morning, as originally planned, we now wouldn't be leaving Baghdad until eleven-thirty. And naturally, Iraqi Airways Flight 15, bound for Kuwait, was running late.

"This isn't going to work," I said to Sadoun as we took our seats in the departure lounge of Saddam International Airport. "Even if we take off by noon, we're not gonna get there until one. The flight back is at three-thirty. It's not going to be possible to do what we'd planned."

"Don't worry," Sadoun assured me. "We will go to a hospital. You will have your story."

"This is fucked," I said to correspondent Doug James. "I'm tempted to forget the whole thing."

"I know what you mean," Doug said glumly. "Here, have a cookie." He reached in his hand luggage and pulled out a bag of Chips Ahoy!

"You're gonna OD on those things," I joked. Atlanta had shipped us two cases of chocolate chip cookies along with a gross of peanut butter. Doug, who was a finicky eater even when not in the Middle East, practically lived on the stuff.

"Are you okay, Stymie?" Cynde Strand asked. "You look so depressed." Cynde was a camera person assigned to our Beijing bureau. A blond, hip-looking rock 'n' roller in her early thirties, Cynde could hold her own with the best of 'em. Before being assigned to China, where she'd had her nose smashed covering Tiananmen Square, her beat had been Beirut.

"This trip's gonna be another nightmare," I said. "I really don't need the aggravation."

"I know," she said, "but do try to cheer up. We're all pulling for ya. C'mon over here, Cybil," she called to Tracy Flemming, in her best Pearl Plum Southern girl accent. "Let's sit by Stymie. He needs some brigh-tenin' up."

The Boeing 727 finally lifted off the runway at twelve-fifteen. A few minutes later, the flight attendant served tepid instant coffee in white china cups—after all, we were flying "first class." Every now and then, Sadoun would glance across the aisle and try to reassure me we'd have plenty of time. After his fifth "Don't worry," I knew I'd just gotten the kiss of death. I was surprised to see so many other passengers. Most were Iraqi soldiers returning from leave, but there were also several "businessmen" on board. One told Doug he'd already "imported" more than ten thousand pounds of frozen lamb chops from Kuwait and was headed back for more.

As we flew over the desert on the outskirts of Kuwait City, I spotted dozens of tanks dug in behind "berms" in the sand. There were also tank formations lined up along both sides of the runway. Sadoun had said we wouldn't be landing at Kuwait International Airport, but he wasn't sure where we'd touch down. It turned out to be at a Kuwaiti Air Force base about forty miles from the city. The Iraqis had concealed the name of the base by hanging a huge tarpaulin over the sign on the control tower. We were told the airport had opened to commercial traffic only the day before.

"QUICKLY, QUICKLY, WE MUST GO QUICKLY," Sadoun said as he shooed us toward the two Chevy Blazers that pulled up beside the plane. "Hurry, please fetch the equipment." Thanks to the efficient ground staff, it took a mere twenty minutes to collect the only two pieces of gear we'd checked: the light kit and tripod. Mercifully, there was no such thing as customs or immigration.

Kuwait looked like a mega-junkyard. The entire place was littered with abandoned automobiles and trucks, all stripped of their tires. There was some obvious war damage; a burned-out truck or tank, a pockmarked building here and there, but not as much as I'd expected. Still, it seemed pretty clear the gang-rape of Kuwait was already well underway. As we drove along the modern highway, at speeds of up to ninety miles per hour, I couldn't spot a single store, large or small, from pizza parlors to video outlets, that hadn't been looted.

Soldiers were everywhere. Sadoun said most of the Iraqi troops in Kuwait were on high alert, but if this were true I reckoned Schwarzkopf and company wouldn't need a coalition to defeat them. The Iraqi soldiers I saw in Kuwait were the most ragtag, undisciplined, misbegotten, slovenly looking bunch of military conscripts I had ever laid eyes on. Compared to any one of these guys, a deserter from SWAPO could qualify for a presidential guard of honor. What's more, few of the soldiers even carried weapons. At a major intersection near the entrance to the city, I watched as dozens of them swarmed like locusts on the back of a truck hauling melons and ice. It was parked under a larger-than-life portrait of Saddam Hussein constructed with tiny colored ceramic tiles.

There was little traffic on the street. Just as well, I thought, since none of the traffic lights worked. But there were no Kuwaitis either. And that made me feel sad. I stared out the window at a deserted amusement park in the "Jara" district and tried to imagine it filled with laughing Kuwaiti children.

"We're almost there," Sadoun said as we drove past a medical complex. It was a little after two o'clock. I opened my notebook and began to scribble.

"What about something like this?" I asked Doug, reading in a whisper from what I'd just written. " 'On a brief trip such as this one, it is difficult, if not impossible, to know what is accurate. But the Iraqi authorities would only permit us to visit this one hospital. Doug James, CNN. . . .' Obviously we can play with the words," I said, "but we'd better say something strong at the end that shows this ain't what you'd call a comprehensive tour. Keep it in mind," I added. "The way things are going, we might not have enough time even to shoot a stand-up."

"I agree with you," Doug said. "It's a good thought."

"We are here now, Robert," Sadoun said over his shoulder. The Chevrolets pulled to a stop in front of a small maternity hospital near the sea. It was typical of many I'd seen in the Third World: small, run-down, in need of a coat of paint. "Hurry, the doctors are waiting," Sadoun exclaimed.

"MOST OF THE NURSES have gone home to India," the Kuwaiti physician explained. "Before August 2, we had twenty-four nurses. Now we have nine." We were strolling through one of the wards while he spoke. "Even during the difficult times, we still do our best to care for our patients. Here," he said, pulling open a curtain to reveal a mother nursing her baby, "you may take pictures if you like."

"Would you please ask if it's all right with her? She might prefer not to be photographed," I said. He and the woman exchanged a few words in Arabic. "It is fine," he assured us. Cynde set up the camera and rolled some tape.

"What shortages are you suffering?" Doug asked.

"Skilled nurses, of course, are our biggest problem, but we actually have enough equipment and enough medicine to provide proper care. Due to the lack of personnel, we find we have to modify the treatment somewhat. That means, instead of staying at the hospital for a few days after the baby is born, we now discharge the mother the next day. If everything is normal, of course," he added.

"Are you finished here now?" Sadoun interrupted as he looked at his watch. "Please, let's go to another place to see the emergency equipment."

"We need a few more shots here first," I said as I watched Cynde and Tracy moving through the ward.

"Would you like to see a baby being born?" the doctor asked.

"Yes. That'd be fabulous," I replied. We walked down the corridor, turned the corner, and pushed our way through two large swinging doors.

"This is Surgery," the doctor said, pointing to a pile of disposable sterile gowns, masks, and shoe covers. "You may help youself." A moment later, we entered the operating room. "She is being prepared for a Caesarean procedure," he explained as we gazed at the patient, a young woman who looked to be in her early twenties.

"Will you be giving her an epidural?" I asked smugly, with the confidence of a father who'd watched both his sons born by C-section.

"Exactly," he replied.

"Oh, Weenie, I can't do this," Tracy suddenly blurted out.

"C'mon, you'll love it," I laughed. "No pain, no gain . . ."

"If you're pressed for time, you may already see a newborn across the hall," the doctor interrupted. I glanced at my watch.

"Saved by the bell," I said to Tracy, as we all stepped next door. For the next few minutes, Cynde took pictures as a tiny brown bundle of wonder was slapped on the fanny, carefully weighed, and wrapped in a white cotton cloth.

"God, I love babies," I said aloud, thinking of Jesse the day he was born.

"If you have finished your pictures, we may now visit the pharmacy," the doctor said.

"Why did you spend so long in there?" Sadoun asked with obvious frustration as we came out of Surgery. "Please, Robert . . . we don't have much time."

"Hey, I told you in Baghdad that we wouldn't have enough time."

"Yes, yes, but we do the best we can. You must see the incubators and then we must go."

"We also need to see the pharmacy and do a quick interview with the doctor," I said.

"Please, Robert," he implored me. "Please do it quickly. We cannot miss the plane."

The pharmacy seemed extremely well stocked. I was surprised. "We already had a huge supply of medicine before August 2," the doctor volunteered. "But obtaining new supplies is a problem. Now the sanctions directly affect us too." We walked over to the "intensive care" unit, a simple, nondescript room that contained about a dozen simple incubators. Only two of them were in use.

"Let's do the interview here," Doug suggested, as we were joined by the hospital director and other "officials." Doug and the Kuwaiti doctor reviewed, for the record, some of the points they'd talked about earlier, then Doug asked about allegations that the incubators had been "misappropriated."

"I have heard about these stories," the doctor admitted, "but I can honestly tell you nothing of the sort has happened here."

"Do you know if it's happened at other hospitals?" Doug asked.

"I have no way of knowing for sure," he said, "because I work here, but we've been very well treated at this hospital." Down the hall, I noticed an Indian nurse filling in charts. I walked over to speak with her. After introducing myself, I asked her about the incubators.

"No one has taken anything from us," she said in a whisper. "But we are always afraid."

"Please, we must go now," I heard Sadoun tell Doug and the crew. "If not, we shall miss the plane."

"We've got to shoot a stand-up," I explained as we walked outside and bid farewell. "It'll just take a minute."

"We have no time," Sadoun insisted.

"We have to do this," I said, as Doug and I walked down the driveway, out of earshot.

"What do you think?" I asked.

"Let's go with your suggestion," he said, as we made some slight changes that strengthened the text. Three takes later, the stand-up was in the can.

By now, it was almost ten minutes to three. "Faster, go faster," Sadoun urged the driver. The Chevy careened down the highway.

"Hey, I didn't come this far to die in an automobile accident," I said as we missed, by inches, colliding with another car. "If we miss the plane, we'll take another in the morning."

"We must make this plane," Sadoun said. "We cannot stay over." He turned on the radio and flipped through the dials.

"Hold it," I said, hearing the familiar tones of the BBC. "Let's listen." A second later, I couldn't believe my ears. The lead story quoted the Iraqi News Agency as saying a CNN team had been to Kuwait and discovered that reports of Iraqi soldiers stealing incubators were unfounded. "What kind of bullshit is this?" I asked Sadoun. He shrugged his shoulders. "I'm serious," I shouted. "This is BULLSHIT!"

"I feel very uncomfortable with this whole thing," Doug said.

"No shit!"

We made it to the airport with just minutes to spare. Luckily for us, the plane was still being loaded. From my window, I watched as a couple of new washing machines wobbled up the conveyor belt into the belly of the jet. A short while later, we were finally airborne.

"CLOSE THE DOOR! Close the door!" I yelled at Ingrid. "I don't want to see anyone until I speak with Atlanta."

"Atlanta wants a phoner from Doug as soon as possible," she said. "It's unbelievable! Everyone's been calling. Everyone wants to do an interview. Everyone's requested copies of our video."

"What a nightmare!" I shouted. "We had less than forty goddamn minutes on the ground."

"How many hospitals did you visit?"

"How many? How many do ya think ya can visit in forty minutes? We only saw one."

"Jesus!"

"Yeah, tell me about it!" I picked up the phone and placed a call to Atlanta. A moment later the telephone rang. I expected it to be the operator, but it was Naji on the line.

"I hear you had problems," he said.

"You heard right," I said, clenching my teeth. "And what's this business I heard on the radio?"

"The Iraqi News Agency reported CNN went to Kuwait. Is that not factual?"

"That's not all it reported," I said. "You know better than that."

"Well, do you have your story or not?"

"Frankly, I don't know what we have. We didn't get what you yourself said we'd have: time to visit several hospitals and do our job properly. . . ."

"It's Atlanta on the other line," Ingrid interrupted me.

"Naji, may I call you back? I've got CNN on the other phone. They're going to do an interview with Doug."

"Fine. Please remember our agreement." There was something odd about the way he said it. I felt it was imperative to double-check.

"We agreed to do a story about the hospitals," I said. "And if we file, we'll honor the agreement. Atlanta also wants to do some Q&A about what we saw in Kuwait . . . general impressions, that sort of thing. We didn't take any pictures, of course, but surely Doug can describe what he saw there on the telephone."

"And what did you see?" Naji asked coyly.

"You know, the conditions in the city, soldiers, abandoned cars, etc."

"This has all been reported before, Robert, has it not?"

"Some of it has, I suppose, but it's still worth mentioning."

"But this is contrary to our agreement," he warned. "You were only permitted to visit Kuwait for a story about hospitals. Not for soldiers. Not for general conditions. Not for abandoned cars."

"And a hospital story is what we will file for television. This is simply a phone interview. . . ."

"Please, Robert, let's be serious," he said, his voice growing cold. "You may do what you like. I cannot prevent you from speaking on the telephone. But if you break our agreement, I do not think it will help with regard to interviewing President Saddam Hussein." It wasn't a direct threat, but the message was clear.

"I quite understand," I told him. "I'll call you back later."

"HOW SOON CAN YOU PUT DOUG on the line for a phoner?" Eason asked urgently.

"I can put him on now, but that's not the problem," I said. "Not only was the trip a total rat-fuck, but we can only talk about the one hospital we visited."

"What!" he exploded. "Didn't you see troops down there, hostages, anything else?"

"Sure, we saw plenty of stuff worth reporting, but Naji says that violates the agreement. As I told you and Earl, we're limited to the hospital. . . ."

"You never told me that," he interrupted.

"Of course I did. . . ."

"No, you didn't!" he bellowed. I had never heard him sound so angry. "Good grief!" he wailed. "Here, talk to Earl. I've got to call Ed."

"Hey," Earl said calmly, as he came on the line. "I gather you've had one hell of a day."

"That and more. Listen, I distinctly remember telling you and Eason about the ground rules for this thing. . . ."

"Sure you did," he said evenly. "But I think Eason was under the impression they applied only to Doug's spot, and not to phoners."

"No, they apply to everything. . . ."

"Ed wants to know what you think will happen if we do the phoner anyway," Eason interrupted.

"Tell him we can kiss Saddam good-bye."

"What a mess!" he yelled. "Stand by."

"Jesus!" I said to Earl. "They don't pay me enough for this. . . ."

"How soon will Doug's report be ready?" Eason asked tersely, coming back on the line.

"Well," I said slowly, knowing full well he wouldn't like what I was about to say. "The fact is, both Doug and I have a problem with that as well. We feel we can't really do a comprehensive story after only spending forty minutes at one hospital."

"What do you mean? I thought you were taken on a tour. . . ."

"It never happened," I interrupted him. "They changed the schedule. . . ."

"Hold on," he said, his voice dripping with disgust. A moment later, Ed Turner came on the line.

"Hi, Robert. What seems to be the problem?" he asked matter-of-factly.

"The problem is, we don't think we have a comprehensive story based on the limited time we spent in Kuwait. I think we'd be better served if I asked Naji if we could go back tomorrow and do what we'd originally planned."

"I don't have a problem with your going back tomorrow," Ed said, "but I still want a piece about what you did today. If you were only taken to one hospital, say so. I'm sure that you and Doug know what to do."

"But . . ."

"That's all," Ed cut in. "Just do it! And one other thing. You tell Naji this: CNN will be pleased to go wherever the Iraqis care to take us. But in the future, we reserve the right to report whatever we see, regardless of the fact we may not be permitted to take any pictures. You tell Naji those are *our* ground rules. Good-bye."

"Robert, it's Eason," he said, coming back on the line. "You can make a dub of the footage for ITN, but that's it. Anyone else who has access must take it off our air."

Under the circumstances, Doug wrote the best script he could. Ultimately, we were saved by the stand-up close, which left our credibility on this particular story intact, but not much more. Naturally, we declined all interviews about the trip, except for a brief soundbite Doug gave to ITN. The upshot was that in the eyes of the rest of the foreign press, we'd been used by the Iraqis.

I checked in with Eason the next day before seeing Naji. "I gotta tell ya," he said, still clearly agitated, "it was the worst day in the history of the network . . . the only time in ten years a reporter has not been able to report what he's seen with his own eyes. . . ."

"Yeah, it's fucked," I agreed. "But let's be honest. If any other news organization were called up and offered a trip to Kuwait under the same conditions, it would accept. You know it and I know it. I'll grant you that, afterward, another reporter might have said to hell with the ground rules. Maybe we would have said it too, if the story were important enough. But face it, we want Saddam Hussein and that's driving the bottom line."

"SO THAT'S THE BOTTOM LINE," I finished explaining to Naji. "We'll be happy to go anywhere, but we reserve the right to report what we see, whether there's a camera there or not."

"The Doug James story implied he didn't know if what he was told in Kuwait was the truth."

"We only visited one hospital. The doctor there couldn't address what may have happened at other facilities."

"I do not agree," Naji said. "You didn't tell the truth because CNN wouldn't let you. We know CNN is run by the State Department."

"*Bullshit! That's bullshit and you know it!* I've had it," I shouted at him. "First, I get hammered by my network. Then I get hammered by you. What do I look like? A fuckin' anvil. . . !"

"Calm down, Robert. Calm down," Naji said, as he burst out laughing. "I know you don't work for the State Department, but, honestly, there are probably people at CNN who feel what you report must reflect Washington's policy. . . ."

"With all due respect, you're way off base," I said, trying to regain my composure. "That's not how it works at all. . . ."

"Let's not be naive," he said. "All governments use the press in one fashion or another. . . ."

"That's not what we're talking about," I interrupted. "Your press is used to serve the state. Our press is there to question it. That's a fundamental difference between our systems."

"Well, I will take up the question of your returning to Kuwait, but frankly I don't believe that Security Services will accept your conditions."

"So be it," I said. "As long as we understand one another."

A FEW DAYS LATER, Iraqi TV broadcast a documentary about hospitals in its "Nineteenth Province." It rejected as "lies" allegations that the incubators had been stolen and Kuwaiti babies left to die. Many physicians were interviewed for the program, but our Kuwaiti doctor was not among them. On March 4, 1991, in a story filed from Kuwait City, CNN's Mark Dulmage reported that the man had been executed, allegedly following Doug's report.

"Apparently, Iraq's going to grant visas to a number of British women to visit their husbands," John Fiegener told me during the morning call to Atlanta. "We'll try to have the London bureau give you a 'heads-up' on the timetable. I'm sure we're going to want coverage of the reunions, if at all possible."

"I'm sure you will," I said bitterly. "I would have thought you'd had enough after Nadia Comaneci."

"Nadia!" he laughed. "Can you hear me, Nadia?"

The live televised reunion I produced between former Romanian gymnast Nadia Comaneci, who was in New York, and her mother, sister, and the brother of her current lover, who were in Bucharest, is not among the highpoints of my checkered career. In fact, in terms of the bullshit factor, it ranked right up there with our recent excursion to Kuwait. I had taken "Captains Wacky's Flying Circus" to Bucharest to cover the revolution. The entire team had risked life and limb to get there; faced potential firing squads at more than one checkpoint; worked like fiends around the clock to keep up with the spiraling pace of events; even dodged bullets to get to the feedpoint. Eason had called me: "I was just reading a press release about Nadia Comaneci," he explained. "Apparently, she hasn't had any word of her family since the revolution began. I was just thinking, if we could find them, get them to the hotel, and put them up live, we could reunite them with Nadia, who we'd bring in to the New York bureau. Whaddaya think?" he asked excitedly. "It could generate a lot of good press. I'm sure it would boost the ratings."

I thought it over. We already had a full agenda of real news that we planned to cover in the morning. A project like this was sure to siphon off men and matériel. On the other hand, along with Olga Korbutt and Mary Lou Retton, wasn't Nadia one of America's favorite little Olympic pixies? Of course she was. Eason was right. It'd be great TV.

"Fine. Let's do it!" I proclaimed enthusiastically. "Get in touch with her and get some addresses and phone numbers—"

"That's the beauty of it," he interrupted. "I've already gotten them from her agent." I copied them down. "You contact the family, and put 'em on ice at the hotel. Lock 'em in a room and give 'em something to eat, if necessary. I've got a feeling the other nets are going to go after them too, and I want this for CNN exclusively."

I rousted our "fixer," Vladimir, out of bed and gave him the details. "Take a driver and make the arrangements right now," I said, handing him the addresses. "None of them has a phone, so you'll have to do it in person. Tell 'em we'll pick them up tomorrow at ten and bring them here. And for Godssakes, tell them not to speak with anyone else."

"I scared the shit out of the mother," Vlad said when he finally returned at 4 A.M. "She thought anyone knocking on her door in the middle of the night had to be Securitate. But it's all set."

By eleven o'clock, the pixie's mother, sister, and the brother of her lover were happily munching on an assortment of cold meats and salad, undoubtedly the best food they'd seen in quite a while.

Meanwhile, Bly was annoyed, not only because I'd canceled his shoot but also because I'd appropriated his crew and producer for the interview. "C'mon, Captain," he complained. "You know this isn't news."

"Fuck the news!" I howled. "It can wait for a few hours. We're talkin' about Nadia Comaneci here!" Bly looked at me as though I'd finally lost my mind, and stormed out.

The live shot was a disaster. CNN had secured the services of a simultaneous translator since no one in Bucharest spoke a word of English, but owing to technical problems and the slight time delay that occurs when someone is interviewed via satellite, the reunion, which CNN had promo'd to the max, consisted mostly of Nadia asking her mother, sister, and lover's brother, "Hello. Can you hear me?" while the three of them in Bucharest held the world transfixed as they replied, "Hello, Nadia. Are you there, Nadia?"

Except for a brief item buried in "USA Today," the Nadia Comaneci Special didn't generate any press, let alone boost the ratings. But it did succeed in generating a lot of laughs, not to mention my colleagues' scorn, as they knighted me the P. T. Barnum of Bucharest.

Ever since, if anyone so much as mentions the word "reunion," I immediately break out in hives.

I TOLD FIEGENER if I didn't hear from London about the British wives it was fine by me, and jotted down some other news items he passed along.

"A group called International Physicians for Prevention of Nuclear War says if a one megaton bomb is dropped on Baghdad, 2.7 million people will die, and another 1.3 million will be injured," he said.

"Glad to hear it," I joked. "You got anything else to cheer us up?"

"I take it you're already up to date on this Four Stage/Four-Day Blitz Plan that's been leaked to some of the newspapers?"

"Someone has mentioned it, but I don't have the details."

"Well, Stage One would last six hours," he said. "The coalition would bomb the shit out of Iraq's Air Force and destroy all of its missile bases.

Stage Two would last twenty-four hours. It'd destroy Iraq's entire military-industrial complex, along with eight bunkers in a Baghdad suburb where Saddam holes up. It would also cut the highway from Basra to Kuwait. Stage Three," he continued, "would be a surgical operation to 'detach' Kuwait from Iraq. Green Berets and Navy Seals would spearhead it. And Stage Four would be the liberation of Kuwait by U.S., British, and French forces. The Egyptians, Syrians, and the Moroccans would be called in to mop up."

"And this is all supposed to happen in four days?" I asked incredulously.

"Yeah. It sounds pretty unrealistic to me too," he conceded.

"Well, getting back to reality . . . Edward Heath's due here soon, and we'll definitely cover him. If Cat Stevens was able to take out four, think how many hostages the former Prime Minister of Great Britain will get!"

"It's getting to be quite a sideshow over there," he laughed.

Indeed it was. Between the weirded-out independent peace activist from Scandinavia—whom we immediately dubbed "Moon Man Martin"—to the more established antiwar group from the U.S.A. called the Fellowship of Reconciliation, it seemed as if everyone was coming to Baghdad to take a stroll in the hostage bazaar. From Japan came a famous wrestler, from Sweden and Finland came officials and parliamentarians, and from France came a vicious little moron named Michel Sargeant, who claimed to be the world's only "volunteer hostage." He was prepared, indeed eager, to be dispatched to a strategic site, if that meant freedom for other French nationals. "Please understand, monsieur," he explained to me one afternoon, "I am not an anti-Semite. But this whole crisis has been created by the media, and, of course, the media is controlled by the Jews."

The Iraqi government established a liaison office called the Organization for Peace, Friendship, and Solidarity to coordinate activities with these various groups and individuals, but the program varied little. If you wanted to take home a hostage, you'd work your way up the line from the Speaker of the National Assembly to the Minister of Culture and Information, to the Foreign Minister, to the Deputy Prime Minister, and, eventually, to President Saddam Hussein, where, more likely than not, if you had gotten that far, your request would be granted. Each night, Iraqi TV broadcast pictures of these meetings, as suitably reverent foreign supplicants made their appointed rounds.

THE DAY BEFORE BERNIE'S ARRIVAL in Baghdad, Mr. Mazin materialized out of the blue. I was genuinely glad to see him. Although Nasir had improved since I'd taken him to task, his performance remained, to say the least, erratic.

"I am here to be of service to you," Mazin explained. "I think you have important interview soon."

"Indeed we do. Where have you been hiding?"

"Why you think I hiding?" he protested. "I working inside the ministry, but when I learn Mr. Bernard Shaw come to Baghdad to interview His Excellency President Saddam Hussein, I say, perhaps I can assist my old friend Mr. Robert." I asked Mazin to accompany me to the airport to meet Bernie's plane.

"Perhaps you could help Mr. Shaw avoid a long and debilitating experience dealing with your associates at customs."

"I do my best," Mazin assured me, as we agreed to meet the next morning.

"OOH, YOU SEE . . . I tell you . . . you here in Baghdad a long time . . . you should know . . . Mr. Shaw's plane is late," Mazin trilled, as we looked up at the board marked Arrivals.

"Only by an hour," I laughed. "For this place, that's right on time."

"Come, let us walk together," Mazin said, steering me toward a small snack bar at the far end of the terminal. "It will be my pleasure to buy you a cup of coffee." Unfortunately, the snack bar was closed. In fact, during the fourteen times I was in and out of Saddam International Airport prior to the war, I don't remember ever having seen it open. "You must to tell me," Mazin said, as we began our trek back to the other end of the hall, "if I am to assist Mr. Shaw when he arrives, I must to know what he looks like, to recognize him."

"Bernie will probably be the only journalist wearing a coat and tie. I'd say he's in his late forties, medium height, has a mustache . . . and he's black."

"A black man!" Mazin exclaimed. "I think that is unusual for American journalists."

"Unfortunately, it is," I agreed. "Certainly for newsmen of Bernie's stature. Injustice and prejudice aren't limited exclusively to your corner of the world, my friend." As Bernie's plane landed, Mazin disappeared into the arrival hall. Nearly two hours later, he and Shaw emerged through the heavy glass doors.

"You look tired," I said to Bernie as I greeted him. "How was the trip?"

"Once we took off it was fine," he said wearily. "But the formalities on this end tended to take time."

"Lucky for you, you had Mr. Mazin to smooth the way. Trust me. It could have been worse." As we threw his bags into the trunk of the Honda, Bernie introduced himself to driver Jasim.

"That's *Mr.* Jasim," I explained solemnly. "Just as I am *Mr.* Robert—"

"And you," Mazin interrupted and pronounced with a flourish, "you are Mr. Bernard Shaw!"

"Bernie will do just fine," Shaw laughed.

"I haven't scheduled anything for the rest of the day," I said as we drove into town. "I figured you'd prefer to relax. Tomorrow, we'll get together with Joe Wilson at the embassy for a private briefing. I've also set up meetings with Naji al-Hadithi and Nizar Hamdoon."

"Ah, Nizar," Bernie mused, glancing out the window. "He must be under a tremendous strain. How's he holding up?"

"He's up and down. It depends on the day. This place is like a roller coaster."

"Yes, that I can believe, my brother. That I can believe."

We checked into the hotel with a minimum of fanfare, but the moment Bernie was spotted in the lobby by a crew from CBS, the word was out: CNN had an interview with Saddam Hussein. Why else, they reasoned correctly, would the network's principal Washington anchor have come to Baghdad? Within hours, the other nets would learn of it too and dutifully inform their desks.

"There's no way we could keep it under wraps," I explained to Eason when I called in. "Bernie's a visible guy. They just put two and two together."

"I don't know what he expected me to do," I said to Bernie later. "Bring you in through the service entrance with a sheet over your head? The fact is, there aren't many secrets you can keep in this town."

"Don't worry about it," he assured me. "In any case, I'm going to stick close to the office. It saves answering a lot of questions from our colleagues."

"So, what's Tom Johnson like?" Ingrid piped up, referring to CNN's new president. "None of us has ever spoken with the guy." Bernie reached for the pack of cigarettes tucked into his sock just above the ankle, an old habit from his days as a Marine.

"Tom Johnson," he intoned, "is the right man at the right time to lead this company." He took a puff on his cigarette. "He's a hard-news, hands-on professional with excellent contacts and superb people skills. By the way, he asked me to convey his congratulations for the job you've already done, and he wants to know if there's anything he can do for any of you."

"He can start with per diem!" Ingrid laughed.

"I don't understand . . ." Bernie said.

"Don't worry about it," I interrupted. "It's just a little sore point."

Actually, it was more than that. Like other news organizations, CNN paid its employees a food allowance while they traveled. In our case, forty-five dollars a day anywhere outside the United States. The amount remained the same, whether in Prague, Johannesburg, or Amman, where forty-five dollars was enough to pay for three meals; or in Paris, Berlin, or Geneva, where it wasn't. Baghdad, of course, was wildly expensive. So expensive that CNN, based on my recommendation, was picking up the tab for everything. It was the fair thing to do. But it also seemed fair that if CNN were paying for the food, per diems should be eliminated. The logic was irrefutable. When CNN cemented a deal for a workspace in Amman, however, the hotel threw in free meal vouchers and the people in Jordan got their per diems on top of that: in essence, a tidy six hundred and thirty extra dollars of pocket money every two weeks. Naturally, no one in Baghdad begrudged the folks in Amman a little something extra. But it irked some people that, by volunteering for Baghdad and risking their lives, they were also "losing" money. I had several conversations with Eason about the situation—neither of us wanted to penalize CNN Amman, where the vouchers were only good for hotel food, and one could chow down better elsewhere, but we were at an impasse over what to do for the folks in Baghdad.

"And all this is over forty-five dollars a day?" Bernie asked incredulously, shaking his head. "Chump change! I'll speak to Tom about it."

"A little tip to remember," Joe Wilson explained as we concluded our meeting, "is that Saddam has a tendency to hold his hand down when you move forward to shake it." Wilson stood up and extended his right hand at arm's length just below the waist. "You don't realize there's anything unusual, because Saddam's very tall. But what he's actually doing is forcing you to tilt your head—in effect, to bow before him. I was cautioned about this before our first meeting and was determined not to let it happen. Well, the damnedest thing," he laughed, "was when I saw myself on Iraqi TV that night, I'd involuntarily done it! It looked like I was bowing while shaking hands. . . ."

"I'll remember that," Bernie smiled.

"Well, the second time we met," Joe continued, "I tilted my head upward and just stuck out my arm. I was not going to let it happen again. But to tell you the truth, I didn't know whether I was going to shake his hand or grab his dick!"

"Presumably, a serious breach of protocol," I surmised.

"Quite serious," Joe laughed.

"Welcome to Baghdad, Mr. Shaw," Naji effused, standing up from his desk for the customary greeting. "May I offer you a cup of tea?"

I had briefed Bernie in full about Naji, including the famous "nipple" story. "He's really quite a piece of work," I'd said. "I think you'll find him fascinating." The two of them discussed Shaw's trip to Iraq, the upcoming interview, antiwar demonstrations around the United States, and congressional debate for some time. Naji seemed to imply that George Bush had neither the support nor the resolve he needed to actually wage war.

"I wouldn't underestimate the President's resolve, nor that of the coalition which supports him," Bernie said flatly.

"So," Naji asked, as if delighting in this delicate verbal sparring, "will there be war?"

Bernie looked Naji straight in the eyes, and in the same low-keyed voice that characterized his early comments said simply, "My balls are not made of crystal." He then took another sip of mint tea.

To this day, I'm not fully convinced Naji understood precisely what he'd heard. I certainly couldn't tell by looking at his face. He didn't smile, he didn't frown, in fact, he didn't react at all. He simply took a sip of tea himself and asked about the weather in Washington.

"I don't mean to be flip," Bernie said, coming back to the question, "but I don't think anyone knows what will happen. Does your President know?"

"Our President does not want war," Naji said. "So only Bush can know what will happen, since Bush will be the one to start a war, if there is going to be one." At this point, I sensed the conversation had gone past its usefulness, and I jumped in to wrap things up.

"Well, with all due respect, Naji, we don't want to take up any more of your time. Bernie and I have an appointment with Nizar and I want to show Mr. Shaw some of the sights before that meeting."

"Of course," Naji said, standing up to say good-bye. "You are most welcome here, Mr. Shaw. We shall stay in contact."

"'MY BALLS ARE NOT MADE OF CRYSTAL?' Jesus Christ!" I laughed. "Where'd ya come up with that one?" Bernie took a drag off his cigarette and looked at me like the cat that swallowed the canary.

"I was simply trying to point out that none of us can predict the future," he said dryly.

"That's their dish over there," I said, pointing to a large satellite dish behind the Ministry for Foreign Affairs. "Nizar's office is on the fifth floor." The satellite dish enabled the folks at the Foreign Ministry to watch CNN, among other things; Iraqi officials also could watch CNN at the Ministry of Culture and Information, and I suspected they watched at the presidential palace as well. (Until we got our four-wire and could hear CNN programming, that was a whole lot more than we who worked for CNN could do.) I had already taken this walk so often, the guards recognized me.

"Ah, Mr. Robert," Bernie chuckled as we breezed through security and were allowed to continue unescorted through the lobby. "If only Atlanta could see us now."

"His excellency Mr. Nizar Hamdoon will be with you shortly," the male secretary said, ushering us into Hamdoon's outer office, which had been newly decorated with black leather couches. "Please," he gestured deferentially, "you may sit down."

"At least we can smoke in here," I said to Bernie, popping a Gauloise into my cigarette holder. "Unlike Naji, Nizar is a Marlboro Man." For the next few minutes, the two of us puffed away contentedly as we admired two arabesque lithographs that graced the wall. "Some of the art is fabulous," I said. "Along with carpets, it's the thing to buy. . . ."

"Hello, Bernie," Hamdoon said warmly as he approached Shaw and kissed him on both cheeks. "Welcome to Baghdad, my friend." Nizar escorted us into his office and called for refreshments.

"My favorite network," Bernie smiled, noting the television set turned to CNN.

"It is on all the time," Hamdoon explained, "both here and in the Foreign Minister's office. It is quite useful to have these days. So, how are you, Bernie?"

"Glad to be here, and looking forward to speaking with your President."

"This is your first trip to Baghdad?" Hamdoon inquired.

"Yes, it is. And hopefully not the last. It's a beautiful city."

"You would like to come back?"

"Oh, very much so. Mr. Robert here has been showing me around."

"Yes, Bob is an old hand by now," Hamdoon smiled.

"So tell me, how are you?" Bernie asked. Nizar lit another Marlboro and sipped his coffee.

"Trying to keep up with these events that seem to have moved so swiftly," he replied thoughtfully. "It is often difficult."

"It must be. Did the world's reaction surprise you?"

"Frankly, yes," Nizar said. "And the unwillingness to have dialogue."

"On Washington's part?"

"In Washington and elsewhere."

"Well," Bernie said, "*we* are looking forward to having a dialogue with your President."

"I am happy to hear that," Nizar replied emphatically. "A dialogue can be useful." The three of us talked in general terms about the format for the interview, after which I broached the subject of having CNN rather than Iraqi TV technicians man the cameras.

"I can assure you the quality of the pictures and overall composition will be greatly improved," I said.

"I agree with Robert," Bernie added. "To be perfectly candid, your technicians are not as concerned about lighting and composition as we perhaps are."

"This still poses a security problem for us," Nizar explained.

"How so?" I asked. "I'm willing to have our people wherever you want them twenty-four hours in advance. That's plenty of time for Security to rigorously inspect the equipment. We could even move it in earlier, if necessary."

"I understand," Nizar said. "I will look into it, but I have no control over Security."

"We'd appreciate whatever you can do for us," Bernie said graciously. For the next several minutes, Bernie and Nizar reminisced about Washington and Nizar's days there as Iraq's ambassador. It was clear he was nostalgic for those easier times.

"Do you think you'll get the top job here?" Bernie asked.

"Which job?"

"Foreign Minister."

"I don't think so," Hamdoon said quietly.

"Why not?" asked Bernie. Nizar became introspective, as if weighing whether to let down his guard.

"You know," he said thoughtfully, "I never trained for a career in government. I was educated to be an architect. But events . . ." His voice trailed off.

"Are you saying you might leave government service?" Bernie probed. Hamdoon became reflective again as he reached for still another cigarette.

"Not now . . . but perhaps one day," he said, almost in a whisper. "So," he added, raising his voice, "we shall get together again soon. I have another meeting I must attend to." He escorted us to the door.

"Ed wants to know what your first question will be," I said to Bernie as I entered his room. He had spent several days preparing for the interview, pouring over a thick file of research material that included clippings, magazine articles, and a copy of Samir al-Khalil's *Republic of Fear*. His table was covered with dozens of index cards on which he had handwritten potential questions, or specific topics he wanted to address. Bernie looked up, took off his eyeglasses, and reached for a smoke.

"I haven't decided yet," he said. "Did Ed have a specific question in mind?"

"I think Ed wants to go with something like 'Will there be war?' but between you and me, I might want to go a different route."

"Well, 'Will there be war?' is certainly viable," he agreed. "It cuts to the essence of things."

"Yeah, but I think it lacks a certain zing. And it's also so, you know, predictable."

"What did you have in mind, my brother?"

"Well, I think we need something that catches Saddam off guard, generates news, and, in turn, headlines; you know, grabs the world's attention. . . ."

"Such as?"

"Such as, 'If Mrs. Saddam Hussein were raped and murdered, would you advocate the death penalty?' Think about it," I laughed as I scooted back to the workspace.

"Which one of you guys is gonna shoot the Heath news conference?" I asked Mark and Cynde, "it begins in twenty minutes." Since Heath's arrival, we'd relied mostly on ITN to cover the visit of the former British Prime Minister, but because this was his final news conference following his talks with Saddam Hussein, we decided to cover it ourselves. Heath was expected to announce he'd be leaving with as many as two hundred British hostages, no small accomplishment if he could pull if off. Naturally, the British press was in a tizzy, with the BBC and ITN eyeing each other suspiciously and jockeying for position over every angle of the story. Upon landing in Baghdad, Heath was bedded down at the Al-Rasheed, but within twenty-four hours he moved to an official government guest house, which afforded not only more luxury but relief from the omnipresent gaggle of media meisters.

I had never met Ted Heath before, nor his foppish male secretary, and I was looking forward to what would surely be a bucket of bullshit served up to the world's press with customary British understatement and civility.

"As soon as we are able to give you the names, we shall do so," Heath explained after stating he'd be leaving with only about thirty hostages plus a puppy. He said he'd covered a lot of ground during his three hours of talks with Saddam Hussein, in an effort to find a diplomatic solution to the crisis. "I will say more in the House of Commons and in Britain when the occasion arises," he announced pompously.

I got up from my seat and sought out his secretary. "How many hostages did you specifically request to be released?" I asked him.

"Two hundred," he said, shuffling a stack of papers that included a neatly typed list of names. I thanked him and sat down, prepared to ask Heath a question when another reporter asked it for me.

"Sir, in light of the fact that you asked Iraq to release about two hundred hostages, aren't you disappointed that only thirty or so will be going home?"

"Who said anything about two hundred hostages?" Heath replied contemptuously.

"We understand, sir, you specifically asked for two hundred . . ."

"That's untrue. We never asked for any such thing," Heath bellowed. I stared at his secretary, who glanced away nervously.

The rest of the news conference focused on the need for what Heath called a "stable order in the Middle East," although Heath admitted Saddam had given him no indication he was ready to withdraw wholly, or even partially, from Kuwait. As the news conference ended, I noticed Saddam's translator standing in the back of the room. I walked up and said hello.

"The former Prime Minister of Great Britain, and you only gave him thirty guys and a dog?" I laughed. "Even Jesse Jackson did better than that." Dr. Zoubaydi chuckled, but was diplomatically noncommittal.

"Please, Mr. Robert," he asked, "could you make me an audio tape of the news conference?"

"No problem," I said. "So tell me, do we have a specific date and time for our interview with the President?"

"Very soon, I assure you," he smiled. "Your patience will be rewarded."

We weren't the only ones whose patience was rewarded. That day, Iraq's National Assembly voted to endorse Saddam's proposal to immediately free all French citizens held against their will.

The telephone call came at eleven in the morning. Sadoun al-Jenabi, Minder of all Minders, was on the line. "Please," he implored in a hushed, urgent tone, "you and your team must not leave the office. The interview may come at any moment."

"This is it!" I shouted as I hung up the phone. "We're all on standby." I'd been briefed earlier by Naji about what to expect. He said we'd receive a telephone call alerting us the interview was imminent. After that, it could happen at any time, day or night. We should be prepared to move within fifteen minutes. Cars would be sent to the hotel to collect us. We had no idea where we'd be taken.

During a second meeting with Hamdoon, Bernie, Bly, and I again stressed the need for CNN to videotape the interview. For almost an hour we'd pressed our case with both Nizar and Dr. Sa'doun Zoubaydi, who had joined the discussion. Finally, a compromise was hammered out. Mark and Cynde would videotape the interview, but with cameras belonging to Iraqi TV.

I walked across the hall and knocked on Bernie's door. I suggested he don the "uniform of the day," as he liked to call it. Three doors away, Bly was already getting dressed in his best gray pinstripe, which had been sent Federal Express from London to Amman, and hand-carried to Baghdad.

Ten minutes later we gathered in Room 906 and waited. Nine hours later we were still waiting. "It's not going to happen today," Bly insisted. "I'm taking this damn suit off."

"Be my guest," I laughed. "So long as you're ready at a moment's notice."

The eight o'clock news carried pictures of Yevgeni Primakov's arrival in Baghdad. The Soviet envoy had returned to the Middle East promoting a new peace initiative. "You might be right," I said to Bly. "He's not going to see us until he's through with Primakov."

"I agree," Bernie said. "But, of course, we don't know for sure." By midnight, my nerves were frayed, but Bernie was cool as a cucumber. "There's really nothing we can do about it," he reasoned. "The man will call when he's ready."

Saddam was not ready that evening, nor the following morning, afternoon, or even the following night. Mark, Cynde, and Tracy passed the time editing some of their best pictures to a Bob Geldof tune called "The Great Song of Indifference." Bernie spent the hours reviewing his notes or listening to Luther Vandross, while Bly burned off energy, if not extra calories, shadow-boxing down the halls of the Al-Rasheed. I, among other things, changed their airline reservations for what I hoped would be the last time, and shot the shit with our Rome bureau chief, Mark Dulmage, who'd arrived to replace me. Every now and then I'd call Ingrid, who'd left for Amman when her visa expired, to give her an update. Once we had satellited the interview from Baghdad, she would have overall responsibility for its final production.

WE WERE HAVING BREAKFAST when a man in an olive-green uniform knocked on the door. "CNN?" he asked. "Please come now. The cars are waiting."

"We'll be right down," I told him as I gave Dulmage some final instructions. "Let Atlanta know we're on our way and be sure they alert Amman. I'll take the tapes directly to Iraqi TV after the interview. Tracy can meet us there. Hopefully, Bernie and Bly can make the 2 P.M. flight. We ought to have a driver standing by." Then the five of us headed downstairs.

For the next twenty minutes, we seemed to be driving in circles from one residential neighborhood to the next. By the time we arrived at what turned out to be a lavish government guest house near the banks of the Tigris, I was thoroughly disoriented. After a cursory frisk, we were escorted into an elaborately furnished salon, where three television cameras were already prepositioned. The room was decorated with expensive oriental rugs, crystal chandeliers, and ornate but contemporary trappings. Several original oil paintings graced the walls. On the small marble bar adjacent to the room, packs of Marlboro and Cartier cigarettes were displayed like canapés. About a dozen Iraqi technicians and security personnel were posted around the room, many of them sporting the same octagonal gold pin with an engraved likeness of Saddam that seemed to serve as a backstage pass. I asked one burly fellow if he'd like to swap one for a plastic CNN lapel pin, but he said no deal.

We immediately got down to business rearranging the "set" that had been arranged for us. "You're gonna want these curtains closed, aren't you?" Mark called out from the far side of the room. "What about this couch? Should we move it back too?" A few technicians stepped in to help.

"How are you this morning?" Dr. Zoubaydi asked amiably, entering the room. "I see everything is well in hand." A few minutes later, Minister Latif Nasif Jassim made an appearance. He seemed intrigued as I sat down in what would be the President's chair while Mark "blocked" the shot. Jassim was accompanied by his official translator from the Ministry of

Culture and Information, who would assist Zoubaydi during the course of the interview. Once Mark and Cynde finished adjusting the lighting, all of us were ushered out of the salon for a security check.

"Take off, please," the guard said, pointing to my watch. "Everything. Also, please empty pockets."

"Everything?" I asked, as we proceeded to offer up wallets, pens, notes, money, rings, bracelets, keys, cigarettes, even the odd receipt, which were placed in individual manila envelopes. "Hey," I said to the guard. "This is just like getting booked." He looked at me quizzically. We tried to explain that some items, especially notebooks, pens, and watches were needed for the interview, but he didn't understand. Dr. Zoubaydi finally interceded on our behalf. "Please, Mr. Robert," he implored. "Just take the minimum of what you really need." Lastly, we were treated to a much more thorough frisk than we'd had before.

We were back in the salon making last-minute adjustments when the security guards began scurrying around like mice. "He's coming. He's coming now," one of them whispered. A few seconds later, more security guards entered the room, followed by the tall, imposing figure of the man we had come to see: Saddam Hussein, the President of Iraq.

No doubt about it, the guy's got a commanding presence, I thought as I eyeballed Saddam in the flesh for the first time. He looked tanned and fit, more handsome in person than in his pictures. He was dressed in an expensive silk suit, a shade between blue and gray, and sported a red pocket handkerchief. His eyes were dark and penetrating. Somehow, I expected to see craziness in those eyes, but I saw nothing of the kind. What I saw instead was resolve and fierce determination. Dr. Zoubaydi hovered around him and made the introductions. There was nothing unusual about the way he shook hands, despite what Joe had told us. I was surprised, however, to see the tattoo on the top of his right hand—a large blue geometric design. After he was seated, I adjusted his microphone. He looked straight ahead and didn't blink. I then took my seat next to Minister Jassim and looked at my watch. It was eleven twenty-nine.

"Mr. President . . ." Bernie began, "to prevent the embargo from destroying your country, will you withdraw from Kuwait?"

"If any embargo could lead the American people to withdraw from Washington, or the British people to withdraw from any city . . . if an embargo could force the Americans to withdraw from Hawaii, it would probably lead the Iraqis to think . . ."

"So your answer is no?" Bernie followed up.

"Naturally," said Saddam. ". . . the issue is not this or that part of Iraq. The issue is the issue of the Arab Nation as a whole. . . ."

"Do you have a feeling that things are moving to a head?" Bernie asked.

"We are working to avoid military confrontation," Saddam said. "But there are those who work for military confrontation to occur . . . in this order: Israel, the Zionist influence, Thatcher and her complex, and Mr.

Bush. And it seems to us that Israel and Thatcher are trying to push Bush into that quagmire."

"What did you think when Bush compared you to Hitler?" Bernie wanted to know.

"This is his view. This is how he thinks," Saddam said. "But when his views are not fair, that is his responsibility. But you, as a citizen, don't you think Bush made an error when talking to a head of state of a country where he has an embassy, and wants diplomatic contacts. . . ?"

"Mr. President," Bernie replied diplomatically, "as a reporter, I can't respond to your question. I am not on the same level as President Bush or yourself."

"I understand your position. I appreciate your position," Saddam said frankly. "But we are in the habit here when we talk to others . . . we forget about titles. I talk to you as a man. . . ."

"May I go further?" Bly pressed. "You've been called 'The Beast of Baghdad,' 'The Butcher of Baghdad' . . . there have been allegations you're responsible for massacres . . . murder. Who is Saddam Hussein?"

"Saddam Hussein is an Arab citizen, a worshiper, a believer in God, fighting for justice and truth, and rejecting injustice. He fears no one but God. In these traits, he becomes at one with the Arab Nation and the Arab people. But as to those references about massacres . . . you can have the answer by roaming the country and asking for yourself. My biography is recorded. . . ."

For the next two hours, Saddam held forth on a wide variety of topics. He characterized his recent dialogue with Primakov as "wide-ranging, deep, and useful," and said it included "practical proposals" for resolving the hostage issue. He talked about his July 25 meeting with Ambassador April Glaspie, insisting he was "very clear" when he expressed Iraq's views on Kuwait. He accused the United States of unjustly pressuring members of the Security Council to pass resolutions that harmed his country. He again called for an international conference "with a view to a comprehensive solution" to settle all problems in the region. And he said neither the United States nor any of the "parties" in the coalition had opted for dialogue. "The parties themselves are occupied with their own arrogant positions. This is a course of action that we find wicked."

Throughout the interview, Saddam sat bolt upright, both feet planted firmly on the floor, his eyes squarely on Bernie and Bly. "There is nothing worse than war," he said, "but to be deprived of liberty, honor, and security . . ."

"If you drag your people into another war," Bernie asked, "will they ever forgive you?"

"I have never dragged my people into a war. And I will never do so," Saddam insisted. "We explain to our people what is right, and what is farce! You know, the United States resorts to misrepresentation and distorting to confuse our people and their way of thinking to undermine morale. But our people's morale is strong. . . ."

"I am grateful for your questions, even your provocative ones," Saddam said finally, trying to wrap things up. Then he added with just the slightest of smiles, "But I remind you, Bush said people will fall asleep during my speech. . . ."

"If you would permit a final question," said Bernie, "when you die, how do you want to be remembered?"

". . . The true believer always believes that God is satisfied with him. And I believe the great people of Iraq and the glorious Arab Nation will remember us favorably."

Bernie and Bly thanked the President for his time, and all of us, including Mark and Cynde, were led into the foyer to pose for official photographs. I couldn't believe my eyes when Bly gave Saddam a "high five."

"Give him a lapel pin. Go ahead, put it on him," Mark whispered, nudging me in the ribs. But my sense of propriety rose to the occasion. Even I considered that just over the line. Moreover, I could only imagine the expression on Ed Turner's face when the PR people came storming into his office.

Bernie and Bly raced back to the hotel while I sped to the feedpoint. "Many people have satellite bookings, but I cancel them so you can feed your material," Mrs. Awattif informed me. "How was your interview?"

"I think it went well," I said. "To tell you the truth, I was taking notes so intently, it was hard to tell." I placed a call to Atlanta while Mark and Tracy furiously racked up more than a dozen tapes. For the next five hours, we pumped the interview, recorded on three separate cameras, down the line. In Amman, Ingrid and Kris made deadline by the skin of their teeth.

BY THE TIME I GOT BACK to the hotel I was exhausted. "There is a present for you from the President," Mazin chirped as he greeted me in the lobby.

"What kind of present?" I asked.

"Ooh, you will see upstairs. It is very nice."

"Congratulations," Dulmage smiled as I entered the office.

"Thanks. I need a drink!" I exclaimed.

"It's already taken care of," Clancy said, offering me a Stoli on the rocks. "This came for you too." He handed me a brown leather album embossed in gold with the emblem of Iraq. Inside were the color photographs taken at the guest house.

"There's one for each of you," Dulmage explained.

"Did Bernie and Bly make their plane okay?"

"Yeah, just. They were lucky it was late."

"Well, great," I said, draining my glass. "I'm gonna check in with Eason one last time before I ascend into the Twilight Zone. ITN's throwing a big one tonight, and I'm in the mood for serious trouble."

"HEY!" EASON EXCLAIMED. "*Great* job."

"Thanks. So, I'm outta here tomorrow. Any last-minute instructions?"

"No. Oh, by the way, it looks like we're gonna put in a four-wire at the Al-Rasheed."

"No way!" I laughed. "You got permission?"

"Well, the PTT in Amman says it can do it. They've already spoken to the Iraqis."

"That's great. But I'll believe it when I see it."

"We'll run it between Baghdad and Amman," he explained, "and order a connecting line between Amman and Atlanta."

"Sounds good to me. Okay, my friend. I've got a rendezvous with destiny. I'll speak with ya soon."

"Get some rest," he advised.

"Not tonight!" I laughed.

PART FOUR

November—December 1990

14

"We go through this every time," I said to the ticket agent at the gate in Amman. "It's obvious my boarding card says 'first class.' Why would I possibly want to travel economy?"

"Okay, you go first class," he said after mulling it over. "Someone else go economy."

"You've made a wise decision, my friend," I said as I picked up my bags and headed downstairs to the tarmac. It never ends, I said to myself as the bus pulled to a stop beside the aging Boeing 707. As usual, everyone's luggage was piled on the ground, where we were expected to identify each suitcase, then personally load it into the cargo hold. Alongside me, a middle-aged, overweight Iraqi looked like a candidate for a hernia as he struggled to lift one of four tractor-trailer tires that lay scattered about him. I threw my bags on the conveyor belt and climbed the stairs to the plane.

"Batteries? Do you have batteries?" the steward asked at our final security check.

"No batteries. No shortwave radios. No modems. No sidearms," I announced, opening my shoulder bag.

"You have been to Baghdad before," he smiled. "Please, you may take your seat." I placed my hand luggage in the overhead rack and walked down the aisle to the lavatory. As I pulled the door closed behind me, the light fixture fell on my head. "Jesus!" I yelped. Then I noticed the lock on the door was broken too. The goddamn plane was falling apart! I stepped back out to try the can next door. The adjacent lavatory was vacant, or so said the sign. Actually, it turned out to be occupied by an elderly gent, about sixty, holding his index finger to his nose as he blew a wad of snot directly into the sink. Welcome aboard Iraqi Airways!

I was looking forward to getting back. Much had happened while I'd been with my family in Europe. Stepping up his rhetoric, President Bush had called Saddam Hussein "more barbaric than Hitler." A few days later, citing the need for "an adequate offensive military option," he'd ordered one hundred and fifty thousand additional troops to the Gulf. In a surprise move, Baghdad had said it would free all foreign hostages over a three-month period beginning Christmas. Washington had called the announcement a "further cynical manipulation of innocent people's lives." President Bush had flown to the Gulf to spend Thanksgiving with his forces. He'd told them if war should come, it wouldn't be another Vietnam. "If anybody's asked to fight, they'll fight to win," the President had assured a group of young soldiers gathered in the desert. Within days, Saddam Hussein had paid a second visit to Kuwait. He'd told his troops that, if attacked, he was prepared to fight the "evil blasphemers."

Meanwhile, "shoppers" continued to elbow their way into the hostage bazaar. The list of VIPs who traveled to Baghdad read like an International Who's Who: Willy Brandt, Yasuhiro Nakasone, former New Zealand Prime Minister David Lange, Ramsey Clark, Daniel Ortega, Jean-Marie Le Pen, not to mention delegations from Switzerland, Denmark, Canada, Belgium, and even Archbishop Capucci, the Greek Orthodox patriarch of Jerusalem. All pressed for release of the hostages and a peaceful solution to the crisis.

As I took my seat, I noticed British politician Anthony Wedgewood Ben sitting across the aisle. A few days later he would leave Baghdad with a promise from Saddam to release fifteen sick and elderly Britons.

I passed on a cold meat platter of dubious origin and sipped my vodka instead. Behind me I could hear Amani giggling away in a falsetto trill as she chatted with Ben's male secretary. Amani Soliman was an Egyptian I'd hired in Cairo to provide simultaneous translation of the emergency Arab summit. She'd done a first-rate job and had found a niche with CNN ever since, especially in Amman, where we had a huge operation. Since Willy Brandt had plucked our translator/hostage Thomas out of Baghdad, we were in dire need of a translator there, and Amani had volunteered to fill in for a few weeks. She was a tall, slightly overweight woman in her late twenties, moderately attractive, and a notorious flirt. Ingrid immediately christened her "Princess Lumpy," a road name that fit to a T. At our Halloween party she'd made her grand entrance clad as Cleopatra, having spent hours in the hotel's beauty parlor to achieve the "right" look. Now it looked like she was out to play another round of what Ingrid called "*Shtup* the Egyptian!"

As I checked back into the Al-Rasheed, I spotted Muhammad Ali in the lobby. "What room am I in again?" he whispered to his aide. The champ looked in even worse shape than when I'd last seen him at a banquet in Los Angeles. There, Ali had accepted accolades from Jesse Jackson, who'd sauntered over to our table to press the flesh. After the two had chatted a few minutes and Jackson had left, the champ had asked the person seated next to him, "Who was that?"

Oh, brother, I said to myself, as I watched Ali walk slowly to the elevators in what seemed like a daze, so it's come down to this! A few days later, I saw him again, this time on Iraqi TV, during his much touted "interview" with Saddam Hussein. Ali's aide-de-champ did all the talking; Ali mumbled only a few words. Nevertheless, he was rewarded with more than a dozen hostages who eventually flew out with him. For the record, Ali was seated in economy, but made no fuss. Presumably the champ didn't know the difference. If they possessed a shred of human decency . . .

"Hey, how ya doin'?" I said to Richard Roth as I entered the office. I was genuinely glad to see him. In addition to being one of the best reporters at the network, Roth is probably the funniest man I know. Once, when shooting at a Baghdad coffeehouse, Richard stood up in the middle of the joint and played maître d'. "Table for four! Antonelli?" he called out. "We have some names of people here we can't read out," he deadpanned, looking at his clipboard. "They must have gone down the street to the deli." On another occasion, when Naji declined to be interviewed after his weekly tennis match, Roth chased after him into the shower. "Don't you agree the Iraqi Women's Union is sanctioning prostitution," he boldly suggested to another official, "by sending women to Kuwait to sleep with the soldiers?"

Although based in New York, Richard had joined the circus in Eastern Europe and we'd pushed him to seek a post overseas ever since. But when it came to making a personal decision, Roth would agonize for days. Eventually he'd turned down Frankfurt. "It just didn't feel right," he explained, after laboriously running down the pro's and con's.

"So that's it!" I exclaimed, eyeing the four-wire. "Fabulous! How's it working?"

"It works fine," Richard said. "Getting Atlanta to pay attention is another story." I sat down in front of the small gray metal box and flipped a switch.

"Baghdad to Atlanta," I spoke into the microphone. There was silence on the other end of the line. Roth looked at me knowingly. "Baghdad to Atlanta," I repeated, raising my voice. "Baghdad to Atlanta," I said again a few seconds later. "Is it always like this?" I asked Richard.

"Frequently," he replied, raising his eyebrows.

"Hello, Atlanta," I said, my voice up an octave. "The bombs are falling, Atlanta. . . . They're coming through the windows. . . . This line's gonna go down any second. . . . We're all dying here, Atlanta. . . . Oops, now we're all dead. . . ."

"Hello, Baghdad. This is Atlanta. Are you trying to call us?"

"Yeah, Will, I was. I think you guys have to monitor this thing a little more closely."

"I'm sorry. We're kinda busy today. What do you need?"

"I need ya to work out some system where you can hear us immediately, no matter how busy things get. We might not have that much time if the shit hits the fan."

"Yeah, I understand. We're working on getting a few more units here on the desk. They should be installed in a few days."

"Great. Well, I'm just checking in. This is fabulous, by the way."

"Yeah. It certainly changes things. So you got in okay, and Amani's there with you?"

"Roger that. By the way, you got any money down on the Ali comeback fight?"

"What? Is he gonna box again?"

"Nah. I think it was just a vicious rumor," I laughed. "Speak to ya later."

"This is great," I said to Roth, flipping the switch on the box. After all those trips to the embassy, the countless hours waiting for calls at the hotel, the disconnections, the poor quality, the endless frustration, we now had instant communications: a direct telephone line, which bypassed operators and switching stations all the way from Baghdad to Amman to Atlanta, and consequently to more than a hundred countries around the world. They ought to give Eason a medal, I thought, as I reached for a smoke. Since early October, Eason and I had been aware that four-wire service was theoretically possible from Baghdad. Mrs. Awattif had said as much when she'd included the use of an Iraqi TV four-wire on her list of available facilities in telexing her confirmation of our live interview with Tariq Aziz. But, skeptical that it could be installed within the twenty-four-hour-notice time we'd been given for the Aziz interview, we had decided to use telephones instead. Meanwhile, Eason and the folks on the satellite desk continued to pursue the four-wire option. For weeks they cajoled the phone company in Amman, which, in turn, made the arrangements with the PTT in Baghdad. Once the Baghdad to Amman line was established, it was a simple affair to order a connecting line from Amman to Atlanta. But keeping it up and running was another matter.

"There is a problem with your special telephone line," Sadoun would inform me confidentially a few days after my return. "The people at the PTT were told it only goes to Amman, but you speak direct to your headquarters in the U.S."

"That's through a second line from Amman," I said. "It has nothing to do with the Baghdad PTT."

"You understand what I am saying, Robert," he said, putting a hand on my shoulder. "You have tricked them."

"I personally haven't tricked anyone," I protested. "But as long as it's up and working, why don't we just let things be?"

"Do not worry, my friend. For now, things will be all right. We like you and the CNN team."

"I appreciate that, Sadoun," I said sincerely.

"By the way, I want to show you something," he said, pulling a piece of paper out of his drawer. "What do you think of this?" He showed me what looked like an application form with spaces for "Name," "Company," "Date of Entry into Baghdad," etc. "We are going to ask all journalists to register directly with the ministry. That way we shall know who is here, and who has been here before. It will help us to help the foreign press."

"I gotta be honest with ya," I said, shaking my head. "All journalists hate filling in forms. It's a swift pain in the ass. However, if you issued official press cards, after filling in the forms—nice, laminated ones with the stamp of Iraq—every journalist in town would be rushing in here to get one—"

"Press cards!" he interrupted. "Now that is a good idea. . . ."

"Yeah. And once you had a press card, every Iraqi would know you're a bona fide journalist . . ."

"Of course. . . ."

"So consequently, if Iraqis on the street can see we're bona fide journalists, then we wouldn't need minders to go with us to explain that to them in the first place."

"No, Robert, no," he laughed. "I see what you are trying to do, but it is impossible."

"I don't know, Sadoun. Think about it. It would cut down on the ministry's overhead."

The four-wire ended our isolation. Not only was Atlanta able to read us the latest wires at the flick of a switch, but now we were also able to listen to CNN. For the first time, we could hear "World Day," the "International Hour," Bierbauer live at the White House, Blitzer at the Pentagon, Begleiter at the State Department: the "killer B's," as they were sometimes called. No longer did we in Baghdad feel trapped in a cocoon. More important, the four-wire gave us a tremendous competitive edge. If news happened in Baghdad, we could alert Atlanta instantly; conversely, if news broke anywhere else in the world, we would know it long before our colleagues and scramble for Iraqi reaction immediately, consistently beating the competition.

Naturally, the four-wire provoked considerable jealousy, if not downright resentment on the part of other news organizations. There were ugly accusations that we'd unfairly curried favor with the Iraqis to obtain their permission, perhaps even offered a bribe. Nothing was further from the truth. But when they couldn't get the necessary permission to install their own four-wires, well after ours was up and working, at least some of the American networks thought it had to be true. It didn't help matters that Minister Jassim would sometimes wait to begin a news conference until CNN had arrived on the scene—even though U.S. military commanders in Vietnam had done the same thing for CBS and the influential *New York Times*. But most of the press corps in Baghdad hadn't covered Vietnam, or had a limited perspective on such things. From where they stood, it looked as if we were in Saddam's pocket. That was the excuse they offered their headquarters, and their headquarters, in turn, wasted no time having their P.R. departments grind out the party line. As Ed Turner so eloquently put it later, "Nineteen ninety-one is a vintage year for sour grapes."

I drove to the embassy to check in with Joe and deliver his usual box of cigars. Steve Thibault had finally left Baghdad, replaced by his immediate boss, Jim Callahan, who had arrived from the States. Callahan was a nice enough fellow, but one look at him in his bureaucratic button-down, short-sleeve shirt and necktie told me he wasn't the sort to shout out that Saddam Hussein was a scum-bag, at least not in front of the press. I missed Thibault immediately. Bill Armbruster, a quiet, nonassuming guy who'd worked in the Public Affairs office at the embassy in Kuwait, was still around. As was Hanan, a sweet-natured and helpful Iraqi national employed as a secretary by USIS. Bill and Hanan had taken upon themselves the care and feeding of Bosh, an orphaned and emaciated little kitty, which, thanks to their constant attention, now resembled more cat than rat. Blystone had featured Bosh in one of his earlier reports, writing "his progress is watched like a fever chart, as if it could foretell what will happen here." Ever since, Ingrid always made sure a box of Tender Vittles from the Amman Safeway was included in every shipment to Baghdad.

"I want to show you something," Joe said, picking up a telex from his desk. It was a congratulatory message from the President of the United States, praising Wilson's professionalism and courage for speaking out against Iraq's treatment of the hostages. "I'd like you to give a copy of this to Richard Roth," he said, signing his autograph. "He's also responsible, you understand. I want to express my thanks."

On Thanksgiving, Roth had been told that the Red Cross planned to deliver turkey dinners to some of the hostages, perhaps even to the so-called "human shields." He had somehow convinced his minder to accompany him and the crew to the Baghdad Hunt Club where he'd heard the dinners might be prepared. At best, he recalls, he thought he might find a hostage who'd already been "presented" to the media. The Iraqis regularly put hostages on television, in a bizarre and extremely twisted production called "Guest News." Instead, what Richard found upon entering the club were about a dozen Americans talking among themselves in small groups. Roth said he was certain they were indeed human shields, a fact confirmed moments later when they asked him to smuggle out mail. Richard spent about six minutes doing interviews with the men before he was told by Sadoun, who had just arrived, to leave immediately. There had been some kind of mistake. Later, other networks protested they had asked for permission to cover the event and were refused.

That evening, in an exclusive interview with CNN, Joe Wilson called the incident "barbaric." He said it was outrageous that American hostages could be brought to lunch just two blocks from the American chargé's home, when they were denied the right to be visited by their own diplomats, another violation of international law.

For the first time, according to Roth, Wison's comments were censored at the Iraqi TV feedpoint. But the following morning, Wilson called a full-blown news conference and, based on the interviews Richard had done, which by now Joe had screened, he again blasted the Iraqis. His latest comments were subsequently broadcast around the world, and prompted the telex from President Bush.

"So, what's your read on the UN resolution authorizing a military strike by January?" I asked.

"I think it's going to happen," Joe said. "The Soviets fully support our position, but there might be some wiggle room over the exact date."

"So it looks like it's coming down to the crunch," I ventured.

"I think so," he said, stepping back to his desk. "Unfortunately, Baghdad's miscalculated once again."

Before heading back to the Al-Rasheed, I asked Kareem to drive downtown. I wanted to buy a carpet. I'd seen a fabulous "runner" from Iran on my previous trip and decided to take the plunge. It was almost twenty feet long, more than a hundred years old, and made entirely by hand: a steal at five hundred bucks. I'd known very little about oriental carpets before coming to Baghdad, but, like the rest of the press corps, before I left I'd become an "expert." It seemed as if everyone was consumed by "rug fever." After obtaining your exit visa, scheduling a little "souk time" was considered *de rigueur*. Depending on the number of journalists in town, the price of carpets would fluctuate wildly. In the early days, for example, you could purchase a magnificent handmade Baktaran or Tabriz for about three hundred dollars. Later, as the "greed factor" rose, one dealer told me, "If you won't pay this, ABC will." After the ritual haggling, over several cups of mint tea, the deal would be done; then the carpet was rolled up, placed in a brown polyurethane bag, and transported back to the Al-Rasheed. Once there, grown men and women would get down on their knees in front of their colleagues and "ooh" and "aah" as they gently stroked the merchandise and counted the knots. The problem was how to get the booty out of the country and on to your final destination. It seemed to matter little to any of us that we were technically violating the trade embargo. Journalists are, if anything, a resourceful lot, and soon my latest acquisition was neatly rolled and stuffed into an empty tripod case that Richard consented to carry to Amman when he departed.

"Hello, Robert," Naji greeted me as usual.

"How are you?" I asked, expecting the usual response.

"Still surviving," he smiled. "As you can see." Naji was indeed surviving but I thought he looked exceptionally tired. When I told him so, he dismissed it with a flick of the hand. "Not tired, just busy," he said, standing up to draw open a curtain. Again I made my pitch about bringing in the flyaway. Again he said there were "security concerns." "But now you have your special telephone line," he reminded me. "Surely that is a good thing."

"Live *pictures* would be even better."

"You always push," he chuckled.

"That's what I get paid for," I laughed. We talked about the general situation and the Aziz trip to Moscow. He dismissed Gorbachev's insistence that Iraq must withdraw from Kuwait as a mere technicality.

"I am hopeful reason will prevail," he added cryptically. He expressed no concern about the UN resolution that would authorize a military strike. "It is true a war will be a disaster for both sides," he said matter-of-factly, "but for us, the Iraqis, at least we know what we are fighting for. I do not think the American people will support a war of these dimensions for oil. You know, Robert," he said, removing his eyeglasses to clean the lenses, "we have many weapons. Not only chemical and biological weapons, but weapons like fuel bombs. Perhaps one thousand fuel bombs. They are very inexpensive to manufacture, and they explode like nuclear weapons. It will not be as easy as Mr. Bush thinks."

"And you're still planning to bring Israel into it?"

"Of course," he said, without a moment's hesitation. "The Israelis are trying to destroy us too."

"What a mess!" I sighed, perhaps a bit too candidly.

"You must not let this affect you like that," he smiled. "After all, it is a poker game. One side will bluff."

"Do you have to do that in here?" Richard pleaded as I popped a Gauloise into my holder. It was an automatic gesture and I apologized profusely. Roth didn't just have an aversion to cigarette smoke; he also had asthma, a fact he reminded smokers of at every opportunity. He also didn't drink, although there were unconfirmed reports he had actually once been spotted downing a beer.

"I'm really sorry," I said. "It's the pressure."

"It's your life," he moaned like a Jewish mother. "And your liver!"

"So what are you having for dinner tonight?" I asked, as if I didn't know. Roth always traveled with a personal supply of tuna fish, preferably canned in water. "How about some lamb chops for a change?" I suggested.

"I don't think so . . . Amani, pleeeeassse," he whined, as she lit up a Marlboro.

"Take it in the next room," I told her. "A little respect, huh, for the rights of others . . . ? It's a good thing we all love ya, Richard. Otherwise I, for one, would slit my wrists."

"I'll be ready in a minute," he said, making some final additions to his script. "Let's see, I can't say 'hostages'—they'll censor that. I'm tired of calling them guests, or so-called guests. Why don't we just end with this?" he said, scribbling away on a yellow legal pad. "What do you think?"

The copy was vintage Roth: straight, lean, no-nonsense, with the occasional zinger that cut to the quick; in this case, it came at the close. It was perfect, I thought. And I had no doubt it would elude the censors. Asking the editor to insert a picture of Saddam Hussein, Richard had written a line that subtly said it all: "Not every kidnapper leaves a ransom note."

At the stroke of ten, Jim Callahan ushered us into the ambassador's office to meet with Wilson. "For those of you who are newcomers," he said to us, all of whom had been there longer than he had, "I'll quickly review the ground rules for this briefing. . . ."

"Good morning, gentlemen," Joe boomed, entering the office. "And lady," he added with a smile, spotting Marie Colvin of *The London Sunday Times*. "I'm ready for your questions. . . ."

"I'm happy to see any, in fact all Americans," he said when asked if he would meet with a peace delegation of U.S. citizens who had come to Iraq to donate medicine. "We're not at war with these pacifist groups. We, like them, want a peaceful solution. The only war, so far, is the war Iraq started when it invaded Kuwait." Wilson was asked his opinion about a group of American wives due in Baghdad within a few days.

"Frankly," he said, "we prefer to discourage these visits. They only serve to help the Iraqis cynically manipulate the hostages. But of course, I'll meet with any of these women should they wish to see me, and the embassy is here to assist them in any way it can." Joe was then asked for an update on the effect of the sanctions.

"Well, we have evidence many factories have closed. Parts of refineries are also shut down. There are shortages in the petroleum industry. They're in need of lubricants. They're in need of spare parts. I think we're beginning to see the end of the stocks looted from Kuwait," he added. "And I understand pilots with Iraqi Airways are having trouble putting in enough hours to maintain their international licenses. So the air embargo is beginning to have an effect too." Wilson said he understood that for foreigners still trapped in Kuwait City, the food situation had improved "slightly," and added that, by some estimates, about fifty-five tons of medicine had been shipped to Iraq since the beginning of the crisis.

Charlene Coutré Williams was not one of the nine American women who had traveled to Baghdad to visit their husbands. Until a few days ago she had never left her husband's side. Charlene had opted to remain in Kuwait with her husband, Stuart, while most other spouses left when Saddam opened the floodgates. "The food was lousy but we were treated fine," she explained, sitting in our office at the Al-Rasheed. She was a thin, pretty woman I estimated to be in her mid-thirties. "Three days ago, the Iraqis brought us to Baghdad and put us up at the Mansour Melia Hotel. I'd heard that's where hostages were taken before they're released. We were overjoyed. I remember telling Stuart it seemed too good to be true. Then, on the second night, some men, I think they were security guys even though they weren't wearing uniforms, took Stuart away."

"To a strategic site?" I asked.

"Yes, that's what I think," she said, sipping her coffee. "All that time together, and now to be separated like this, it all seems so cruel. Stuart's daughter from his first marriage, Jennifer, decided to come to Baghdad with the other American women. She wanted to get her dad and me out. Now we don't quite know what to do. What do you think?"

"Well, don't give up hope. I imagine there's still a good chance he could be released. You should just attach yourself to the other American women and go through the ritual, you know, the meetings with the Iraqis, the

Speaker of the National Assembly, and other guys I imagine the women will see."

"They actually have a meeting with the Speaker tomorrow," she perked up.

"There ya go. That's usually the first step. Have you spoken to the embassy, by the way?"

"I spoke to them," she said bitterly. "But it seemed they didn't want to do anything. This woman said there was nothing she could really do. When I see what the British embassy does for the British wives staying at the hotel, the visits, the concern, even the small packs of cigarettes and candy, the contrast makes us feel so forgotten. . . ."

"You should call Joe Wilson personally," I suggested. "He's a decent guy. There are so many different stories in this place. Maybe the person you spoke with at the embassy was just feeling overwhelmed."

"Perhaps. Each story's different, I suppose," she said, standing up to leave, "but each story has the same sadness to it."

"Where the fuck is Amani?" I howled. "We need this translated *now*." Iraqi TV had suddenly come on the air with a special bulletin. "Get me that Egyptian slut-meister immediately!"

"She went out shopping again," Tracy said. "But I think she's back in her room. I'll call her." All that woman does is shop, I thought. Not more than twenty-four hours after arriving in Baghdad, Amani had gleefully discovered that everything looted from Kuwait could be had for a song. She'd already purchased a new 35-mm camera for about eighty dollars and every day, it seemed, she was heading back for more. Lucky for her, she was a fabulous translator. Even so, I was concerned that my usual admonishments about playing the black market had probably gone unheeded. I reminded myself to have another talk with her later.

"I'm here. I'm here," she twittered breathlessly, running into the office. "What's going on?"

"How the fuck do I know what's gone on?" I roared. "If I spoke 'worm,' I wouldn't be employing you as a translator, would I?"

"Oh, Robert!" She batted her eyes, pulling up a chair in front of the television set.

"I hear you gave another performance last night for ITN. You know, I don't mind if you belly dance till 4 A.M., but when Iraqi TV goes on the air, it'd be nice to have you here."

"Shush," she snapped. "I'm trying to hear." She looked at the screen and listened intently.

"Sooo?" I asked a few minutes later. "Care to give us a hint?"

"The Belgians," she explained after a moment. "The National Assembly has voted to free all the Belgians."

"That's it?"

"That's all. No more Belgian hostages."

"Belgians! Big fuckin' deal," I laughed. "Baghdad to Atlanta," I spoke into the four-wire.

"Atlanta here. Go ahead."

"Iraq's National Assembly has just voted to release all Belgian hostages. It's hot off the presses. Do you want Roth to go live?"

"You said Belgian hostages?" the voice from the desk queried.

"That's right. Belgians. You heard correctly."

"Hold on, I'll check with the producers." I began to reach for a cigarette, then thought of Richard. "Atlanta to Baghdad," the four-wire crackled.

"Baghdad here," I responded.

"Forget it."

"So, Wienerish, what's with the no-smoking signs?" Ingrid, back for her fourth tour of duty, laughed as she lit up a Camel Light. "Has Roth got you brainwashed?"

"Uh-oh," Richard sighed, as he watched the smoke curl from her mouth. "It's a good thing I'm leaving soon."

"I was just trying to respect the rights of nonsmokers. . . ."

"Give me a break," she wailed. "If Richard doesn't like it, he can write next door. He's got a perfectly good . . ."

"That's my cue," Roth winced, as he fanned the air with a sheaf of papers. "If you need me, I'll be in my room."

"You're one tough customer," I said to Ingrid as I put my feet on the table and prepared to savor a smoke myself.

"I'm serious, Wienerish," she yelped. "I love Richard to pieces but this is not an operating room. So, what's going on?"

"They're gonna want Roth on the four-wire to react to the UN vote. It's gonna come down late, our time, so getting any Iraqi to respond immediately is doubtful."

"What about Naji or Nizar?" she asked.

"I've spoken to both of them, but they won't have anything to say, I suppose, until Eric puts out the official word." Eric was a code-word for Saddam used at the Australian embassy. Ingrid had learned it from an Aussie spook who occasionally was a good source of information. "I'm sure Jassim will hold a news conference tomorrow," I said.

"Anything new at the embassy? How's Joe doing?"

"Joe's fine. Thibault's gone. They finally gave him that assignment in Thailand. His replacement is Jim Callahan, a real Mr. USIS type."

"How's Bosh?" she asked, dipping into the carton she'd brought from Amman to pull out a box of Tender Vittles.

"Bosh is just fine," I assured her. "Is there something in there for us, I hope?"

"Do I ever forget you, Wienerish?" She picked out two liters of potato juice.

"Thank God!" I joked. "Between Richard and Dulmage, this place has the feel of a temperance league."

"That's all in the past," she assured me, placing the bottles on our makeshift bar. "Let's look to the future!"

"A minute to you, Richard," Bob Furnad barked over the four-wire from Atlanta. Furnad was CNN's senior executive producer. Among his duties was supervising important live shots, especially if they involved several "remotes." Remotes for reaction to this historic Security Council vote, which officially drew the line in the sand, would include the United Nations, the White House, the State Department, the Pentagon, and Capitol Hill, as well as Baghdad, Saudi Arabia, Amman, London, Moscow, and Israel. "You'll be talking to Susan Rook," he told Richard as we gathered around the table.

"I'll be back in a second," I said, walking across the hall to look out the window. It was well after working hours at the Foreign Ministry, but the lights in the fifth-floor offices of Tariq Aziz and Nizar Hamdoon were shining brightly. I walked back into Room 906 and informed Richard.

"Thirty seconds," Furnad said as Susan began her introduction. For an instant, Roth looked up at me as if he had something to say, but he apparently changed his mind. Then I heard Susan say, "We go live now to Baghdad and CNN's Richard Roth. . . ."

"Susan," Roth intoned in his deeper than normal broadcast voice, "this city has a lot of flies and tonight I'd like to be one of them on the walls of the Foreign Ministry. . . ."

Jeez! What the hell was that? I said to myself. I could see Ingrid was having a similar reaction. Possibly worse, since she'd buried her head in her hands. Roth, catching a glimpse of both of us, stumbled a second, before he continued to expound on what Baghdad's reaction to Resolution 678 was expected to be.

"A lot of flies?" I shouted after he'd signed off. "A lot of *flies*? Have you entirely lost your mind?"

"What was wrong with it?" he asked sheepishly. "It's a perfectly good analogy. I said, I'd like to be—"

"Spare me," I pleaded. "I know what you said. What I don't understand is *why* you said it."

"I knew you wouldn't like it," he said. "You know, I was going to tell you what I had in mind before we went on, but I was sure you'd insist I say something else."

"Bingo! You're a genius! Well, that's a wrap for tonight," I said as I poured a vodka into my glass. "See, Richard, you've pushed me over the edge. You've driven me to drink."

"When it comes to that," he deadpanned, "a ladybug could push you over the edge."

"Bush is going to speak later today," Fiegener said. "We'll let you know when we get a time. Lemme see," he drawled on, "reaction to the vote . . . U.S. forces have been placed on a higher state of readiness . . . Japan welcomed the resolution . . . Shevardnadze said the resolution's impact gives both sides time to think again. He said it also pledges to the victims in Kuwait that help is on the way, that the countdown has started."

"Anything else, John?" I asked.

"No. That's about it. Oh, when does Holliman get in?"

"He should be here this afternoon. You could check with Amman."

"Amman to Baghdad and Atlanta," came John Holliman's voice over the four-wire.

"Go ahead, John," I said. "We're both here."

"Just wanted to let you know all is indeed confirmed for the flight, and I will see you this afternoon."

"That's fine, John. I'll have a driver out at the airport."

"Fine and dandy. Amman out."

"Okay, John Fiegener," I said, wrapping it up. "We'll be in touch."

"Right. Atlanta out."

IT WAS ALREADY SHAPING UP to be a busy day. In addition to seeking on-camera reaction to the Security Council vote, we'd have to be prepared to react in case President Bush had a surprise or two up his sleeve. But there was something else on my mind. The January 15 deadline gave the world some breathing space, including all of us in Baghdad. But after the fifteenth, who knew? Since August, we'd all been on visas that expired every few weeks or so. Extensions were possible, of course; on my last tour I had stayed more than a month. But any visa extension required writing a letter to the Ministry of Culture and Information, a meeting with Sadoun, or even Naji, and a trip to the Directorate of Residence for the appropriate stamp in the passport. In short, it was a pain in the ass. I didn't want to be going through that as January 15 rolled around. Moreover, by the fifteenth, I wanted a team in place who worked well together and could count on each other should the worst occur.

Eason had already telexed Naji asking that I, as the senior CNN representative in Baghdad, be granted a multiple-entry visa, but Naji had reluctantly said no. No multiple-entry visas were ever granted to journalists, he explained. Now I had another idea. If I could obtain Naji's promise that those of us in Baghdad by the fifteenth could stay indefinitely, it would solve a lot of problems. I wouldn't risk having Blystone, for example, missing the war due to a bureaucratic snafu. What also had to be decided was who the members of the team would be. CNN was limited to seven people: two correspondents, two producers, a cameraperson, a sound technician, and a videotape editor. Naturally, it would be a voluntary assignment. Baghdad always was. But the right mix was critical.

Obviously Ingrid and I were in, and surely Bly, I thought, though Atlanta would have to get his okay when he returned from vacation. But I couldn't see Bubba saying no. Mark, Cynde, and Tracy seemed a natural for the crew; "Axel," "Pearl," and "Cybil" were almost like family. It would be a shame to break them up. The problem would be choosing a second correspondent. Of all our reporters who'd been to Baghdad, only Clancy was second to Bly in terms of war experience. But Jim was in Saudi Arabia and his wife was expecting a baby. Baghdad would be too impractical. We might be stuck in here for months. Doug James was not available either. He had promised his worried daughter that his previous trip to Baghdad would be his last. It would have to be Richard Roth, I decided. Yes indeed, "the Dick of Death" fit the bill. He and Bly got along swimmingly, and Ingrid and I adored him. On top of that, Richard was among the most popular reporters with all the crews. There was only one problem. Richard would have to make a personal decision. Oh well, I thought. We still had a month and a half to go.

"SO, WHADDAYA THINK?" I asked Ingrid, explaining my plan.

"It's a great idea," she agreed. "And Richard would be perfect."

"I can see it now," I laughed. "Roth chained to the wall in the bomb shelter, with you and I on either side of him, smoking to beat the band."

"You're cruel, Wienerish."

"Hey, seriously, we should ask Mrs. Nihad if one of the shelters will have a No Smoking section. That's probably the first thing Roth will want to know."

"I'll get right on that after the briefing," she joked. "Well, I'm off to see Joe."

"I am almost positive the minister will see journalists later," Naji said. "Only he can make such a statement."

"Surely you must have some reaction to the resolution," I insisted.

"Of course I have a reaction, Robert. This resolution is another attempt to intimidate us, another form of pressure. And you know, we have said many times we will never succumb to pressure."

"The consequences after January 15 seem very real," I suggested.

"I have no way of knowing that. For me, January 15 is just another date on the calendar."

"May I use some of this, Naji? How about on background? My network's hurting for Baghdad reaction."

"No, I wish you wouldn't. These are my personal views. The minister will speak officially."

"In any case, I have your agreement about visas for a final CNN team."

"Yes, you have my agreement," he said. "Give the names to Sadoun as soon as you can and I shall make the necessary arrangements."

"So that's the deal," I said to Eason, having made the call from my room, to avoid the whole world listening in on the four-wire. "You'll have to check with Bly and run it by Cynde. I'll speak to Tracy and Mark here, but I think this is the best team for the job."

"Understood. By the way, did Earl have a chance to speak to you yet about our plans for the night of January fifteenth?"

"No. Whaddya got cookin'?"

"Well, keep this under wraps but on the night of the fifteenth, we're gonna blow everything out. Live from everywhere. In addition to our own reports, we're bringing in experts, analysts, you name it. We're really gonna make it something special. Anyway, what we'd also like to do is have a live interview with Saddam Hussein. . . ."

"On January fifteenth . . . ?"

"Yeah, coinciding with the deadline," he emphasized.

"Live . . . ?"

"Yeah, live."

"You know, Saddam hasn't done live," I reminded him. "We went through this before for the first interview."

"Well, maybe he will now. It's worth a try. Just get the flyaway in there and make it happen," he said blithely.

"Will Bernie be doing the interview?"

"I don't know if he'll want to be in Baghdad on January 15. Ed's gonna speak with him."

"Anything else?"

"Isn't that enough?" he laughed.

"You just love it, don't ya," I quipped.

"Well, if anyone can do it, you can, my man. Good luck!"

"So this is it! Yeah," Holliman exclaimed, bounding into the office. "This is all right. This is okay." He surveyed the workspace before peering out the window at the swimming pool and gardens. "What's that over there?" he asked, pointing to the futuristic-looking, fifty-four-meter-high Baghdad Tower in Zawra Park.

"That's a revolving restaurant and discotheque," I explained. "We call it the Giant Mushroom. If there's war, you'll be able to inform our viewers, 'Chevy, the Giant Mushroom is on its ear. . . .' "

"Yeah. Okay. I understand," he chuckled.

"If you look to the left over there, on top of that hill, you'll notice a small missile site."

"I see. A missile site. Right in your own backyard. That's just great," he laughed nervously.

"Please, where you want these?" the porter called from the hall.

"Oh, those two go in here," John told him, pointing to two large boxes balanced precariously on the luggage cart. "The bags go in my room." He looked at his key and gave the porter the number. "How much do I give this j'moke?" he asked, pulling out an Iraqi ten-dinar note.

"That's thirty dollars," I explained. "Hell, I don't tip that well at the Ritz."

"Uh-oh," he said. "Thirty dollars. No, I don't want to tip this gentleman thirty dollars just for unloading two bags. Do you think he'd take American?"

"I'm sure he will," I smiled.

"Good. Then here's five dollars for your trouble, sir," John said after fishing into his wallet for a portrait of Abraham Lincoln. "Oh, before I forget," he said an instant later, "this is for you." He reached into his duty-free bag and came up with a bottle of Finlandia. "Clear liquid. I believe that is your preference, sir."

"Indeed it is," I laughed. "And yours?"

"I'm a brown liquid man, myself. But they didn't have Jack Daniels at Amman duty-free."

"Play your cards right and you can probably get some from Joe Wilson at the American embassy. That's assuming the 'dips' haven't already polished off what was stocked in the commissary."

"Okay. I'll remember that," he said, walking over to study the huge collage that hung on the wall in the edit suite, titled "Dream-O-Vision: TV at Ground Zero."

"I think Mark and Cynde started that, and it just kept on growing," I explained.

"Whose bra and panties are those?" John asked, with a gleam in his eye.

"Cynde's," I smiled. "She used to do her laps in them because she forgot her bathing suit. It created quite a stir."

"I'll bet," he laughed.

The collage had become the focal point for everyone's "wish list," and included magazine pictures of such things as pizza slices and an automatic ice-making machine; wrappers from chocolate bars, Oreo cookies, Pepto-Bismol, and Imodium for diarrhea; erotic passages from a Sidney Sheldon novel; bowling scores, stickers from other news organizations, cartoons, news clips, an artistic smear of peanut butter, and a plastic tube of orange drink, which we had fitted with a battery and dubbed The Baghdad Vibrator.

By the time the war started, Cynde's brassiere would disappear from the board. Popular paranoia had it that the culprit was Iraqi Security. But realism seemed to dictate it was probably nicked by a Brit journalist on his way to a party.

"We are hopeful for a peaceful solution," said President Bush, "but if there must be war, we will not permit our troops to have their hands tied behind their backs, and I pledge to you there will not be any murky endings. Let me assure you," the President added, "should military action be required, this will not be another Vietnam."

As usual, we were gathered around the four-wire when suddenly Bush announced he was going the "extra mile." The President said he would issue an invitation to Foreign Minister Tariq Aziz to come to Washington during the latter part of the week of December 10, and he was asking Secretary of State James Baker to go to Baghdad, where he hoped Saddam Hussein would receive him "at a mutually convenient time between December 15 and January 15 of next year."

"Holy shit!" I blurted out. "This is terrific news!"

"These are not negotiations," the President stressed. "I hope what it does is demonstrate that we are prepared to go face-to-face and tell him how committed we are to the United Nations resolutions. I don't think Saddam has felt this commitment." Uh-oh! Quit while you're ahead, George, I said to myself. "When you've done what he's done," Bush continued, "I don't see that there's room for concession, there's room for giving something to save face. That's not the way you treat aggression, and we're not going to treat it any differently than I've outlined here." Bush said he was not optimistic about the diplomatic effort he had just proposed. "I can't tell you that I think we're going to have great success on all this," he added frankly.

"Well, it's a good first step, but Jesus Christ . . ."

"And that thing about not 'saving face,' " Ingrid wailed.

"Doesn't he realize that in this part of the world—"

"Hello, Baghdad," Will King interrupted over the four-wire.

"Go ahead, Will," I answered.

"E.T. just called down to the desk. For tonight's feed, he wants you guys to put together a profile of Tariq Aziz."

"You know, the feed's in less than two hours . . ."

"I know. I know. That's what I told him, but he's insistent."

"Look, it's a fine idea, Will, but we don't have much time."

"I understand," he said sympathetically, "but what could you do?"

"Let's see," I said, trying to think quickly as I looked at my watch. "First of all, you'll have to edit most of it in Atlanta. Pictures shouldn't be a problem. We've got plenty of stuff of Aziz with Primakov, Aziz with King Hussein, Aziz at Revolutionary Command Council meetings, you know, that sort of stuff. Have the library run a search and pull tape now. What I'm really gonna need is some editorial information, background stuff, a detailed biography. And I'm gonna need sound. We can pull a bite from Aziz himself, but we really should have someone talking about Aziz, his qualifications, his skill, you know what I mean—"

"Hold on. Hold on," he interrupted. "We're doing an interview in a half-hour or so with a guy named Ken Katzman. He's a former CIA type who's been to Baghdad and has followed the Iraqi leadership."

"Has he ever met Aziz?" I asked.

"I don't know if he's met him, but he certainly knows who he is."

"My mailman knows who Aziz is too," I joked, "but I'm not putting him on television."

"No, no," Will protested. "This guy Katzman is a legitimate expert, analyst, whatever."

"Then Katzman will have to do," I said. "I know for sure Joe Wilson's not gonna go on camera. He'll defer to Washington. And Naji or Nizar won't go on TV either. That's not the way it's done over here."

"Do you need anything else?" he asked.

"Just that editorial information as soon as you can get it."

"I've already got Aziz with Primakov, Arafat, Waldheim, and on TV the other night," Tracy hollered from the other room. "What else do you want?"

"Aziz and Saddam!" I shouted. "Also, rack up that bite about pride, the one he gave to Bly and Clancy. I don't know if we're gonna use it, but I want it just in case."

"What do you want to do about my 'nightwrap'?" Richard asked. "We're almost two-thirds done." Richard's piece covered Iraq officially rejecting what it called "the U.S.-imposed Security Council resolution." After chairing a meeting of the Revolutionary Command Council, Saddam had issued a statement saying Iraq "would not bow to the policy of arrogance and terrorism."

"Finish it," I said. "We'll give 'em two for the price of one tonight. John here will handle Aziz."

"We can do this!" Holliman eagerly agreed.

I walked into the other room and placed a telephone call to Nizar. His secretary said he was in a meeting and I left a message. I picked up the phone again and called Naji. "I'm really under the gun," I explained. "Can't you give me something . . . even on background?"

"The minister might have something to say tomorrow," he said.

"With all due respect, I can't wait that long," I pleaded.

"Well," he said after a pause, "it would be very difficult to turn down Bush's offer. We are not happy with the ground rules, but we shall probably accept. What is important is if Baker comes to listen, not just to lecture. . . ."

"Thanks a million," I said. "I really appreciate it."

"Atlanta to Baghdad," Will called over the four-wire.

"Tell Will I'll be right there," I shouted as I double-checked my notes. I ran into 906. "Go ahead, Will," I said, taking my seat.

"I've got a biography of Aziz here, when you're ready for it . . ."

"We're ready now, Will. Shoot!"

"Tariq Aziz is the only Christian among Saddam Hussein's inner circle. . . ." Holliman and I furiously took notes. "He received a degree in English literature from Baghdad University. . . ."

"This'll make great TV," I laughed to Ingrid.

"In 1968, after a power struggle . . ."

"Keep writing, John," I said. "I've got to take a piss." By the time I sat down again, Will was wrapping things up. The biography added little to what I already knew about the man.

"And that's all there is. Now let me tell you what the library has," Will said, reviewing a shot list. "I'll get back to you when I have the Katzman bite. One other thing," he added. "I know you guys are pressed for time, but if you could let us know as soon as possible what you'll need inserted here, it'll help a lot. The producers want to turn this around and get it on the air right after the bird."

"We haven't even written the piece yet," I said curtly.

"I know. I know," Will said. "But when you can . . ."

"Okay, let's go to work," I said to Holliman, who was seated at his computer. I lit a Gauloise and paced around the room. "Tough, shrewd, and articulate," I began, "have all been used to describe Tariq Aziz, the only Christian in Saddam Hussein's inner circle . . ." For the next twenty minutes, the two of us hammered out a script, including the soundbite about Arab pride that I thought might work well with John's stand-up close. The close would be based on the comments from Naji, "a high-ranking Iraqi government official."

"It's Will for you," Ingrid called out to me.

"Go ahead," I said, rushing to the four-wire.

"I've got that Katzman bite. Is now a good time to—"

"Go," I interrupted.

"He's pretty well up in the Iraqi government hierarchy," Will read at dictation speed. "His influence on the President of Iraq will be positive and constructive."

"That's it? That's the best you could come up with? It's a bullshit bite!" I fumed. "We already know Aziz is quote pretty well up in the Iraqi government hierarchy. Naturally, he's got influence."

"Yeeaaah, I agree it's not the best. I think there was some kinda miscommunication about what we wanted from the interview."

"Will, it ain't brain surgery!"

"I know. I know. Well, what do you want to do?" he asked plaintively.

"Piss on it! If you have to, you can throw it in after the first graph, but we probably shouldn't use it at all."

"So, are you guys okay? Will ya make it all right?"

"I don't know. We haven't started writing yet," I joked. "We were waiting for the bite . . ."

"What! You're kidding me, right . . . ?"

"Will, have I ever once missed deadline?"

"No. I can't think of a time . . ."

"So why do you always ask me?" I laughed. "Seriously, we'll be fine."

We finished the script, John shot his stand-up, and Tracy edited as much as she could. I gave Atlanta final instructions about what needed to be "covered." We made deadline just under the wire, but we made it. And in the news biz, that's what counts.

"YOU SEE, we couldn't have done that without the four-wire," I said to John as we relaxed over a drink. "If you had to rely on the telephones here, no fuckin' way!"

"I don't know about the four-wire, my friend, but we couldn't have done it without you. That was mighty impressive."

"Well, it's a team effort. And everyone on this team is pretty solid."

"I'll say," he agreed. "I could grow to like the place."

"Well, this clear liquid, as you call it, certainly makes it palatable at night," I laughed. "How about dinner?"

I called room service.

"THAT WAS WORTH $180, wouldn't you agree?" I smirked as we polished off the last of the lamb chops.

"Gee whiz, $180!" John laughed. "I don't think I've ever had a $180 meal on CNN since I joined the company."

"Well, neither did I, until I came to Baghdad. I shudder to think what they're gonna say in the accounting department."

TRADITIONALLY, THERE'S ALWAYS SOME TENSION between the people who cover the news and the people who pay for the people who cover the news. At other networks, this tension probably exists on a grand scale. But at CNN, where the budget is smaller and the grip on the dollar is tighter, it truly goes from the sublime to the ridiculous. To cover the landing of the space shuttle *Columbia* back in 1981, "The World's Most Important Network" booked me into a foul-smelling, roach-infested, horrid little scumbox near Edwards Air Force Base, a bargain, or so CNN thought at the time, at $17.50 a night. I was profoundly jealous of my colleagues at the other nets who were permitted to spend another few dollars to repose at a Travelodge up the road. But, being a good company man, I just sent another roach to roach heaven with the heel of my shoe, pulled a semen-stained blanket over my head, and attempted to get some sleep. When we returned to the hotel late the following night, having been up since four in the morning to prepare for the landing, I was astonished to find that my room was occupied. Another guest's suitcase stood next to mine. But that was nothing compared to what our engineer at the time, Jerry Koch, was greeted by when he unlocked his door. His room was also occupied, by an elderly couple fornicating on his bed. Naturally, I protested to the management, which said it would discount the room. CNN was so delighted with this unexpected bargain, it booked me into the same motel on the next trip.

CNN had come a long way from those days to a $180 lamb chop dinner at the Al-Rasheed, but the bean counters were still sticklers. My archnemesis in accounting, the formidable Alma Knott, vice president of finance, called me into her office after our award-winning coverage of Eastern Europe and asked me to explain just why I'd spent the equivalent of $54 a day per person to feed our staff during the violent Romanian revolution.

"You had several drivers over there. Why couldn't you have sent one of them to a convenience store, like a 7-Eleven, for cold cuts and a case of Cokes?" she wanted to know. "If you bought luncheon meats and made sandwiches, the company wouldn't have to pay for expensive hotel food." I attempted to explain to Alma that one of the reasons the Romanians were so hot under the collar was that there was absolutely nothing to eat in their country. The only item that could have been displayed in a convenience store, had there been one, would have been a loaf of moldy week-old bread, or perhaps a boiled egg.

"I understand," Alma finally drawled. "Maybe Romania was exceptional, but keep in mind what I've said. On the road, those convenience stores could save us a bundle."

(Note to future journalists: Although Alma has long since retired from CNN, since this little anecdote appeared Ms. Knott expended considerable effort to make my tenure at CNN a nightmare, as far as her accounting department was concerned.)

Nevertheless, remember this golden rule: You will never run afoul of a credible news executive spending what's necessary to cover a story . . . but you will be in a whale of trouble saving money and missing the story.

John already had coffee brewing by the time I arrived in the office.

"What kind of play did we get on the Aziz piece?" I asked. "I assume you've checked in with Atlanta."

"Yeah. Good play," he said cheerily. "The 'International Hour,' 'The World Today,' 'NewsNight.' I think they used it on most every cast."

"Great. Any other news break overnight?"

"Let's see," he said, reviewing his notes. "Three thousand Marine reservists are being called up . . . A flight of Stealth bombers is being sent to the Gulf . . . Bush postponed his trip to Japan. That's about it."

"Any official word on whether Iraq has accepted Bush's offer?"

"Not yet," he replied. "At least Atlanta says there's nothing on the wires."

"Well, as Naji pointed out, they'll probably have to accept." An instant later we were interrupted as loudspeakers at mosques throughout the city blared and church bells tolled. "Martyrs' Day," I said, looking at my watch. It was 8 A.M. "We'll try to get something from Wilson when he appears at the service." All ranking members of the diplomatic corps were expected to attend a memorial ceremony later in the morning at the Martyrs' Monument, dedicated to the fallen of the Iran-Iraq War. In Baghdad it was called the Gulf War.

"Morning, boys!" Ingrid saluted us, as she entered the room. "Did you guys order any Turkish coffee?" Ingrid preferred Turkish in a tall glass with milk to get her engine started.

"Sorry darlin'," I said, calling room service. "You disappeared early last night."

"Yeah, I had a couple of drinks with my friend Norbert, then stopped up at ITN."

"Was Miss Amani on stage again?" I inquired.

"Jesus! Was she ever!" Ingrid laughed.

"Ya know, we're really gonna have to find a permanent translator. When her visa's up, we're outta luck."

"I know," she agreed. "I'm gonna speak to Mr. Petros about it—you know, my Arabic teacher."

"You have time for Arabic lessons along with everything else you have to do?" John marveled. "Ingrid, you're amazing."

"Gee, John," I laughed. "I didn't know you were an investigative reporter."

"So that's the deal," I said to Richard. "It'd be you and Bly, me and Ingrid, and Mark, Cynde, and Tracy. Whaddya think?"

"It's tempting," he said with a grin. "I'll have to think about it."

"So, what else is new?" I laughed.

"What do you mean, what else is new? This is potentially a life or death decision."

"For you, every decision is a matter of life and death."

"C'mon," he smiled. "There are a lot of factors to consider."

"There aren't that many factors," I said. "Either you decide to stay here and cover a war 'live' from behind the lines, a journalistic first, or you'll go to Saudi Arabia to join a 'pool' of *shmegeggies* led around by the nose by the U.S. military. C'mon, Richard, you've seen those news conferences: 'General, how are *we* doing? Are *we* prepared? Jesus, those guys are already brainwashed. It's embarrassing!"

"Yeah, I know. You're right," he sighed.

"Talk about fuckin' cheerleaders!"

"Well, I wonder just how much we'll be able to do here," he said.

"I don't know. Obviously, there'll probably be some restrictions. There already are. It's a gamble, but no one's ever done this before. So, think about it—but I need an answer soon. I thought I had more time, but Naji wants me to submit a list of names as soon as possible."

"Hmmm," he murmured, tapping a pencil on his legal pad.

"I can just see it," I laughed. "Trapped in a bomb shelter for months with me, Ingrid, and Bly chain-smoking till we dropped."

"Don't think that hasn't occurred to me," he smiled.

"Trust me. That would be the least of your worries."

"I'm afraid of that too."

"C'mon," I whispered. "Aren't you 'one of the good Jews'?"

"Joe didn't have much to say," Ingrid said, returning from the ceremony. "As of this morning, he still hadn't heard from the Foreign Ministry. There's not going to be a briefing today, but we can call him at the embassy."

"How were the festivities?" I asked.

"Oh great, Wienerish. Great pictures. I cut a deal with CBS to share tape so we'd have two crews. There was a lot of color."

"I spoke to Roth about January 15," I said.

"Oh yeah, good. What'd he say?"

"What do you think he said?"

"He'll have to think about it," she laughed.

"Exactly. Well, Richard's outta here tomorrow and I'll need an answer by then. I don't know what we're gonna do if he says no. You agree we shouldn't go with someone who hasn't been here before?"

"Absolutely, Wienerish."

"I suppose we could just have one correspondent and I could begin reporting again. . . ."

"You don't want to do that, do you? Anyway, you've got too many other things to take care of."

"Yeah, I know. We really should have two full-time reporters. Earl wants to go that route too. You never know what could happen. What do you think about Holliman?" I asked.

"Hmmm, I don't know . . . he's sort of . . . um . . ."

"Gee whiz?"

"Yeah, gee whiz," she smiled.

"That he is, but he's got a great fuckin' attitude and his work last night was fabulous. Furthermore, he's easy to get along with."

"I agree. I guess Holliman would be okay."

"All right, let's pencil him in if Roth says no. I haven't even spoken to John about it yet. But based on what I've seen so far, I think he'd go for it."

Iraq said it accepted Bush's offer for face-to-face talks but would seek "serious and deep dialogue," not "informal meetings, as the U.S. President wanted to use as a pretext for American public opinion, the Congress, and the international community to achieve his preplanned objectives." The Revolutionary Command Council said the proposal was accepted "even though the arrogant President of the United States, George Bush, has already rejected dialogue, voicing his contempt for the Arabs and Muslims and all those who believe in God and human values."

The RCC added that any serious discussion would be based upon Saddam Hussein's initiative of August 12. "Palestine and other occupied territories would remain before our eyes, and at the forefront of the issues that we will discuss in any dialogue," the statement read.

"That's a hell of an acceptance," I laughed.

"I'll say," John agreed.

"Well, a lot of that's for public consumption, I suppose. I remember something Begleiter once told me. I think he'd heard it first from his college professor. 'If you don't believe in a double standard, don't practice diplomacy.' "

"I see you're almost packed," I said, walking into Richard's room. "You want to leave any of those here?" I asked, looking at a huge pile of copies of *Newsday*, the *Village Voice*, and *New York* magazine.

"I haven't finished reading them yet," he said.

"So, I take it you won't be coming back." Richard had informed Atlanta he was taking a few days off in Rome before tentatively heading for Dhahran.

"I might come back for one more rotation," he explained, "but I can't make a decision about the fifteenth. I'd have to see how it feels if I come back the next time."

"I'm sorry I can't wait that long, but I wish you a lotta luck. I assume you can recognize a jeep?"

"I'm afraid that's about all I can recognize," he smiled. "I don't know anything about that military stuff."

"Don't worry about that. They'll tell you what you're seeing as they personally take you around to see it," I laughed.

"I know . . . I know . . . I know it's going to be awful," he admitted. "This story has so much more . . ."

"Texture!"

"Yeah, texture," he agreed.

"You got it. . . . What did Bernstein call it? 'The Capital of Dread.' "

"HEY, WIENERISH, we're gonna wanna do the World Peace Festival tomorrow, right?" Ingrid asked as I stepped back into the workspace.

"Absolutely. It's a giant!" I laughed. For days, the lobby of the Al-Rasheed had been festooned with posters, banners, and other paraphernalia promoting the festival, which would feature rallies and sports competitions between participants from several countries including Japan, the United States, Canada, India, and Mexico. Saddam's son, Uday Hussein, was expected to attend in his capacity as president of the Iraqi Sports Federation, along with a number of high-ranking Iraqi government officials. The festival was supposed to coincide with World Peace Day, but when the desk checked with both the United Nations and the Associated Press they said they'd never heard of the event. "This is not a political thing," an American basketball player named John Quigley had told me in the hotel lobby. "We just felt peace beats the alternative."

THE END OF A CREW'S ROTATION was always a good reason to hoist a few and since Richard didn't drink we all felt obliged to celebrate for him. It had been another long day, and by midnight we were suitably anesthetized. Roth's background was in radio and he was forever entertaining us with one broadcasting shtick or another. His latest became known as RADIO WIENER, which he recorded on audio tape and left behind for us to remember him by. Though it began as a joke, hardly a word was uttered on the four-wire from Baghdad to Atlanta from that day on until the war began, without Roth's "Sign On" and "Sign Off" at the beginning and end of the day.

In the morning Atlanta was greeted by:

> Good morning. This is W-I-E-N-E-R beginning its broadcast day. We are operating on an assigned frequency of Baghdad 439899, general licensing number 4501. Comments on the schedule can be made to general manager Achmed Bob Wiener, 431 Friedrickstrasse. Thank you very much. This is your announcer, Richard Roth, speaking.

And when the day was "wrapped" they'd be treated to this:

> This is W-I-E-N-E-R concluding its broadcast day. Thank you very much for joining us. We will be signing on in just a few hours with the best of Baghdad. If this had been an actual alert, you would have been instructed where to tune in your area for news and official information. This has only been a test. Join us later today with the entire cast, crew, secretaries, and general manager of the earth station. Thank you very much. This is your announcer, Richard Roth, speaking. Good night.

"One trip doesn't hinge on the other," Wilson explained. "Whatever results from the Aziz meeting in Washington, Baker's still going to come to Baghdad." I had accompanied John to the embassy for a private briefing with Joe, part of an "orientation" tour that would also include paying a courtesy call on Naji and perhaps Nizar. A few hours earlier Iraq had test-fired three or four Scud missiles, creating momentary panic as coalition forces were immediately placed on a state of high alert. Though the warheads landed within Iraq's borders, Joe was still reeling from the effects of the launch.

"When that telephone call came . . . in 'real time,' and the guy on the other end of the line said, 'The balloon is up!' my heart almost stopped," he recalled with a muted laugh. "One thing I've learned is from now on, I'm going to bring an extra pair of undershorts with me to the office."

"So are you saying when Aziz gets to Washington there'll be no negotiations at all?"

"Exactly. Off the record, Robert, we're gonna hose him! We're going to reiterate our public position, what we've been saying all along, and that's all. We want him to be able to report back to Saddam to assure him that we're serious, that we're not bluffing. Now, when Baker comes to Baghdad, that's something else. That's the meeting you want a ticket to," he smiled.

"What happens then?"

"Baker will offer Saddam four things. One, he'll guarantee his army won't be attacked, that he can leave Kuwait without fear of reprisal. Two, he'll guarantee there'll be dialogue between the U.S. and Iraq, real dialogue like Saddam wants. Three, he'll promise President Bush will tone down the rhetoric, the references to Hitler, that sort of thing. And four, Baker will promise the Palestinian question will be put on the front burner, after a 'suitable' period of time—"

"That's linkage," I interrupted.

"We'd prefer to call it 'loose-linkage,' " he smiled.

"If you don't believe in a double standard, don't practice diplomacy," I muttered.

"What was that?" Joe asked with a grin.

"It's not important," I said. "But Baker's four promises are only contingent on Saddam first accepting to withdraw from Kuwait?"

"That's correct," he said.

"What have you heard about a special videotape that's been prepared for Aziz that will give him a pretty graphic impression of the military hardware Iraq's up against?" John asked. "I'm told the tape shows things like the M1A1 Abrams zooming through the desert, and the Tomahawk missile and Stealth fighters doing their thing. . . ."

"I think I heard something about that," Joe said. "But I'm not sure."

We spent a few more minutes discussing the hostage situation and the specific concerns expressed by Charlene Coutré Williams.

"I disagree with her," Joe said. "I've been over to the Mansour Melia twice already to meet with the wives, and I'm going back this afternoon. But if you speak with her before then, tell her to please feel free to give me a call."

"I'LL BE WITH YA IN A MINUTE," I said to John as we walked out of the chancery. "I need to stop by USIS for a sec." I strolled over to the building and went upstairs to Callahan's office. There was something I'd wanted to copy down in my notebook ever since I'd first read it several months before. His office was empty as I carefully took the reference book down from the shelf. It was a guide to protocol and decorum for foreign service officers and diplomats that had been written long ago. The first chapter was entitled "Diplomacy."

"Diplomacy," I copied down, "is the application of intelligence and tact to the conduct of official relations between governments . . . the conduct of business between states by peaceful means."

The meeting with Naji was uneventful, but it gave him and Holliman an opportunity to meet face to face, important in the long run. John told Naji he was anxious to speak with him or Latif Nasif Jassim as often as possible, and Naji promised to arrange an exclusive interview with the Minister of Culture and Information. The highlight of the afternoon occurred just before seeing Naji. As we first entered Sadoun's office to pay our respects, I reminded the portly Iraqi I'd soon need to extend my visa. "Robert, my friend," Sadoun joked as he playfully slapped my shoulder, "you do not need a visa extension. We will send you home in a coffin." Holliman was not amused.

"This guy, Mr. Alla, is really okay," John proclaimed. "I think we can work with him. He seems to understand the Western press." Alla had become our latest minder, since Mazin and Nasir suddenly found other commitments. He claimed to be a journalist, although Ingrid was convinced he worked for the secret police. "Well, everything's possible," I said when she mentioned it. "The Iraqi Mind Fuck has a long reach."

"That's good to hear," I said to John. "Still I wouldn't jump to conclusions. These guys aren't called minders for nothing. Take Mr. Mazin, for example. He was often very helpful, but he never forgot who he was really working for."

"Well, this guy Alla seems all right," John insisted. "I think he wants to help us. He also said he'd like to get together for dinner tonight. He's gonna stop by later."

"Why not?" I laughed. "You should try *masgouf* at least once while you're here."

I sat back down at the computer and continued drafting my letter to Naji. What I hoped would be the final letter. The final rotation. Mark and Tracy had tentatively agreed to return in January, though I sensed Tracy was still uneasy and Mark needed to break the news to his wife. But Cynde, on R&R back home in Beijing, had eagerly agreed by phone, and Tracy, I think, was swayed, knowing her buddy "Pearl" would be right beside her. As expected, Holliman had eagerly agreed too, though his wife Diane was understandably dismayed by the news. "I'll see you by Christmas, honey," John had told her on the phone. "I'll explain more about it then." In fact, most of us were going home for the holidays and planned to return to Baghdad the first week of January. Earl Casey and I were in the process of figuring out who'd man the store while we were gone.

"Fifty-fifty," Saddam said in English when asked whether there'd be peace or war. The Iraqi President had made the statement during an interview with French TV. ". . . If they want to make this meeting [the U.S.-Iraqi talks] a path to dialogue, we are closer to peace. But if they want to make this meeting nothing other than a formal exhibition for the American Congress, the American people, or international public opinion, simply to give themselves good conscience to say, 'There, we've tried to dialogue with Iraq without Iraq renouncing its position'—in that case, we are closer to war," Saddam told the two correspondents from Antenne-2.

I'd spoken with Nizar on the telephone a couple of times since the Bush announcement. Eason had suggested we try to put a reporter on Aziz's plane, but Hamdoon was not optimistic. Nevertheless, he readily agreed to meet me and John in his office for a short chat. Nizar, whom I'd often found reticent, was more forthcoming than I'd ever seen him. He clearly had something to say, and voiced no objection when we opened our notebooks. "This is on background," he reminded us. "You may call me a senior Iraqi government official." The Aziz-Baker meeting could be a positive step, he declared. His President was under "tremendous pressure." He did not elaborate. He said that during the upcoming talks "everything is on the table." Did that include withdrawing from Kuwait, we asked? Hamdoon wouldn't say. "Everything is on the table," was as far as he would go. I asked him if Iraq would still insist any withdrawal from Kuwait be "linked" to the Palestinian question.

"It need not be linked directly," he said slowly. "We might be willing to accept a loose-linkage, so long as the issue was responsibly addressed." Jesus! I couldn't believe my ears.

"A loose-linkage?" Holliman repeated.

"Yes," said Nizar. "What is important is the Palestinian question eventually be part of an agenda." I was almost too stunned to speak. I couldn't mention what Joe had said, since that was off the record, but holy shit! What was going on here? I asked Nizar if he, like I, had noticed a perceptible softening of rhetoric in the latest issues of *The Baghdad Observer*.

"Perhaps," he said, but he seemed to attach little importance to it.

We talked about CNN doing another interview with Saddam Hussein on January 15 and the importance, perhaps now more than ever, of getting the flyaway into Baghdad. "If for nothing else than the Baker visit," I stressed. "We're going to want to hear from officials on both sides." Nizar politely promised his help on both these matters.

"As usual, I thank you for your time," I said.

"Not at all, Bob," he smiled. "We shall be in touch."

"DID YOU HEAR WHAT I think we just heard?" John asked immediately after we'd left Nizar's office.

"Jesus Christ! You've got a hell of a story," I whistled. "I want to touch base with Ed on this one, and I want him to approve the script." We raced back to the hotel with that gloriously giddy feeling that comes from knowing you have something no one else has, and what you have is hot!

THE SCRIPT WENT through a couple of revisions before Ed finally signed off on it. He insisted Naji be identified as a "high-ranking Iraqi government official who has usually been reliable in the past."

"That's just covering his ass," John huffed. "Why do we need it?"

"If anything, he's covering the network's ass," I said, "but I don't have a serious objection to it. This story's so goddamn sensitive." Ed also suggested we include the fact that using journalists as conduits to test the waters on potential bargaining positions was nothing new. Former Secretary of State Henry Kissinger had effectively used the technique during his so-called "shuttle diplomacy." Every line of the script was meticulously crafted, quoting Nizar precisely. There was no wiggle room for anything less.

"We're gonna want Holliman on live," Will said shortly after we filed. "We're also efforting reaction from the White House, but we don't expect that for a few hours. How soon can John be ready?" As usual, Holliman was ready at the drop of a hat. He pulled up a chair in front of the four-wire.

"Be careful," I advised him. "Keep your answers confined to the script exactly as we've written it. Atlanta may throw you a curve ball." He gave me a thumbs-up as we listened to the introduction.

"John, when you reported the official said Saddam Hussein was under quote tremendous pressure, what did he mean?" the anchor asked. "Is that pressure from inside or outside the government?"

"Probably both," John said. "These have got to be tough times for the President of Iraq." Damn, I thought. Holliman was probably right, but that's not what Hamdoon had told us. He had simply said under "tremendous pressure." Period. Case closed. We weren't accurate if we reported where the pressure was coming from. For all I knew it could have been from other Arab leaders. The day before, Saddam had hosted what was billed as a mini-summit, attended by Yasir Arafat, King Hussein, and Yemen's vice president, Ali Salem al-Baidh. According to the Iraqi News Agency, the four agreed to seek "a permanent and comprehensive peace based on legitimacy and principles of justice and fairness. . . ." The rest of the live shot passed without incident, but I was worried by that "pressure" line.

"A senior administration official cautioned CNN not to take too seriously the idea that some sort of deal might be found," Will told us a few hours later. "The official said Iraq is a one-man show. They might be trying to float rumors to avoid a military strike as long as possible."

"C'mon, Hamdoon was your source on that, right?" Allen Pizzey of CBS asked slyly. Pizzey and his producer, Joe Halderman, had stopped by the workspace for a nightcap of scotch, with a splash of information.

"You know I can't reveal our sources," I smiled, as I replenished his glass.

"Well, it had to be either Nizar or Naji," Pizzey surmised, as he lit his cigar. "They're the only two 'high-ranking Iraqi government officials' who will talk on background."

"Is that right?" I laughed. "What do I know?"

"What does he know?" Halderman smirked. "You guys work hand in glove with 'em."

"Spare me the bullshit, Joe," I said curtly. "I'm really tired of having to go around on that."

"All I'm saying is—"

"All I'm saying is that's beginning to sound like a broken record," I interrupted.

"So what are you guys planning to do after the fifteenth?" Pizzey asked, changing the subject.

"We plan to be here. Holliman, myself, Ingrid, Tracy over there," I said.

"You're crazy," Halderman said.

"What about you?" I asked Allen.

"Not me," he said flatly. "They can get themselves another boy. I went through the same bullshit in Libya. They're just going to lock you in the hotel. You're not going to be able to report. Not to mention the danger. It ain't worth it." Pizzey was a veteran CBS correspondent who'd paid his dues in countless hellholes around the globe. His words had a sobering impact, especially on Tracy.

"You might be right, Allen," I said. "But then again, you never know. In any event, we've made our decision."

"Well, good luck. I've already told CBS this is my last rotation."

Holliman had finished the morning "call-in" show and we were having a snack. More precisely, John was preparing to sip his snack, a malted diet drink he swore would help him drop ten pounds. "Where's my marital aid? I need my marital aid," he joked, looking around the room for the hand-held, battery-powered miniature mixer he used to prepare the concoction.

The call-in show, called "Crisis Conference," usually linked correspondents in Baghdad, Saudi Arabia, and Amman with an anchor in Atlanta. The phone lines were then thrown open and viewers could ask the reporters anything they chose. Sometimes the questions were pretty bizarre, like the time Mark Dulmage in Amman was asked, "Isn't it true Muslims are taking over the world and that's why we have this crisis?" To his credit, Mark diplomatically deflected the query, rather than call the viewer a bigoted coprophagist. I personally never got behind the call-in concept. Invariably, reporters would get suckered into giving their personal opinions, which meant little, or in the case of Saudi Arabia, assuring the American public "the troops are ready over here." But "Crisis Conference" was very popular, or so I was assured by the home office.

Amani, who was quietly listening to the radio, abruptly put down her cigarette and turned up the volume. By the look of astonishment on her face, it was clear she'd heard something important.

"What is it?" I asked with a start.

"All the hostages have been released," she said, straining to hear more. "Yes, that's it," she said, "they're going to release all the hostages."

"Which is it?" I snapped. "They have been released or they're going to be released?"

"I'm not sure," she confessed. "Those were just the headlines. They're going to repeat it again during the newscast." Well, fuck me, I thought as I made for the four-wire.

"Baghdad to Atlanta," I called urgently.

"Atlanta here, go ahead."

"Will, we're getting a report, and this is still unconfirmed, not for broadcast, that all of the hostages have either been released or are going to be released. Amani is listening to the radio right now. I'll keep you posted the moment we nail it down, but it sounds like we've got a major one."

"Okay, let me know," Will said. I raced back to Amani, who I was pleased to see was now taking notes.

"The Iraqi News Agency says Saddam has asked the National Assembly to allow all foreign nationals who are currently banned from traveling outside Iraq to leave the country," she translated. ". . . the pleas by certain brothers and the decision by the democratic majority in the American House of Representatives and the invitation to our Foreign Minister for dialogue with the European parliament all encouraged us to respond to these positive changes which will have a great influence on Western public opinion, particularly in America, to restrain the evil attempts by the warmongers . . ."

"Unbelievable," I shouted, as I proceeded to call Atlanta.

"Yeah, it just came over as a bulletin on Reuters," Will said. "We've already got it on the air." Shit! I muttered to myself. I wished we were first, although I didn't regret double-checking with Amani. It's great to be first, but more important to be right. "How soon can Holliman be ready?" he asked.

"Give him two minutes," I said, "to be sure he's got everything."

"We're probably gonna want reaction from any hostages you can find over there. . . ."

"No shit! And I was planning to take the rest of the day off," I laughed. "Here's Holliman," I said, turning the mike over to John. "Ingrid," I screamed. "Round up the crew!" Within minutes, they were out the door, while I began working the phones.

For the next ten hours John was on the air at least once every half-hour, and his stellar performance still ranks, in my mind, as among the best I've ever seen on a breaking story. He was masterful. At one point, "calling our translator Amani Soliman to the microphone," he recapped the news for our audience and then had Amani herself translate the official announcement. He ad-libbed like a pro, in an easy, laid-back style that nevertheless conveyed the appropriate sense of urgency. No fool, Holliman. He knew this was history. "For those of our viewers just joining us," he said, "let's explain just how we happened to learn of the news. Amani, you were listening to the radio, as you do every hour. Right?"

"That's correct, John," Amani said with impressive self-assurance. "Usually the Iraqi News Agency uses the radio to make announcements that will be broadcast later on the evening television news . . ." It became the "Holliman and Soliman Show," and Atlanta loved it.

"I've just been handed a note by my producer, Robert Wiener," John said during another beeper. "Quoting a senior Iraqi government official now, he says the decision to ask the National Assembly to release the hostages was prompted by what he called positive changes in public opinion abroad. The official said Iraq was watching these changes. . . . It was time to take action. That," he repeated, "from a senior Iraqi government official." Thank you, Naji, I smiled.

"Is this CNN?" an American I guessed to be in his early thirties asked.

"Yeah," I whispered, moving him into the next room away from the microphone. He introduced himself as Tom Van Balle. He'd just seen Ingrid at the Mansour Melia Hotel and she'd told him to come by. Tom was in Iraq trying to free his father-in-law. Within five minutes, he was seated at the four-wire next to John.

"Well, they're drinking beers in the bar, they're buying everybody else beers," he said in answer to Holliman's question. "The hostages, the guests, or whatever you want to call them, they're slapping each other on the back and tellin' war stories. Everybody's just so happy," he beamed. "They know they'll be home for Christmas." Atlanta arranged for Tom to be connected with his wife Cathy in Des Moines. I knew what was coming, but even a cynical prick like myself was moved. "Honey," Tom cried on the air. "It's true. I'm bringing your dad home." I noticed Holliman was crying too.

Between newscasts, John worked on his TV script, which included several interviews with hostages or their wives. "It's absolutely marvelous," said Barbara Smiley of Los Angeles, "but my husband's afraid to celebrate about it until he's told it's really true." "We're so overwhelmed," said another woman. "It's absolutely tremendous."

Iraqi TV advised all members of the National Assembly to gather the following morning for the formal vote. Once the motion was approved, the hostages would be free to depart immediately.

Throughout the afternoon, I hadn't had any luck reaching Hamdoon. I'd left several messages, but none of my calls were returned. What the hell? I thought. I'd give it another shot. When he finally came on the line, Nizar was like ice.

"I must tell you, I am very upset and angry," he said bitterly. "Not only did I not say that Saddam Hussein was under pressure from inside this government, but how can you say that I used to be reliable?"

"With all due respect, Nizar, what we said was an 'official who has usually been reliable in the past . . .' "

"No, no," he protested. "That was not what was said, but even if it were, it was still wrong. And that black box," he seethed. "It is an insult."

"What black box?" I asked incredulously. I had no idea what he was talking about.

"The black box with a silhouette," he explained. "Next to my quotes about 'everything on the table.' " Oh, Jesus! I thought. The graphics department strikes again.

"Look, Nizar, I promise I'll look into this. In the meantime, could you spare me a minute or two to talk about today's developments?"

"No, I have nothing to say," he shot back, as he hung up.

What a nightmare. After months of cultivating Hamdoon as a source, it was up in smoke. I lit another cigarette and pondered my next move.

"To blacken someone's face is considered an insult," Mr. Alla explained. "It is not done here."

"Is there anything I can do?" John asked. "I feel like I'm responsible for—"

"Nah, forget it," I said. "I've got to find out about that graphic."

"Good grief," Eason sighed when I related the news.

"How bad was the graphic?" I asked.

"Well, it wasn't the best," he admitted. "So, what do you propose we do now?"

"I don't know. Is the report still airing? Can we change the graphic?"

"No, we stopped running the piece a while ago."

"Fuck!" I exclaimed. "Maybe you could send Hamdoon a telex. Apologize for the graphic. Assure him we meant no disrespect. Even Alla the minder says it's a big faux pas in these parts."

"Okay, I'll do it," he said. "Anything else?"

"Yeah, ya better get a second correspondent in here ASAP. Between the packages and the live stuff over the four-wire you'll want as the hostages are released over the next few days, we're gonna need help."

"I don't have another correspondent in the region."

"Why not bring in Leopard from Amman?" Mitch Leopard was a producer/reporter normally based in London. "I know Mitch would love to do it and have the opportunity to get on the air."

"Okay," he agreed. "We'll put him on the next flight."

"IT'S NAJI FOR YOU," someone called. Now what? I thought, picking up the phone.

"Hello, Robert," Naji said, a little chillier than usual.

"Hi there," I answered, trying my best to sound upbeat.

"Do you know what the name of our legislative body is?" he asked disdainfully.

"You mean the National Assembly?" I asked.

"Yes, it is the National Assembly. That is its correct name. Why then does CNN refer to it as Saddam Hussein's rubber stamp parliament?" he asked. "Is this proper journalism? Is this fair or accurate?"

"Thanks for calling, Naji. I'll take care of it right now." I got on the four-wire and alerted Will King. "Tell the writers to call it by its proper name," I said. "If they want to add that it rarely or perhaps never has been known to overrule Saddam, fine. But 'rubber stamp' is a wire service cliché and Naji has a point."

"I agree," he said. "I'll pass it on."

As expected, the National Assembly voted to free all the hostages. The decision wasn't unanimous. Eighteen of the two hundred and fifty members of the Assembly voted against the proposal. Nevertheless, anticipating the outcome, Iraq had already begun busing hostages during the night from their strategic sites to hotels in Baghdad. Most of the Americans would be moved to the Mansour Melia.

Ingrid and the crew were up early to gather interviews, but "General Stu," still holed up in the Bechtel Bunker, continued to deny permission to his charges to speak. "What an asshole!" Ingrid howled when she called in from the embassy. We'd again made arrangements with CBS to pool our videotape. Along with other crews, the Columbia Broadcasting System was staked out in front of the Mansour Melia, but the Iraqis said the hotel was off limits to the press—except for the Japanese. Naturally, this only prompted another round of Jap bashing by the more liberal members of the Fourth Estate.

"This is good day," a low-level Information Ministry official told me in the lobby of the Al-Rasheed. "The hostages are going home."

"You mean the 'guests'?" I smiled.

"Guests . . . hostages, you call them what you like. Iraqi people never want to keep the foreigners. Is not right to do," he whispered.

By late afternoon, Ingrid, CBS, and a few other intrepid souls finally managed to talk their way into the Mansour Melia. Although confined to the lobby, they shot a few interviews, including one with our old friend Bob Vinton and his wife, Sue. Sue had arrived with the last delegation of American wives. A few months in captivity hadn't broken Bob's independent spirit.

"I'm a goddamn resident of Baghdad!" he shouted at a guard who tried to block his path as he attempted to leave the hotel. "I'm going home to pick up my things." Naturally, the outburst made for great TV, which

Mark, as well as CBS, immortalized for posterity. Mr. Alla, meanwhile, displaying his astute understanding of the workings of the Western press, threatened to smash our camera.

"Gee!" Holliman exclaimed, viewing the videotape in which Alla lunged at Mark's lens like a crazed weimaraner, "I guess . . . yeah," he said, shaking his head. (At the feedpoint that night, while Ingrid distracted the censor, CBS managed to satellite the sequence showing Vinton and Alla. Feeling guilty that CNN had already made things difficult enough for Bob, I'd ordered the sequence held. Once Vinton was safely out of Baghdad, we used it in a story about censorship in general, which Mitch Leopard hand-carried to Amman and filed from there.)

At the American embassy, Joe and his staff were in the thick of it, organizing charters to fly down to Kuwait. "We're trying to move this along as quickly as possible," he said. "We hope to have everyone out within a week or so."

The decision to free the hostages was welcomed around the world. British Prime Minister John Major called it "wonderful news." Japanese Prime Minister Toshiki Kaifu said "it should be a truly joyous occasion and a happy event." King Hussein hailed the decision as "courageous" and "a step in the right direction." At the Soviet Foreign Ministry, spokesman Vitaly Churkin said he was "very happy indeed." And President George (Read My Lips, I'm No Wimp) Bush told reporters that now that the hostage issue was out of the way, it'd make it that much easier for America to kick some ass, or words to that effect.

"If it undermines the war effort, that's not necessarily a bad thing," Wilson said candidly after a couple of beers. Joe had stopped by the workspace for a "purely social visit," bringing along with him a gift of two magnums of California wine. He wanted to thank CNN for its "help" over the preceding months. "If we truly listen to each other and understand each other maybe this thing can be settled at the table," he said. "If not, well, I don't want to comment on a final [embassy] withdrawal, but we'll probably pull out of here too."

IN THE MIDST OF THE HOSTAGE STORY, Nizar telephoned to ask if we'd be interested in another interview with Tariq Aziz. It wouldn't be live, he informed me. We could tape it at the Foreign Minister's office. I suspected Hamdoon had received Eason's telex, since his tone was dramatically different from our last conversation.

"Again, I apologize for the graphic," I said. "I hope you understand no malice was intended."

"Yes, yes," he agreed. "I received Mr. Jordan's telex, thank you. Bob, let us just say it is all in the past."

We assembled in Aziz's suite and began rearranging the furniture as usual. While the crew set up, I meandered into the conference room.

"Hey, check this out," I whispered to Ingrid, waving her over to a long sideboard across from the mahogany table. There, on display, were over a hundred tiny flags: the member states of the United Nations.

"I'd say they're a little behind the times," Ingrid smiled as she plucked out the banner of the German Democratic Republic. "Let's see, what else is screwed up?"

"This," I said, pointing to an empty hole in the stand, meant for the flag of Israel.

"You didn't expect to find that here, did you, Wienerish?"

"I suppose not," I admitted. But it bothered me nonetheless.

"The Foreign Minister is coming now," his secretary said, snapping me out of my thoughts.

As in our previous encounters, Aziz was articulate and impressive. Unfortunately, if Begleiter's interview had seemed like a debate, John allowed Aziz to conduct a monologue. Holliman's questions were far too soft, and he neglected to follow up. Aziz said Iraq had decided to release the hostages because of "positive changes in world opinion." He explained Baghdad had taken advantage of the time and was now "fully deployed" in Kuwait. He insisted we'd been misinformed when we'd reported "everything is on the table." "Our position remains the same," he added, referring to Saddam's initiative of August 12. "We will never succumb to pressure." Throughout the interview, Aziz often glanced at me or Ingrid. I didn't know if he expected us to jump in with a question, but based on the way the interview was proceeding, I figured now was as good a time as any.

"Sir," I asked, "with regard to the misunderstanding you mentioned earlier: are you categorically stating that Iraq will never, under any circumstances, withdraw from Kuwait?"

"That is our position," Aziz said, "until we sit at the table. . . . When you sit at the negotiating table, then you listen to the others, what the other parties are offering. And then you judge if the other parties are offering something which is going to satisfy the needs of peace, and settlement, and justice; then you've got to make your contribution. . . . Our position is a steadfast position. But at the same time, we have said clearly, and my President has said clearly, that Iraq is ready to make its contribution to the cause of peace and justice and stability in the whole region."

"And that could include withdrawal from Kuwait?" John followed up.

"Well, I'm not commenting on that," Aziz said, raising his hand, "because we should not anticipate what's going to be put on the table by all sides. We shouldn't rush or jump to judgments before the negotiations have taken place."

"A final question," I pressed. "The state of Israel has said it will never sit down at an international conference, that it favors direct negotiations with its Arab neighbors. If there were such a conference, could Iraq assure the Israelis that they would have the direct negotiations they sought, looking for recognition in an atmosphere of peace, so that all parties could benefit?"

"Well," Aziz smiled, "I think you are making a lot of hypothetical questions. First of all, there is no international conference . . . but an international conference is a necessity in this case for the Palestinian question because people in this region wanted to get guarantees, and who can provide the guarantees? The superpowers or the members of the Security Council. Therefore our Palestinian brothers insisted on the formula of an international conference in order to get the guarantees for the future. The Israelis don't like that formula because they would like to impose their own policies. . . ."

"But," I persisted, "it would probably go a long way to satisfying Israel's fear and insecurity if it heard that its Arab neighbors would sit down face to face, for direct negotiations. After all, Israel is a country here in the region."

Aziz shook his head and shrugged. "Well," he said, "to my knowledge, those who are involved directly have not refused that within the context of an international conference. . . ."

"But none of the Arab countries surrounding Israel, with the exception of Egypt," I countered, "has recognized Israel's right to exist. . . ."

"The Israelis have not recognized the right of the Arab states," Aziz chuckled. "They have to recognize the right of the Palestinians to exist, the right of the Palestinians to have their own state. If they do that, well, then they can complain about the position of the others. But they haven't done what they have to do first of all . . ."

"Mr. Minister," John jumped in. "We're almost out of time . . . when your children, when your family asks you, 'Will there be war?' what do you tell them?"

"I tell them it's up to Mr. Bush," he smiled. "Honestly, I don't know what Mr. Bush is going to do. As far as Iraq is concerned, we don't want war, and we're not building for a war. We would like to avoid war, not because we are afraid of it, as might be interpreted by the cynics in Washington. We are a brave people, we have gone through hard experiences, we have shown endurance, a great capability for endurance in times of war with Iran. . . .

"As human beings and believers in God, we have to try to do whatever we can to avoid war. But not by capitulation. We're not going to surrender to avoid war. And they have to make a clear-cut distinction between the genuine willingness for peace in this country and the cynicism they resort to when we show readiness to talk. They shouldn't make any mistakes about that."

"I'M SORRY," John said as we packed up to leave. "I don't know what happened at the beginning there, but thanks for jumping in."

"He's a tough bird to nail on that Israel stuff," I sighed. "I felt like we were beginning to get into another debate."

"Yeah, I know what ya mean."

"The fact is, it's all so fucked!" I said, genuinely discouraged. "Neither side can see the other's point of view."

Over the next several days, John and Mitch shared four-wire duty and split the workload, which included constantly updated packages. Ingrid and the crew virtually camped out at the airport to record the exodus. Even Bosh the cat was going "home."

The American embassy in Kuwait would remain "open but unstaffed." Ambassador Nathaniel Howell would be on the final American charter, an Iraqi Airways 707 from Kuwait to Frankfurt.

"You'd better get someone to Frankfurt," I told Tom Fenton on the desk. "Where's Roth, by the way?"

"He should be in Paris, heading back to Amman. He's about to get on the plane." So Richard had changed his mind yet again, I laughed. Goodbye, Saudi Arabia. Welcome to Jordan.

"If I were you, I'd pull him," I said. "Unless you've got any other ideas." Thirty minutes later Tom called back. He'd managed to page Richard just in time and reroute him to Germany.

"I've been reading a number of books for a reality check," Joe laughed, a few days after the hostage release. "One of them is *1984*. The other is *Alice in Wonderland*." Iraq had proposed that Tariq Aziz meet Bush in Washington on December 17, while Baker and Saddam would meet in Baghdad on January 12. But after saying a Baker visit to Iraq was acceptable any time between December 15 and January 15, the White House now indicated January 12 was too close to the UN deadline.

"You know, I'm not surprised by what Aziz said and what your source told you in that first report," Joe explained. "Those conflicting signals, it's part of their negotiating tactic."

"Well, it is sometimes tough to get a 'read' on this place," I admitted.

"It's often tough for us too. We've only had an ambassador accredited to Iraq since 1984. Remember, diplomatic relations were severed in 1967."

"So, what's gonna be on this date bullshit?" I asked.

"I don't know," Joe said. "Aziz wants to spend four days in the States prior to meeting the President. He wants a maximum time to present his case to the press."

"So?"

"Well, nobody knows how this will play out."

"It's like having a knife pulled out from between your ribs," one hostage said.

"This is my passport to freedom," said another, holding up a special travel document issued by the American embassy. "I've been upset for four and a half months, but God willing, today's the day."

And then there was Joe Wilson's take on the proceedings. Said the American chargé d'affaires: "The emotional roller coaster I've been on has been as good as anything I've experienced since I stopped doing drugs."

In the blur of the final departures, a few images stand out: an incongruous bus tour to Babylon, laid on by the Iraqis for a contingent of British wives; Ingrid buying sandwiches for dozens of Vietnamese waiting at the airport; Bosh being gently slipped into a cardboard box by Hanan; dozens of potbellied, tee-shirted, bearded oil workers in baseball caps waving to beat the band as their buses pulled out of the Mansour Melia driveway, bound for Saddam International Airport.

And then they were gone.

The day after Bosh blew Baghdad, Will King came on the four-wire. "Hey, I hate to bother you with this," he said, "but before you say no, please listen." I prepared myself for the worst.

"This has nothing to do with Nadia Comaneci, does it?"

"No, no," he laughed, "but here's the story. We're hearing that before one of the hostages boarded the plane yesterday, her puppy got away. I mean, the dog was at the airport . . . probably is still at the airport. The dog just got spooked because of all the excitement and jumped out of the woman's arms. I'm just thinking . . . if by some chance we had the time to go back to the airport and find the dog, it would make a great human interest story. You know, the response we've had to Bosh the cat has been amazing." A few days earlier, Holliman had done a stand-up holding Bosh, and Roth had documented the pussy's arrival in Frankfurt.

"Will, I gotta tell ya . . . I'm not going to dispatch people to the airport to look for a dog. With all due respect, fuck the dog!"

"All right, sure, I understand," he stammered. "I just thought, if we were going to be there anyway, it would be a good little story . . . that's all. So, what are you up to today?"

God bless Will. The man had a heart of gold. In fact, of all the people who worked on the International Desk Will was the one who always looked on the bright side. During the Velvet Revolution in Prague, for example, while we were still waiting for our flyaway to arrive after the other nets had already gone live, Will had tried to convince me we weren't getting our butts kicked.

"Tell me," he had implored. "What do we gain editorially just by going live? We're all over the story. You tell me, what does going live gain us?"

"Will, that's not the point," I'd bristled. "We promote ourselves as the *live* network. For Chrissake, as Roth says, 'We go live to cockroach races!' If the other nets are live in Prague, we should be live too!"

"Well, we're working on it," he'd sighed.

"Yeah, I'm sure we're working on it. But while we're working on it, the other guys are doing it."

"We'll be okay," he'd assured me.

Always the optimist, I thought. As one colleague put it, if someone marched into the Atlanta newsroom and proceeded to mow down the entire staff with a submachine gun, Will would try to promote the fact there may have been survivors. But he was a dedicated and talented newsman, whom you could always count on in a pinch.

Although Earl still hadn't spoken to Blystone, I submitted my letter to Naji with the names for the final rotation. "All of the people listed below," I'd written, "have been to Baghdad before. You are familiar with their work, integrity, and professionalism."

"Very well," he said, after reading the list. "The visas will be waiting in Amman." We talked at length about the flyaway and our proposed interview with Saddam Hussein, which Naji said was being "favorably considered."

"I must tell you frankly, though, we do not understand why it was necessary to have a psychiatrist analyze His Excellency, the President."

"What psychiatrist?" I asked. "I really don't know what you're talking about."

"The psychiatrist. The man you had after the last interview with Mr. Shaw, who gave his opinion about Saddam Hussein's so-called state of mind."

"I'm sure you're mistaken," I protested. I remembered ITN put a shrink on the air following their one-on-one with the Iraqi leader, but CNN usually refrained from that sort of thing.

"No," he insisted. "It was CNN. Maybe you had nothing to do with it—"

"Honestly," I interrupted. "I'm in the dark. . . ."

"If you want to have people react to the interview, or even analyze the interview, you could get other statesmen, or politicians," he suggested. "It is irresponsible to have a doctor interpret what may be going on in the President's mind. Do you not agree?" he asked. Personally, I did. That sort of thing might be interesting, I thought, but it wasn't news.

"It's not for me to agree or disagree," I said, "but I'll speak to my network and find out what happened. In any case, it's my understanding

CNN is going live from world capitals on the fifteenth, and a remote from a psychiatrist's office doesn't figure into our plans."

"All right," he laughed. "You understand, we are not dictating the people you choose to interview, but the doctor serves nothing, in my opinion."

"I'M SORRY TO TELL YA, IT'S TRUE," Eason said when I called in later. "I didn't like it either."

"Jesus!" I wailed. "That's really bush!"

"Do you think it's gonna louse up the interview?" he asked, with obvious concern.

"Well, if you don't plan to have Sigmund Freud on again, you might drop Naji a telex and reassure him."

"Understood. By the way, we've made a final decision about the per diem situation." The topic had come up again when Holliman mentioned he'd been told by accounting he'd receive forty-five dollars a day in Iraq.

"Yeah?" I asked expectantly.

"We're gonna pay per diem to everyone," he said. "And it'll be retroactive."

"That's great," I said. "It's really gonna boost morale."

"It should. We're also gonna pick workspace food."

"Well, you're doing the right thing," I said. "Thanks for your support on this."

"Just try to keep the costs down as much as you can," he admonished me. "You wouldn't believe what it's costing to cover this story. We're spending a small fortune every week."

Joe had invited most of the American press corps to his house for champagne, a celebratory toast to a successful evacuation, but I'd decided to pass on the festivities, opting instead for a stroll through the souk. I was feeling elated as I made my way out of the Al-Rasheed. Every now and then, when time permitted and a car was available, I'd ask Jasim or Kareem to take me for a short spin around the city. One of the disadvantages of being "circus master" was getting stuck in the workspace for days. Still, it was far preferable to being bureau chief in, say, Los Angeles, where I'd supervised a staff of over seventy and eventually felt weighed down by the bureaucracy and paperwork. No, on the road was where I longed to be, as long as my legs and my liver held out.

Both sides remained deadlocked over the timetable for the upcoming talks. The United States, still rejecting January 12 as too close to the UN deadline, offered fifteen alternative dates between December 20 and January 3. President Bush said that was the latest he'd be willing to send James Baker to Baghdad. Iraq rejected the U.S. President's latest appeal, saying while Washington could decide when Aziz went to the United States, Saddam Hussein would determine the date of the meeting in Iraq. It began to sound like the International Conference on Vietnam, when talks were bogged down while all sides yammered on about the shape of the table.

"Our leadership is busy until January 12," Latif Nasif Jassim told John Holliman during an interview in the minister's office.

"Is there anything else more important than this?" John asked.

"Do you think this meeting will mean war will be avoided?" Jassim countered.

"I don't know, Mr. Minister," John answered honestly. "Is Iraq prepared to withdraw from Kuwait?"

"It is too late to withdraw," Jassim insisted. "This is a fact. Kuwait is part of this country . . . in the past and in the future."

"Well, what about this dialogue . . . ?"

"We want dialogue, but no one will force a solution upon us. I assure you we do not want war. We want peace. We do not want anyone to die and we do not want our population to be wounded. We want to develop our country, but our dignity, sovereignty, and our right to choose come above everything. The U.S. government does not understand this mentality, the mentality of the Iraqi leadership. I have a message for Bush," the minister smiled. "Don't go to war. If you go to war, you will go to hell!"

"JESUS! THAT WAS TOUGH TALK," I said to Naji as we walked to the elevator. "It seems a much harder line than Mr. Aziz was taking the other day when he talked about Iraq's willingness to make a contribution at the negotiating table."

"Well, do not forget there is a difference between Minister Aziz's job and Minister Jassim's job," he smiled.

"And who swings the most weight?"

"In matters of foreign policy, I think it is obvious. Mr. Aziz is our Foreign Minister."

"So why is Minister Jassim turning up the rhetoric?"

"Do not forget what his job is," Naji said with a wink. "But I will tell you something, Robert, and this is my personal view. It is too late for us to withdraw from Kuwait. It could have happened in August, perhaps even in September, but now it is too late. We will not succumb to pressure."

"But war will be such a catastrophe . . ."

"Yes, war will be hard, but do not forget: we lost more than fifty thousand in the battle for Faw. And what was Faw? A dirty little town. You know these people think when they die they go there," he said, pointing upward, "to Allah. So, in terms of human life, we are prepared for the consequences. Do you think the people of the United States or the members of Congress are willing to accept thousands of American dead? No, Robert. I will tell you this off the record, you understand, but my personal view is that it is too late."

"SOMEBODY'S GONNA HAVE to blink and it ain't gonna be us, it ain't gonna be the Western coalition," Joe Wilson said when I told him about the interview with Jassim. "Off the record, we're gonna go to war. Now that we have no more Americans here, we ought to drive it right to the brink!"

For months, the American networks had been trying to get Wilson to go on camera for a wide-ranging interview, but he'd always declined on orders from Washington. Now that the hostages were gone and his efforts in that regard had been successful, the State Department had finally said yes.

"I'm only going to do it with you and CBS," Joe explained, "you guys who put your asses on the line when no one else would come in here."

We arrived at his home around eleven in the morning and set up on the front lawn. "By the way," he said, "I decided to let NBC in on this too. Boettcher's on his way over but we can start without him."

"There were a lot of frustrations," he declared as we began the interview, "especially when the Iraqis changed the rules, for example with our diplomats from Kuwait."

"Any high points?" he was asked.

"I think when they called for a jihad, and of course, when those scuds were launched. When the guy said, 'The balloon is up. This is not a drill.' That's something I won't soon forget.

"I've learned a lot about myself," he admitted in answer to another question. "This wasn't an institutional thing, we were dealing with human beings. When you're dealing with issues of war and peace, you deal like two lawyers before a trial. But with the hostage issue, which was a humanitarian issue, you deal passionately."

Joe was asked if he'd like to remain in the region.

"Sure, I'm attached to this part of the world," he said. "The people are more passionate, the issues are more passionate, and the problems are more passionate. As a diplomat, I'd like to reestablish a relationship with Iraq. They're a tough, resolute people, but it's possible to achieve that. Look, I haven't flinched," he laughed, "but I don't know where we go from here. There have been a lot of mixed signals from the other side, but in the absence of substantive change, we don't know what to make of it. This is the one country in which I've served where I didn't have a friend or colleague in the President's inner circle."

Joe said he had gone from being "indispensable to expendable" now that the hostages were gone, and he said he worried about Hanan and the other Iraqi nationals who worked for the embassy. "They've been absolutely courageous," he said.

When the interview concluded, Joe invited us inside for drinks. "The vodka's in the freezer," he said to Ingrid. "Help yourself. I'm afraid it's not Russian," he laughed. "You'll have to settle for Smirnoff."

The foreign ministers of the twelve European Community countries canceled the planned meeting between the EC president and Tariq Aziz, stipulating the Iraqi Foreign Minister must first meet with President Bush. The ministers, gathered in Brussels, said they wanted to send a "clear signal" to Baghdad that the United States and Europe were in full accord on the issue of Iraqi withdrawal from Kuwait. Meanwhile, Yasir Arafat was back in town, sending Ingrid into another tailspin as she attempted to track down the peripatetic PLO chairman. Atlanta had finally told her to forget about Abu Nidal, who, rumor had it, might also be in Baghdad.

The ninth floor of the Al-Rasheed began to take on the spirit of Christmas. Biello set up an artificial tree, and a crew from Sky News decked the halls with strands of twinkling lights. And what would Christmas be without Christmas office parties? There was plenty of cheer, but without the hostage issue to focus on, the constant free-floating anxiety that was a by-product of the Iraqi Mind Fuck now took on a nasty edge.

"Fuck these people," Joe Halderman ranted. "I hate 'em. I want to provoke 'em."

"Hey, if you don't mind, I'd appreciate your keeping your voice down," I cautioned. "Moreover, I think what you're saying is irresponsible, especially for a newsman."

"What? Are ya afraid they're gonna hear? Let 'em," he bellowed. "I'm sick of this place and I'm sick of them. You guys are nuts if you stay here. You, Joe Wilson, all of you." He picked up his glass and took another large swig.

"Well, I don't think Joe's going to be around on the fifteenth," I smiled. "Not if things are going the way they are now."

"He'll be here," Halderman insisted. "Where else is he gonna go?"

"I'm sure they'll close the embassy and evacuate the 'dips.' "

"Bullshit! They don't give a fuck about Joe Wilson in Washington. Baker will let him hang," he sneered. "Baker doesn't give a shit. He wants him to hang!"

"I disagree with you," said Nancy Lane, who'd arrived in Baghdad that same afternoon. Nancy would be filling in for me over the holidays.

"You!" Halderman shrieked. "You don't know what you're talkin' about! Don't forget, I hired you! You used to work for me! Anyway, I'm not talkin' to you, I'm talkin' to him and I say the embassy's not gonna close. And even if it did, no one gives a fuck about Joe Wilson. You wanna put money on it?"

Halderman wasn't the only person who seemed to be unraveling. Reached late at night and asked to comment on a report that Aziz might cancel the talks altogether, Joe Wilson simply shouted into the phone, "Fuck him!"

"IT WAS DEFINITELY TIME FOR A BREAK," I said to John as we boarded the jet for Amman. "Ah, tomorrow," I sighed, thinking about the short trip we'd be taking to Jerusalem, and a night at the fabulous American Colony Hotel. "Tomorrow you'll see paradise."

"WELL, GUYS," Arnett said shortly after we sauntered into the Jerusalem bureau, "I'd love to be there with you. Just say the word, Robert, and I'll hop on a plane."

"Baghdad? What are you, *meshugge*?" Mouli laughed as we walked into Fink's later that night. The sixty-year-old restaurant had been my favorite watering hole when I'd been based in Israel, and Mouli Azrieli, the manager, was a close friend.

"Well, it's a hell of a different beat," I agreed as he seated us at our table. Peter Arnett and his friend Kimberly Moore were joining us, along with Michal Zipori, the bureau's senior producer.

"So, what's going on here?" I asked. "Are you guys set up in Tel Aviv?" In the event of war, the Israel Defense Forces' spokesman would brief reporters at the Tel Aviv Hilton.

"Larry hasn't made a decision yet," Michal said. "He's trying to keep costs down, and he's going on vacation."

"What!" Peter exclaimed. "On vacation now? If things aren't set up properly, I'm the one who's going to look foolish."

"Well, someone should speak to Register," I suggested. "Based on what we've just seen, time is running out."

PART FIVE

December 1990–January 1991

18

I had a brief, bittersweet holiday with my family in Berlin. It was the first time in years I'd been home for Christmas, but I couldn't put the Baghdad story out of my mind and give them the attention they deserved. The television was constantly tuned to CNN, and more times than I'd care to admit I insisted the boys be quiet so Daddy could watch the news . . . again.

Elaine and I went shopping for presents, electric trains for Jesse, a cable car set for Jake, but even then my thoughts were elsewhere. I looked at the fat and happy shoppers in Ka De We and thought of the people in the Baghdad souk, and what probably lay ahead for them.

I couldn't sleep but I didn't want to talk, especially about the "what if's." Although Elaine held firm to her conviction that war would somehow be averted at the last minute, her greatest fear was my being cut off for weeks if communications went down. I tried to assure her that if that happened, she shouldn't necessarily assume the worst. Someone would eventually get through to Amman with news.

As anxious as she was, Elaine fully supported my returning to Baghdad for the "duration," as I euphemistically called it. I couldn't discuss it with the boys, of course, not in great detail anyway. But they knew quite a bit already. After the war started, Jake announced to his kindergarten class, "My daddy's the boss of Baghdad."

One afternoon I watched the news as Baghdad staged a mock evacuation drill in the eastern part of the city. Allegedly more than a million people were moved from their neighborhoods to the "safety" of the suburbs. Iraq's Minister of the Interior claimed it was the largest evacuation in the country's history, but Roth (who'd been sent back to Baghdad rather than Saudi Arabia for one more rotation) and other journalists covering the event reported that the figures seemed inflated. They saw only a few hundred evacuees, who appeared to have been "dumped" just outside the capital. Nevertheless, Iraq proudly proclaimed that in the event of a U.S. airstrike, the entire population of Baghdad could be moved.

Another day I watched as Richard reported on a "blackout." Electricity was cut throughout the city, including the Al-Rasheed. "Did the four-wire go down?" I asked Atlanta. "If it did, tell Roth or Nancy it also works on batteries." From that day on, a supply of fully charged BP-90's was kept next to our communications "lifeline."

For his part Saddam Hussein gave a series of interviews to Spanish, German, and Mexican TV. He affirmed Iraq would not abandon its "Nineteenth Province" and said as Muslims, the Iraqis had faith in their cause and would defend their principles. "Have you thought for a moment, as we do," Saddam asked one reporter, "about the possibility that the United States might be defeated?" He said Iraq still wanted dialogue with the United States but insisted only Baghdad could choose the date for James Baker's visit.

The boys spent Christmas Day playing with their presents and I spent it in front of the TV. Iraq's Christian community celebrated midnight mass while Secretary of Defense Dick Cheney told troops in Saudi Arabia, "the clock is ticking." A few days later, the United States and Britain announced they would begin vaccinating their forces against germ warfare.

On New Year's Eve, Roth and his crew shot parties in Baghdad. Some Iraqis told Richard it might be their last chance to whoop it up. At the stroke of midnight, the nightclub they were in erupted in a frenzy as the band played its rendition of that perennial New Year's Eve classic "Jingle Bells." New Year's Day saw Saddam Hussein back in Kuwait. He told his soldiers Iraq would mass sixty divisions along the border with Saudi Arabia. Later, in an address to the nation, the Iraqi President lambasted President Bush: "In the same way as Judas betrayed Jesus, so has Bush—through his aggressiveness and deep-rooted evil—betrayed the teachings of Jesus Christ."

In Washington, President Bush told David Frost the invasion of Kuwait was the biggest issue to face the United States since World War II. "It's that big, it's that important," said the Commander-in-Chief. ". . . There's been nothing of this moral importance since World War II." The President branded Saddam "a dictator, an aggressor, the rapist of Kuwait." Then, two days later, he gave Iraq an ultimatum: accept talks in Geneva by January 9, or prepare for war.

I hardly slept my last night at home. Around three in the morning I tiptoed into the boys' room, sat on the floor, and just stared at them. God, how I loved them, I thought. What a fucked-up world! Each of them purred as I kissed his head. The night before they had presented me with a large drawing . . . animals, spaceships, airplanes, and ladybugs . . . to decorate my room in Baghdad. I rolled it up and packed it carefully in my suitcase.

Elaine and the boys stood by the window as I loaded the taxi in the early morning dark. I thought she was crying but I couldn't tell for sure. We continued to wave to each other until the cab disappeared down the street.

"Stymie! Hey, Stymie, over here," "Pearl" shouted in the Lufthansa lounge. She threw her arms around my neck and gave me a warm, friendly kiss.

"I was so sorry to hear about your dad," I said, returning her embrace. A few weeks earlier, Cynde's father had died suddenly in Texas. "How are you holding up?"

"I'm okay," she said, but she looked exhausted. "The flight over was a bitch, first from Dallas to New York, and then here to Frankfurt. It was impossible to sleep."

"Love the haircut," I laughed, running my hand over her new crew cut.

"Yeah, I look just like a guy, don't you think . . . with tits!"

"It's fabulous!" I laughed, "but there's still no chance you could pass for a guy. So, what else is doin'?"

"You wouldn't have believed security in the States. It was a nightmare. They wanted to look at everything, including in there." She gestured toward a small bag beside the couch. "My father!" she explained. "I'm carrying my father in there."

"What?"

"Yeah, my dad . . . his ashes. When this is all over, I'm going to scatter them in Tibet."

"Are you going to take him to Baghdad too?"

"I don't think so. The scene at customs would be too bizarre. Bad karma. I think I'm just going to leave him in Amman."

"A wise decision," I laughed. "Unless you want Mazin to check him through."

"Oh, Stymie," she said, giving me another hug. "It's so good to see ya."

Cynde and I hooked up with Ingrid in Amman and we quickly obtained our visas. The three of us were booked to Baghdad on the morning flight.

"This is great," I said as we checked in at the airport. "Two fabulous women, the best story in the world, and first class to boot." As if on cue we were informed the entire flight had been downgraded to economy. Shortly afterward the loudspeaker announced our flight would be delayed at least seven hours. "It never ends," I said to Ingrid. "What do you want to do?"

"I say we go back to Amman," she declared. "I feel like having lunch in a pine forest. There's that restaurant just outside of town."

After surrendering our passports to Immigration, which assured us we could retrieve them later, we hopped a cab back to the city. "Listen, fuck the outing in the forest. How about the buffet at the Intercon?"

"ADMIT IT, wasn't that better than having pine needles up your ass?" I joked as we called for the check.

"Ah, you're losing your sense of adventure, Wienerish," Ingrid laughed. "C'mon, let's go over to WTN and say good-bye." We walked downstairs and entered the office of Worldwide Television News, just off the swimming pool.

"Hey, I'm glad you stopped in," said Faradoun Hemani, who headed WTN's operation there. "Maybe you could do me a favor. I need some 'green' taken into Baghdad. I'll be there in a day or two, but my guy there needs it now."

"No problem," Ingrid said. "How much?"

"Could you handle twenty-five thousand dollars?" he asked.

"Sure. My commission is usually 10 percent."

"That's okay with me," Faradoun joked. "But I think London may have a problem. By the way, you're just in time for lunch." A few minutes later, his driver arrived with an assortment of *mesa* and other Arabic delicacies.

"There's only twenty-four here," Ingrid said, counting the bills.

"Let me see that again," Faradoun said, swallowing the bait.

"Just kidding," Ingrid insisted. "It's all here. I'll give it to Michel [Haj]." We hung around another hour or so before heading back to the airport.

"There will be another short delay," the manager of the lounge told us, "but the plane is here and it will be flying."

"It'd be nice to get there before Baker meets Aziz," I responded. The Iraqis had finally accepted Bush's proposal for a sit-down in Geneva.

"Please be patient," he said. "It will not be much longer."

"YOU TAKE CARE of the rest of the bags," I shouted at Ingrid and Cynde, after I'd tossed my suitcase on the conveyor belt. "I'll run up and find us

The Interview. Cynde Strand, Richard Blystone, Saddam Hussein, Bernard Shaw, Mark Biello, and the author following an interview with the Iraqi President on October 29, 1990. *Author's collection*

President Saddam Hussein, Minister of Culture and Information Latif Nasif Jassim, and the author on October 29, 1990. *Author's collection*

Sound technician Ben Coyte, correspondent Richard Roth, and camera person Cynde Strand in the lobby of the Al-Rasheed Hotel. *Alec Miran*

Bernard Shaw and the author in the CNN supply room a few days before the war. *Nic Robertson*

Iraq's Foreign Minister Tariq Aziz and U.S. Secretary of State James Baker shake hands at the start of their meeting in Geneva on January 9, 1991. *Reuters/Bettmann*

Yasir Arafat, Bernard Shaw (back to camera), and Peter Arnett following Bernie's live interview with the PLO Chairman on January 13, 1991. *Nic Robertson*

Translating Saddam. Ingrid Formanek and the author look on as John Holliman transcribes and Mr. Alla of the Ministry of Information provides simultaneous translation over the four-wire of President Saddam Hussein's news conference with Iraqi journalists on January 14, 1991. John Holliman was tragically killed in an automobile accident in September, 1998. *Mark Biello*

The Boys of Baghdad. For almost seventeen hours, Bernie, John, and Peter reported the start of the Gulf War live and uncensored from Room 906 of the Al-Rasheed. *Courtesy CNN*

The Powers That Be. Eason Jordan, vice president, International News Gathering; Tom Johnson, president; Burt Reinhardt, vice chairman; and Ed Turner, executive vice president of CNN, gather in the Atlanta newsroom to watch the coverage from Baghdad. Ed Turner succumbed to cancer in April, 2002. *Kelly Mills, Copyright CNN 1991*

Iraqi officials, including Dr. Sa'ad (center), chief censor at Iraqi TV, and Sadoun al-Jenabi (right) of the Ministry of Information display fragments of a Tomahawk cruise missile to reporters in the bomb shelter of the Al-Rasheed Hotel, January 20, 1991. *Author's collection*

CNN Baghdad, January 19, 1991. Nic Robertson, Ingrid Formanek, the author, Bernard Shaw, Mark Biello, Kris Krizmanich, John Holliman, and Peter Arnett in front of the Al-Rasheed. *Jana Schneider/Sip*

CNN Baghdad, January 21, 1991. The author, Peter Arnett, Nic Robertson, and CNN's INMARSAT. Except for a Spanish newspaperman and a few Jordanian reporters, all other journalists had left Baghdad. *Author's collection*

Don't Shoot, It's Us! The CNN flyaway departs Amman for Baghdad. *CNN*

Deputy Prime Minister Tariq Aziz and the author stroll through one of the presidential palaces in 1998. *Author's collection*

The author with actor Michael Keaton on the set of HBO's Live from Baghdad. *Ron Batzdorff*

good seats." I double-timed it into the plane and headed for the emergency exit. If we had to travel economy, at least we'd have extra legroom.

"You cannot to sit there," the flight attendant said after Ingrid and Cynde had joined me. "Emergency exit only," she insisted, pointing to the sign.

"Yes, we understand," I said, "but these are our seats. We're comfortable here."

"You cannot to sit there," she repeated. "Please, move one row in back. Is good for you."

"Jesus Christ!" I said to the Damsel and Pearl as we gathered up our bundles. "There's got to be a better way." But no sooner had we taken our new seats than three Iraqi men took our old ones.

"What the fuck is this?" Ingrid wailed, as the passenger in front of me reclined his seat, pinning my arms against my chest. She called for the flight attendant. "Excuse me . . . Excuse me," she said. "I thought you said that was the emergency exit. What are they doing there?"

"Oh, is good for them there," she said sweetly. "Is good for you here."

"Save your breath," I laughed. "The Iraqi Mind Fuck strikes again!"

THE ANCIENT 707 wheezed down the runway and headed up into the night. Almost two hours later, the captain announced Baghdad was socked in by a blanket of fog and we were now heading south. "This plane is not equipped with an automatic instrument landing system," the captain explained, "but we think we have enough visibility to land in Basra."

"Hold on to your seats," I said as I belted back a last hit of duty-free booty.

THERE WAS A GREAT DEAL of confusion at the airport in Basra. The control tower had neglected to inform Customs and Immigration of our unscheduled stop, and for almost two hours we sat sprawled in the Arrivals Hall while hastily summoned officials debated what to do next. Finally, they decided to bus us into Basra to spend the night. We'd continue to Baghdad in the morning. "Your luggage will stay on the plane," the man in charge announced.

"WOMEN AND CHILDREN ONLY," said the driver bound for the Sheraton.

"You mean, 'Women, children, and Wiener,' " Ingrid laughed as we climbed on board the bus. "Tallyho!"

Basra was crawling with soldiers, more Iraqi soldiers than I'd ever seen in one place before. Thousands of them jammed the darkened streets or gathered en masse at intersections or bus stops. Most wore heavy coats to ward off the cold. Here and there, groups of them huddled around fires set alight in waste bins. We seemed to be driving in circles, though I thought that couldn't be possible. Wrong again, I laughed, as the driver stopped to ask directions. A few minutes later, the bus limped into a service station. I couldn't believe it. We had run out of gas. Finally, at 12:45 A.M., we pulled up to the Basra Sheraton.

"We'll need three rooms," I told the reception clerk, "and a large bucket of ice. And if we could have the ice *immediately,* so much the better. . . ."

"I will send someone right up," he said, forking over the keys to our rooms on the second floor.

The Basra Sheraton obviously had seen better days. The Christmas decorations were still up, the place was dark and grim, and in each room the telephone line had been yanked out of the wall to discourage "guests" from calling out. But after the trip we'd had, the bed, at least, looked inviting. A few minutes later, Ingrid and Cynde joined me and we opened the Finlandia. "Where the hell is the ice?" I muttered, peering down the hall. "This is the worst . . ."

"Chill, Wienerish, chill!" Ingrid laughed as she inspected the bathroom. "At least you got a bar of soap."

"Room service," called the man at the door. I thanked him for the ice, then noticed two platters of Oriental "mixed grill" on a serving cart beside him.

"This is fabulous," I said, picking up one of the plates. "We're all starved."

"This for you?" he asked with a look of astonishment. "You only ice," he said, as he double-checked his order.

"This is definitely for us," I lied. "Look at my companions here. They're faint with hunger." I quickly signed the check and shut the door.

"This is delicious, " Ingrid cried as we immediately devoured most of the meat. Then there was another knock on the door.

"Please," the man from room service insisted, pointing to our platter, "this not for you."

"You may be right," I said, "but we're almost finished—"

"No, no, this no good," he said, in obvious distress. "Kitchen now closed and other room ask for two orders." I noticed the second platter was still on his serving cart.

"Don't worry. We can handle this," I said, picking up our almost empty platter and putting it on his cart. "We'll just take a little from here and a little from there. . . ." I scooped up portions from the second platter and heaped them on the first. "And presto, my friend, now you have two orders and everything is fine."

"This is good now," he smiled. "Thank you very much."

"Oh, Stymie, I can't believe you did that," Cynde wailed.

"Well, we wouldn't want the guy to get into trouble," I smiled, "but we've all got to eat." I turned on the TV and up popped the movie *Papillon*.

"This is too bizarre," Cynde said as I refilled our drinks.

We decided to pack it in about 3 A.M. The three of us were in the hall working out a wake-up plan when a short, dark-skinned man wearing a suit approached us. His name tag identified him as the night manager.

"You are Americans?" he asked in a whisper.

"Yes, American journalists," Cynde said.

"Ah, journalists!" he exclaimed. "Yes, now I understand." He told us he was an Egyptian and used to work at the International Hotel in Kuwait. The Iraqis had taken him to Basra and confiscated his passport. "They took everything," he complained bitterly. "They would take the air if they could." He said he'd been forced to work at the Sheraton and couldn't leave. "They don't have anyone else qualified to run the hotel," he smirked. "The whole world thinks the hostages are gone, but I'm still a prisoner."

"Have you tried contacting your embassy?" Ingrid asked.

"What can they do?" he sighed. "Egypt and the United States are on the same side. The Egyptians cannot help me."

"So, what are you going to do?"

"Sit out the war, if it comes, I suppose, then try to return home."

"There's a good story there," I told Ingrid as I bid her good night.

"But how can we tell it?"

"Unfortunately, we can't," I said. "Not now, anyway."

AFTER A FEW HOURS SLEEP, a cold saltwater shower, and a cup of tepid Nescafé, we boarded the bus and returned to the airport. This time the driver didn't get lost; in fact we were given an official escort. But it would still be several hours before the plane eventually took off. "As far as I know, Baghdad remains fogged in," the pilot said when I spotted him in the terminal. "We apologize, but you will have to be patient."

"THANK FUCKIN' CHRIST!" I sighed as we taxied to a stop at the gate in Baghdad. "I hope Mr. Jasim's here. I'm in no mood for any hassles." As we waited for our baggage, a planeload of soldiers disembarked from Kuwait. They were mostly young recruits, home for what would turn out to be their final leave.

"So, do you think there'll be a war?" I asked a nineteen-year-old who said his name was Omar.

"No war. No war," he laughed, shaking his head.

"*Insha'allah,*" said his friend, as he struggled to lift a large canvas bag off the rotating belt. The tip of a silver candelabrum was poking out through the zipper.

"Standard issue in Kuwait?" I asked, but he didn't understand.

We zipped through customs in an Iraqi flash—an hour and a half—to be greeted by Jasim's smiling face. "I be at airport last night till much late," he said. "And I here very early in morning."

"I apologize for the inconvenience. How are you and your family, my friend?"

"I may have to go Army soon," he said matter-of-factly. "Is no good if there is war."

"Do most people think there'll be war?"

"All Iraqis wait to see what happen tomorrow in Geneva," he said, as we drove into town. They're not the only ones, I thought, as we passed the by now familiar sign, "WELCOME TO BAGHDAD, Capital of Arab Saddam."

"So this is the safe," I said as I entered the workspace.

"Yeah," said Holliman. "We've got about a hundred thousand in there. I'll show you how it works a little later." The safe, an electronic, digital combination affair imported from Amman, had been Atlanta's idea, and a good one at that; except that when the war began and the electricity was cut, short-circuiting the system, Holliman would spend the first few minutes running around naked in a panic as he attempted to extract the loot.

"Well . . . well . . . well," I said to Roth, who was due to depart on the morning plane, "just couldn't keep away, huh?"

"It's been interesting," he admitted. "Did you see our piece on New Year's Eve?"

"Indeed I did, but I thought your remark on 'Crisis Conference' was the most provocative. Let's see, what did you say? The only requirement for joining the Popular Army was you had to be overweight!"

"Ah . . . that," Roth smiled. "Yes, Eason wasn't too happy . . ."

"I'll bet," I laughed. "What were you auditioning for? The Comedy Store?"

I UNPACKED MY BAGS in 909 and taped the boys' drawing up on the wall. I counted my Gauloises, fifteen cartons in all, and a two-month supply of filters for my cigarette holder. I took out the shortwave, put the travel clock on the night table, placed a new bottle of Eau Sauvage in the bathroom, and a volume of W. B. Yeats—a gift from Elaine—on the desk. I lit a cigarette and turned to "The Valley of the Black Pig." It seemed appropriate.

The dew drops slowly and dreams gather: unknown spears
Suddenly hurtle before my dream-awakened eyes,
And then the clash of fallen horsemen and the cries
Of unknown perishing armies beat about my ears.

We who still labour by the cromlech on the shore,
The grey cairn on the hill, when day sinks drowned in dew,
Being weary of the world's empires, bow down to you,
Master of the still stars and of the flaming door.

". . . by the cromlech on the shore," I read again. What the hell was a cromlech? Why can't these guys keep it simple? I took a quick shower and headed for the workspace.

"Let's see," Edith Chapin said, reviewing her notes. Chapin had come to Baghdad along with Nancy Lane to produce our coverage over the Christmas holiday. "There are only six 'dips' left at the U.S. embassy . . . the last flight of Soviets leaves the day after tomorrow . . . oh, that Peace Camp in the desert, there's like, about fifty people down there . . . it looks good for Bernie's interview with Saddam, but Naji needs to see you . . . what else . . . ?" Edith, who'd been filling in for Ingrid, planned to leave in the morning with Roth.

"What else is going on?" I asked.

"There's supposed to be another evacuation exercise," Edith said. "This one's at the Saddam Hussein Medical Center. Oh, and you ought to keep on top of flights, if anyone needs to get out. There's hardly any space left."

"I heard several guys may be driving out," Holliman said. "You need what's called a 'Land Permit.' Maybe we should get one for all of us, just in case . . ."

"Fine. Ingrid can look into that," I said. "I want to check in with Atlanta."

"YOU GOTTA PUSH HARD for the interview," Eason insisted. "I'm hearing Rather may be heading your way."

"I'll do my best. Where's Bernie right now?"

"He should be in Egypt doing Mubarak. After that he's got King Hussein, and then Shamir."

"Well, I'll be in touch after I speak with Naji. Anything else going on?"

"Here, let me read you something," he said, as he ticked off the figures from the latest Gallup survey. Thirty percent of the television audience was now getting its news from CNN; ABC came in a distant second. "Tell Naji about the poll. I can't believe they'd rather do CBS."

"Whaddaya hear about Koppel?" I asked.

"I think he's still in Amman. He's not going to Baghdad unless Saddam is definitely a 'go.' So, ya gotta push."

"I'll push, I'll push," I laughed. "Although all the pushing in the world couldn't get our plane to Baghdad on schedule."

"Yeah, I heard. How was Basra, by the way?"

"A fuckin' paradise. Well worth a visit. And don't pass up the 'mixed grill' at the Basra Sheraton if it ever comes your way."

"DO NOT BE CONCERNED about the interview," Naji assured me. "If the President does it, he will do it with CNN. Perhaps you should have Mr. Shaw here within a few days."

"That won't be a problem," I said, as I sipped my tea. "Now I'd like to talk to you about another matter that, frankly, has me worried."

"You have worries here in Baghdad?" he laughed.

"It's hard to believe," I joked, "but yes, every now and then . . ."

"Tell me what worries you," he said, turning serious.

"Naji, as you know, our four-wire is working, but I have my doubts as to how long it will last in the event of war. We need to have a backup. I know that you've tried to help us bring in the flyaway, which we still hope to get in here by the way, and I appreciate that, but at the very least, as a backup I want to bring in an INMARSAT phone."

"Which is what?"

"A small satellite telephone. It comes in a suitcase."

"Satellite? But that is how your television station works. Security will not permit it . . ."

"This is not for pictures, it's for communications."

"But you already have your four-wire . . ."

"Yes, we have it now, but for how long? Who knows? There's no point asking people to remain in Baghdad during a war unless we can communicate, unless we can do our jobs. Now, here's what I propose, and I'd like you to consider it very seriously: I will make arrangements to have the INMARSAT brought to Baghdad, but I give you my word it will not be used unless all other communications go down. Furthermore, your security people would be free to inspect the phone to satisfy themselves it's no threat. I think that's a fair proposal. What do you think?"

"Well," he said, mulling it over. "I cannot give you an answer right now, but I will speak to the minister. . . ."

"I'd appreciate that. If he has any questions, I'd be happy to address them. So," I said, changing the subject, "any predictions on what will happen in Geneva?"

"I gave you my predictions the last time we spoke. I see nothing that has changed them."

"It all seems so crazy," I said sadly. "So immoral . . ."

"You must understand, my dear Robert, war is not fought for moral or humanitarian reasons. If it were, there would be hundreds of thousands of people at that Peace Camp in the desert, instead of just a few dozen of those crazy people."

"They're still meeting," Adrian Braun of TV-AM said. "That's a very good sign. I'm optimistic."

"I'm optimistic too," Ingrid agreed. "They wouldn't be spending all that time in there unless something positive was happening."

"Sweetheart, you're always optimistic," I said, "but it wouldn't surprise me in the least if both sides came out of the conference room and declared there wasn't a single issue on which they could agree."

"Well, I'm staying optimistic," Ingrid laughed, "considering the alternative . . ."

The Baker-Aziz powwow in Geneva sent emotions careening in Baghdad. The longer it lasted, the greater the prevailing feeling a breakthrough was imminent. Throughout the day it seemed as if every reporter in town popped into the workspace to listen to the four-wire and the continuous updates from Geneva.

"Well, at least they're talking," I said to Holliman, as the hours dragged on. "Maybe those cockamamy Indians actually did some good." A few weeks earlier, a delegation of Native Americans had come to Baghdad to offer prayers for peace. They were unsuccessful, however, in their efforts to convince Saddam Hussein to puff their ceremonial pipe, which they'd then planned to offer to President Bush.

"THEY'RE FINISHED," Will exclaimed over the four-wire. "Begleiter says Baker's going to speak first."

"Pipe down! Pipe down!" I yelled, as we waited for the Secretary of State to approach the microphone. I turned up the volume as several reporters around me opened their notebooks. As usual, Holliman was hunched over his computer, ready to transcribe. James Baker began by saying he had come to Geneva "to communicate, and communicating means listening as well as talking. We did that, both of us," the secretary said, describing his marathon session of talks with Tariq Aziz as "serious and direct."

"Regrettably, ladies and gentlemen," Baker continued, "I heard nothing today that in over six hours suggested to me any Iraqi flexibility whatsoever in complying with the United Nations Security Council resolutions." I felt my stomach muscles tighten. "There have been too many Iraqi government miscalculations," Baker told reporters. "They miscalculated the response to their invasion of Kuwait, expecting the international community to stand idly by while they pillaged a peaceful neighbor. They miscalculated the response to what I think was a barbaric policy of holding thousands of hostages; that cynically doling them out a few at a time would give them political advantage. So let us hope that Iraq does not miscalculate again . . . the choice is Iraq's. If it should choose to continue its brutal occupation of Kuwait, Iraq will be choosing a military confrontation that it cannot win and will have devastating military consequences for Iraq. I made these points with Mr. Aziz, and I did so with no sense of satisfaction.

"We genuinely desire a peaceful outcome. The people of the United States have no quarrel with the people of Iraq. I simply wanted to leave no room for another tragic miscalculation by the Iraqi government.

"Now the choice lies with the Iraqi leadership," Baker stressed. "The choice really is theirs to make, and let us all hope the leadership will have the wisdom to choose the path of peace. It's time for Iraq to act and act quickly by getting out of Kuwait."

A few minutes later, it was the Iraqi Foreign Minister's turn to speak. "When I arrived in Geneva," Tariq Aziz told reporters, "I said that I had come with open-mindedness and that was my intention. I also came in good faith. The most important fact about these talks I would like to draw your attention to is that they are taking place after five months of occurrences of the latest events in the Gulf, and I drew Secretary Baker's attention to this important fact. Also, that this meeting took place after the last resolution that was taken under American pressure by the Security Council, which makes limits on diplomacy. If we had had an earlier opportunity several months ago, I told the secretary, we might have been able to remove a lot of misunderstandings between us. There was a chance for that." Aziz said Iraq had not miscalculated anything. "We have been very well aware of the situation from the beginning.

"From the professional point of view, it was a serious meeting," Aziz continued. "We gave each other time to explain and convey the information we both wanted to convey. On this aspect of the talks I am satisfied. I told [Baker] very clearly that what is at stake in our region is peace, security, and stability. What's at stake is the fate of the whole region . . . a region that's been suffering from wars, instability, hardships over several decades. If you are ready to bring about peace to the region, comprehensive, lasting, just peace to the whole of the Middle East, I told him, then we are ready to cooperate.

"I have no problem with international legality," Aziz insisted. "I have no problem with the principles of justice and fairness. On the contrary, those principles are in the best interests of the people of Iraq, and in the best interests of the Arab Nation. We have been seeking for decades to have those principles respected and implemented in our region, but they have not been respected and implemented by the Israelis and in that, they have had continuous strong American support." Aziz went on to decry what he called "the double standard used to address questions in the region. . . .

We are fed up with this policy of double standards. We shall not accept to be treated as a nation of underdogs. We are a proud nation; we have our history; we have our contribution to human civilization, and we would like to be treated in a dignified and just manner." Again, he reiterated that the Palestinian question was inextricably linked to an overall settlement of the crisis and said Iraq would "boldly" defend herself if attacked by the United States.

Aziz said he'd declined to accept a letter President Bush had written to Saddam Hussein, a letter Baker had shown him, saying the language was "not compatible" with correspondence between heads of state. "Politeness need not compromise substance," the Foreign Minister added.

Asked if Iraq would attack Israel in the event of war, Aziz said, "Yes, absolutely, yes."

The tension in the workspace was palpable, as was the disappointment. Barring a last-minute change, all of us knew what probably lay ahead. A box seat at Ground Zero. I looked at Ingrid, strangely quiet as she smoked a cigarette and stared out the window. Cynde too seemed lost in thought. Holliman just reread his notes and shook his head. I was overcome by an overwhelming sense of sadness and emptiness, tinged with no small measure of fear.

"Well, that's the ball game," I said to Pat Tyler of *The New York Times*.

"You're probably right," he agreed. "By the way, Wilson said if it came down to this, he'd probably be out by Saturday."

"Have any embassies closed?" You could always count on Pat to be on top of things on the diplomatic front.

"Malaysia, New Zealand, and Argentina are now officially unstaffed," he said. "And I hear Turkey is reducing its staff to two."

"That's only the beginning," I said. "In a few days, there'll be a stampede."

"WE'VE GOT TO KEEP TRYING," President Bush said during a news conference later, "but this was a total rebuff. I can't misrepresent this to the American people. I am discouraged." Bush characterized his letter to Saddam Hussein as "proper and direct."

"I'll bet," I smirked. "It probably began, 'Dear Adolf . . .' "

It was by no means rude, the President insisted, and yes, he might be willing to release it. Still, "I have not given up," said the President. "It is not too late." Less than twenty-four hours later, his supporters on Capitol Hill drafted legislation on his behalf that would authorize George Bush to lead the United States of America to war against Iraq.

With the failure of the Geneva talks, UN Secretary General Javier Pérez de Cuéllar announced he was flying to Baghdad in a last-ditch effort to avoid war. In Paris, François Mitterrand said France would also pursue its own independent diplomatic effort. "The United States and France," Mitterrand told reporters, "do not have the same vision with regard to an eventual international conference to settle the Arab-Israeli conflict. I well understand this position, but it does not entail a weakening of France's point of view on the same subject, especially as I have been calling for such a conference for six or seven years." Nevertheless, the French President insisted he would not oppose the use of force after January 15, if Iraqi troops were not withdrawn from Kuwait.

In Baghdad, people began hunkering down for the inevitable. Long lines formed at gas stations and grocery stores, where, despite skyrocketing prices, citizens stockpiled essentials. Hospitals were told to admit only cases requiring urgent attention; the beds would be needed for military casualties. Civil defense programs, by now a staple on Iraqi TV, were broadcast more frequently and people were instructed to clean out and prepare their shelters. The Ministry of Culture and Information announced that every Iraqi male over the age of fifteen would be issued a weapon, including Kalishnikov submachine guns.

The capital suddenly became Rumor Central: Iraq was closing its airspace; the road to Amman had been sealed. These unconfirmed reports further jangled the nerves of an already uneasy press corps, many members of which besieged Sadoun's office in pursuit of exit visas.

"I NEED THAT INMARSAT now more than ever," I said to Naji. "Have you received an answer from the minister yet?"

"I am still waiting to hear," he said, "but you assure me, correct, that it is not to be used without our authorization?"

"It's not going to be used as long as the four-wire's working," I said, trying to mask my frustration. "I've given you my word. But with all due respect, I need an answer within twenty-four hours."

"I will give you the answer tomorrow," he promised. "You may telephone or come by."

AS WE DROVE BACK to the Al-Rasheed, I skimmed *The Baghdad Observer*. As usual, a picture of Saddam Hussein graced the front page. Today he was exhorting senior members of the Arab Ba'ath Socialist party. "If the Americans attack," Saddam warned, "Iraq will make them swim in their own blood." He said the upcoming battle would result in changes for the Arab Nation and "would lift oppression from the whole of humanity."

"It's damn good to see you," I said to Bly, giving him a hug. "This place has been going nuts since the talks collapsed. I'm happy you're finally here." I gave him a quick "read" on where things stood, and plans for the final evacuation of the American embassy. "Wilson's personally taking it very hard," I explained. "I think he's beginning to unravel. As for the long run, I think there's a good chance I can bring in the INMARSAT, but I don't know about the flyaway yet. In any case, we're finally all together," I said, trying to sound upbeat. "This is gonna be a tough one." As usual, Bly had been listening intently; but now I sensed he was oddly distracted.

"I've got a problem," he said a few minutes later, after calling me into his room. "I promised Helle I'd only be away three weeks. I want to stay, and I'm prepared to stay, but that last six-week stint took an awful toll. . . ."

"Weren't you told this was the final rotation?" I asked in disbelief.

"No one ever mentioned it to me," he said. "Maybe they just assumed—"

"Jesus Christ!" I exploded. "How could they assume something of this importance . . . ?"

"Oh, hell," he muttered. "Maybe I could extend it. I really feel awful about this." We talked for a moment about Bly's personal reasons for not being able to remain for the long haul. I agreed they were compelling.

"Look, you and I are not here to make a reputation," I said, sympathizing with his dilemma. "Helle has probably put up with more shit from you than anyone could reasonably expect. More than twenty years on the road, Bly . . . the missed holidays, birthdays. You owe it to her if she asked you directly. God knows I'd do the same for Elaine if she ever asked me. The fact is, I don't know what's gonna happen. We could conceivably get stuck in here for months. I can't guarantee I could get you out, even by land."

"Yeah, you're probably right," he said glumly. "I feel like such a twit about this."

"Fuck that!" I groaned. "You owe it to Helle. Don't worry about us. We'll be okay." But privately, I wondered if we would be. All of the staff looked up to Bly and with good reason. He was a veteran correspondent. He instilled confidence. He had covered wars before. Moreover, he was a key part of the dynamic for the final team. His leaving would take away a fundamental cornerstone. "Well, you better call Eason and let him know. We'll talk again later," I said.

"WHAT'S GOING ON WITH BLYSTONE?" Holliman asked. "Is there anything I can do?" I filled him in but asked that he keep it to himself. "So, what's your plan?" he asked.

"I think there's only one thing to do," I said. "We need to bring in Arnett."

"GOOD GRIEF," Eason moaned when I suggested he call Peter in Jerusalem. "You know, he's got a job to do where he is, and anyway, what makes you so sure he'll even want to come?"

"Trust me! He'll come. He already said as much when Holliman and I saw him last month."

"Okay, I'll have to run it by Ed. Give me thirty minutes."

When will it ever fuckin' end, I thought, as I lit a cigarette and tried to relax. We'd need an entry visa for Peter, an exit visa for Bly, reservations for Bly; I still needed to arrange a pickup for Bernie; finalize the Saddam interview; bring in the INMARSAT; push for the flyaway, and God knows what else! Grace under pressure, I reminded myself.

"IT'S A GO FOR ARNETT," Eason said. "He'll be there the day after tomorrow, assuming you can get him a visa."

"Consider it done. What do you want to do with Bly?"

"We're gonna send him to Jerusalem. He can always get to London from there if he has to."

"So, what did Peter say?"

"I don't know. Ed spoke with him, but I gather he was . . . er, enthusiastic."

"I'll bet," I laughed. "Batt'n down the hatches!"

"EXCUSE ME, Robert, may I have a word with you?" John Simpson of the BBC asked. I waved him into the workspace, and offered him a cup of coffee. "If we could speak privately . . ." he began, glancing around the room at the usual hubbub.

"Sure, no problem," I said as we moved into 908. "What's up?"

"The fact is," he said quietly, leaning forward and clasping his hands, "we intend to remain in Baghdad whatever may occur, and I gather CNN does too. Frankly, I don't know how many others will stay, but it's safe to assume that in the event of hostilities, we'll all be fairly limited in what we can actually do. What I'm proposing is that we pool our resources. We have certain facilities at our disposal that may be helpful to CNN, just as you have . . . er, things that we're interested in—"

"The four-wire's not up for discussion," I interrupted.

"No, no, I quite understand. Frankly, communications shouldn't be a problem for us. . . ."

"How so?"

"Well, we already have an INMARSAT here."

"You do?" I asked, genuinely shocked.

"Yes, it's set up at another location. But please," he stressed, "this is quite confidential. You must promise you won't let ITN know."

"No problem. And the Iraqis gave you permission to bring it in?"

"Not really. We smuggled it in piece by piece over a period of time. . . ."

"Jesus!" I said. "*Chapeau!* Not even Naji knows?"

"I believe he knows something's up. I made a vague reference to it the other day and he sort of winked, if you know what I mean."

"Have you actually used it yet? It's working?"

"Oh, we know it works," he said flatly. "We've tested it but we haven't used it to file. . . ."

"Well, my hat's off to you, John, but just how do you think you're going to use it without permission?"

"As I said, we're set up at another location . . . a secure location, it shouldn't be a problem."

"Get real! You're telling me that if there's a war, you're simply gonna sit in a backyard someplace with your satellite phone and that's it? C'mon. Even if you could get away with it, somebody's eventually bound to discover you. They'll think you're a spy!"

"Not where we're going to be," he said tersely.

"And where's that?"

"For now, I prefer not to say." I guessed it was the British Embassy.

"Well, depending on the situation, I might be amenable to pooling tape, but I'm not gonna risk my people's lives by having them secretly transmit from Baghdad during a war. I think it's foolhardy and irresponsible."

"Then what are you going to do for communications?" he asked. "Once the PTT is hit, your four-wire goes down with it." I thought for a second about whether to answer his question, and decided to tell him the truth.

"I've asked Naji for permission to bring in our INMARSAT," I said. "Now, that stays between us, agreed?"

"And what did he say?"

"I don't have an answer yet but I think it will happen." Simpson whistled softly.

"And where would you set it up?"

"Right here at the Al-Rasheed. I can't see us zippin' around Baghdad while the bombs are falling. . . ."

"Well, I'd appreciate your letting me know if your efforts are successful," he said. "That would certainly change things for us." John stood up and shook my hand.

JEEZ, I WONDERED AFTER SIMPSON LEFT, have I screwed up? The BBC had shown great enterprise by bringing in their satellite phone. John and his colleagues had taken a considerable risk and they'd succeeded. Of course if it came to the crunch, whether they would actually be able to use it was another story. But one thing was clear: The BBC already had an INMARSAT in Baghdad, and CNN didn't.

Still, I felt we should continue to pursue things as we'd done in the past . . . openly and honestly. We'd established a professional relationship with the Iraqis that was built on trust. To deviate from that now could have serious consequences. Obviously, I couldn't mention the BBC to Naji even if John thought he might already know. No, I would simply press al-Hadithi on our behalf, and let the chips fall where they may.

I was mulling over my conversation with Simpson when I received a call from Brent Sadler of ITN. "Certain decisions have been made between London and Atlanta," he said. "We should probably discuss them." We made an appointment to talk later, after I'd spoken with Eason.

"I TOLD THEM USING THE FOUR-WIRE is out of the question," Eason said, "but we might be interested in some kind of 'pool.' It's up to you guys on the ground. You should talk to Sadler. I understand ITN already has an INMARSAT there, or will have one in place in a day or two . . ."

"That's a strange coincidence," I laughed. "Simpson of the BBC just proposed the same thing."

"Well, if we make any arrangement, we'd obviously prefer to do it with ITN," he said, "because of our relationship."

"How did they get their INMARSAT in?" I asked, already knowing the answer.

"Piece by piece. By the way, what's the latest with ours?"

"I've been told we'll know soon—"

"Robert, hold on a sec," he interrupted. "I've got something here that's important. The U.S. just officially announced it's going to close its embassy. Fitzwater is urging all Americans . . . including journalists . . . to leave Baghdad."

"Yeah, well we all knew that was in the cards."

"I suppose," he said. "I just wanted to make sure you were in the picture."

"SO, IF YOU'RE AMENABLE," Sadler said, "we could share footage, and perhaps technical facilities . . ."

"Have you tested your INMARSAT yet?" I asked. Sadler looked at me suspiciously. Brent always played his cards close to the vest.

"Did London tell you about that?" he asked pointedly.

"No, the BBC did," I laughed. "Of course Nigel [Handcock of ITN] mentioned it to Eason."

"You understand, if we enter into this agreement, the BBC is out. I know Simpson's been trying to organize something on his own. . . ."

"Don't worry," I said. "That's not a factor. So, have you tested the thing?"

"We're going to try it tonight. We think we can get a signal from one of our rooms."

"Great. Please let me know. We plan to bring in ours and I'd like to set it up at the hotel too."

"You're bringing in an INMARSAT too?" he asked, with a faint trace of envy.

"I hope to, as soon as we receive permission."

"So then I gather you don't need ours," he snapped. "But you still want to pool—"

"Look," I interrupted. "Here's what I propose. I'm not going to pool anything while the four-wire's up. I consider that our competitive edge and I want to keep it as long as possible. However, when that line goes down, I suggest we do this: if, for some reason, your INMARSAT isn't working, you can use ours. By the same token, if we have a problem, then we'll use yours. That way, we're both backstopped in terms of communications. As for videotape, we already share material so that shouldn't be a problem. Agreed?"

"In principle that sounds fair. One other thing. If Naji gives you permission for your phone, will you let us know? Then we'd obviously ask Naji for permission to use ours."

"You guys are somethin' else," I laughed, getting up to leave. "You've been bad-mouthing CNN, accusing us of being in bed with the Iraqis. So you sneak and scheme to get your INMARSAT in while we've been open and frank. And now, if we get permission, you're gonna hop on CNN's coattails and say to Naji, 'If CNN can do it, why can't we?' "

"Well . . ."

"Well, nothing. I don't begrudge you the goddamn INMARSAT. I just find it amusing that CNN's policy of doing business in Iraq, a policy you've been quick to condemn, will probably make it possible for you and others to eventually broadcast from Baghdad. Ironic, no?"

"Believe me, I haven't criticized—"

"Spare me," I said. "We're both professionals. You're well aware of some things that've been said. Let's just put it behind us and move on. I'll stay in touch."

After nearly five months in Iraq I thought I was immune to surprises but the pictures on Iraqi TV that night stopped me cold. There, walking down Rasheed Street in the center of Baghdad, as if out for a Sunday stroll, was Saddam Hussein, accompanied by Kenneth Kaunda, the President of

Zambia. Saddam looked as if he hadn't a care in the world as he pressed the flesh like any politician working the crowd. Naturally he was surrounded by a phalanx of bodyguards who tried to keep the faithful at bay, but several Baghdadis broke through the cordon to reach out and kiss the hand of their President. "Saddam . . . Saddam," they shouted, as Hussein escorted Kaunda, who gripped a white handkerchief in his hand, on a walking tour of the capital. Unlike most other presidential appearances I'd seen, this one wasn't stage-managed in advance. In fact, the crowd seemed as astonished to see their leader out pounding the pavement as I was.

"He did this before the Iran-Iraq War," Mr. Petros commented. "He show people he not afraid." Ingrid's Arabic teacher had taken over Amani's job as translator.

Saddam certainly looked convincing. He might have been caught in the cross hairs of the entire world, but you would never know it by his expression and demeanor. Maybe Wilson was right, I thought, as I sat transfixed in front of the television. Maybe Saddam *has* reached the messianic stage.

"THAT GUY'S GOT BALLS OF STEEL," I said later over drinks. "Either that, or he's a certified . . . well, I'll leave it at that."

"So, Weenie," Tracy said, "you heard Fitzwater told journalists to leave . . ."

"You mean, 'urged' journalists to leave," I corrected her.

"So what do you think, huh?"

"To tell ya the truth, I haven't thought too much about it. I suppose it was the proper thing for him to do."

"C'mon, Weenie, what he's saying is, they're gonna bomb Baghdad!"

"We already know they're gonna bomb Baghdad, sweetheart. What else is new?" The moment I said it, I knew I probably sounded too flip and I didn't mean to. I sensed Tracy might be having second thoughts and, if anything, I should have tried to be more reassuring. God knows we all had our mood swings, but Miss Cybil's seemed to hit big highs and big lows. A few months earlier, when she was especially down in the dumps one day, we'd conspired to throw her a surprise birthday party, though none of us knew her actual birthdate. We'd showered her with presents, not to mention good cheer, and Pearl had arranged for a magnificent cake. Doug James, aka Willard "Three Scoops" McHenry, had composed a witty special edition of the *Pearltown Times* on his computer, which lauded Cybil's achievements and made for great laughs. The next day Tracy was back to normal. This time, I knew it was going to take more than a party to cheer her up. She was literally crushed by Bly's impending departure. Thank God, I thought, she still had her soul sister Pearl nearby.

BEFORE TURNING IN, I decided to give Wilson a call. Despite the lateness of the hour, I had no doubt he'd still be awake. Getting no answer at his home, I dialed his office. After about a dozen rings he finally picked up.

"Yeah, whaddaya want?" he barked into the phone.

"Hey, Joe, I'm just checking in with ya. . . ."

"Whaddaya want? Who is this?" he wailed.

"It's me. It's Robert. . . ."

"Robert? Robert who?" he asked. I could tell he'd been drinking but it wasn't so much drunkenness in his voice as anguish.

"It's Robert . . . Robert of CNN," I said again.

"Oh Robert, yeah, how ya doin'?"

"I'm doing fine, Joe. I was just calling to see how you were doing. . . ."

"Aah, we did everything we could, Robert. Every damn thing we could. But we couldn't do enough. And now it's over. . . ."

"I understand. . . ."

"We got the hostages out but we couldn't make peace," he slurred. "Fuck it. Now Saddam's gonna learn a lesson."

"Well, Joe, you did the best you could. You should be proud of what you accomplished. . . ."

"But we couldn't do enough," he moaned. "And now we've run out of time."

"We've had some bad news," John said the moment I arrived in the workspace. "Pearl's mother has had a heart attack."

"Oh, shit," I cried. "What's her condition?"

"She's in the hospital, in intensive care."

"Where's Pearl right now?" I asked, looking around the office.

"She's downstairs in her room. She'll be back up shortly."

"Christ Almighty! First her dad, and now this. . . ."

"SHE'S OKAY," Cynde tried to assure me. "I spoke to my sister and Mom's okay, really."

"Well, I think you should get on a plane and fly home," I suggested.

"It's not necessary, Robert. She's okay. I want to stay here. Listen, we'll talk later, all right? We need to leave for the shoot."

"Sweetheart . . ."

"I placed a call to Texas. If it comes through tell 'em I'll call back later." She gathered up her gear and left the room.

"This is fucked," I said to Holliman. "God forbid she takes a turn for the worse and Cynde is still in Baghdad, she might not be able to get home . . ." Just then the phone rang.

"United States on the line," the operator said.

"Hello, is Cynde Strand there?" asked the voice at the other end.

"No, I'm sorry she's not. This is Robert Wiener. Is this Cynde's sister?"

"Yes. Hi, Robert. . . ."

"How's your mom?" I asked.

"The doctors say the next twenty-four to forty-eight hours are crucial. But Mom's a pretty strong person. . . ."

"I spoke to Cynde about flying home. . . ."

"What did she say?"

"Essentially, she said she'd play it by ear, but my feeling is she should be there with you. . . ."

"I think you're right," she said. "I don't know what she can do but I know it only means more pressure on Mom knowing Cynde is where she is. . . ."

"Well, consider it done. I'll tell Cynde when she gets back. Don't worry. I'll have her in Amman tomorrow, then on the first flight out to Texas. . . ."

I CALLED SADOUN and asked him to issue Cynde an immediate exit visa, and pull whatever strings were necessary to get her on the morning flight. "This is terrible news," he said. "Please tell Cynde we are all very sorry." I then got on the four-wire to Humi in Amman and asked Peter to make reservations for her trip to the States.

"Please make sure she's as comfortable as possible," I said. Though we often flew first class on Third World airlines, it was company policy that we should travel "business." But considering the strain Cynde had been under recently, I knew an upgrade, especially on a long flight, would make a difference. Peter got the message immediately.

"I quite understand," he said. "Consider it done!"

"LISTEN," I said to Cynde, putting my hands gently on her cheeks, "I don't put on my executive hat very often, but I'm doing it now. I'm telling you that you have to go home. Please don't make me say 'order.' "

"Oh, Stymie," she said, "you're such a good friend. But I feel like I'm leaving ya in the lurch. . . ."

"I could never be in the lurch having a friend like you. I'd only be in the lurch if I didn't." I held her tight before she left for her room to pack.

First Bly, now Cynde, I thought selfishly as I headed for the elevator on my way to the embassy. This could throw everything off. Who was next? Tracy, I supposed. Without Cynde, it would be only a matter of time before she'd probably want to leave too. Despite the best-laid plans, a delicate balance had been shattered. Shit, I muttered, bad fuckin' luck!

I was almost out the door of the Al-Rasheed when who did I see but none other than one of the world's *major* certified bad guys: terrorist chieftain Abul Abbas, so-called mastermind of the *Achille Lauro* hijacking and the murder of Leon Klinghoffer (played with great conviction by Karl Malden, I might add, in a TV Movie of the Week). Jeez! I thought. Now this would be a hell of an interview. Abbas seemed to be alone. I looked for a bulge under his gray Members Only windbreaker, wondering if he were armed.

"Hi. I'm Robert Wiener of CNN," I said, extending my hand.

"Hello," he said. "Good to meet you."

"I was wondering if you'd be available for an interview? You know, perhaps about plans for your . . . er, organization should war break out."

"Yes," he said instantly. "Tomorrow?"

"Nah, Pérez de Cuéllar is due in tomorrow. How about the day after?"

"It is possible."

"Fabulous. Do you have a telephone number handy where I can reach you?" The moment the words were out of my mouth, I realized the absurdity of my question.

"We contact you," he corrected me. "You are here at hotel?"

"Room 906. If the line's busy try 902, 904, or 908."

"You will have translator?"

"What translator? Your English is terrific."

"Is not so good," he said. "You must have translator."

"C'mon, your English is great."

"Is not so good," he insisted.

"Okay, we'll have a translator when you come to us." I thanked him for his time and moved on. A second later, I noticed former Nicaraguan President Daniel Ortega standing by the Guest Relations desk. Should I . . . ? No, I concluded, it was too bizarre.

However late he'd been up the night before, Joe seemed none the worse for wear as he began his final briefing. In fact, Wilson sounded downright aggressive.

"There will be a 727 leaving tomorrow at 11 A.M. with room for 126 people," he intoned. "As of this moment, 32 places are booked. If you wish to obtain a seat, we can probably accommodate you. I strongly suggest you take advantage of the opportunity. This will be the final evacuation."

"Can you tell us who else will be leaving with the U.S. embassy staff?" a reporter asked.

"This is not a news conference," Joe said tersely. "I'm here to tell you there's a 727 leaving tomorrow with 126 places. If you wish to obtain a seat, we can probably accommodate you."

"Joe, we understand this isn't a news conference. . . ." the reporter said.

"Then put away your notebook," Joe lectured him. "You don't need to be taking notes. I'm going to say this one last time: we have a 727 leaving tomorrow with 126 places. If you wish to obtain a seat, you can sign up here. Exit visas or other documentation are your responsibility."

"What time will you be leaving the embassy?" I asked.

"Between eight and eight-thirty," Joe said.

"Will you be taking the flag with you?" a reporter wanted to know.

"A flag will continue to fly over the embassy," Joe stated emphatically.

"So you won't be taking the flag . . . ?"

"I may be taking a flag with me," he said cryptically. Jesus, I thought. Why doesn't he just say he'll be taking the embassy's flag, but will raise a second one in its place? What was this? A state secret?

"Will other allied diplomats be on the flight?" Joe was asked.

"Look," he said, getting up from the couch and moving toward his desk, "this is the last time I'm going to say it: this is not a news conference. The United States government has chartered a 727 and there are seats available. If any of you feel like white wine, I'm offering a standing invitation to join me in the front of the plane." It was apparent the "briefing" had come to a swift conclusion. Several of us walked up to Joe to say good-bye.

"I just received this present from a former hostage," he said, reaching into his pocket and pulling out a black, palm-sized electronic device. *"Fuck you!"* a computerized voice sputtered when he pressed a button. *"You're an asshole!"* it said, when he pressed it again. "It's called 'The Final Word,' " he explained, clearly delighted with what he thought was a most appropriate gift. I was one of the few onlookers not surprised by the gadget. A few months earlier, Roth had given one to Ingrid. That morning, it happened to be in my bag.

"Hey, Joe," I laughed, as I pressed the button. *"Fuck you!"*

"Eat shit!" his machine responded to mine. For an instant, I imagined Baker and Aziz armed with similar devices.

"It could do wonders for diplomacy," I joked.

"I agree," he laughed. "I wish I had gotten this earlier."

I lingered a few minutes until most of the others had gone. I wanted to thank Joe privately and wish him well.

"So you're going to stay?" he asked after shaking hands. "Well, the best of luck. Just be careful you don't end up a pound of ground round!"

"We'll see each other again, I'm sure. Hopefully in better days."

"I'm looking forward to it, Robert," he said, walking me to the door. "CNN has really been terrific. I can't thank you enough."

I came out of the embassy to discover that Baghdad suddenly had been transformed into a veritable armed camp. Hundreds of soldiers and militiamen were posted on every street corner and at every major intersection. Anti-aircraft batteries had been rolled into position near mosques and government buildings. One was even set up directly in front of the Sheraton. The troops didn't look like the middle-aged overweight men of the Popular Army, the butt of so many jokes. They looked young; and they looked fierce. It was a frightening scene.

"What's this all about?" I asked Mr. Jasim.

"They prepare," he said, gunning the Honda to pass a truck filled with soldiers. "They show they ready." I don't know if *I'm* ready for this, I thought, as we headed for the Al-Rasheed. The embassy was closing and now these guys were on the streets. It didn't feel good.

"It's a hell of a scene out there," I said, entering the workspace. "We need to shoot it." Ingrid and Mark left to find Mr. Alla.

"You know, Louis Farrakhan is here," Holliman said. "I think he'd make a pretty good guest." Farrakhan had come to Baghdad to attend an international Islamic conference being held across from the Al-Rasheed. Saddam Hussein was expected to address the gathering later that afternoon.

"Let's give it a shot," I said, calling his room after Atlanta said yes to the interview. Farrakhan, who headed the Lost and Found Nation of Islam, based in Chicago, was a controversial figure. The "give and take," even over the four-wire, was bound to generate sparks.

Farrakhan said he'd be happy to oblige and would send his security chief to our office to oversee arrangements. "His name is Leonard Farrakhan Mohammed," I said to John. "You play producer for a while. I'm off to see Naji."

"YOU MAY BRING IN YOUR SATELLITE PHONE," Naji said, "but only under the conditions we discussed. I have personally promised the minister, on your behalf."

"That's great," I said. "Will your office inform customs so there'll be no problems?"

"We will make the arrangements," he assured me. Out of the corner of my eye, I noticed a picture of Farrakhan on CNN. The interview was evidently going as planned. Naji picked up the remote control and turned up the volume. A second later he turned it down again.

"Who is Mr. Peter Arnett?" he asked abruptly. I knew Naji had seen Peter's name when I'd applied for his visa.

"Peter is one of the finest reporters in the world," I said. "He's won the Pulitzer prize and is a man of absolute integrity."

"He has not been to Baghdad before?"

"I think this might be the only country he hasn't reported from. But he's coming at an interesting time."

"And Mr. Shaw?"

"Bernie's due in this afternoon. Is there any news about the interview?"

"In principle, it will be fine," he said. "We shall talk more after Mr. Shaw arrives."

I CALLED EASON and gave him the news about the INMARSAT. We conferenced with engineer Nic Robertson in Amman, who volunteered to bring it in, though he cautioned his decision was not to be construed as a long-term commitment. Nic also expressed concerns about getting out of Baghdad if he had to.

"That shouldn't be a problem," Eason assured him. "Peter Humi has a lead on a charter." I told Nic I'd call Sadoun to ask that permission for a visa be telexed that very afternoon. With any luck we'd see him and the INMARSAT the next day.

"I GOT YOU A SUITE THIS TIME," I said to Bernie as we walked down the hall. "I figured you'd be more comfortable."

"Mr. Robert, Mr. Robert," he smiled. "You always take such good care of me. Here, I have something for you." He opened his Halliburton and pulled out a tiny bottle of Blephamide. "For your eye," he said, handing me the antibiotic. "Though you know, you really should see a doctor."

As usual, I was glad to see Bernie. While he continued unpacking, I brought him up to date on the day's events, the bad news about Bly and Cynde, and the good news about the INMARSAT. I told him the interview with Saddam was expected to happen but he shouldn't count on it precisely on the fifteenth. "The party line is, 'that's just another date on the calendar,' " I said. I doubted Saddam would acknowledge its significance by talking with CNN.

"You're probably right," he said philosophically. "We'll just have to see."

We talked some about our families and the strain we'd put them under by accepting this particular assignment. I ventured the pressure on Bernie's wife Linda and their two children was more acute. "Why would you say that?" he asked.

"Well, you're an anchorman, after all. They've got a right to feel you're beyond the Nick Danger stage . . . you know, taking unnecessary risks."

"We're both reporters, my brother. I'm sure your family is as worried as mine. So tell me, Mr. Robert," he said, steering us onto safer ground, "do they still serve those lamb chops with the red wine sauce? Tonight, I feel up for a treat."

"WE FIGHT FOR THE SAKE OF DIGNITY," Saddam told the Islamic Conference. "Our paradise is the promised one for believers. All our youth, our students, and our farmers are armed and will fight this holy war. This is not a showdown over land or territory. It is a showdown for the sake of human objectives."

In Saudi Arabia, Secretary of State James Baker told U.S. forces, "You will not have to wait much longer." Said Baker: "At midnight on the fifteenth, we pass the brink."

There was no real reason for me to be in the workspace by 5 A.M., but I couldn't sleep. It promised to be a busy day. Wilson and the other "dips" were leaving, Pérez de Cuéllar was due in at night, and sometime within the next twenty-four hours the Congress of the United States would vote on whether to give Bush the authority to use force to eject Iraqi troops from Kuwait. We would all earn our pay today.

Naturally, the workspace looked like a disaster area. The night before, we'd been up exceptionally late, doing our journalistic duty and shooting the shit with Bernie. If Roth had walked into the place, he'd have had a stroke.

After swallowing my daily overdose of Excedrin, I set about airing out the office and straightening up. There was a small mountain of empty ice trays due, in large part, to my new propensity to order more ice than we actually needed. Mr. Petros had taught me to say *Thelliche min fadlach*, or "More ice, please" in Arabic. My fractured accent had room service in stitches: I half-expected Mrs. Nihad to ask me if I wanted to moonlight as a lounge act in the Scheherezade Bar. Mr. Petros also taught us such handy phrases as *Rye-yaa* (fabulous), *Mumtaz* (excellent), *Mish moohshkila* (no problem), and one that I would have occasion to use once the war began: *La toe drope, ana sahafi* (Don't shoot, I'm a journalist).

I put up some coffee and threw the cassette in the tape recorder. It was time to check in with Atlanta. "Good morning. This is W-I-E-N-E-R beginning its broadcast day. . . ."

"The U.S. embassy in Tel Aviv is urging Americans to leave Israel," John Fiegener said. "They're potentially talking about tens of thousands of people. Let's see, what else? There's a report out of Moscow that the Kremlin may be pursuing a new diplomatic initiative, but they're not elaborating. I guess you heard what Baker said about passing the brink? It looks like it's getting serious. . . ."

I went over the day's game plan with Fiegener, then joined Bly and Holliman for breakfast. Bly was still torn over his decision to leave, but what was done was done. He'd be flying out with Wilson on the U.S. embassy charter. Atlanta wanted him to stitch together an evacuation piece he would file from Frankfurt. Ingrid and the crew left for the embassy and from there headed to the airport. The Damsel would ferry back tape as soon as possible for the morning feed. I sat down at the four-wire and called Humi in Amman. I wanted to be brought up to speed on his efforts to find us a plane.

"Essentially," Peter said, "the charter is ours twenty-four hours a day from the fourteenth to the eighteenth. There's a period on the fifteenth when it isn't available, around 6 P.M., Amman time, but that's well in advance of the UN deadline. The jet is a Rockwell Sabreliner. It can carry six to eight people and approximately a hundred and fifty kilos of luggage. The company says it needs four hours 'scramble time' to prepare for the flight."

"What's the range of the plane?" I asked.

"There are actually two jets available. Both fly at about four hundred miles per hour. One can cruise for three and a half hours without refueling, the second, about four. That should easily get you to Amman, Cairo, Turkey, or Cyprus."

"Tail numbers and markings?"

"Right. The first one is JYAFP, the second JYAFH. Both planes are painted white, with red and gold stripes on the livery near the portholes." God bless Humi, I thought. In addition to being terrifically well organized, Peter had a head for details. "Let me give you some names and numbers in Baghdad," he added. "These are the local representatives of Arab Wings." I copied down the telephone numbers, both office and home, of the station manager and his assistant.

"So how much is this little venture costing the home office?" I asked.

"Ten thousand dollars a day to keep the plane on standby. Actual flights are about fifteen."

"Well, it's certainly a new CNN," I laughed. "In the old days, they'd have tried to evacuate us by camel."

"THE PLANE STILL HASN'T TAKEN OFF," Ingrid said, calling in from the airport. "They're saying something about airspace being officially closed."

"What?"

"Yeah, that's what they're saying, Wienerish. I'm going to check again with the Air Operations Director. I'll call you back."

"The charter's still on the ground," I informed Atlanta. "Ingrid's trying to confirm a report the airspace might have been closed."

"We're also hearing that here in Amman," Peter cut in on the four-wire. "They're saying it's because of VIP travel." What VIP? I wondered. Pérez de Cuéllar wasn't due for hours.

"Robert, this is Eason," he said, jumping on the line. "We need to see about getting Naji or someone else over to the four-wire for a live interview following the congressional vote."

"I've asked Naji several times about going live," I said, "but he's always declined."

"Whaddaya mean? I heard him do a radio interview with the BBC. . . ."

"I know, but he says that was exceptional. They just caught him at the right time. . . ."

"Give me a break," Eason exploded. "Those fuckers . . ." The four-wire suddenly went dead.

"Baghdad to Atlanta," I called. "Baghdad to Amman."

"Way to go, Eason," Holliman smirked.

"Baghdad to Atlanta! Baghdad to Amman! Baghdad to Atlanta! Baghdad to Amman!"

"It's down," Holliman said, turning up the volume. "Listen, there's not even any 'white' noise."

"This is just great," I said, as I lit a Gauloise.

"Yeah . . . *Mumtaz*, as they say," Holliman joked.

"Baghdad to Atlanta . . . !"

"Hello, Robert." Eason came back on the line. "I'm very sorry about that. . . ."

"This is the Iraqi Federal Communications Commission," I lampooned in my best Richard Roth impersonation. "The use of profanity on this channel is in direct violation of IFC regulations. Consider this a warning. . . ."

"I hear ya," Eason said. "I'm really sorry. . . ."

"Forget it," I laughed. "Listen, I'll do my best to get Naji for you, but it's damn near impossible."

"Understood. Hey, Ed wants to have a word with you. . . ."

"Hiya, Robert," Ed said, taking over the line. "How are you and the gang holding up?"

"Just great," I joked. "Can we go home now?"

"Why sure," he laughed. "That's why we chartered that plane in Amman. . . ."

"That plane is a hell of a gesture . . ."

"Well, we would have preferred several camels. . . ."

"Funny that you mention it. I was just telling Humi the same thing. . . ."

"How's Bernie doing?" he asked, turning serious.

"He's fine, Ed. He's in his room right now going over some material. Do you want me to get him for you?"

"No, that's not necessary. Please tell Bernie to stay 'up' as much as possible. We'd love to have him on the four-wire whenever he's available. John or Peter can handle the packages and 'Crisis Conference.' We'd like to have Bernie on from the 'International Hour' through the prime-time shows."

"That shouldn't be a problem. So, how are you guys doing?"

"Oh, we're fine. We're all thinking of you people in Baghdad. . . ."

"That's nice to hear. I'll pass it on to Ingrid and the others when they get back."

"OKAY, THEY'RE FINALLY 'WHEELS-UP,' " Ingrid called in from the airport a few hours later. "There were forty-four passengers, including six American 'dips,' seven private U.S. citizens, and three journalists." She ticked off the nationalities of the other passengers to relay to Atlanta. "We're on our way back to get something to eat, then we'll come back out here to meet the Secretary General."

So that's that, I thought. It was odd. I certainly never had any intention of running to the U.S. embassy in the event of war, but now that it had closed and our diplomats had left, there was a certain chill in the air that hadn't been there before. To his credit, Joe had gone out of his way to see to it that journalists could continue to use the telephones at USIS; at the airport he also told Ingrid he'd left keys with Hanan to a couple of apartments he suggested we might use. Unfortunately, there must have been a misunderstanding because when we checked with Hanan, she knew nothing about it.

I KNEW WHAT TRACY was going to say before she'd even said it, but it still gave me a headache. "I'm sorry, Weenie . . . I really am, but I've been giving it a lot of thought and I'd like to leave."

"No problem," I lied. "Could you at least hang around until we find a replacement?"

"How long do you think that will take?"

"It will have to be within the next couple of days. I presume you don't want to be here past the deadline."

"Oh, Weenie, I feel so terrible about this," she said, giving me a hug. "Will you ever forgive me?"

"There's nothing to forgive. It's a very personal decision. I'm in no position to second guess—"

"Of course, I'll stay until the fifteenth," she said, "but you know, you should think about leaving too—"

"Please," I interrupted. "I don't want to have this conversation. Listen, Cybil, I don't mean to sound curt, but these past couple of days . . . all these changes, it's drivin' me nuts. Now you have to do what you have to do, but please, even out of concern, don't tell me what I have to do. I know what I have to do. I'm just trying to do it the best I can." I walked back to my room and placed a call to Atlanta.

"SO WHAT'S YOUR SUGGESTION?" Eason asked.

"I think we should call Krizmanich. God knows Kris would be entitled to say no. She's probably pissed at not being the first choice for the final rotation, but that was also a matter of personnel dynamics. It had nothing to do with her work, which is fine. . . ."

"Understood. I'll call her," he said.

"Fine. And I'll activate the visa process with good ole Sadoun."

We're going to need some serious morale boosting after these latest changes, I thought after I returned to the workspace. Losing Tracy was bound to have a ricochet effect. Shit. Time was running out. What to do? Almost as if on cue, Peter Arnett appeared at the door.

"Hey, guys", he bellowed, giving us all his greeting. "This is terrific." He looked around the office. "What a setup!" I gave Peter the five-dollar tour, pointing to the generator, flashlights, and tape recorders Holliman had brought from the States; the food stocks, dispensary, converter, Still Store, four-wire, and other equipment. "I love it!" he boomed. "This is just perfect. You've thought of everything. This is better than anything I ever had in Vietnam." I showed him to Bly's former room across the hall and briefly reviewed the latest changes.

"Let her go," he said about Tracy. "We don't want anyone here who isn't ready to give their all. Now, if you ask me, what we need is a small core of—"

"Everything's under control," I interrupted. "Hopefully Krizmanich will come in to replace Tracy. . . ."

"This is quite a hotel," he said, changing the subject while continuing to unpack. I pointed out some of the more unusual "security" features that distinguished the Al-Rasheed. "I love it!" he laughed, inspecting the tiny red and green lights above the bathroom. "What a trip, Robert! Don't you agree?"

Peter's just what the doctor ordered, I thought as I crossed back over to the workspace. People who'd never worked with him before might find his style a bit abrasive, but there was no doubt in my mind we'd made the best possible choice by asking Arnett to join us.

The congressional debate seemed to drag on for hours, as did the voting in both the House and the Senate. Bernie monitored the proceedings on the four-wire while I called Naji in search of quotes.

"I think Bush would go to war with or without this approval from the

Congress," Naji said. "Even if the world is against us, we will not succumb to pressure."

I knew they were following the story closely on CNN at the Ministry of Culture and Information. Sadoun had already called twice asking me to explain some of the finer points of legislative protocol. I did my best to accommodate him, though my knowledge of these matters was rather limited. At best, I hoped not to confuse him any further.

Both the U.S. Senate (52–47) and the House of Representatives (250–183) gave President Bush a vote of confidence as they endorsed the use of force. "No, technically this is not a declaration of war," I'd told Sadoun. But for all intents and purposes, that was precisely what it was.

Bernie took to the air for the evening shows, setting the scene in Baghdad and updating Iraqi reaction. Hafez al-Assad of Syria promised Saddam Hussein that if Iraq were attacked after withdrawing from Kuwait, Syrian troops would fight alongside him. "We do not trust this Assad," Naji said after I'd reached him for comment. "Look what he promised the Palestinians and Lebanese. Would you trust Assad after that?"

INGRID RETURNED AROUND MIDNIGHT. Pérez de Cuéllar's arrival had been a zoo. "They weren't prepared for the press," she explained. "Here, check out this tape." The UN Secretary General was greeted by Aziz but the two men quickly disappeared under the crush of reporters. This was more than a typical gang-bang. With so much riding on the Secretary General's eleventh-hour mission to Baghdad, crews were literally climbing on top of each other to get their shots. At one point they broke through security, only to be physically restrained by the Iraqi guards. At a brief impromptu news conference, Pérez de Cuéllar said he carried no specific proposals with him but was looking forward to discussing a wide range of issues with Saddam Hussein when the two met the next day. Then he and Aziz sped off to their own meeting.

"IS BERNIE AROUND?" Larry Doyle asked, stopping by the workspace. He and Shaw went back many years to when they were both at CBS. Allen Pizzey was standing behind him.

"Jeez, what are you doing here?" I laughed. "You're the last person I expected to find . . ."

"Well, I had some time off with my family in Rome," Pizzey said. "That helped a lot. Then I figured, what the hell?"

"No crew though," Doyle explained. "CBS can't find a single crew willing to come back here."

"Goddamn," I whistled.

"Actually, they can find a crew," Pizzey corrected him. "They just don't want to pay for them."

"Free-lance guys?"

"Yeah," Doyle said. "They're still trying to work out the details in New York, about insurance and that kind of thing, but in the meantime, we are it for CBS."

"So, what are you going to do?"

"What CNN used to do ten years ago," he smiled. "Beg for footage wherever we can get it."

For the second night running I couldn't sleep. The deadline was just two days away and much remained to be done. It occurred to me if Naji had given us permission to bring in the INMARSAT on condition we wouldn't use it until the four-wire went down, maybe he'd say yes to the flyaway under similar ground rules. After all, it was widely assumed if war broke out, Iraqi TV would be a primary target. Once it was bombed, the only way to transmit pictures from Baghdad would be through a portable uplink. I made a note to call Naji and pitch him hard.

Nic and the INMARSAT would arrive within hours. Barring any last-minute hitches, Krizmanich would arrive the following day. Tracy had already made reservations to fly out on Iraqi Airways the morning of the fifteenth, and, of course, we always had the charter.

I jumped in the shower and stood under the water for almost fifteen minutes, juggling the taps from hot to cold. I'd heard somewhere this was meant to be therapeutic, but it did nothing for me. I gathered up my laundry and debated whether or not to send it in. Same-day service was by now only a pleasant memory, but you could usually get your clothes back the following afternoon. Still, if there were a fuck-up . . . what would I wear to the war? I decided to chance it anyway. I pulled back the curtain and looked out on the anti-aircraft battery set up on the roof of the building directly across from us. Several soldiers were drinking coffee. I noticed that overnight they'd reinforced their position with additional sandbags. Here's looking at you, I toasted, taking a swig of cold mineral water.

The Saddam-Pérez de Cuéllar tête-à-tête was the lead story, of course, but the Iraqis weren't permitting coverage. At most, we hoped to get another airport statement from the Secretary General upon his departure later in the day. Bernie and I also had an appointment to meet with Naji, and perhaps even Minister Jassim, to firm up details for *the* interview. And at some point, I wanted to bring Peter over to the ministry as well for a personal "meet and greet."

"You're up early," I said to Holliman as I entered the workspace. "What's going on?"

"They've finally clarified the exact timing of the deadline," he explained, double-checking his notes. "It's midnight on the fifteenth, New York time . . . that's 8 A.M. for us, the morning of the sixteenth."

"So we can expect the planes at 8:01?" I joked.

"I guess," he chuckled. "Gee, it's getting close, huh?"

A few minutes later Peter joined us and we ordered breakfast. John asked Arnett if he'd care to take over the four-wire for the morning broadcast of "Crisis Conference," but Peter declined. "Just give me some time to get up to speed, guys," he smiled. "Perhaps I could do it the next time around."

"Morning, boys!" Ingrid whooshed into the workspace.

"Hey there, darling," I greeted her. "How's your vaginitis?" Out of the corner of my eye, I saw Peter do a double take.

"My vaginitis?" Ingrid laughed. "It's . . . acute!"

"Very cute?" I deadpanned.

"I see why you came to Baghdad," Peter roared with laughter. "What's with you two?"

"Don't mind them," Holliman explained. "You'll get used to it. It's a running gag."

"I love it!" Peter wailed.

"Well, don't love it too much," Ingrid smirked. "It ain't war yet!"

AFTER BREAKFAST, Ingrid left to buy provisions. Anticipating the worst, we'd been stockpiling as much mineral water and canned goods as we could find. Peter eagerly joined the Damsel on this excursion. It would give him a good opportunity to take a look at the city firsthand. I listened in while John did "Crisis Conference," which, among other topics, prompted the usual questions about working "behind the lines." Naturally, this subject intrigued many of our viewers, though their queries sometimes focused on our patriotism, or rather, our supposed lack of it, as well as their concern for our safety.

While John was on the air, I fielded two telephone calls that took me by surprise. The first was from Abul Abbas, confirming our interview around midday; the second from the PLO. Would we, the caller asked, be interested in talking with Yasir Arafat? The Chairman had returned to Baghdad the night before last. As usual, we had telephoned his people the moment we'd learned Arafat was back in town, but until now we'd heard nothing. I tried to mask my eagerness as I made arrangements for Arafat to come to the Al-Rasheed that evening and sit down with Bernie in front of the four-wire. Goddamn! I thought, as I concluded the call, it was shaping up to be one hell of a day.

"There was a bit of trouble at customs," Nic said, helping the porter with the INMARSAT. "Nothing serious, but they lifted a part. I'm fairly certain it can still work without it."

"That's bullshit," I groaned. "We had permission—"

"Yes, I know. Here," he said, handing me a slip of paper. "I had the fellow at customs give me a receipt."

"Ya know, this isn't fair," I said, picking up the phone to call Sadoun. "I want that part back as soon as possible."

Sadoun apologized profusely, but insisted it must have been a simple misunderstanding. "Robert, I promise to take care of this. I will come to the hotel personally to see you later." I thanked him politely, then placed a second call to Naji.

"I know we'll see each other later," I said, "but I wanted to run this by you now." I gave him my thoughts about bringing in the flyaway.

"It is an interesting proposal," he admitted. "In principle there should be no problem, but please, do not do anything until I learn for certain."

As much as I wanted to accompany John to see Abul Abbas, I couldn't get away. For the past couple of days I'd been considering moving CNN out of the Al-Rasheed to potentially safer quarters. One option we'd discussed was the Soviet embassy. Though most of its diplomats had left, a skeletal staff remained. I'd had a meeting with a senior Soviet diplomat to pursue the matter; CNN had even asked our Moscow bureau to sound out Primakov. There were pros and cons to moving, of course. The biggest plus was that the Soviet embassy was unlikely to be a strategic target. The downside would be abandoning the four-wire, but with an INMARSAT in place, that wasn't insurmountable. In principle, we'd still be able to broadcast. But there was also an ethical question. As independent journalists would we be compromising ourselves by seeking shelter under a Soviet protective wing? True, there were no Soviet troops in the allied coalition, but Moscow had signed on to the UN's mandate. Having done that, the Soviet Union had chosen sides. Our presence on Soviet "soil" could therefore become an issue. As it turned out, we never had to make the decision; the answer from the Russkies was nyet. They claimed their embassy had neither the space nor the personnel to accommodate us.

We also considered moving back to the Sheraton. It was on the other side of town, away from the presidential palace and several key ministries, but the shelter there was for shit. And if the bridges across the Tigris were bombed, we'd be isolated. Renting a room at the Sheraton might provide a second camera location, but I didn't want to split up my troops. It seemed to me we'd be better off if we all stayed together, wherever that might be.

Saddam Hussein responded to Hafez al-Assad's offer to support Iraq militarily once it pulled out of Kuwait by calling on Assad to side with Iraq against the forces of evil. "Our Nineteenth Province has become a battlefield for the showdown," Saddam said over Baghdad radio. "The Arab world will be triumphant . . . we are filled with joy and hope when the gathering of the faithful expands and when the crowds increase at the door to virtue." He said the distance between "the camp of the faithful and that of the enemies had become wider" and reminded his listeners that "jihad," or holy war, was a duty for every Muslim.

Meanwhile, Iraqi TV devoted most of its evening news broadcast to showing antiwar demonstrations around the world. From London to Bonn to Paris to the United States, tens of thousands of people rallied for peace. The footage, most of it from CNN, was "looped" and shown again and again throughout the night.

It was well after dark when Bernie and I finally headed over to the Ministry of Culture and Information. As usual, we walked unescorted through the building and took the elevator to the seventh floor.

"Good evening, Mr. Shaw," Naji said, rising to greet us. "Hello, Robert, how are you?"

"Fine, Naji. Still surviving?"

"Yes," he said, smiling, "still surviving."

Bernie and Naji exchanged the usual pleasantries and discussed the congressional vote, which Naji dismissed offhandedly as simply another threat. He had little to offer in the way of information about the meeting between Saddam and Pérez de Cuéllar. Only later would we learn the Iraqi President had kept the UN Secretary General cooling his heels most of the day, while Saddam met first with Yasir Arafat, Daniel Ortega, and Japanese Socialist leader Takako Doi. Naji told Bernie he had come to Baghdad at a "historic" time, but he could not confirm a specific date for the interview with his President. "Let us go see Minister Jassim himself," he suggested. "Perhaps he has some news."

The three of us took the elevator to the ground floor and entered an enormous mausoleum of a room. It was empty except for a white marble bust of Saddam Hussein and two tan leather couches in the far corner. On one sat Minister Latif Nasif Jassim, wearing a heavy green overcoat over his Revolutionary Command Council military uniform. As always, his bodyguards hovered nearby. Naji translated while we made small talk, then Jassim told Bernie the interview would probably take place on the sixteenth or seventeenth . . . not before. As far as Iraq was concerned, he smiled, "January 15 is just another date on the calendar."

Suddenly Jassim turned to me and asked in English, "Robert, why do you look so sad?"

His question took me by surprise, but I answered him as honestly and directly as I could. "Mr. Minister, as you know I have great affection and respect for the Iraqi people, and it grieves me that many of them . . . many of them will die here if there's war."

Latif Nasif Jassim leaned forward and looked me squarely in the eyes. "Robert, my friend, there is no need to be worried. American planes will never reach Baghdad."

By the time we returned to the workspace, I was in serious need of a reality check. A few minutes later it was provided by the PLO.

"We are from President Arafat," a security guard announced. "We here to look . . ."

"We'll be doing it right here," I said, pointing to the four-wire.

"This all CNN?" a second man asked, pointing to Rooms 904 and 908, whose connecting doors to 906 were open. "Please, when President Arafat come, these doors stay close. No person go in or out."

"That's just the bathroom," I called to the first guard, who'd poked his head inside.

"Please, this door stay close too," he insisted. The two spent another few minutes inspecting the premises, then left.

"We ought to put this on tape," Mark suggested. "I can stay tight on Arafat; we could use the soundbites in a package."

"Makes sense to me," I said, as he and Nic began setting up the gear.

ABOUT THIRTY MINUTES LATER there was a rustling in the hall as first the security guards, and then Arafat, along with his entourage, made their way into the workspace. This was the first time I had ever met the PLO leader and what struck me were his eyes. They twinkled. There's no other word for it. He was dressed in the familiar olive-green uniform and sported his trademark black and white checkered *kaffiyeh*. "Hello, hello," he said enthusiastically, shaking hands round the room. I showed Arafat to his seat beside Bernie. "This is live?"

"Indeed," Bernie said, moving the four-wire closer to both of them. "They'll have a picture of you on the screen while we're talking on this line."

Arafat told Bernie he did not believe there would be war. "You will see," he smiled, emphatically nodding his head. "I will be here in Baghdad on January 15." He again stressed the need for an international conference on the Middle East and lauded Saddam Hussein for his support. He blamed the United States and Israel for hindering efforts to achieve a comprehensive settlement to problems in the region and said the congressional vote hurt Pérez de Cuéllar's efforts to seek peace. He said little that was new or startling, except for his conviction that hostilities would ultimately be avoided.

Following the interview, Holliman asked Arafat to pose for a photograph and a few moments later the Chairman and his coterie were gone.

"Awww, SHIT," Ingrid muttered when she returned from the airport. "I'm pissed I missed Arafat. . . ."

"Never mind him," I snapped. "What'd de Cuéllar have to say?"

"Well, it doesn't look good, boys," she said glumly. That was an understatement.

"God only knows if there will be peace or war," the Secretary General told reporters before boarding his plane. From the tone of his voice it was obvious his mission had been a bust.

Bernie did live "cut-ins" throughout the rest of the evening until we finally called it quits just after 2 A.M. We shared a nightcap and talked awhile before he turned in. I fixed myself another drink and lingered in the workspace. "American planes will never reach Baghdad." I couldn't get it out of my head. Jassim didn't actually believe that, did he? I was about to call it a night when Iraqi TV suddenly came back on the air. Saddam Hussein was holding a news conference with Iraqi journalists. "Fuck!" I shouted. Holliman, who'd been relaxing in his room, ran into the workspace. "Get Alla," I shouted as the telephone rang. It was the control room at Iraqi TV telling me the pictures of Saddam, recorded earlier, were being simultaneously transmitted to Jordan. I got Atlanta on the four-wire and passed on the news. A few minutes later, John returned with Alla. "What's your President saying?" I asked frantically.

"As American law seeks to dominate the world . . ." Alla translated, "it seems America wants to use this new illegitimate privilege to wave its big stick, which it successfully tried with others, imagining it will succeed in a similar manner with the Arab Nation, including Iraq. . . ."

"Atlanta to Baghdad," came a voice over the four-wire.

"Baghdad here."

"Okay, we're seeing it in Atlanta. Can we take it live?"

"Go ahead," I said. "Here's Holliman for an intro." I passed John the mike.

"This is John Holliman in Baghdad. What you are seeing are pictures of Saddam Hussein now being broadcast on Iraqi television. We understand this is a news conference that was held earlier today. Let's listen in. . . ." John moved the microphone in front of Alla and held it there.

"Our planes are capable of striking from long distance and hitting their targets," he translated. ". . . If they want war, no other party can prevent it because things have turned out this way. On one side there is Iraq and its supporters, and on the other side there is the United States and its allies. Bush speaks about capitulation, capitulation of Arabs, capitulation of Iraq. The time of capitulation has gone forever. It does not exist in the Iraqi vocabulary. . . ." Alla, who in the past had been reluctant to provide any translation, let alone live and simultaneous, was now getting into it. He motioned to John to hand him the microphone.

"We presented Pérez de Cuéllar with a review of our stand, tackling all political and legal aspects of some issues before the second of August, and after that date until this day. Iraq encouraged the Secretary General to continue his visits and dialogue if there was a desire to search for peaceful means. However, it should be known that the kind of peace we mean is comprehensive peace, and in the forefront of peace comes the Palestinian question."

Saddam said he was confident of an Iraqi victory, and said American technology would not be the decisive factor. He said the real battles would be fought by the infantry and tanks, and Iraq would emerge victorious because it was defending its homeland.

When asked if Iraq was about to make a surprise move, Saddam said no. "We are not the type to make surprises and initiatives under pressure and threat . . . We want peace but we also want Palestine, and we have nothing to barter for. We want all our rights. . . ."

"THAT WAS TERRIFIC," I said to Alla when the news conference concluded.

"Yeah, what a pro," John applauded.

"This calls for a drink," I laughed.

"No, I must return to my bed," Alla protested.

"I won't take no for an answer. You've just done excellent work. We must observe tradition. . . ." I reached for the Stoli and a couple of glasses.

"Okay, just one," he relented. "Very small."

"To Mr. Alla," John toasted. "And a job well done."

"To Mr. Alla," Ingrid chimed in. I looked at my watch. It was nearly 3:30 A.M. . . . January 14.

"I don't think that from today there is much room for undertakings for diplomacy," UN Secretary General Pérez de Cuéllar told reporters in Paris where he'd stopped off to brief French President François Mitterrand. "Unfortunately, I don't see any reason to be optimistic. I have no hope. The hope that I had is already gone."

"Jeez!" I said to Fiegener in Atlanta as I copied down the quotes. "He's not pullin' any punches."

I reviewed the checklist I'd scribbled in my notebook: Exit visas for everyone, distribute money (ten thousand dollars each), flashlights, and tape recorders; part for INMARSAT?; emergency packing for shelter, if necessary; call Naji and Nizar.

I got on the four-wire to Peter Humi in Amman. Although Tracy was booked out on commercial, we'd decided it was safer to bring in the charter.

"Let's plan on an 8 A.M. departure tomorrow," I said. "I'll have her at the airport an hour before." Peter said he'd take care of everything and get back to me.

"WHEN DID YOU GET those pictures of the Saddam news conference?" Brent Sadler asked, stopping by the workspace. "London's been after me."

"They popped up last night after two. We translated them live."

"Damn," he muttered. "Any chance of a dub?"

"Sure," I said. "See Tracy next door."

SINCE TRACY HAD DECIDED TO LEAVE, she'd been spending a lot of time huddled with Mark and Nic. Though I wasn't certain, I suspected she'd been advising her friends to think twice about what they were doing. Nic, of course, had already made it clear he'd be leaving by the deadline; now I sensed Mark was also wavering. I decided to have a word with both of them.

"The thing is," Mark said, "I didn't even get a raise when they promoted me from soundman to cameraman and moved me to Berlin. Not a dime. Look at ABC. They're paying their techs three hundred and fifty dollars a day extra to take this assignment. But what do I get from CNN? Nothing. Not even a raise. And now they expect me to risk my life—"

"Hold on a minute," I interrupted. "You're dealing with apples and oranges here. A raise is one issue. Being in Baghdad's another. If you'd like, I'll speak with Eason."

"Well it would help if the company did something . . ."

"What about you, Nic?" I asked. "Still plan on leaving tomorrow?"

"I'm not sure. We can speak later when you get an answer about the flyaway, but I agree with Mark. I'd feel a lot better if the company made a gesture. . . ."

"GOOD GRIEF," Eason moaned. "Are you telling me he's willing to risk his life for three hundred and fifty dollars a day? Is that what he thinks his life is worth?"

"Well, it's the principle of the thing," I said. "And to tell ya the truth, he does have a point about his raise . . ."

"That's a separate issue," Eason snapped. "This other thing sets a bad precedent. If we pay bonuses to Mark and Nic, what about all the other people who are risking their lives, in Saudi for example?"

"I hear ya, but I think a case can be made that Baghdad's unique . . ."

"Yeah, maybe. Okay," he sighed. "Lemme go speak to Tom and Ed."

EASON CALLED BACK AN HOUR LATER. Atlanta gave Mark his raise and agreed to pay both Mark and Nic a bonus for each day they were in Baghdad after the fifteenth. (When the fighting ended, CNN paid everyone who was in Baghdad during the war a "Special Baghdad Premium" equivalent to three times his/her daily wage for each day spent in the Iraqi capital.)

"I appreciate what you've done, Robert," Nic said. "It shows the company really cares."

"Please, keep this to yourselves," I admonished them. "I have more than enough to deal with, without having to negotiate any more contracts."

THE SPECIAL MEETING of the National Assembly had everyone transfixed. Since the session had been announced there were persistent rumors it might be used to spring a plan that would, at the very least, forestall the war. After everything we'd heard recently from Saddam, it was undoubtedly wishful thinking, but for those of us hunkered down at Ground Zero, well, as they say, hope springs eternal.

That hope faded moments after the session began. The two-hundred-and-fifty-member assembly voted by acclamation to go to war rather than abandon Kuwait. "This is a historic confrontation," its resolution declared. "Your steadfast Iraq led by President Saddam Hussein has resolved to fight . . . Iraqis will fight valiantly to be martyred or achieve victory. The aggression will be repelled by the experienced Iraqi Army." The speaker of the assembly, Saadi Mahdi Saleh, asked deputies to swear allegiance to Saddam, whom he called "the knight of the Arab Nation." A few hours later, the Iraqi News Agency reported that Saddam had ordered the words *Allah Akhbar,* God is great, added to the national flag.

"*And to Kuwait—Any day now.*" Watching the commercial for Kuwait Airlines on CNN while sitting in Naji's office has to rank as one of the more bizarre moments of the Baghdad countdown. Naji said he was close to obtaining permission for the flyaway and assured me he'd have an answer in the morning. He seemed more concerned by the flight of journalists that was already underway. "I do not understand why they are all leaving. We shall provide daily briefings. People can do their work."

"There's a considerable fear factor in the air," I said. "The bombing will probably be massive."

"That is war, but we have no plans to evacuate Baghdad now. Look," he said holding up a sheet of paper, "these are requests for visas from reporters, many I have never heard of, from Taiwan, Turkey, and Korea. They still want to come here even if the Western press leaves—"

We were interrupted by the arrival of two Japanese journalists, both of whom I recognized from TV Asahi.

"I received your kind invitation," Naji said, standing up to greet them. "I look forward to attending the reception." From what I gathered it was a party to celebrate the opening of TV Asahi's new Baghdad bureau.

"That is why we have come," one of the Japanese explained. "Excuse please, but we must leave Baghdad. We will have the party, um, later, when we return, after the war."

"That is up to you," Naji said without a trace of emotion.

"Excuse please, our company ordered us to leave. What will CNN do?" he asked, turning to me.

"We're staying," I replied, prompting a satisfied grunt from Naji.

"Well, good-bye then," he said, shaking hands. "And good luck."

After they'd left the room I turned to Naji. "I'll tell you honestly, I'm very frightened. And I'm also concerned about my people . . ."

"Do not worry, Robert. I assure you, you will be able to work. We will make every effort to help you do your job. You now have your telephone; you will soon have your flyaway, we have done our best for CNN."

"I appreciate that. I really do. But I still need exit visas for all my staff. Just in case."

"See Sadoun," Naji said. "He will take care of it."

"JUST COULDN'T STAY AWAY?" I laughed, giving Kris Krizmanich a hug.

"Well, I figured nothing was going to happen for at least a week, so I said to myself, why not?"

"I appreciate your coming, Kris. I really do. I hope you're not upset about not being asked earlier."

"Oh, that's okay. Don't worry about it."

"So, what's going on in Amman?"

"The same old thing. There have been a few demos lately. When are we doing Saddam?"

"Either the sixteenth or the seventeenth, I think . . ."

"We're not gonna edit it here, I hope?" she asked with some concern.

"Nah, you're off the hook," I laughed. "See, there is a plus to being here."

WHILE JOHN WORKED on the evening package and Peter handled live shots on the four-wire, Bernie and I drove to the Foreign Ministry to meet with Nizar. From the moment he greeted us, it was apparent Hamdoon had seen better days. He was exceptionally low-key and seemed depressed. "I feel like I'm watching a fiction movie," he admitted after Bernie asked Nizar if he had ever imagined things would go this far. "It is all very strange."

As usual, the television in his office was tuned to CNN. As we reviewed the day's developments, I asked Nizar about the meeting in Geneva. "From the diplomatic point of view, Baker handled himself correctly, but these weren't negotiations. He gave us ultimatums." Nizar said Iraq was willing to negotiate, even now. He said Baghdad was prepared to discuss all issues . . . all issues, he repeated. We then chatted about Iraq's ambassador to the United States, Mohammed al-Mashat, who Nizar said planned to return to Baghdad. The United States had told the Iraqis to reduce its Washington embassy staff to four. (al-Mashat spent the war in Vienna, where his wife allegedly underwent medical treatment; he subsequently sought political asylum in Canada.) Throughout the discussion Bernie took notes. Nizar said he could be quoted as "a senior Iraqi government official."

BERNIE DROPPED ME OFF at the Information Ministry before returning to the hotel. I needed to pick up the exit visas from Sadoun and see about a generator. And we still hadn't secured the missing INMARSAT part from customs. By the time I got back to the Al-Rasheed, Bernie was about to go on the air. He showed me his script, based mostly on the meeting with Hamdoon, and sat down at the four-wire.

What happened next was an indication not only of the power of CNN, but of how desperately the world wanted to believe there was still hope. Though Bernie quoted Nizar accurately about Baghdad's willingness to discuss all issues, the stock market soared as people interpreted his report as meaning Iraq was ready to withdraw from Kuwait. It didn't help any that a writer for the Dow Jones wire also misunderstood what Bernie had reported and moved the story as a bulletin. Shaw immediately went back on the air and clarified his report, but he was angry. "I worked on this script for thirty minutes. I can't be responsible for what people want to believe . . ."

"I hear ya," I sympathized. "But let's fine-tune it even more so there's not a shred of doubt." We made some minor adjustments to the script, which Bernie reported again during his next live shot, and put the issue behind us.

"I JUST STOPPED BY TO SAY SO LONG," Pat Tyler said. "I'm leaving in the morning."

"Are all of you print guys pulling out?"

"I think so. *The Washington Post, The L.A. Times, The Baltimore Sun, The Wall Street Journal,* for sure. I think *The Daily Telegraph* has already left, and I heard something like two-thirds of the Japanese are going tomorrow as well."

"TV-AM is leaving too," I said pointing to the room across the hall. "We're gonna take over their space. It'll give us camera positions on both sides of the hotel."

"So, you're definitely staying?" he asked.

"It looks that way."

"And you're staying too?" he asked Bernie.

"Yes, I am," Bernie said.

"What about Saddam? Do you know when you'll be doing your interview?"

"Don't know for sure," I shrugged. "We're still waiting."

BERNIE HAD JUST FINISHED the 2 A.M. live shot when Atlanta said Ted Turner wanted to speak to us. He was calling from California. It took a few moments to transfer the call to the four-wire before the familiar Southern accent came over the line.

"As far as I'm concerned, you're all *heroes!*" Ted shouted. "You're heroes for being there up to now, but especially now since it's January 15 where you are. I'm very proud of you."

Bernie thanked Ted for his support and assured him he'd pass the word to the rest of the team. Then he put me on the line.

"Hi, Ted," I said, doing my best to sound casual.

"You're doin' a helluva job over there, Robert. Congratulations!"

"Thanks. I think it's important that we're here—"

"We *have* to be there!" he interrupted. "We're a global network! Also, if there's a chance for peace . . . personally, I'm afraid it's too late for that, but if there is, it might come through us. Hell, both sides aren't talkin' to each other, but they're talkin' to CNN. We have a major responsibility. . . ." I agreed with Ted the situation didn't look promising and told him we were prepared for the worst. "Well, keep up the good work," he boomed. "And best of luck."

BERNIE AND I HAD a late snack before the next cut-in. "Did you speak to Linda today?" I asked.

"Um-hmm, we talked earlier."

"How's she holding up?"

"All right, but it's difficult."

"You know, Bernie, you're a valuable asset to this company. I'm concerned about something happening and your getting stuck in here if war breaks out . . ."

"That's occurred to me," he admitted ruefully.

"Ya know, the Saddam interview notwithstanding, it might be in the best interest of the network to have you back in Washington, sitting at that anchor desk . . ."

"Perhaps. But so long as there's a possibility of doing the interview . . ."

"I understand. But look, the fact is Peter could do the interview; John could do the interview; I could do the interview. Obviously, it'd be better if you did it, but I'm terribly concerned about your getting trapped . . ."

"It's a risk."

"Well I might mention it to Ed, although I have a feeling I already know what he'll say."

SHORTLY BEFORE BERNIE'S LAST LIVE SHOT at 4 A.M. Tracy wobbled into the workspace. Her suitcases were in the hall and she'd checked out of her room. Driver Jasim was due at the hotel around six, and I'd planned to accompany Tracy to the airport shortly afterward. Although she'd been up all night saying good-bye to friends, Tracy didn't seem drunk; but she didn't seem quite right either. She was having trouble standing and was slurring her words.

"What's going on, sweetheart?" I asked, as I tried to steady her. "Have you taken something?"

"I'm so afraid," she cried. "I took some tranquilizers but they didn't help . . ." She slumped into a chair. Clearly, she was in no condition to fly.

"Oh, shit," I muttered as I gently led Tracy into the edit room before Bernie went back on the air.

"Oh, Weenie, I don't want you to die," she moaned. "Please, Weenie, please get out of here. You're crazy. I don't want you to die!"

"I'm not gonna die and you're not gonna die either," I assured her, "but I think it's best if you lie down . . ."

"I've already checked out . . ."

"Please, you can use my room," I insisted. I helped her across the hall where she collapsed on my bed. "Where are you going?" she mumbled. "I don't want you to leave, Weenie." I told Tracy I had to check on the charter and kissed her on the forehead.

"I'll be right across the hall," I said. "Everything will be okay. Try to get some sleep."

"IS THERE ANYTHING I CAN DO?" Bernie asked before heading back to his room. "Anything at all?"

"I don't think so. She needs to sleep it off. I'll speak to Humi about the charter but I'm worried about the weather." Baghdad was socked in by a thick layer of fog.

"Well, let me know if you change your mind," Bernie insisted. "Don't hesitate to wake me."

"TOO MUCH FOG," Mr. Ra'ad, the Arab Wings representative, reported when I telephoned the airport. "The plane cannot come from Amman. Maybe in a few hours." I silently cursed this turn of bad luck, then remembered Tracy also had a confirmed reservation on Iraqi Airways. Their jet was already on the ground, scheduled to depart later in the morning.

I was thinking about putting Tracy on board when Helena St. James, a producer for CBC, stopped by the workspace. She was also supposed to fly out on our charter and I'd promised her a ride to the airport.

"Goddamn it," she swore when I told her about the fog. "I don't like the sound of this. I think I'll also try to get on Iraqi Air. I've got a backup reservation."

"Could you give me a hand with Tracy?" I asked as we strolled over to my room. "She's gonna need some help." We tried to rouse Tracy but it was impossible.

"She can't fly like that," Helena protested. "They'll take one look at her at the airport and think she's on drugs. I wouldn't risk it. I'm sorry," she said, nervously checking the time, "but I'd better grab a taxi."

I walked back to the workspace and called Humi. Peter said he'd stay in close touch with Arab Wings and get back to us as soon as the charter was cleared to leave. I was exhausted. I'd been up all night and now that there was nothing more I could do, my nervous energy disappeared. I went back to my room, set the alarm to ring an hour later, and fell asleep next to Tracy.

"We've got a problem," I said to Ingrid as she joined me for breakfast. "Could you take Tracy out to the airport? Peter says the plane should be in around ten. I've got to meet with Naji, and then we have the demos." Radio Baghdad had called on Iraqis to take to the streets in a show of support for Saddam Hussein.

Meanwhile, Kris began moving provisions into 905, directly across the hall. The room, abandoned by TV-AM, offered a perfect view of the antiaircraft battery and the adjacent roof. "I'm putting all the food and water in here," Kris said. "It's better to keep it in one place."

"I'm going to start distributing the water," Mark said. "I think everyone should keep at least a case in his room." He went downstairs to borrow a cart from the porter.

Nic continued to tinker with the INMARSAT, which we'd successfully tested the evening before. Two officials from the PTT had stopped by to marvel at this heretofore unseen piece of Western technology and left suitably impressed. John and Peter split four-wire and package duty while I returned to my room to shower and change. The deadline was now less than twenty-four hours away.

Throughout the day we stayed glued to the four-wire as Atlanta kept us abreast of the latest developments. A last-minute flurry of diplomatic activity on the part of the French fizzled, as Paris conceded the time for talk had passed. In Washington, President Bush was described as "reflective and resolute." Charles Bierbauer, our senior White House correspondent, reported the President had walked around the grounds of the executive mansion at dawn, then met with his top advisers. "I would say the President is at peace with himself, ready to make the tough decisions ahead, if necessary," Charles quoted presidential spokesman Marlin Fitzwater. The White House said military action was likely "sooner rather than later." In Amman, King Hussein sadly concurred war was imminent and said it would result in a terrible catastrophe.

Naturally, we constantly updated the news from Baghdad. The state radio claimed millions of Iraqis demonstrated throughout the country, chanting "Kuwait is ours! Defeat the criminal Bush!" Iraqi TV's evening newscast showed American flags being torched as the announcer methodically ticked off a list of cities and provinces in which demonstrations had taken place. In Baghdad itself, several hotels were hosting so-called "Night of Challenge" parties where Iraqis were encouraged to sing the praises of Saddam while they danced till dawn. "You are the light; you are the challenge" went the refrain at the Babylon Oberoi, where revelers were charged the equivalent of sixty dollars each to get in the door.

THE IRAQIS weren't the only ones celebrating. After nearly five months since I first set foot in Baghdad, and just hours before the deadline, CNN finally received permission to bring in the flyaway. "I am sorry it has taken so long," Naji said dryly. "We have been very busy."

"Please, it's no problem at all," I blurted out, trying to contain my enthusiasm before hanging up the phone. So we did it! I thought to myself. Hot fuckin' damn! I jumped on the four-wire and conferenced with Eason and Peter Humi.

"I still need to line up a generator," I crowed. "Holliman's isn't powerful enough to run the flyaway. By the way, will everything fit on the plane?" The flyaway traveled in about twenty separate cases.

"I suspect we may have to make two trips," Peter said.

"Check it out and let me know," I said. "We should bring it in tomorrow."

CNN'S SPECIAL COVERAGE of the countdown to the deadline was extraordinary television. Virtually all the network's resources were mobilized as CNN hopped around the globe from the United States to the Middle East, to Europe, the Soviet Union, and Asia. With live and taped reports, interviews and analysis, official pronouncements and reaction from people on the streets, the network captured the mood and the moment precisely. CNN's reach was impressive but as far as I was concerned there was only one dateline that counted; and whenever an anchor in Atlanta intoned, "We go live now to Baghdad and CNN's Bernard Shaw," I felt I was living history.

"I do not think there will be war," Bernie told Larry King just three hours before the deadline. "I have been very reluctant to express personal opinions about this crisis. I studiously avoid infusing my reporting with anything personal, anything subjective . . . but I'm going to take the opportunity now to express a few thoughts . . . and the reason I do not think there will be a war . . . are my impressions of Saddam Hussein. This is not a man who would destroy what he has so assiduously worked to build up," Bernie said. "This man wants to be the Pan Arab leader. He wants Iraq to be a dominant force in the region. When you go against the kind of armament that is arrayed south of Kuwait, you risk destruction. That is what the American government has said to the Iraqi government time and time again. The problem here is a cultural one, the perception of having been dictated to, the perception of having been subjected to a double standard vis-à-vis the U.S. policy toward Israel . . . Well, we're coming up on H-Hour and we'll see . . . So, am I hopeful? Yes, I am hopeful."

After being awake all night listening to Bernie recap the news and the mood in the Iraqi capital, when the deadline finally rolled around at 8 A.M., it seemed almost anticlimactic. I stared out the window. The capital was again blanketed in fog but people were out on the streets. Arnett and the crew were out there too, to capture the scene on videotape for our morning television spot. As it turned out, it was the last spot we would file for days.

While Bernie tried unsuccessfully to nap, John took over as official "live meister." I went downstairs to pick up a copy of *The Baghdad Observer*. I half-expected to see screaming headlines about the deadline, but then I remembered what Minister Jassim had said about the fifteenth being just another date on the calendar. Naturally, a picture of Saddam graced the front page, but there was nothing in the January 16, 1991, edition of the paper that seemed, well, historic. The headlines were typical: ANTI-U.S. PROTESTS SWEEP THROUGH IRAQ; DOCUMENTS SHOW SAUDIS WERE AGAINST AL-SABAH OIL POLICY; CHINA, BRAZIL WARN OF GULF WAR CONSEQUENCES; THREE SENIOR PALESTINIAN AIDES MURDERED IN TUNIS; YEMENIS WANT IRAQ TO LIBERATE PALESTINE; ANTIWAR MOOD PREVAILS THROUGH THE WORLD. The editorial was entitled "A Matter of Principles, Not Policy."

"U.S. President Bush says the last peace initiative should come from Iraq," it read. "It seems that the long stick policy has blocked Mr. Bush's mind from admitting the reality that, for Iraq and for the Arabs, the time of submission to America's threats has gone forever. . . . There is a big difference between actions motivated by deep-rooted principles and those guided by a narrow-minded policy of interests. Regrettably, Mr. Bush appears unable to differentiate thanks to his blinkered way of handling the affairs of the 'most powerful' of the world's superpowers."

For the record, page five of the *Observer* featured its weekly "Music Roundup." According to Billboard's Top Twenty, the best-selling tune was Madonna's "Justify My Love."

"HUMI SAYS THERE'S A SNAG over insurance and landing rights," I said to Holliman. "He thinks it'll be sorted out by the end of the day but we probably won't get the flyaway here till tomorrow." With the expiration of the deadline, insurance rates for the charter, indeed all private and commercial aircraft, skyrocketed. There was now a real possibility the network would have to put up a bond of almost $1.5 million to get our plane in.

"Chicken feed," I laughed to Ingrid. "Your travel advances are bigger than that."

I placed a call to Naji to ask about Bernie's interview with Saddam. We had hoped it might happen within hours. "I am afraid it is not possible today," he said. "You must call me tomorrow." Unable to sleep, Bernie trundled down to the workspace every half-hour or so in his maroon Christian Dior pajamas. We were commiserating with one another over the timing of the interview, when Eason came on the four-wire with the news: "Fitzwater just urged all journalists to leave immediately. He said it worries him to see his colleagues on TV from Iraq. He even said, 'God be with you!' "

PART SIX

January 16, 1991–January 23, 1991

22

Bernie and I were the only ones in the workspace when a flash of red light suddenly exploded in the sky beyond the Giant Mushroom. I knew it had started but for a nanosecond my mind didn't want to accept it. Maybe, just maybe, it was a drill. Then, the anti-aircraft batteries on the rooftops around us opened up, filling the sky with a barrage of hot white light, and there wasn't any doubt. More explosions and flashes . . . green, red, and white. Bernie and I locked eyes for a split second, then lunged for the four-wire. "This is Bernie Shaw," he called to Atlanta. "Something is happening outside."

God, I hope Atlanta is hearing us, I thought.

I could hear screams in the corridor as panicked guests threw open their doors and ran for the stairwell. I ducked as the incessant tat-ta-tat-tat of anti-aircraft fire reverberated around the room. I was scared to death the fire from the adjacent roof might hit the workspace. My chest was pounding and I found it difficult to breathe. Behind me, I spotted Mark, crouched down, cautiously moving toward the camera. Arnett was behind him.

"Peter Arnett, join me here," Bernie called over, his voice quivering. "Let's describe to our viewers what we're seeing . . . the skies over Baghdad have been illuminated . . . we're seeing bright flashes going off all over the sky . . . Peter . . ."

"Well, there's anti-aircraft gunfire going into the sky . . . However, we haven't yet heard the sound of bombs landing, but there's tremendous lightning in the sky, lightning-like effects. Bernie."

"I have a sense, Peter, that people are shooting toward the sky and they are not aware or cannot see what they are shooting at. This is extraordinary. The lights are still on. All the streetlights in downtown Baghdad are still on . . . We're getting starbursts in the black sky . . . Peter."

"Now the sirens are sounding for the first time . . . Turn the lights out!" Peter yelled at Krizmanich. "We're trying to get the lights out in our hotel room yet the streetlights are on, and the firing is continuing, and the sirens are continuing," he coolly reported an instant later. "Here with us now is John Holliman . . ." He handed the microphone to Holliman, who had come running into the room.

"Good evening, gentlemen . . . or rather good morning," John said, as if he were sitting on his front porch rather than at Ground Zero. "I cannot see any aircraft in the sky here . . . a lot of tracer bullets going up in the sky, but so far no planes . . ."

"The four-wire's down. The four-wire's down," I screamed as the electricity suddenly went out, plunging the entire hotel into darkness. The little yellow light on the four-wire was out too. "Quick, plug in a battery!"

"Where the hell is a battery?" John shouted as he groped around in the dark. It took a few moments to make the connection. "Wow! . . . Holy cow!" he cried, hitting the floor as a giant explosion shook the hotel. "That was a large airburst that we saw . . . it was just filling the sky—"

"And I think, John, that burst took out the telecommunications," Peter interrupted. "You may hear the bombs now. If you're still with us, you can hear the bombs now. They're hitting the center of the city!"

The explosions were deafening. I crawled closer to the window to get a better view, but found myself edging back each time another dull "thump thump thump" echoed through the air. I pulled out my tape recorder and began to speak into it. I didn't know how long the four-wire would keep working.

"This is Robert Wiener in Baghdad," I found myself panting. "The attack has started. The sky is filled with tracers illuminating the night. A lot of anti-aircraft fire, machine gun fire. Earlier today, the White House had advised reporters to leave Baghdad. Many reporters felt they had time to do so . . . obviously that did not happen. There are flashes all over the sky now, an almost perverse version of the Fourth of July. . . ." I looked around the workspace. Holliman and Arnett were crouched on the floor, peering out the window. Where were the others? I needed to check on my people. I crept out to the corridor and ran hunched over toward the elevators. Bernie was standing there, his suitcase by his side.

"I'm sorry, my friend. I truly am," I apologized. My worst fear about getting Bernie stuck in Baghdad had come to pass.

"Please, it's not your fault," he said with an air of resignation. "We should probably get to the shelter."

"Not the elevators," I cautioned, even though one was still working. "We'll be safer using the stairs." We walked down the nine flights, stopping at the lobby. All the lights were off. "You go down," an Iraqi said, signaling with his flashlight.

The shelters were already jammed. Hundreds of people had sought refuge in the cavernous basement: hotel guests, journalists, employees of the Al-Rasheed and their families, Ministry of Information officials, militiamen, members of the Gulf Peace Team, a few Third World diplomats, and others. Bernie and I walked into the shelter closest to the stairs. Ingrid, Mark, Kris, and Nic were already there.

"Over here, we saved you a place," Mark called out as we tiptoed over dozens of people reclining on the floor. Jesus, I thought, what a scene!

Ingrid looked at me and just shook her head. She was clearly distressed. "I don't believe it, Wienerish. I really don't."

"Are you okay?" I asked Nic. He looked white as a sheet.

"I've never seen anything like that," he said. "I hope I never do again."

"Well, I think we'll be seeing it for a while," I ventured. "But we should be safe down here." I needed a cigarette; I stood up and left the room.

BY THE TIME I RETURNED from my walk around the basement, Bernie had left the shelter. "I think he went back upstairs," Mark said. Maybe it's over, I thought, as I climbed the stairs. But by the time I reached the third floor, the bombing and anti-aircraft bursts began again, and continued with a fury. I crawled down the now deserted ninth-floor hallway and slipped into the workspace. The noise and explosions seemed even heavier than they were before. Bernie, John, and Peter were huddled by the four-wire, reporting what they witnessed as they passed the mike around. After about ten minutes or so I began to feel useless just sitting there watching them. I was tempted to jump in and do some reporting myself but it hardly seemed necessary. The Boys of Baghdad, as David French in Atlanta dubbed them, were the perfect combination. To do it alone would be tough, I thought, but together they really brought the fear, facts, and fascination of war home. I crawled out of the room and went back down to the shelter.

THE MOMENT I reached the basement, I realized I'd made a mistake. The doors were now guarded by armed Iraqis, men I'd never seen before, who prevented anyone from leaving. "This for your safety," one shouted at a British cameraman trying to get out. "You, away from door," he said, pushing me with his submachine gun. Instinct told me to back off; they were in no mood to discuss the issue. I walked into the shelter and tried to relax.

I thought about Elaine and wondered what she must be going through. I was also worried about my parents. My father had not been well. God knew this was bound to be an additional strain. Every few minutes I stepped into the hall to grab a smoke. Occasionally, even in the basement, I could hear the dull thud of falling bombs. In the shelter itself, many people were napping, including some of my colleagues. But I was too keyed up to rest. I felt guilty and somewhat foolish not being upstairs with Bernie, John, and Peter. I ambled around the basement in search of another way out but all the exits were now blocked by gun-toting guards. At the end of the corridor a group of reporters gathered around a shortwave radio listening to the Beeb. The BBC had picked up CNN and the Boys of Baghdad as they continued their unprecedented reportage from Room 906. "This is fabulous," I said. The others agreed.

About 6 A.M., the Iraqis permitted us to return upstairs. I picked up Bernie's suitcase and began the long climb up, stopping every few flights to catch my breath.

Bernie, Peter, and John were clearly exhausted but literally beaming when I arrived in the workspace.

"Robert, you would have loved it," Peter howled, throwing his arms around me. "It was fantastic. We've been on the air all night. Atlanta says everyone picked up the broadcast. They've never seen anything like it!"

"Yeah," Holliman agreed. "It was something else, all right."

"He's the real hero," Bernie said, pointing to Arnett. "When the Iraqis tried to make us go down to the shelter, he just went, well, er, crazy."

"I told them I was nuts," Peter laughed. "That shelters drove me cuckoo ever since I'd been to Vietnam." He pointed his finger to his head and made the familiar circular motion.

"They took the cameras," Mark said, joining us. "Both handycams are gone. Oh, shit!" he exclaimed, "they took the tapes out of the Sonys too."

"I know," Holliman said, "but they said we'd get the stuff back later today."

"What can I tell you guys? I'm really proud of ya," I crowed.

"Well, you made it happen, Robert," Peter shot back. "You and this damn four-wire of yours. You know, Bernie even did an interview with Brokaw, and Atlanta says Rather wants to speak with him too."

"Jesus!" I whistled. "I heard you guys on the BBC, but we must have creamed everyone—"

"By the way," Bernie interrupted. "Atlanta knows that you're all okay; we asked that the desk call your families . . ."

"Gee, what a night!" Holliman exclaimed again. I sat down at the four-wire and called Atlanta.

"You better figure out some way for those guys to get some rest," Eason said, "but we're gonna want someone on the air all the time."

"No problem. We'll set up a rotation. How's the network looking?"

"You wouldn't believe it," he said. "The phones have been ringing off the hook. We made history!"

The import of Eason's words was largely lost on me—only later would I learn the full extent of the impact we'd made. Spearheaded by the Boys of Baghdad, the network's gripping coverage of the start of the Gulf War was carried around the world. Television stations in Britain, Germany, France, Israel, Brazil, and Sweden for example, preempted their regular programming and punched up CNN instead. It was the same story in the United States. Across the nation, affiliates dropped their network's coverage to rely on CNN. In Littleton, New Hampshire for example, you could watch CNN on the station that usually carried NBC. And in Atlanta, you couldn't watch anything but CNN, as NBC, CBS, and ABC affiliates all made the switch to "the world's most important network." The memo from then CNN vice president Paul Amos said it all: "For the first time in history, CNN has beaten all three broadcast networks on a twenty-four-hour basis in the CNN universe."

"Are you guys still on the air?" Allen Pizzey asked as he dropped by the workspace. "I couldn't get through to New York."

"Well, don't worry about it," I smirked. "I think Rather's gonna interview Bernie." The moment I said it, I realized it was a cruel and insensitive remark, but before I could apologize, Pizzey turned on his heel and left.

"You were awfully tough on him, my brother," Bernie chuckled.

"Yeah, you're probably right. But that son-of-a-bitch and all his talk about us being crazy to be here was part of the reason Tracy freaked out in the first place. Well, fuck it," I sighed. "What's done is done."

WE DECIDED that Bernie and Peter would get some rest while John stayed at the four-wire. We listened to CNN as Wolf Blitzer at the Pentagon reported that almost the entire seven-hundred-plane Iraqi Air Force and much of the elite Republican Guard had been "decimated." Wolf said all of Iraq's fixed scud and ballistic missile sites were put out of commission and Baghdad's nuclear, chemical, and biological weapons arsenal had been "wiped out." He quoted Pentagon officials as believing Iraq might actually surrender within "a number of days."

A short while later, speaking on Baghdad radio, Saddam Hussein said, "The mother of all battles has started and victory is very near."

Looking out the window, John reported he could see little sign of damage but an acrid smell filled the air. A huge cloud of white smoke, almost a giant smoke screen, really, was pouring out of a building a few miles away and wafting into the air. He counted only seven cars on the highway in front of the Al-Rasheed.

Unable to sleep, Bernie kept coming back to Room 906 to join John on the air.

"It was one hell of a night," he said. "Wave after wave of planes. It shook you to your soul. If this was surgical bombing, I don't like being this close to the operating table."

TWO IRAQI OFFICIALS stopped by the workspace and asked us to accompany them to the television station. They said we could feed the tapes that had been confiscated overnight along with a televised message from President Hussein. Because phone service at the Al-Rasheed was nonexistent, Kris went with Nic to the TV station with orders to return as soon as possible to let us know when the actual feed would begin.

About thirty minutes later she was back. There was some kind of snag, a problem with communications. "I don't think anyone should be there," she huffed. "It's not the safest place in the world, ya know."

"I agree," I said and left to find Nic.

NO SOONER WAS I OUT the door of the hotel than the rat-ta-tat-tat of anti-aircraft fire began again and far out in the distance I heard the dull thuds of falling bombs. The lull in the action hadn't lasted long. The allies, it seemed, were going to keep up the bombing around the clock. None of our regular drivers was around, but for fifty dollars a man I had never seen before agreed to take me to the television station and wait. My hands were shaking as we sped down the streets, weaving around cars that were pulling off the road helter-skelter.

IRAQI TV WAS RINGED BY TANKS. "Stop here! Stop here!" I yelled as we arrived at the entrance, but the troops guarding the building waved us by. "No . . . stop . . . stop," I shouted at the driver. As I jumped out of the Honda three soldiers lifted their weapons and took aim. Slowly and deliberately, I put my hands above my head and approached them.

"La toe drope, ana sahafi . . . Ana sahafi," I cried. The soldiers motioned

me to stop where I was but I continued toward them. *"Ana sahafi . . . Ana sahafi,"* I repeated. An instant later an officer joined their ranks and waved his hands to indicate the building was "off limits."

"Please," I implored him. "*Ana sahafi*. I must go inside."

"Finish, finish," he said in English.

"Please, you don't understand. I have a colleague inside."

"Finish, finish," he said again.

"Please," I said, edging closer to the door. "Please come with me, they know me in there." I tapped my chest and pointed to the door.

"You wait," he ordered as he entered the building.

A moment later he stepped back out, and motioned me to join him. "You come."

I didn't recognize any of the guards but after five minutes of explanations in broken English and sign language, they made me understand that Nic had left. I was uneasy about the situation but they were adamant about not letting me go any farther than the lobby. I thanked them and left, walking back to the car under the now bemused smiles of the Iraqi tank crews. On the way back to the hotel I noticed that several microwave dishes on a nearby communications tower had been destroyed. There was also some civilian "collateral" damage to an adjacent building. We had to back up and take another route to avoid the rubble.

Iraqis were on the streets but the atmosphere was anything but normal. All of the shops we drove past were shut; only a cigarette stand remained open. The sky was gray and overcast; a perfect frame for a somber scene.

"WHERE'S NIC?" I asked with alarm the moment I entered the workspace and didn't see him. Kris shook her head. I began to get really worried. But just as Atlanta was about to put me on the air to describe what I'd seen, Nic showed up. He hadn't been able to feed the tapes but he did have news to report. While at the television station, he'd seen Saddam Hussein.

"Initially I met Minister Jassim," Nic reported over the four-wire, after John introduced him. "I was waiting at the feedpoint. Then President Saddam Hussein walked by, I think to record a message to his people. I saw him within the last hour . . . I believe [Iraqi TV] is trying to make contact with Amman, Jordan, but there's no communication."

"What can you tell us about how Saddam looked. What were your impressions?" Susan Rook in Atlanta asked.

"He was very resolute and there was determination in his step . . . the people with him were walking apace to keep up with him."

"There you have it," Holliman took over. "Our man, Nic Robertson, probably the only Western journalist to have seen Saddam Hussein since the war began."

AROUND 10 A.M. the bombing started again and John was back on the air. "I wish I didn't have to tell you this," he said to anchorman Patrick Greenlaw, "but there have just been two very loud explosions that rocked us here in downtown Baghdad . . . I can't tell you exactly what just happened but it shook us up a bit . . . There's a rumbling coming from the west, like a herd of horses. I hear now what sounds like big bombs falling but I don't see anything. But I hear this rumbling. I'm going to stick this microphone out the window and see if you can hear it too . . . There's a lot of thunder and it's obviously not coming from the heavens but from the coalition forces."

I ran across to 903 and peered out the window. "They've hit something," I called over to John.

"Now our producer, Robert Wiener, says there has been some damage. I'm not able to get my microphone over to you, Robert, you'll have to come to me and describe what you see . . ."

I walked over to John and took over the mike. "Out beyond the Foreign Ministry, there has been an attack," I reported. "There are thick billowing clouds of black smoke in the distance. The anti-aircraft battery positioned on the roof of the building in front of us has been at alert. They fired off several rounds. I don't know if you could hear that, John, when you were on the other side of the hotel, but people are bracing for another attack . . ."

THE LATEST FLURRY of fire brought Bernie running back to the workspace. "I'm afraid to go to sleep," he explained to the world. "Number one, as a journalist, I don't want to miss anything . . . and two, I don't like to go to sleep where bombs are falling." But he was so tired that during an interview with Israel's Deputy Foreign Minister Benjamin Netanyahu, Bernie started to drift into a sort of stream of consciousness that sounded more like someone talking in his sleep than someone conducting an interview.

"Please, put him to bed," Bob Furnad ordered during a break, but it was impossible to keep Bernie in his room and he wandered back and forth all day, almost in a trance.

It didn't make any sense to risk another trip to Iraqi TV, I thought, and even if communications were up—a doubtful proposition—we weren't going to have anything new to feed. The Iraqis would not permit cameras outside the hotel, which limited our coverage to what we could do on the four-wire. All afternoon, John, occasionally joined by Bernie and Peter, reported on the continuing air raids, which by sunset, would number about seventeen.

"John Holliman is trying to see every bomb that falls for the benefit of our viewers," Peter explained wryly at one point. "This latest raid has been going on about seven to eight minutes, and these raids usually last a quarter of an hour."

During lulls in the air war, I busied myself opening cans of tuna and preparing sandwiches. There was plenty to eat and drink, but with electricity still out making hot coffee was a problem. Nic finally came to the rescue, connecting a three-hundred-dollar generator to a five-dollar hot water coil, and presto, we were in business. Misters Alla and Nasir occasionally stopped by to look in on how we were doing, but it seemed they were motivated more by the need for Marlboros and Nescafé than by any official obligation. In any case, they voiced no objection when John left for a drive around town.

"This city is not in ruins," Holliman reported after returning from his tour. He saw damage, but only to selected targets. "None of the shrines have been hit."

"If this were indiscriminate bombing, believe me, ladies and gentlemen, the world would not be hearing what you are hearing now," Bernie agreed. "Ask yourself this question: why is CNN able to get out these reports . . . and if this is happening during the day," he said, referring to the bombing, "what are we going to go through tonight?" According to the Pentagon, there had already been over one thousand sorties.

"I think the reason we've been able to broadcast is a unique acknowledgment of the role CNN is playing in the Middle East, at least," Peter surmised. "In the country where I usually work, authorities tell me they watch CNN because they want to know what their allies and enemies are thinking." Unfortunately, CNN's live and uncensored broadcasts from Baghdad were coming to an end. Alla informed me there was an urgent meeting in the lobby.

"YOU MUST STOP IMMEDIATELY," Sadoun said, after politely shaking hands. I was joined by John Simpson of the BBC, Brent Sadler, ITN, and Tom Aspell, a correspondent for NBC, which was using the BBC's INMARSAT. "And you three must shut down your satellite telephones. We have to prepare a new system and we will review your reports, which you must record in advance."

"What about CNN?" Aspell asked. "Are you going to review their reports as well?"

"Everyone will follow the same rules," Sadoun explained. "We shall decide times when you can do your reporting . . . one or two times a day . . . the rest of the time, the satellite telephones must be shut."

"What about CNN?" Aspell nagged. "Their four-wire is always open. They don't have to lug the phone outside. Why can't we all just file over CNN's line? It's already in place and it's more convenient." Sadoun began to mull it over, but I stopped him in his tracks.

"You," I said, pointing to Aspell, "would do a greater service to your network if you worried less about CNN and more about NBC. Except for humanitarian reasons the four-wire is not going to be used by you or anyone else." Sadoun threw up his hands and shrugged.

"So, please," he said, "close everything now." Aspell and the others left to inform their networks.

"There has got to be a better system," I said. "Why can't Mr. Alla just stay in our room when we're on with Atlanta? It makes no sense for us to record stuff in advance. We can show you a script, but why can't we read it live?"

"These are the rules—"

"I know they're the rules," I interrupted. "But frankly, what difference does it make if we report live or on tape if you see our copy in advance?"

"I understand but . . ."

"I'm not going to deceive you at this stage of the game. I've always been straight with you . . ."

"It is not you, Robert," he said. "We are under orders from the PTT."

"I am going upstairs," Alla said, "to tell CNN to stop . . ."

"Hold on a sec," I stopped him. "I'll go with you. Just give me a minute or two to finish speaking with Sadoun." I motioned to Sadoun to walk with me in the lobby while I tried to think of a compromise he might accept.

"Look, these other people are bitter about our four-wire," I said. "You just saw that for yourself. The fact is, we have greater demands than they do. We're on the air twenty-four hours a day . . ."

"Yes, I know . . ."

"So, why should we be penalized if they don't have the technical facilities, or can't give the story the same amount of airtime as we can? Surely, there's got to be a better way."

"What *is* the latest news?" he asked plaintively. Earlier, Sadoun seemed almost devastated when I told him the Pentagon said the Air Force and Republican Guard had been "decimated."

"So far, the coalition has flown more than a thousand sorties . . . all the scud sites . . . and chemical, biological, and nuclear facilities have reportedly been destroyed. And this is just the beginning . . ."

"My God," he sighed.

"How is your family?"

"They are fine, thank God. They are out of the city."

"What a mess, huh?"

"You know, Robert, we did not start this . . ."

"Please, this is not the time or the place to begin debating the cause of this bullshit," I insisted, as the air raid siren began to wail.

"No, no, you are right," he said. "But please, Robert . . . stop your transmissions now. We will talk again later."

WELL, I GAVE IT MY BEST SHOT, I thought as I climbed back up the nine flights of stairs. Mr. Alla preceded me. "Hold on," I yelled. "I'm older than you are, it takes me more time." When I finally reached the workspace, Mr. Alla had already signaled John and Peter to stop reporting but they were still on the air.

"Our executive producer, Robert Wiener, has just walked into the room," John said, as I tried to catch my breath. "Robert, tell us what's going on."

"We have unfortunately been ordered to cease transmitting," I said, gasping for breath. "We have been told that we may no longer transmit live to our audience, and that in the future, taped reports will be subject to censorship."

"Well, that's that," Holliman sighed. "Obviously this is something that's just abhorent to all of us. We'll talk to you as soon as we can."

"John, I will make the decision to cut communications since I'm the senior man here," Peter said, sounding remarkably like Al Haig as he grabbed the microphone. "So for Bob Wiener and John Holliway, er, John Holliman and Bernie Shaw and myself, Peter Arnett, signing off from Baghdad for CNN, and we hope we can resume our communications in the very near future." It was 6:59 P.M. local time. We had been on the air almost seventeen consecutive hours.

"Hello, Baghdad! Hello, Baghdad!" I heard Eason call over the four-wire. I cast a long glance at Mr. Alla. "Hello, Baghdad!" Eason called again.

"Please," I said to Mr. Alla. "Surely I can speak to the desk. This is not being broadcast." After some hesitation, he slowly nodded his consent.

"Baghdad to Atlanta," I called. "Go ahead, Eason."

"Robert, you need to get everyone out of the hotel immediately. We've just gotten word that the Al-Rasheed may be bombed. You need to get out of there *now*!"

"Jesus!" I screamed. "We're on our way! Everybody out! . . . Out!" I yelled to the others in the room. "Meet me in the lobby." I picked up my flashlight and ran down the hall to find Bernie. "Grab your things," I yelled, pounding on his door. "We've got to leave the hotel."

Where to go? Where to go? I thought as I double-timed it down the stairs. By now it was well after nightfall and we didn't have a driver. And even if we did, there were eight of us! I raced through the darkened lobby to the hotel's entrance. This is fucked, I said to myself, staring into the night. There wasn't any place out there that was safe. "Goddammit," I cursed aloud.

"What is the matter, Robert?" Sadoun asked, seeing me at the door. "You look very frightened."

"I am. We've just received news the hotel may be bombed. Is there someplace else . . ."

"My God!" he cried. "Why would they do such a thing? There are only civilians here and journalists."

"I don't know. But that's what we heard . . ."

"Quickly, to the shelter," he urged. "I will tell the staff . . ."

"WE'LL JUST HAVE to sit it out downstairs," I said to my colleagues, who were waiting at the other end of the lobby. "We don't have any choice, really . . ."

"Well, these shelters are pretty good," Peter said. "Unless they drop something directly through an airshaft, we should be okay." Now there's a comforting thought, I said to myself as the sirens began to wail.

"Uh-oh," Nic exclaimed. We instantly raced downstairs.

"So, we shall die together," Sadoun said, putting his hand on my shoulder as we sat on the floor along with hundreds of others gathered in the shelters of the Al-Rasheed. A moment later the basement reverberated as a two-thousand-pound bomb landed outside.

"Jesus!" I whistled. "That was close." I looked over at Ingrid, who rolled her eyes.

"You have saved many lives by telling me what you did," Sadoun said. "Otherwise, we may not have been able to get these people downstairs so quickly." By now our shelter was jammed. Those who couldn't find a spot in the actual shelter simply camped out on the hard basement floor, using bedding from their rooms to make a nest. There were more infants and children than the previous night. Officials from several ministries now had their families with them. I noticed Mr. Fouad, who worked in Sadoun's office, among them.

Mark picked up his camera and began rolling tape. Many Baghdadis were gathered around an old television set watching a broadcast of Saddam at prayer. Evidently the television station was functioning again, but for how long? Others nibbled on fruit and bread as they settled in for the night.

MOST OF THE REMAINING JOURNALISTS were also in the shelter. I walked over to John Simpson, who, even under these circumstances, still managed to look surprisingly well groomed. "Hey, did you guys hear this story about the hotel being bombed?" I asked.

"Yes, indeed. As a matter of fact we actually left the Al-Rasheed, but after driving for fifteen minutes, we realized there was nowhere else to go. So we came back."

"Where'd this damn story originate?"

"I'm not quite certain," he said. "Our desk in London got a call from someone, I believe it was NBC."

"Well, it sure scared the shit out of us."

"Us too."

"So what's the Beeb [BBC] reporting?" I asked, eyeing his shortwave.

"Several scuds have been fired at Tel Aviv. There's no mention yet of casualties."

"Jeez, so Saddam really did it, huh? Goddamn! If the Israelis get into this thing, this ain't gonna be a great place to be."

THE TIME PASSED even more slowly than the previous night, when the couple of hours I spent locked in the shelter seemed like forever. Most of our group was sleeping now; Peter, John, Nic, and Mark were stretched out at one end of the room while Ingrid and Kris dozed nearby.

"I know this is heresy," I whispered to Bernie, "but in a way I'm damn happy they pulled the plug . . . at least for tonight. We can all use the rest."

"I concur," he said. "I'm somewhat relieved too. By the way, I think we should plan on some of us leaving tomorrow. I, for one, would like to get home as quickly as possible."

"Agreed. You know, about twenty journalists left today for Amman, CBS and ABC among them."

"So I hear. Well, Mr. Robert, we should do the same." He opened his suitcase and offered me some crackers and cheese.

"I'm pretty sure Peter's gonna want to stay," I said, forgoing the snack. "And I have no problem staying with him. I think Nic would be up for it too."

"Well, that's up to you, of course," Bernie said, "but first thing in the morning let's get cars for those of us who want to leave."

AS EXHAUSTED AS I WAS, it was impossible to sleep. I tried closing my eyes, but I couldn't block out the events of the past twenty-four hours. I finally gave up and walked out of the shelter to smoke a cigarette. Bernie joined me a few minutes later. The two of us were chatting quietly when an Iraqi approached us. I wasn't certain but I thought I'd seen him before at the Ministry of Culture and Information. He introduced himself and asked us what news we'd heard of the war. When I told him about the Air Force and Republican Guard, he was incredulous. "Is impossible," he stammered. "Too many soldiers there."

"Well, if they were hit by the B-52's, the reports could be true," I said.

"Plane so powerful?" he asked.

"Oh yes," Bernie said. "These planes were used in Vietnam . . . but in the jungle you can hide. There's nowhere to hide in the desert."

"Jesus," I sighed. "Can you imagine those guys just sitting there while that shit was dumped on top of them."

"If that's what happened," Bernie said, "they never had a chance. Those planes fly so high you can't even hear them until they're on top of you. In fact, I'm not so sure you can hear them then. Then a moment later . . . the bombs. When I think of all those men . . . fathers, husbands, sons, brothers . . ." Bernie began to weep. "They didn't die like soldiers. They didn't die like fighting men. They just died at their posts. They never knew what hit them." He took out his handkerchief and wiped his eyes. "They never knew what hit them," he said again softly.

"HEY, WHERE HAVE YOU BEEN?" I asked John a few hours later.

"Upstairs," he whispered. "I let Atlanta know we're all right."

"How'd you get around the guards? They just let you out?"

"No. First I tried to explain that I needed my medicine, but they didn't buy it. Then Sadoun helped me out. I promised him I was only going to pass on a personal message and he told the guard to let me up."

"That's great. I'm impressed. So what's going on outside? Is there still bombing?"

"It's quiet right now," John said. "But who knows how long that'll last."

SOMEWHERE AROUND 6 A.M. I finally managed to doze off, only to be awakened an hour later when someone stepped on my hand. "Excuse, please," said an elderly woman, who, along with most everyone else in the shelter, was preparing to leave. I reached for my bottle of mineral water only to discover someone had finished it for me. My mouth tasted awful, my bones ached, and I longed for a hot shower. My clothes felt sticky. Come what may—bombs or no bombs—I swore to myself I would change my socks. I staggered out of the basement and up to the lobby, to be greeted by the sight of driver Jasim, resting in one of the chairs.

"Good morning, Mr. Robert," he said, pumping my hand.

"How are you?" I asked.

"Everything good now. No go Army for some days."

"I'm happy to hear it. Now, Mr. Jasim, can you round up some cars for a trip to Amman?"

"You go Amman today?"

"Not me, but Mr. Shaw and some others."

"I can, but trip to Amman very expensive . . . between three and four thousand each car."

"Fine, we'll talk about that later. I'll need three cars, including your own, and make sure they all have gasoline."

"I bring jerry cans," he said. "You want I go now?"

"Please . . . and come back with everything as soon as possible."

"I agree with Robert," Peter said as we all gathered for breakfast in the workspace. "The Iraqis are only going to let us file once, perhaps twice a day at most. There's no reason for all of us to be here."

"Well, I'm ready to stay," John said. "You know my rule, Robert, just tell me what to do. . . ."

"I appreciate that," I said, "but I don't see a need for two correspondents. Also, who knows how long the highway to Amman will be open? I think it's best to go, John . . . while the going is good."

"I agree," said Bernie. "I'd like to get on the road as soon as possible."

"Well, Jasim's getting the cars . . . I just need to update the exit visas and then you can be on your way."

"What about you, Nic?" Peter asked.

"I'm happy to stay. But I'd like to move the four-wire downstairs."

"Can you do that easily enough?" I asked.

"Oh sure, I've got reams of cable."

"Well, let's set up in the bar," I laughed. "It'll make the perfect command post. . . ."

"In the bar!" Peter exclaimed. "I love it!"

"I'll give you a hand with the four-wire," Mark said to Nic. "Maybe we should also take some equipment back to Jordan."

"Let's keep most of the stuff here," I cautioned. "We'll just move it downstairs. After all, we're not abandoning Baghdad, we're just paring down. . . ."

"Ya know, Wienerish, I'm not so sure I want to leave," Ingrid piped up. "I'm gettin' used to all this."

"Well, I'm gonna miss ya, sweetheart, but there's no point having two producers here with just one correspondent. I'd also feel better knowing you'll be shepherding the rest of the group to Amman. Your savvy on the road could come in handy."

"I agree," said Bernie.

"Me too," Holliman smiled.

"Well, just so it's on the record, I'm now prepared to stay—" Ingrid interrupted.

"Duly noted," I laughed. "I'll alert the historians!"

BECAUSE THE ELEVATORS WEREN'T WORKING, it took several hours to move the INMARSAT, generator, Still Store, and other gear downstairs as well as to reconnect the four-wire. I felt sorry for the porters as I watched them struggle with the cases; they had to make more than a dozen trips up and down the nine flights before everything was moved. As I packed my suitcases, I discovered that my shortwave radio and alarm clock had been "appropriated" from my room. The clothes I'd last sent to the laundry, of course, were gone for good. Finally, everything was in place. I pasted a CNN decal below the sign that read Scheherezade Bar . . . and we had an office. With Mr. Alla at my side I tested the four-wire to call Atlanta. It worked perfectly, but Eason had sounded better.

"We sort of got caught with our pants down in Jerusalem last night," he sighed. "After the great start you guys gave us, it's really a shame." In a classic example of poor planning, bureau chief Larry Register had apparently worked everyone into the ground before the war even started; when Israel came under the scuds the bureau was unstaffed. Out of his element and totally panic-stricken, Larry had gone on the air himself, a disastrous moment in broadcast history (later immortalized by several comics who mimicked him hyperventilating in his gas mask, looking like a giant aardvark run amok). I updated Eason on our current plans before he put Tom Johnson on the line. Tom had several concerns.

"Robert, it is very important that I know the make and color of the cars carrying Bernie and the others. I also need to know the specific order in which those cars will be traveling, and there must be no deviation from that order. Do you understand?" I did. Presumably, CNN would try to get some protection for the convoy.

"They'll be traveling in three large Hondas," I said. "White . . . metallic blue . . . and red."

"In that order?"

"In that order, unless you hear differently."

"How are you, Peter, and Nic doing?"

"Just great," I laughed. "We're all set up here in the bar. . . ."

"That's what I just heard," he laughed. "Aside from the obvious, why did you choose that location?"

"For one thing, it's close to the shelter, Tom. There's running water. And you can even sleep on the banquettes. It's really not a bad setup."

"Well, I don't think we'll introduce Arnett as reporting from the bar, but it sounds like you've made the right choice. When will you be able to file your next report?"

"Probably this afternoon. We're working out the details now. . . ."

"Enough . . . enough," Mr. Alla interrupted, waving his hands.

"Tom, I'm being told I have to sign off now. I'll be in touch later . . ."

"I understand," he said. "We'll be waiting."

"WE NEED A GROUP PHOTO," I said to everyone as we gathered in front of the Al-Rasheed. "Let's get one for posterity."

"I want one too," Kris said, handing her camera to Jana Schneider, a photographer for Sipa.

"One more . . . one more," Jana said, as she took one shot after another before handing back our cameras.

"Well, this is it," I said to Bernie, giving him a hug. "Have a safe trip and I'll speak to you soon."

"You be careful, Mr. Robert. Don't stay here longer than you have to."

"Hopefully, we'll see you in Jordan," Mark said, as he hopped into Jasim's car beside Bernie.

"Krissie, you take care," I said, putting my arms around her.

"I'm sorry," she cried. "I really am."

"Shush. There's nothing to be sorry about. Thanks for being here."

"Well, as you say, it's been *mumtaz,*" John laughed as we exchanged bear hugs. "I'll call Elaine when I get to Amman."

"Oh, Wienerish," Ingrid moaned. "I don't want to leave."

"I want you to make sure they get safely across," I whispered as I kissed her good-bye. "You can always come back. You'll have to," I laughed. "I'm down to my last bottle of vodka."

Nic, Peter, and I continued to wave until the cars pulled well out of the driveway.

"WELL, I'M GLAD THAT'S OVER WITH," Peter snapped as we returned to the bar. "It's going to be much easier, now that we're three." After all we'd just been through together, Peter's remark seemed more than a little cold-blooded and I guess it showed on my face.

"Don't misunderstand," he explained. "It was wonderful having Bernie and John here, but there's no longer a need. As things stand now, this is a one-reporter operation . . . and of course, you can report too, Robert, if you like."

"What I'd like now, is to change my socks," I laughed, "and have some lunch." The hotel had announced it was serving a buffet.

"This is the first communiqué from the General Command of the Iraqi Armed Forces," Naji explained to the few of us who'd gathered for his impromptu briefing. He had come to the hotel dressed in a faded military uniform topped by a brown civilian overcoat. He looked extremely haggard, and for the first time since I'd known him, he was in need of a shave.

"At two-thirty in the morning on January 17, the treacherous Zionist-American enemy, encouraged by the traitor of the holy sanctities and their servant King Fahd . . . this enemy has started its aggression against the state of Iraq. . . . In their air raids, the evil people were aiming at some densely populated civilian areas in Baghdad, and a number of air bases. Despite the heavy raids, our brave men forced the criminals to mid-level and higher altitudes to escape the intensive fire of our air defenses." As he translated the statement, the Al-Rasheed's Muzak tinkled softly in the background. "And then we praise God for His victory," Naji paraphrased, "and we praise the steadfastness of our heroes and our people who will frustrate the infidels and traitors." The communiqué, as well as what Naji called an "open letter" to the people of the United States, went on to denounce President Bush in even harsher terms and said the war was a "showdown with Satan. . . . Bush has pushed the situation to be in accordance with his own considerations and feelings as if it is a personal showdown. He neglected all the chances that we opened for him, in the forefront of which was our initiative of the twelfth of August, which, if he had taken advantage of it, he would have saved himself from the impasse and would have found a face-saving formula for himself."

Naji claimed forty-four allied aircraft and twenty-three cruise missiles had been destroyed and said Iraqi citizens had been instructed not to kill any downed American pilots.

I RELAYED THE INFORMATION to Peter but we still couldn't file. The Iraqis had finally decided we could now report only twice a day, once between noon and 2 P.M., and again between 4:30 P.M. and 7 P.M. It was now after 3 P.M. "You will have more news later," Sadoun assured us, stopping by the bar. "There is a press conference with the Minister of Culture and Information."

"Will Minister Jassim be coming here?" I asked, somewhat alarmed.

The last place I wanted to be during an air raid was in a government building.

"No, we will go to the ministry," Sadoun said emphatically. "We shall leave in an hour." He then walked off to inform the other reporters.

"I don't know about this," I said to Peter.

"I'll be glad to go alone if you like," he suggested. "You can stay here."

"Nah, I don't mind going. I just don't like it."

"Frankly, neither do I," he confessed, "but we have no choice."

Naturally, the news conference had just gotten underway when the sirens began to sound. Unlike some of us, Minister Jassim seemed unconcerned by the raid. He assured reporters they could remain in Baghdad and indicated we would be able to interview some captured pilots. As journalists hotfooted it to the parking lot, Jassim grabbed my arm. "Robert, did CNN leave today?"

"A few of our people did. But Peter and I are here, along with Nic."

"That is good," he said, giving me a paternal pat on the cheek. "You must to stay, Robert. You are welcome here." By the time Arnett and I got to the parking lot, the car we had come in had left.

"What a mess," I moaned. Standing outside, the sirens sounded even more ominous.

"Maybe we can hitch a ride," Peter said.

"It looks like the only possibility . . ."

"Mister . . . mister," an Iraqi yelled from a car in the parking lot. We quickly jumped inside. I had butterflies in my stomach as we drove back to the Al-Rasheed. I could hear bombs falling in the distance. We made it back to the hotel in minutes, but my nerves were shot. "Jesus H. Christ," I whined to Peter. "Who needs this shit?" We headed straight for the shelter, where Nic was already waiting.

IN THE BASEMENT of the Al-Rasheed Peter reviewed his notes and listened to the news. Iraq now claimed seventy-two allied warplanes had been shot down, a dramatic increase from the forty-four Naji had reported. Then Peter and I went up to the bar to file. Mr. Alla, who was with us, reviewed the script but allowed Peter to read it live. Just as Arnett began his report, the sirens sounded again.

"It's good to be back in touch with you again from here in Baghdad," Peter reported while I held a flashlight over his copy. "The Gulf War, of course, is going into its second day. At the moment, however, there has been an air raid alert siren. We're in the lobby of the Al-Rasheed Hotel. Everyone else has been told to go to the basement shelters. They presume an attack is coming at any moment.

"In the morning today there were a series of bombings in the suburbs against targets unknown to us. During the previous evening, raids were close to the city center and they shook the hotel where we are staying. Government officials say the General Command of the Iraqi Armed Forces has released a battle communiqué. It claims Iraqi air defenses have knocked down seventy-two American and other multinational aircraft since the first bombing raids began in the early morning hours of Thursday.

"Today, the government claims seven aircraft were shot down: five on the battlefront and two inside Iraq. The communiqué also says that in response to the aerial bombardments of the multinational coalition, Iraq launched what it called its own effective strikes, setting fire to enemy targets and inflicting casualties—they are their words.

"We've just been talking to the Minister of Information, who's given a brief press conference. He was asked by the press to show us some of the wreckage and if there were any captured American pilots, and could we meet them. He said there were captured American pilots; we could meet them soon. But he added no further clarification.

"Now, the international press corps is operating under censorship as from today. Under this policy, we are required to submit our stories in advance to officials from the Information Ministry to read. Reporters have been permitted to travel around the capital. CNN has reduced its personnel here from eight to three, as the international press corps continues to dwindle. The Al-Rasheed Hotel has become a haven for foreigners—some unintentionally caught up in the hostilities—and they're now trying to seek escape overland to Jordan. Peter Arnett, CNN, reporting live from Baghdad." The anchor in Atlanta thanked Peter and we were through for the night.

"What timing!" Peter shouted as the sirens continued to wail. "It was perfect, Robert. Absolutely perfect. I love it!" he laughed as we headed back to the shelter.

When the air raid ended we went back up to the bar. I lit a few candles, opened the last bottle of vodka, connected the Walkman to Nic's portable speakers, and settled back to unwind. Within the hour we were joined by Sadoun, Mr. Alla, Nasir, British reporter Patrick Cockburn of *The Independent*, and a reporter for *The Irish Times*. "We're going to need more to drink," Peter said, eyeing the group. "I've got some scotch in my room." The Iraqis had never heard of Patti Austin before, or songs like "Smoke Gets in Your Eyes," "Cry Me a River," or "They Can't Take That Away from Me."

"This is, how you say, fabulous," Mr. Alla joked as the melodies carried us away, to better times under better circumstances. It was a special moment. With remarkable candor we talked about our families and exchanged intimacies about our lives. As the hours passed, it seemed to matter little that the bombing had started anew. None of us was in a rush to return to the shelter.

"Please, play that song again," Nasir asked after Billy Eckstine's rendition of "Summertime" had obviously struck a chord. "I wonder how long it will be before . . . before living is easy for us?" he asked wistfully.

"Quite a while, I'd imagine," I said sadly.

I don't remember when I fell asleep, stretched out on the soft banquette while Harry Connick, Jr., sang softly in the background. I do remember it was one of the best nights I have ever spent anywhere, a unique occasion, to be savored forever.

"We have responded with surface-to-surface missiles to liberate Palestine and avenge the death of Abu Jihad," said the latest Iraqi military communiqué. "Palestine, we are coming to liberate you. Our grandfathers are happy in their graves when they see their grandsons defending Palestine."

Shortly after Peter filed his first report of the day, a rumor began circulating through the Al-Rasheed: the Iraqis were about to order all journalists out of Iraq. My first reaction was one of relief. I wouldn't be sad to leave. The previous evening notwithstanding, the effects of the day-in, day-out bombing were taking a toll. I thought it was only a matter of time before the hotel might be hit. I strolled into the garden to find Sadoun. He was sitting next to an INMARSAT as Simpson, Sadler, and Aspell filed their early reports. "Is it true?" I asked. "Everyone has to leave?"

"Yes, yes, but we must talk," he whispered. "I will come to see you soon."

"This is it!" I said to Peter, rushing into the bar. "They're kicking us all out. I'm gonna round up some cars."

"Damn," he seethed. "I thought this might happen, but not so soon—"

"Please," Nasir interrupted. "Do not worry. There is good news for you. You must be patient."

"Well, I'm gonna find some cars anyway," I said to Peter. "If we have to leave, we better have transportation."

As I walked through the lobby, Mrs. Nihad stopped me. "Are you really going?" she cried plaintively. "Oh, please, Mr. Robert, if you leave we will all die."

"What makes you say that?" I asked, alarmed.

"The only reason the hotel has not been bombed is because you are here. With no journalists, they will kill us all."

"I don't think that's going to happen," I tried to assure her. But I wasn't certain.

Naji was coming into the Al-Rasheed as I was going out. "Good morning, Robert," he said wearily. "How are you today?"

"Barely surviving," I joked. "What's this about journalists having to leave?"

"It is only temporary," he explained. "At present, we do not have the means to properly care for many reporters. In ten days, perhaps, we shall permit them back. Of course, Robert, CNN may stay. Has Sadoun told you?"

"Not yet, but I think he was planning to. Tell me, Naji, why is CNN being allowed to stay?"

"Your coverage has always proved impartial and balanced. From your first days in Baghdad, you have always been fair. . . ."

"I tell ya, this is gonna provoke a shit storm with the others. . . ."

"That is not our problem," he said. "We are granting this permission only to you."

"WELL, I GUESS WE'RE IN FOR THE LONG HAUL," I whispered to Peter. "God help us."

"This is terrific news," he blurted out. "What a fantastic opportunity!"

"Please," Sadoun cautioned. "You must not tell the others. It will create big problems. When they leave in the morning, you should go up to your rooms . . . do not stay here by the bar where they will see you and begin asking questions. . . ."

"You're not going to be able to keep this a secret," I said. "You're dealing with reporters here. . . ."

"We shall do our best. Please," he said, putting his finger to his lips, "not a word."

THE AIR RAIDS CONTINUED IN WAVES, perhaps not as frequently as during the first two days, but enough to send us scurrying to the shelter on several occasions. It was during one of those raids that we lost the four-wire. I was on with Atlanta relaying some personal messages when the line abruptly went dead. No hum. No "white noise." Nothing. "Whaddaya think?" I asked Nic, who fiddled with the unit and immediately came to the same conclusion.

"It's gone," he reported.

"I'm gonna check something out. I'll be back in a few minutes." I rushed up to Room 906 and peered out the window. The landscape had changed. Something was missing. Beyond the Giant Mushroom, the tall telecommunications building had disappeared. It had been totally obliterated. "Holy shit," I swore to myself. "Well, that's that." I stopped into 903 and picked up a couple of bottles of mineral water.

BY THE TIME I RETURNED TO THE BAR, the air raid had ended. "Ask NBC to please send a message on their INMARSAT," I said to Nic, spotting their producer, Victor Solis, on the lawn. "Explain that our four-wire went down while we were talking with Atlanta and the desk is probably worried. Tell him to pass on that we'll call in on our INMARSAT as soon as it's set up." I began rearranging the mineral water amid our other supplies.

Nic returned less than a minute later. He looked shaken. "That guy Victor pushed me aside," he explained. "He said he's not doing anything for CNN."

"Did he understand you were talking about a humanitarian message?"

"He understood . . . and so did Sadoun. He was right there."

"That little fuck!" I exploded. I spotted Victor walking into the lobby and took off after him. "Hey, you sorry son-of-a-bitch," I yelled. "How dare you push Nic around? How dare you not pass on a humanitarian request . . . ?"

"I didn't push Nic . . ." he protested.

"Bullshit! Nic says Sadoun was there. He saw it all. And how come you wouldn't pass on the message . . . ?"

"We're under no obligation to help you—"

"Obligation? Obligation to pass on a humanitarian message? Listen, you little fuck, who the hell do you think you are? I swear to you, Victor, I don't know how . . . I don't know when, but I promise you that one day I will get your ass. If I personally have to go to Brokaw, or to [NBC News president Michael] Gartner, or whoever. I promise you that one day the world will know that you, Victor Solis, are a Class 'A' prick!" For good measure I added that he should go fuck himself, and stormed back to the bar.

IT TOOK A COUPLE of hours to set up the INMARSAT. Although the actual unit was outdoors, Nic hooked things up so we could telephone from the bar. Peter's second and final report of the day quoted an Iraqi military spokesman as claiming 101 allied planes had been shot down since the war began. Baghdad also called on the population to be on the lookout for pilots and said the government would pay ten thousand dinars "to any Iraqi or Arab" who captured one and twenty thousand dollars to any foreigner who turned one in. "Search for them," a military spokesman said, "but do not harm them." Iraqi TV that night showed pictures of civilian homes reportedly damaged by cruise missiles. Iraq claimed "dozens of cruise missiles" had been downed by Baghdad's air defenses. We were not permitted to report that the telecommunications building had been destroyed.

THE AIR RAIDS SEEMED HEAVIER than usual that night, which we spent mostly in the shelter. At one point, Brent Sadler wandered over and asked me point blank if CNN had been given permission to remain in Baghdad. He and the others would be leaving in the morning. I saw no point in lying and told him the truth.

"Look, Robert, is there any way you can ask the Iraqis to let us stay too?" he asked.

"I'm sorry," I said, "but that steps over the line. We don't work with these guys. . . ."

"I know, but perhaps if you asked—"

"I'm sorry," I cut him off. "I can't do that. I hope you understand."

On the morning of January 20, 1991, virtually the entire foreign press corps pulled out of Baghdad. Remaining behind were CNN, a few Jordanian journalists, among them Michel Haj, a seasoned combat photographer for WTN, and a Spanish newspaperman named Alfonso Rojo. CNN and the Jordanians had permission to remain; Rojo initially did not. He had avoided the exodus by simply playing possum in his room. Before the caravan departed for Amman, I scribbled a note to be delivered to Peter Humi. Though we would inform Atlanta by INMARSAT, if communications faltered, I wanted to set the record straight. "Robert Wiener, Peter Arnett, and Nic Robertson have been invited to remain in Baghdad to continue our coverage for CNN," my message said. "It is a unique journalistic opportunity and we have decided to take advantage of it. We will assess the situation on a day-to-day basis and determine future plans accordingly. Hopefully we will inform Atlanta by phone of this decision but just in case . . . be assured we're well and in good spirits."

THOSE GOOD SPIRITS DIDN'T LAST LONG. It began in the distance as a kind of rumbling, which grew progressively louder as it made its approach. Within seconds the rumbling turned into a high-pitched whistle that whooshed through the air. I looked over my shoulder, then turned toward Nic, who stood several feet away, at the same time instinctively moving away from the window. I had barely taken a step when a deafening explosion, louder than anything I had ever heard before, shattered the plate glass and sent me hurtling across the bar. In that brief instant I was literally picked up and thrown from one side of the room to the other. I landed on my stomach with my arms outstretched, and grabbed for my shoulder bag, which was luckily within reach. Then Nic and I raced down to the shelter as if our lives depended on it.

I was terrified. I couldn't stop my hands from shaking. I used my right hand to steady my left, then my left hand to steady my right. This was not the first time I had been under fire, not the first time I could have been killed, but the sheer force of the Tomahawk cruise missile that impacted on the grounds of the Al-Rasheed, blowing out or at least shattering almost every window in the lobby and bar, brought me fact-to-face with my mortality like nothing I had ever gone through before. In the space of that one frightening, horrendous, and dangerous second, I saw Elaine, Jesse, Jake, and everything I loved and held dear disappear. I reached for a Gauloise but couldn't even get the cigarette into the holder. I was a nervous wreck. "If you could have seen yourself," Nic said, shaking his head. "You actually sailed across the room. Are you okay?"

"I think so," I sighed.

"If you hadn't started moving when you did, you could have been a goner, or at least cut up real bad by the glass."

"Tell me about it. Jesus, what a nightmare!"

Everyone was running into the basement now as the air raid continued. The hotel shook as two more explosions detonated outside. They weren't as close as the first, but their force was enough to shatter one's peace of mind about the safety provided by the shelter. "Oh, God! Oh, God!" moaned a member of the Peace Team. "Make it stop." A few minutes later Peter appeared. He'd been napping in his room when the bombing began.

"This sounds like a big one, guys," he said as the Al-Rasheed continued to shake. "Are you all right?" he asked me, sensing something was wrong. Nic and I related what had just occurred upstairs.

"But you're all right, aren't you?"

"I'm not hurt if that's what you mean, but—"

"We shot down a plane! We got a plane!" Sadoun cried from the other end of the shelter. "It's true, Robert, we shot down a plane. In the back of the tennis courts." He was squealing like a kid who had gotten exactly what he wanted for Christmas. Oh, Jesus, I thought. This is worse than the Twilight Zone. What was I supposed to say, Congratulations?

"How do you know it was a plane," Peter asked, "and not a cruise missile?"

"It was a plane," Sadoun insisted. "Our people saw it and shot it down."

"It was a missile," Michel Haj whispered a moment later. "I saw it come down when I was in my room."

"Was it shot down?"

"Difficult to say," he said. "It could have been, but it might have just missed its target. I'm sure some people were killed though. The thing came down in the middle of the [hotel] workers' quarters."

"Fuck . . ."

"Here, Robert, here is the plane," Sadoun shouted as two officials from the Ministry of Culture and Information ran into the shelter carrying pieces of smoldering debris. "Look, see for yourself. Here, look at the serial numbers. This is proof!" he exclaimed. "You may take pictures."

By this time the air raid had ended. We asked Sadoun if we could see the "plane" for ourselves and asked after the whereabouts of the pilot. "Later, later," he promised. "The area is closed off . . . for security."

"This is bullshit," Nic whispered. "Can we talk a second?"

"Sure," I said, as we moved away from the others, "what's up?"

"I'm starting to have second thoughts about being here—"

"So am I," I interrupted. "But let's discuss it later . . . calmly, away from all this. . . ."

"That's fine," Nic said. "Just so long as you're aware of it."

NEEDLESS TO SAY, the entire bar was littered with broken glass. The force of the explosion had even uprooted some plants outside and sent them flying through the window. As we surveyed the damage, I concluded I'd indeed been lucky. Peter and Nic agreed. It could have been much worse. "Now tell me again what happened, guys," Peter said, as he sat down to write. "We'll lead with the fact that our colleagues are gone, then talk about this latest raid. I'm not going to say it was a plane. There's clearly no evidence of that. You agree, don't you, Robert?"

"Absolutely. But I think you're on safe ground if you call it a missile. After all, Michel says he saw it. . . ."

"Yes, you're quite right," he said, as he continued to hammer away at his script.

Mr. Alla reviewed the report and Peter went on the air. I wondered what my family's reaction would be when they heard Peter describe how "CNN producer Robert Wiener was blown across the room." Although he quickly added I was unhurt, the news was bound to be unsettling. Still, flush with the thrill of survival, I also relished listening to Arnett's account of my latest derring-do.

"WE THINK IT IS BEST that you leave the hotel," Naji said later that afternoon. "This is for your safety. We will take you to another location. You may continue your work from there."

"Where's that?" I asked.

"I cannot tell you the location. We have different places, some are even outside Baghdad. But they are all secure," he insisted. He glanced around the bar. "You will avoid something like this, I promise you." I didn't like the idea of leaving the Al-Rasheed, and, I could tell, neither did Nic. For his part, Peter seemed unconcerned.

"We can't pick up and move just like that," Nic said. "Don't forget, we have the INMARSAT. You need certain coordinates to find the satellite. If we switch locations, those coordinates automatically change. And we also need the generator. . . ."

"We can put everything on a truck," Naji said. "It will not be a problem."

"I don't know, Naji," I said. "I don't like the idea of moving from one place to another, not knowing where we're going. . . ."

"It is not important to know where you are going; what is important is that you are safe," he chuckled.

"This is something that we need to discuss among ourselves," Peter wisely interrupted. "Gentlemen, if you don't mind . . . What's your concern, Robert?" he asked once the three of us were alone.

"My concern is being carted around the countryside for weeks on end with absolutely no say-so as to where we are going. . . ."

"I agree," Nic said. "Once we leave this hotel, we're completely dependent. We don't have our drivers. We don't have anything, really. . . ."

"Well, it could be an interesting experience," Peter ventured, "and a hell of a story. . . ."

"If you can report it," Nic said. "I doubt they're going to allow you to say where you are. . . ."

"Well, guys," Peter asked, "what do you propose we do?"

"I gotta tell ya, my friend, and it makes me unhappy to say so, but I'm inclined to pull out. It's not only because of what happened to me today; I also can't see putting my family through the agony of wondering where I am if we hopscotch around Iraq. I'm concerned about that, Peter. I really am. You know, I've always said that I have to follow my instincts and my instincts are telling me to leave, at least for now."

"I feel the same way," Nic said. "If I didn't, Peter, I'd stay here with you."

"That's fair enough, guys," Peter said. "I understand. But I think it's important one of us stays and I'm still prepared to do that, whether we're here at the Al-Rasheed or not. This story is too big to abandon. But what about the INMARSAT? You'll have to teach me how to use it."

"It's very simple," Nic said. "We can run through it this afternoon."

"You better run through it a couple of times," I laughed. "Arnett didn't win a Pulitzer prize for engineering."

"A Pulitzer prize for engineering," Peter howled. "I love it!"

"ROBERT, HOW ARE YOU PERSONALLY?" Tom Johnson asked when I telephoned Atlanta. "Are you hurt . . . at all?"

"I'm fine, Tom. I just had the shit scared out of me, that's all. But Nic and I are coming out tomorrow. Peter's gonna remain."

"Is there anything I can do for you? Should I call Elaine?"

"I'm going to try her after we hang up. . . ."

"I'll need to know the make and color of the car, or cars," Tom said, "and what time you plan to leave. . . . I don't have to tell you that the road to Amman is becoming increasingly dangerous. There are all kinds of things on either side of the highway that the coalition is interested in . . ."

"I understand. We plan to leave around 7:30 A.M. in two Hondas. The lead car is red, the second one is white. With any luck we should reach Trebil around one."

"We'll make sure Amman sends someone up to meet you," Tom said. I gave Johnson the lowdown about leaving the hotel and put Peter on the line. He told Tom he was prepared to stay for the sake of the story, whatever the conditions. As I listened to him, I couldn't help but feel admiration for Arnett. There wasn't another reporter in the world, I thought, who would do what he was doing. To say Peter is unique is an understatement. He often said he hoped what he did would inspire future generations of reporters, but as far as his contemporaries were concerned, Peter was the last of a dying breed.

"Jesus Christ! Look at this," I called to Arnett as the pictures came on the screen. One after another, seven captured pilots—three Americans, two Brits, one Italian, and a Kuwaiti—were being interviewed on Iraqi TV. It was a chilling and powerful scene as the airmen, still wearing their uniforms and looking like dazed hunted animals who'd been bagged for the kill, responded to questions. A Navy flight lieutenant identified as Jeffrey Zaun looked especially bad. His face was terribly bruised and we wondered whether his injuries resulted from the downing of his plane or if he'd been tortured. "Our leaders and our people have wrongly attacked the peaceful people of Iraq," Zaun said in a stilted monotone.

"I condemn the aggression against peaceful Iraq," said Marine Chief Warrant Officer Guy Hunter, Jr., whose swollen left eye was almost closed. ". . . I think this war is crazy and should never have happened."

A British flight lieutenant named John Peters looked to be in the worst shape of all. As he appeared on screen, his face black and blue, his head hunched down, his eyes averted, I thought he was missing an ear. "Goddamn," I said to Peter, "is it possible they cut it off?" Mercifully, a moment later Peters straightened up, revealing he hadn't been maimed. But he was totally demoralized as he explained how he'd been shot down by a ground to air missile. "I really feel for these guys," I said. "They look frightened to death."

"It's not easy," Peter recalled. "I remember interviewing American POW's in Hanoi. It was a strange sensation."

"May we get a dub of this?" I asked Sadoun. "I'd like to bring it to Amman."

"Mr. al-Hadithi is bringing the tapes to the hotel right now," Sadoun said. "You will have them shortly."

"You know, we could feed the audio to Atlanta tonight," Nic suggested, "if we had a PAL tape machine. It would be relatively easy to hook it up to the INMARSAT."

"You could borrow mine," Michel Haj volunteered. WTN worked in a standard compatible with Iraqi TV.

"That's great," Nic said, and left with Michel to bring the machine to the bar.

The news also featured pictures of what the announcer said was the Martoma Church in the northern city of Mosul. "This was one of the oldest Chaldean churches in all of Iraq," Sadoun explained. "Look how it has been bombed." Naji arrived with the tapes a short time later and we fed the pilot interviews to Atlanta. Naturally the network was thrilled. It was another exclusive for CNN; and proof that the missing airmen were still alive. Despite their desperate circumstances, this had to be a relief to their families. But it prompted another wave of criticism against CNN, whose detractors claimed it was being used as a tool by Saddam Hussein.

"So, Robert," Naji said, "you are leaving in the morning . . ."

"I'm afraid so, but not without misgivings."

"You may come back, of course, whenever you like. Sadoun will give you a special permit."

"Naji, I can't thank you enough for your assistance. You know, I'm going to miss Baghdad . . . not necessarily under these circumstances . . . but this city and its people have become special to me."

"And we have become friends," he smiled.

"You've kept your word and you've been fair to us. I couldn't ask any more of a friend. I know that you'll do the same for Peter."

"Of course. . . ." He reached out and gave me a hug.

"My thoughts are with you . . . and with your family," I whispered. "God willing, we'll all survive."

"May you have a safe trip. We are sending Nasir with you to make certain there will be no problem at the border."

"Great service up to the end," I laughed.

"For a friend we would do nothing less."

Driver Kareem was outside the hotel promptly at seven-thirty but our second driver was running late. "Goddamn," I said to Kareem. "If Halaf's not here in fifteen minutes we'll get someone else." Then I remembered we were now locked in by the colors of the cars. "Well, shit," I moaned, "let's take some pictures." Peter, Nic, and I posed in front of the INMARSAT while a hotel porter took the snap. "It's obviously up to you," I said to Arnett, "but I'd really think twice before leaving the hotel. I still maintain it's not a wise idea."

"We'll see," he said. "You may be right." We had talked about it again the night before in the shelter, but Peter was determined to stick it out no matter where the Iraqis moved him. Again, I found myself marveling at his tenacity and courage.

"Excuse, please," Halaf apologized when he finally arrived at the Al-Rasheed. "Very hard to find gasoline . . . every place closed."

"Do you have enough for the trip?" I asked.

"We must to stop, maybe at Rutba."

"Will the station there be open?"

"Yes . . . no problem," Kareem assured me.

"Okay, then let's hit the road." We said good-bye to Peter and Mr. Alla and several other Iraqis who had gathered on the steps outside. Nic, Nasir, and myself hopped in with Kareem. Halaf would ferry the luggage. I think the sun was peeking through the clouds as we pulled away, but I'm not certain.

The modern highway to Amman was practically deserted. About ten minutes out of town we passed the bombed-out hulk of what was once a large building; its twisted and blackened steel infrastructure was still smoldering.

"What was that?" I asked Nasir.

"Factory," he said. "For textiles."

I had no way of knowing whether it was or not, but I noticed there was no shortage of strategic targets along the road. All of the communications relay towers were still standing and appeared to be virtually untouched. Even the bridges and highway overpasses were unscathed. Every now and then we'd pass a car going in the opposite direction and a surprisingly large number of huge lorries from Jordan. Despite the war and despite the embargo, the business of commerce continued.

"They make much money now," Nasir said as one semi rushed by. "Much, much money."

Kareem drove at a fast steady pace. I constantly looked over my shoulder to make certain Halaf was behind us. Every now and then I'd poke my head out the window to scan the skies. Based on what Tom had said, I figured we were being tracked. I'd heard somewhere that the United States had satellites powerful enough to take pictures of an automobile's license plates. I hoped it was true.

We stopped for gas at Rutba, about one hundred and forty kilometers from the Jordanian border. The town's one service station was adjacent to a huge communications facility. "I don't believe this," I said to Nasir as we pulled behind more than a dozen cars waiting to fill their tanks. "Trust me. This is not where we want to be." Nasir jumped out of the car and, after speaking with the attendant, motioned us to cut in line. His identification from the Ministry of Culture and Information had done the trick. If he hadn't been with us, I don't know what would have happened. By this time, I was so nervous that I mistook the sound of a chain saw in a furniture shop nearby for an air raid siren. Nic says I literally jumped out of my seat.

We made it to Trebil a little after one. The border was jammed with hundreds of people attempting to get out. Many of them were Indians or Pakistanis, but Jordan, already teeming with refugees, had sealed its border. Nasir helped us with customs and departure formalities. I paid Kareem and Halaf several thousand dollars each and gave everyone, including Nasir, a huge tip. Each had risked his life to see to our safety. We then said good-bye.

A car from WTN drove us through approximately forty miles of "no-man's-land" between Trebil and the Jordanian checkpoint at Ruweishid, where Dan Furnad, one of our Amman producers, and a couple of CNN drivers were waiting. After what seemed like an interminable amount of time going through Customs and Immigration, we finally got on the road again, reaching the Jordanian capital well after dark.

"Here, Wienerish," Ingrid laughed as I entered the CNN bureau on the tenth floor of the Philadelphia Hotel. "I imagine you could use one of these." She offered me a tall glass filled with my favorite libation.

"Welcome back, Weenie," Tracy cried, giving me a hug.

"It's great to see you again," said Kris.

There were hugs and warm welcomes from the rest of the staff before I picked up the phone to call Elaine.

"You're really in Amman," she sighed with relief. "Oh, babe, I'm so glad . . . and so proud of you. And you're okay?"

"I'm fine. How are the boys?"

"They're great . . . as always," she laughed, but her laughter sounded nervous.

"Is there anything wrong?" I asked. "You sound strange."

"It's your dad," she said softly. "He's had a heart attack. He's in the hospital. I spoke to your mom of course and I'll give you the information I have, but you should check with the doctors yourself." She gave me the number in Florida.

"Oh, Jesus, when did it happen?"

"A couple of days ago," she said. "I thought about getting a message to you in Baghdad, but . . ."

"I'm glad you didn't. I couldn't have dealt with it there." I told Elaine I would call her later and dialed the number in the States. My father was in critical condition, breathing through a respirator. "We're attempting to wean him off it," said the nurse. "He's moving in the right direction."

"ROBERT, I'M PROUD THAT I KNOW YOU," Earl Casey said before transferring the call up to Tom Johnson's office where Ed and Eason were gathered.

"Do you need to leave for Florida tonight?" Tom asked when I told him about my father.

"No. I'm gonna check with the hospital in the morning," I said. "I'll take it from there."

"Well, anything you need, you just let us know," Ed cut in on the conference line.

"We heard from Peter earlier," Tom said. "He's going to remain at the Al-Rasheed after all. He told the Iraqis he wouldn't budge. Peter also says we can still bring in the flyaway. What are your thoughts?"

"I think we should do it. Visas shouldn't be a problem. I've got a special letter from Naji. Essentially it says Ingrid or I can obtain visas for whomever we want. I'll stop by the embassy here in the morning and see the press guy."

"Who would you recommend we send in?" Eason asked.

"I don't know yet. I'd have to give it some thought. I'd go back myself based on what Peter says but I'm concerned about my father—"

"That should be your first priority," Tom interrupted. "But if you could help organize things . . ."

"That goes without saying. We can talk more in the morning . . ."

BEFORE I GOT TOO DRUNK I telephoned Cynde in Texas. "Oh, Stymie," she wailed. "I'm so glad to hear from you." I told her about my dad and asked after her mother. "Robert, I'm only going to say this once, so you better remember it. I will always love you because you saved my mother's life. If you hadn't insisted that I leave Baghdad, I think she would have died. But I lay on her bed and held her hand, and she survived. Now, you need to do the same for your father."

"I want this truck painted like a circus wagon," I said to Peter Humi. "Candy-colored stripes, stars . . . even a big yellow sun. Stencil CNN all over the fucker. When this puppy goes down that road, I want every allied pilot to know what it is." Before I left for Florida I needed to do three things: choose the people for Baghdad, make sure the truck carrying the flyaway could be recognized from the air, and meet with King Hussein to obtain his permission to drive our equipment through what was technically Jordanian military territory, heretofore off limits to the press. Apparently, the King was the only person who could make it happen.

Within two days, everything was done. Vito Maggiolo, the network's assignment desk czar in Washington, agreed to take over for me in Baghdad. The cameraman would be Dave Rust, an old colleague based in Los Angeles. Nic, God bless him, would be going in too, along with his fiancée, correspondent Margret Lowrie. If necessary, Lowrie could backstop Peter and work as a second producer. Jay Ayers, a free-lance engineer on assignment to CNN, would assist Nic on the technical side.

I called the King's press secretary and made an appointment; I was told the palace would send a car. King Hussein and Queen Noor greeted me in a small, elegantly furnished salon dominated by a table on which were displayed framed autographed photos of assorted heads of state, Saddam Hussein's most prominent among them. (Both the Pope and George Bush were discreetly tucked behind Prince Phillip of England.) The royal couple were dressed casually, the King in a black turtleneck and sports jacket, the Queen sporting a silk blouse and slacks. Both were intensely curious about the situation in Baghdad and obviously concerned about the long-term ramifications of the war. "There is a perception in the West that I supported Saddam when he invaded Kuwait," the King said wearily. "This is simply not true. Jordan condemned the invasion and the violence that ensued, but what am I to do?"

"We are caught in the middle," Queen Noor explained. "We share a border with Iraq and most of our population is Palestinian. There are certain political realities . . ."

"It might help if you did another interview with CNN," I suggested, "to help set the record straight."

"You should, you know," the Queen agreed.

"Not now," the King sighed. "This is not the time. So, how may I assist you?" I explained that we needed his permission and a military escort to accompany our truck to the Iraqi border. "This will be done," he said, jotting a note to himself. "Have your office contact my press secretary, Mr. Ayoub." We chatted some more about the situation in the region and the prospects for peace. The King agreed what was needed on all sides were leaders of vision, leaders who would take a risk for the sake of peace. I had requested a ten-minute meeting; when the King signaled it was time to leave, I'd been at the palace an hour.

"It's a 'go' from the King," I said to Tom Johnson after the meeting. "As far as I can determine, everything's in place. After the charter drops me in Athens, it's going to Cyprus to pick up Vito and Rust. I think you're in good hands."

"I'll have a car meet you in Florida," Tom said. "I want you to stay in touch with me. If there's anything you need . . ."

"LET'S GO!" I called to Doug James and Mark Biello, who were joining me on the charter. The two of them would be taking a morning flight to Berlin, while I had a three-hour layover in Greece before catching another jet to London and the Concorde on to Miami. We hopped in a car and drove to the airport.

"HEY, THIS ISN'T BAD," Mark laughed, shortly after takeoff, as he sampled another canapé of smoked salmon and caviar. "And it's included in the price of the plane?"

"That's what they tell me," I smiled. "It better be, or Eason will have my ass!"

"We've just cleared Jordanian airspace," the pilot announced. "You can all relax." I poured myself another drink and stared out the window. For the first time in months, I could finally begin to decompress. Still, I couldn't get my colleagues out of my mind. I admired the courage of the team that was going back, and had some regrets about not going with them.

IN A MATTER OF DAYS, CNN would be back in Baghdad in force . . . and this time with a flyaway . . . to broadcast, for the first time in history, live pictures to the entire world of a war in progress from behind enemy lines.

Murrow would have loved it!

EPILOGUE

The war ended on Feb 28, 1991; a triumph but still a hollow victory. Kuwait was liberated with a minimum of American and coalition casualties (mostly the result of "friendly fire") but one could hardly say democracy was restored to Kuwait since it wasn't democratic even before Saddam gobbled it up. But eventually the oil began to flow again, which is why Bush drew his line in the sand in the first place.

During the ceasefire talks in Safwan, General Norman Schwarzkopf was snookered by the Iraqis by permitting them to use helicopters, which effectively helped put down rebellions against Saddam by the Kurds in the North and Shites in the South. The much-trumpeted Republican Guard managed to get away pretty much unscathed, while the bulk of Iraqi casualties, pummeled by six weeks of air strikes followed by one hundred hours of ground assault, were a pitiful ragtag collection of ill-trained, poorly equipped, unmotivated GIs who offered relatively little resistance and eagerly surrendered as soon as they had the chance.

And President Saddam Hussein, the man who faced down the greatest allied coalition since World War II, remained in power—winning, from his point of view, The Mother of All Battles by his singular act of survival.

Iraq left Kuwait an ecological disaster, "Hell's National Park," as correspondent Richard Blystone aptly reported, and, though much of Baghdad was left in shambles, Iraq's ability to quickly rebuild was nothing short of astounding. Not only were buildings and bridges repaired, electrical grids and oil facilities restored, but Iraq's president commissioned even more grandiose projects as a tribute to himself and his regime.

During the almost forty trips I made to Baghdad since the war, there was always something new to oggle at . . . be it the Saddam Clock Tower, more life-size statues of the Maximum Leader, additions to the capital's Palace (or Palaces for the cognoscenti) and perhaps the grandest undertaking of all . . . construction of what is purported to be the world's largest mosque. Like Hanoi in the nineties, Baghdad's national bird too had become the crane.

But the Iraqi people, as gracious and hospitable as ever, suffered terribly. Squeezed by economic sanctions and endless airstrikes by U.S. and British jets in the unilaterally declared "no fly zones" on one hand and the brutality of their own government on the other, Iraqis did whatever it took to survive. Iraq became a vast "fire sale" with everything up for grabs. First to go were any precious possessions, from heirlooms to art, jewelry to personal libraries. Next on the block were simple household goods from furniture to kitchenware. Then the absurd, including sets of false teeth. Finally, much of Iraqi society just sold themselves as prostitution, thievery, begging, and corruption burred in at virtually every level. It was not uncommon for parents to bribe their children's teachers to assure advancement to the next grade, even the third. Then the University of Baghdad, once renowned and respected throughout the Arab World, lost credibility while academics rightly reckoned it cost a small fortune to graduate and qualifications be damned; and, as economic privation hit a deep nerve, the cultural isolation of Iraq also took an enormous toll.

The French opened a Cultural Center, which offered language lessons, film festivals, and a library. Much of my luggage was used to haul in material for this worthwhile endeavor, but for the most part the French were out there on their own.

For years Iraq claimed it was cooperating with United National Weapons Inspectors, and indeed a vast arsenal of dangerous weaponry (including chemical and biological) was destroyed or dismantled. But even the most optimistic inspectors agreed one could spend a lifetime combing Iraq and not find everything. For its part, Baghdad maintained that UNSCOM was riddled with U.S. spies, and often it was. In fact, Scott Ritter, perhaps the most (in)famous of inspectors, admitted to not only spying for Washington but also for the Mossad. Not that Iraq didn't play its own game of cat and mouse, but officials justified it by the need for national security and survival in a region where America's principal ally, Israel, was an atomic power.

Baghdad came under major attack three times following the war—in 1992 (for allegedly not cooperating with the UN), in 1993 (after Clinton concluded Iraq tried to wack Pappy Bush during a visit to Kuwait), and in 1998 after the Clinton administration warned UNSCOM to pack its bags since the cruise missiles were going to fly again. As this book goes to press, Baby Bush, like his father and Clinton before him, has called for the removal of Saddam Hussein—even if it means the United States will act on its own and defy the wishes of the United Nations, the European Community, the Arab League, and anyone who thinks it insane to send 250,000 Americans to fight a war with no logical endgame in sight. But since George W. Bush has as much foreign policy know-how as my pet cat, I suppose Gulf War Round Two is a distinct possibility. Let's face it: there's no question that Saddam Hussein is a brutal dictator who poses a threat to his own people and ultimately the Middle East, but anyone who would publicly call Ariel Sharon "a man of peace" (as Bush did) lacks a certain . . . well, historical perspective.

THE UNITED STATES BASKED in the glory of its Gulf War victory with all the hoopla and patriotism it could muster, and pundits pontificated that America finally "put the Vietnam syndrome behind us." The parades and accolades seemed endless, but lost to the majority of Americans was a new policy that ultimately did a great disservice to its citizens.

After effectively putting the lid on news coverage in Granada and Panama, the Pentagon pulled out all the stops in Saudi Arabia and prevented the media from properly doing its job. In a convoluted system of "pools" that precluded responsible coverage on the battlefield and didn't work anyway, journalists were not only denied reporting about their fellow Americans put in harm's way, but were also subject to censorship sometimes even more rigorous than censors imposed in Tel Aviv or Baghdad. It didn't help either that news conferences were covered "live," allowing the public to see the press at work, warts and all—usually not a pretty picture. With so many inexperienced reporters sent to Dharhan, even veteran war thugs were tainted by the absurd and moronic questions posed to briefers, so much so that *Saturday Night Live* felt compelled to parody the scene, thereby reinforcing the notion that most reporters were a bunch of ill-informed, unpatriotic rubes.

After the ground-breaking achievement of CNN's coverage of the beginning of the war, those of us remaining in Baghdad were denounced as Iraqi lackies or worse. Peter Arnett was labeled a "sympathizer" by Senator Alan Simpson (who later apologized) and was often criticized by the White House. But Arnett and CNN stayed the course, and though it meant reporting the war through a "dirty window," in most cases journalism was best served by our coverage there, along with others whom the Iraqis eventually allowed back in to join us.

CNN's opening night coup put Ted Turner's network on the map—a global media force to be reckoned with—and the network proved itself time and time again over the following years, providing comprehensive coverage from Somalia to Haiti, Rwanda to Zaire. But when the Gulf War ended, so too did the guiding philosophy behind CNN—that news was the star, not personalities. It also influenced the network's decision to go "live" as often as possible. That in itself was not necessarily new, but now we often went "live" simply for the sake of "live" and often at the expense of textured, insightful reporting. Naturally management wanted it both ways, and to his eternal credit Eason Jordan never said "no" when I asked for additional personnel to cover a major story responsibly. But Eason, Ed Turner, and Tom Johnson could only do so much. The Gulf War established a mind-set that filtered down the line and eventually onto the air. Reporters like Richard Blystone were still considered terrific writers and journalists, but not necessarily "live meisters."

So the money and the PR went to those whose "live" skills were considered paramount, like Wolf Blitzer or Christiane Amanpour, and the craft of actual writing took a backseat. This is by no means a criticism of Kissy, a dear friend who is both courageous and dedicated to the finest traditions of our trade. Still, she too was often frustrated at being tethered to a satellite dish on an obscure rooftop rather than being out in the field. But we had entered the age of the "dish monkey," and there was no turning back.

Naturally, along with the star system came its inevitable bedfellow: ego. And this, too, irked many of us who fondly remembered the Farewell to Communism Tour following the collapse of the Berlin Wall in 1989 when it mattered little if Blystone did the morning "live," Tom Mintier carried the evening, and Roth delivered the taped daywrap. The order was interchangeable, just like that. No muss, no fuss, no demands from Atlanta. CNN used its money and newfound clout to open a slew of bureaus following the war, but since we would forever be associated with Baghdad the network made a vigorous and costly effort to stick to covering Iraq full-time. Eason himself made eleven trips to Baghdad to meet with officials and successfully lobby to open a bureau there—the first ever by a Western television network. Even Tom Johnson made the ten-hour trip by car through the desert from Amman in the hopes of securing an interview with President Hussein but Iraq said "no dice."

By Eason's estimate, to date CNN has spent ten to twelve million dollars on our Baghdad coverage. Like any relationship, CNN and the Iraqi government had its ups and downs. Eason was actually accused of being the CIA station chief by the Minister of Information and at one point the network was expelled, forcing Jordan to fly from Asia to the Middle East and then drive to Iraq alone . . . convincing officials to allow us to return. On top of that, he was taken to Basra on a government dog and pony, where he did an admirable job of reporting under tough conditions, only to be criticized by one of our more pompous anchors for supposedly buying the Iraqi line.

During the Clinton Administration CNN was repeatedly hammered by the president's National Security Advisor Sandy Berger and Secretary of State Madeline Albright for allowing Iraqi officials to express themselves on our air, but there's no question in my mind we did the right thing by doing so. Though working in Iraq remained a challenge, we did our best to cover events in a balanced and responsible way and if we made mistakes, we corrected them as we would covering any beat. But eventually the relationship with the Iraqi government soured. Eason recently offered up a few theories. Among them, a feeling on the part of the regime that it had given up trying to sway the United States leadership into seeing Iraq's point of view, and a series of documentaries that CNN claims was "tough reporting" but Baghdad viewed as biased. And Naji al-Hadithi, the former Undersecretary at the Ministry of Culture and Information who over the years helped CNN obtain visas, not to mention being a friend, was promoted to Foreign Minister and now feels CNN has become a mouthpiece for the U.S. Administration.

Naji is not the only Iraqi official to share this perception. Nizar Hamdoon told me the same thing, not regarding Iraq per se, but of CNN's coverage in Kosovo. And, if the truth be told, since Ted sold CNN to Time Warner and then AOL bought them all, there is indeed a change to the overall tone of the network. In our line of work perception can be as important as reality. With Ted, CNN was perceived as an independent entity, delivering the news without fear or favor, as *The New York Times* originally put it. But how can the Iraqi government believe that today, when anchors like Lou Dobbs sport American flag lapel pins, which may be understandable to a domestic audience still reeling from September 11, but is anathema in places like Iraq or Lebanon. Not only is it inappropriate journalistically, but it also puts CNN's people in danger. I have written to both Lou and Walter Issacson, CNN's president, several times about this. To date, I have yet to receive a response.

AND WHAT BECAME OF my CNN colleagues who helped shape coverage that historic night? John Holliman, whose good-natured infectious optimism and cheer brought smiles to all who knew him, was killed in an automobile accident in September of 1998. Ed Turner, who I considered almost as close as my father, succumbed to a particularly vicious form of cancer last April. Bernie Shaw retired from CNN two years ago to write his autobiography and spend more time with Linda and his family. Tom Johnson, dismayed by the eroding journalistic standards demanded by the network's new masters, came to the conclusion he could not preside over the "Fox-izing" of CNN and also tendered his resignation. Ingrid Formanek said farewell to the network several years ago for many of the same reasons, moved to Africa, and got married (the ceremony was conducted on elephants), though CNN is fortunate that she sometimes still freelances for us. Kris Krizmanich is gone too. Mark Biello, our cameraman, is now based in Atlanta, where for a long while he hung up his flak jacket to work the "Features" beat. Peter Arnett got his dick caught in a ringer (for reasons not necessary to dwell upon here) during the infamous Tailwind documentary and also left CNN, but I have every expectation Peter will resurface elsewhere as the talented and hard-charging journalist he's always been. Nic Robertson went from Baghdad engineer to field producer in our Chicago bureau, married former CNN correspondent Margret Lowrie, fathered two girls, moved to London, became Christiane's full-time producer, and is now a senior correspondent working out of London. I am particularly proud of Nic, who has displayed tremendous courage over the years, especially covering the recent war in Afghanistan. The fact that he was voted the "Sexiest Correspondent of the Year" by *People* magazine impresses me little. However, his work in Afghanistan and his superb investigative documentary on Northern Ireland, which won the Alfred E. Dupont Award, does. Keep it up, Nicky.

AS FOR MYSELF, the decade following the war found me kicking around the globe producing virtually every major story I cared to. I literally spent years in Africa covering the bleak (Somalia, Rwanda, Zaire, Congo, Sierra Leone) to the uplifting, like the first all-race elections in South Africa. I produced documentaries and specials as varied as traveling the River Congo by barge one thousand miles downriver from Kisangani to Kinshasa, a two-and-a-half-hour "live" special on the twentieth anniversary of the end of the Vietnam War, a week of unprecedented access living with the Dalai Lama, the fiftieth anniversary of D-Day, and the 1997 handback of Hong Kong to China. There were countless trips to the Middle East, not only to Baghdad but to Israel and the Occupied Territories too. There were papal trips, the death of Princess Diana, a week in Tahiti following France's resumption of nuclear testing, the World Conference Against Racism in Durban, and the opening of America's National D-Day Museum in New Orleans, where Bruce Morton introduced me to the delights of *crayfish étoufée*. It was not unusual for me to receive a call in Africa telling me to hotfoot it to Afghanistan, and I reveled in the excitement and challenge of it all. In addition, I had sold *Live from Baghdad* to Doubleday for a bundle, saw the book translated into several languages and then sold the film rights to Universal for even more. I was courted in Hollywood, spent weekends with Dustin Hoffman and Barry Levinson and hours with directors as varied as Penny Marshall and Francis Ford Coppola, who literally shut down production on Bram Stoker's *Dracula* so he and I could stroll around the studio lot to chat.

The book and movie money allowed me to by a *peniche* in Paris anchored at the Place de la Concorde and vacation with my family in Africa, Asia, Polynesia, and Cuba. My children had the privilege of meeting some of the people who've influenced our times, like General Vo Nguyen Giap, President Clinton, author Stephen Ambrose, Tom Hanks, Pamela Harriman, and the Dalai Lama—not to mention a slew of journalistic pals and colleagues such as Flora Lewis, who added perspective and insight to the boys' formal education.

But in 1997, following a month in cold and miserable Bosnia, my world collapsed. I suffered my first bout of depression, a darkness so terrible I would not wish it upon my worst enemy. I was laid up for almost four months, spent mostly in bed crying endlessly like a baby, seeing *everything* in the negative while putting my family through hell to boot. Tom Johnson was particularly supportive (I didn't know it at the time but he has been down the same road), offering introductions to psychopharmacologists, information about new medication not yet available on the French market, and good advice that only someone else who experienced what Bill Styron dubbed "Darkness Visible" can truly understand. Eventually the cloud lifted.

For a while I cut back on the potato juice, but following the death of my friend Kurt Shork in Sierra Leone on May 24, 2000, I started to hit the bottle hard. It was always after work, of course, but for the first time, I experienced blackouts. This, coupled with another bout of depression, eventually caused Elaine to lay down the law: Stop drinking or move out.

Give up alcohol or lose my family? It was really a no-brainer. So following Ingrid's wedding in Botswana I stopped drinking on December 13, 2000. Contrary to most expectations, it wasn't difficult. I just stopped. Both Ed Turner and my friend Sandy Kenyon assured me that Alcoholics Anonymous was the only treatment for the disease that had a proven track record, and I attended a meeting to discover the uplifting support system AA offers. I read the *Big Blue Book of Booze* and other literature but felt no inclination to attend a second meeting. But neither did I feel an inclination to drink. I was clean and sober, as they say, but there is a difference between that and being happy in one's sobriety. AA might have helped me achieve that goal sooner, but perhaps out of pride, stubborness, or Pete Hamill's wonderful memoir, *A Drinking Life,* I simply did it on my own. It took about three months, as I recall. I still serve alcohol at home, am a regular at the Hemingway Bar at the Ritz, occasionally hold down the fort at Harry's Bar, but I still haven't taken a drink—or, more important, wanted or felt the need for one. What touched me the most, however, was how proud Jesse and Jake said they were when I told them of my decision. I had not realized the extent my drinking had unsettled their lives. To them, as well as Elaine, I apologize.

IT'S SAID one should never make any major changes in one's life before being sober at least a year, and I didn't. Instead, I added to my journalistic skills by learning to operate a camera. After budget cutbacks following the AOL-TIME merger made CNN reluctant to spend money on "nonessential" stories, I signed a new contract that allowed me to shoot, write, and broadcast in addition to my producing role when duty called. I thoroughly enjoyed this new challenge and the engineers and camerapeople at CNN (who saw this one-man band shit as a threat to *their* true professionalism and eventual livelihood) couldn't have been more supportive and gave me the technical equivalent of the Masonic handshake: When there are no porters, tip yourself!

Still, like so many others I was dismayed about the new direction of television journalism, the way the line between news and entertainment was not only being blurred but often obliterated. I began to feel that the values and public service that prompted me to become a journalist in the first place were sliding down a deep and dangerous slope. On the night of September 11, 2001, I was on my way to Pakistan/Afghanistan to supervise our coverage, and during the next several months came to the realization that it was perhaps time for me to hang up the spurs. Naturally, after twenty years at CNN this was not an easy decision, but following a U2 concert in Atlanta I attended with Eason, he reluctantly but graciously allowed me to retire to write, teach, and perhaps speechify. He has always been a fair boss and a good friend.

My friend Mr. Jordan has come a long way since his first trip overseas as Foreign Editor to visit me in Jerusalem in 1988—and wasn't sure if he heard correctly (he did) when the manager of the American Colony Hotel asked Eason if he wanted his bar bills listed as laundry as Mr. Clancy always did. Upon his shoulders, as the network's chief news executive, now rests a major responsibility: to maintain the standards we and likeminded others share and restore Ted Turner's vision of CNN as a vibrant, independent, public-spirited global news organization to foster understanding and make our world a better place. You got your work cut out for you, pal.

And no, in real life, unlike the movie, Eason never asked me if I was fuckin' Ingrid.

—PILAR TOO
Paris, August 2002

THE MEN AND WOMEN OF CNN BAGHDAD
August 23, 1990—Ceasefire

CORRESPONDENTS

Christiane Amanpour
Peter Arnett
Richard Blystone
Jim Clancy
John Holliman
Charles Jaco
Doug James
Margret Lowrie
Tom Mintier
Richard Roth
Rick Sallinger
Bernard Shaw

PRODUCERS

Edith Chapin
Mark Dulmage
Ingrid Formanek
Elisa Gambino
Peter Humi
Nancy Lane
Mitch Leopard
Vito Maggiolo
Alec Miran
Rob Reynolds

CAMERAPERSONS

Mark Biello
Rich Brooks
Stuart Clark
Tyrone Edwards
David Heaberlin
David Rust
Steve Sorg
Cynde Strand
Phil Turner

SOUND TECHNICIANS

Ben Coyte
Paul Deitrich
Trey Haney
Neil Loeb
Rod Nino

VIDEOTAPE EDITORS

Neil Broffman
Tracy Flemming
Kris Krizmanich
Dan Morita

ENGINEERS

Jay Ayers
Nic Robertson
Paul Shulman
Peter Norris Smith

INDEX